Programming in
ANSI C

Revised Edition

Programming in
ANSI C

Revised Edition

Stephen G. Kochan

SAMS
PUBLISHING

A Division of Prentice Hall Computer Publishing
201 West 103rd Street, Indianapolis, Indiana, 46290

To my mother and father

01   11

Composed in Palatino and MCPdigital
by Prentice Hall Computer Publishing

Printed in the United States of America

Overview

Appendices

Contents

Preface

When the original edition of *Programming in ANSI C* was written, the ANSI C specification still existed in draft form. Since that time, not only has the standard been adopted, but the ANSI C form of the C programming language has become ubiquitous as well.

Over the years, I have had many requests to offer answers to the exercises at the end of the chapters. I have been reluctant to do so since that would make the book less suitable for use as a classroom textbook. As a compromise of sorts, I have decided to include answers to the odd-numbered exercises.

The other significant change made to this edition of the book has been the addition of "Quick Tips" throughout the text. These were added to reinforce some key ideas and to help you avoid pitfalls commonly made by C programmers.

This year marks 10 years since the originial *Programming in C* book was published. I am grateful to anyone who has used my book. I hope it has achieved its objective of trying to make learning to program in C easier and more enjoyable.

1

Introduction

The original version of the "C" programming language was pioneered by Dennis Ritchie at AT&T Bell Laboratories in the early 1970s. It was not until the late 1970s, however, that this programming language began to gain widespread popularity and support. This was because until that time C compilers were not readily available for commercial use outside of Bell Laboratories. Initially, C's growth in popularity was also spurred on in part by the equal, if not faster, growth in popularity of the UNIX operating system. This operating system, which was also developed at Bell Laboratories, has C as its "standard" programming language. In fact, well over 90 percent of the operating system itself is written in the C language!

The enormous success of the IBM PC and its look-alikes soon made MS-DOS the most popular environment for the C language. As C grew in popularity across different operating systems, more and more vendors hopped on the bandwagon and started marketing their own C compilers. For the most part, their version of the C language was based on an appendix found in the first C programming text—*The C Programming Language*—by Brian Kernighan and Dennis Ritchie (Prentice-Hall, 1978). Unfortunately, this appendix did not provide a complete and unambiguous definition of C, meaning that vendors were left to interpret some aspects of the language on their own.

In the early 1980s a need was seen to standardize the definition of the C language. The American National Standards Institute (ANSI) is the organization that handles such things, so in 1983 an ANSI committee (called X3J11) was formed to standardize C.

With an ANSI definition for C, you are assured that anyone who sells a true ANSI C compiler has incorporated all of the features of the language specified by the standard. It also means that programmers who are careful can truly write C programs that will run without modification on any system that has an ANSI C compiler.

C is a "higher-level language," yet it provides capabilities that enable the user to "get in close" with the hardware and deal with the computer on a much lower level. This is because, although C is a general-purpose structured programming language, it was originally designed with systems programming applications in mind and, as such, provides the user with an enormous amount of power and flexibility. In fact, programming applications exist that could be easily handled by the C language, but that would be difficult to develop in other languages such as Pascal, FORTRAN, or BASIC.

This book proposes to teach you how to program in ANSI C. It assumes no previous exposure to the language and was designed to appeal to novice and experienced programmers alike. If you have previous programming experience, you will find that C has a unique way of doing things that probably differs significantly from any language you have used. Even if you are coming from a Pascal background—a language that C superficially resembles—you will quickly discover many features that are unique to this language, such as pointers, character strings, and bit operations.

Every feature of the C language is treated in this text. As each new feature is presented, a small *complete* program example is usually provided to illustrate the feature. This reflects the overriding philosophy that has been used in writing this book: to teach by example. Just as a picture is worth a thousand words, so is a properly chosen program example. If you have access to a computer facility that supports the ANSI C programming language, you are strongly encouraged to enter and run each program presented in this book and to compare the results obtained on your system to those shown in the text. By doing so, not only will you learn the language and its syntax, but you will also become familiar with the process of typing in, compiling, and running C programs.

The style used for teaching ANSI C is one of posing a particular problem for solution on a computer and then proceeding to develop a program in C to solve the problem. In this manner, new language constructs are introduced as they are needed to solve a particular problem.

You will find that program readability has been stressed throughout the book. This is because I strongly believe that programs should be written so that they may be easily read—either by the author or by somebody else. Through experience and common sense, you will find that such programs are almost always easier to write, debug, and modify. Furthermore, developing programs that are readable is a natural result of a true adherence to a structured programming discipline.

Because this book was written as a tutorial, the material covered in each chapter is based on previously presented material. Therefore, maximum benefit will be derived from this book by reading each chapter in succession, and you are highly discouraged from "skipping around." You should also work through the exercises that are presented at the end of each chapter before proceeding on to the next chapter.

Chapter 2, which covers some fundamental terminology about higher-level programming languages and the process of compiling programs, has been included to make sure that we are speaking the same language throughout the remainder of the text. From Chapter 3 on, you will be slowly introduced to the ANSI C language. By the time Chapter 16 rolls around, all the essential features of the language will have been covered. Chapter 16 goes into more depth about I/O operations in C. Finally, Chapter 17 includes those features of the language that are of a more advanced or esoteric nature.

Appendix A provides a complete summary of the language and is provided for reference purposes. Appendix B provides a summary of most of the standard library routines that you will find on all systems that support ANSI C. Appendix C summarizes the major differences between the ANSI C language described in this text and the "older" C. In Appendix D you'll find a list of common programming mistakes. Appendix E is a single-page ASCII chart. Finally, Appendix F contains the answers to the odd-numbered exercises found at the end of each chapter.

This book makes no assumptions about a particular computer system or operating system on which the ANSI C language is implemented. The text makes brief mention of how to compile and execute programs under MS-DOS and UNIX. The best reference for more detailed information is the documentation that came with your compiler.

I wish to thank the following people for their help in the preparation of the original text, *Programming in C*: Douglas McCormick, Maureen Connelly, Jim Scharf, Henry Tabickman, and, above all, Ken Brown. I also wish to thank

Henry Mullish of New York University for teaching me so much about writing and for getting me started in the publishing business. I'd also like to thank Dick Fritz, who has generously given comments for many books I have written, including the original and revised editions of this text.

Finally, I wish to thank my wife Leela, who provided her patience and understanding through three versions of this text.

2

Some Fundamentals

This chapter describes some fundamental terms that you must understand before you can learn how to program in C. A general overview of the nature of programming in a higher-level language is provided, as is a discussion of the process of compiling a program developed in such a language.

Programming

Computers are really very dumb machines indeed, since they do only what they are told to do. Most computer systems perform their operations on a very primitive level. For example, most computers know how to add one to a number or how to test if a number is equal to zero or not. The sophistication of these basic operations usually does not go much further than that. The basic operations of a computer system form what is known as the computer's *instruction set*. Some computers have very limited instruction sets. For example, the older DEC PDP-8 computer has a very limited instruction set, while the modern DEC VAX machines contain instruction sets consisting of hundreds of basic operations.

In order to solve a problem using a computer, we must express the solution to the problem in terms of the instructions of the particular computer. A computer *program* is actually just a collection of the instructions necessary to solve a specific problem. The approach or method that is used to solve the problem is known as an *algorithm*. For example, if we wish to develop a program that tests if a number is odd or even, then the set of statements that solves the problem becomes the program. The method that is used to test if the number is even or odd is the algorithm. Normally, to develop a program to solve a particular problem, we first express the solution to the problem in terms of an algorithm and then develop a program that implements that algorithm. So the algorithm for solving the even/odd problem might be expressed as follows: "First divide the number by two. If the remainder of the division is zero, then the number is even; otherwise, the number is odd." With the algorithm in hand, we can then proceed to write the instructions necessary to implement the algorithm on a particular computer system. These instructions would be expressed in the statements of a particular computer language, such as BASIC (Beginner's Algorithmic Symbolic Interchange Code), Pascal (named after the famous mathematician Blaise Pascal), or C.

Higher-Level Languages

When computers were first developed, the only way they could be programmed was in terms of binary numbers that corresponded directly to specific machine instructions and locations in the computer's memory. The next technological software advance occurred in the development of *assembly languages*, which enabled the programmer to work with the machine on a slightly higher level. Instead of having to specify sequences of binary numbers to carry out particular tasks, the assembly language permits the programmer to use symbolic names to perform various operations and to refer to specific memory locations. A special program, known as an *assembler*, translates the assembly language program from its symbolic format into the specific machine instructions of the computer system.

Because a one-to-one correspondence still exists between each assembly language statement and a specific machine instruction, assembly languages are regarded as low-level languages. The programmer must still learn the instruction set of the particular computer system in order to write a program in assembly language, and the resulting program is not *portable*; that is, the program will not run on a different computer model without being rewritten. This is because different computer systems have different instruction sets, and since assembly language programs are written in terms of these instructions sets, they are machine dependent.

Then, along came the so-called higher-level languages, of which the FORTRAN (FORmula TRANslation) language was one of the first. Programmers developing programs in FORTRAN no longer had to concern themselves with the architecture of the particular computer, and operations performed in FORTRAN were of a much more sophisticated or higher level, far removed from the instruction set of the particular machine. One FORTRAN instruction or *statement* would result in many different machine instructions being executed, unlike the one-to-one correspondence found between assembly language statements and machine instructions.

Standardization of the syntax of a higher-level language meant that a program could be written in the language to be machine independent. That is, a program could run on any machine that supported the language with few or no changes.

In order to support a higher-level language, a special computer program must be developed that translates the statements of the program developed in the higher-level language into a form that the computer can understand—in other words, into the particular instructions of the computer. Such a program is known as a *compiler*.

Operating Systems

Before we continue with compilers, it is worthwhile to understand the role that is played by a computer program known as an *operating system*.

An operating system is a program that controls the entire operation of a computer system. All I/O operations that are performed on a computer system are channeled through the operating system. The operating system must also manage the computer system's resources and must handle the execution of programs.

One of the most popular operating systems today is the UNIX operating system, which was developed at Bell Laboratories. UNIX is a rather unique operating system in that it can be found on many different types of computer systems. Historically, operating systems were typically associated with only one type of computer system. But because UNIX is written primarily in the C language and makes very few assumptions about the architecture of the computer, it has been successfully ported to many different computer systems with a relatively small amount of effort.

Microsoft's MS-DOS is another example of a popular operating system. That system is found primarily on the IBM PC computer and compatibles.

Compiling Programs

A compiler is a software program that is, in principle, no different from the ones you will see in this book, although it is certainly much more complex. A compiler analyzes a program developed in a particular computer language and then translates it into a form that is suitable for execution on your particular computer system.

Figure 2.1 shows the steps that are involved in entering, compiling, and executing a computer program developed in the C programming language and the typical UNIX commands that are used.

The program that is to be compiled is first typed into a *file* on the computer system. Computer installations have various conventions that are used for naming files, but in general, the choice of the name is up to you. Under UNIX, C programs can be given any name provided the last two characters are ".c". So the name prog1.c would be a valid file name for a C program running under UNIX.

A text editor must usually be used to enter the C program into a file. Some C compiler vendors supply a text editor when you purchase their software. vi is a popular text editor used on UNIX systems. In order to be able to try the programs presented in this book, you will first have to learn how to use such an editor. Check the documentation that comes with your system for more information about the text editors that are available.

The program that is entered into the file is known as the *source program*, since it represents the original form of the program expressed in the C language. Once the source program has been entered into a file, you can then proceed to have it compiled.

The compilation process is initiated by typing a special command on the system. When this command is entered, the name of the file that contains the source program must also be specified. For example, under UNIX, the command to initiate program compilation is called cc. The cl command activates many of the C compilers found on PCs running MS-DOS. Typing the line

```
cl prog1.c
```

would have the effect of initiating the compilation process with the source program contained in prog1.c.

In the first step of the compilation process, the compiler examines each program statement contained in the source program and checks it to ensure that it conforms to the syntax and semantics of the language. If any mistakes are discovered by the compiler during this phase, then they will be reported to the user and the compilation process will end right there. The errors will then have to be corrected in the source program (with the use of the text editor), and the compilation process restarted. Typical errors reported during this phase of compilation might be due to an expression that has unbalanced parentheses (syntactic error), or due to the use of a variable that is not "defined" (semantic error).

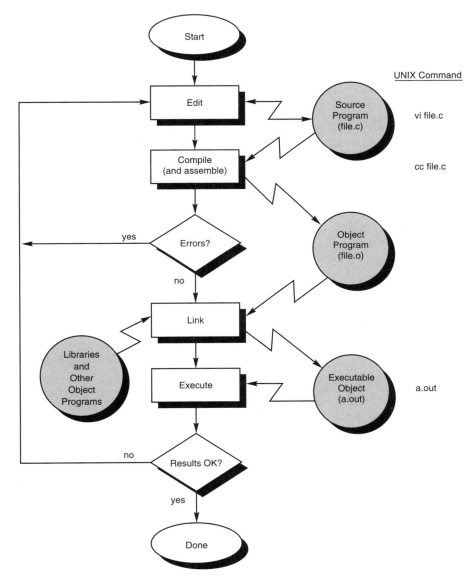

Figure 2.1. *Typical steps for entering, compiling, and executing C programs.*

When all of the syntactic and semantic errors have been removed from the program, the compiler will then proceed to take each statement of the program and translate it into a "lower" form. On most machines, this means that each statement will be translated by the compiler into the equivalent statement or statements in assembly language needed to perform the identical task.

After the program has been translated into an equivalent assembly language program, the next step in the compilation process is to translate the assembly language statements into actual machine instructions. This step may or may not involve the execution of a separate program known as an *assembler*. On most systems, the assembler is executed automatically as part of the compilation process.

The assembler takes each assembly language statement and converts it into a binary format known as *object code*, which is then written into another file on the system. This file will have the same name as the source file under UNIX, with the last letter an "o" (for *object*) instead of a "c".

After the program has been translated into object code, it is ready to be *linked*. This process is once again performed automatically whenever the cc command is issued under UNIX. Other operating systems may require another command to perform this task. The purpose of the linking phase is to get the program into a final form for execution on the computer. If the program uses other programs that were previously processed by the compiler, then during this phase the programs are linked together. Programs that are used from the system's program *library* are also searched and linked together with the object program during this phase.

The final linked file, which is in an *executable object* code format, is stored in another file on the system, ready to be run or *executed*. Under UNIX, this file is called a.out by default. Under MS-DOS, the executable file usually has the same name as the source file, with the c extension replaced by an exe extension. To subsequently execute the program, all you do is type in the name of the executable object file. So the command

```
a.out
```

would have the effect of *loading* the program called a.out into the computer's memory and initiating its execution.

When the program is executed, each of the statements of the program is sequentially executed in turn. If the program requests any data from the user, known as *input*, the program will temporarily suspend its execution so that the input may be entered. Results that are displayed by the program, known as *output*, will normally appear at the terminal from which the program was executed.

If all goes well (and it probably won't the first time the program is executed), the program will perform its intended functions. If the program does not produce the desired results, then it will be necessary to go back and reanalyze the program's logic. This is known as the *debugging phase*, during which an attempt is made to remove all the known problems or *bugs* from the program. In order to do so, it will most likely be necessary to make changes to the original source program. In that case, the entire process of compiling, linking, and executing the program must be repeated until the desired results are obtained.

Before leaving this discussion of the compilation process, we should point out that there is another method used for analyzing and executing programs developed in a higher-level language. With this method, programs are not compiled but are *interpreted*. An interpreter analyzes and executes the statements of a program at the same time. This method usually allows programs to be more easily debugged. On the other hand, interpreted languages are typically slower than their compiled counterparts, since the program statements are not converted into a low-level form in advance of their execution.

The BASIC programming language is the most popular language in which programs are typically interpreted and not compiled. Other examples include LISP (LISt Processing), the UNIX system's *shell*, and PostScript. Some vendors also offer interpreters for the C programming language.

3

CHAPTER

Writing a Program in ANSI C

In this chapter you are introduced to the C language so that you can see what programming in C is all about. What better way to gain an appreciation for this language than by taking a look at an actual program written in C?

To begin with, let's pick a rather simple example—a program that displays the phrase "Programming is fun" at the terminal. Here is a C program to accomplish this task.

Program 3.1

```
#include <stdio.h>

main ()
{
     printf ("Programming is fun.\n");
}
```

In the C programming language, lowercase and uppercase letters are distinct. In most other programming languages, such as FORTRAN,

COBOL (COmmon Business Oriented Language), PL/I (Programming Language I), or BASIC, uppercase letters are used exclusively. If you are used to programming in any of these languages, the use of lowercase letters may take some getting used to.

Also, unlike many other programming languages, C does not particularly care where on the line you begin typing. Some languages, such as FORTRAN and COBOL, are very fussy about such things, but in C you may begin typing your statement at any position on the line. This fact can be used to your advantage in developing programs that are easier to read.

Returning to our first C program, if we were to type this program into the computer, issue the proper commands to the system to have it compiled, and then execute it, we could expect the following results or output to appear at the terminal:

```
Programming is fun.
```

Let's take a closer look at our first program. The first line of the program

```
#include <stdio.h>
```

should be included at the beginning of just about every program you write. It tells the compiler information about the printf output routine that is used later in the program. We'll talk in detail about what this line does in Chapter 13, "The Preprocessor."

QUICK TIP

Remember to put this special include statement at the beginning of all your programs and to type it in precisely as shown in the text.

The line of the program that reads

```
main ()
```

informs the system that the name of the program is main. main is a special name that indicates precisely *where* the program is to begin execution. The open and closed parentheses immediately following main specify that main is the name of a *function*. (This concept will be explained in more detail in Chapter 8, "Functions.")

Now that we have identified main to the system, we are ready to specify precisely what this routine is to perform. This is done by enclosing all program statements of the routine within a pair of curly braces. (For those readers who are familiar with the Pascal programming language, the braces in C are some-what analogous to the `Begin` and `End` block declarators of that language.) All program statements included between the braces will be taken as part of the `main` routine by the system. In Program 3.1, we have only one such statement. This statement specifies that a routine named `printf` is to be invoked or *called*. The parameter or *argument* to be passed to the `printf` routine is the string of characters

```
"Programming is fun.\n"
```

The `printf` routine is a function in the C library that simply prints or displays its argument (or arguments, as you will see shortly) at the terminal or on the video screen. The last two characters in the string, namely the backslash (\) and the letter n, are known collectively as the *newline* character. A newline charac-ter tells the system to do precisely what its name implies—that is, go to a new line. Any characters to be printed after the newline character will then appear on the next line of the display. In fact, the newline character is similar in con-cept to the carriage return key on a typewriter.

All program statements in C *must* be terminated by a semicolon (;). This is the reason for the semicolon that appears immediately following the closed pa-renthesis of the `printf` call.

QUICK TIP

Remember to place a semicolon at the end of all your C statements.

Now that we have finished discussing our first program, why don't we modify to also display the phrase "And programming in C is even more fun." This can be done by the simple addition of another call to the `printf` routine, as shown in Program 3.2. Remember that every C program statement must be terminated by a semicolon.

Program 3.2

```c
#include <stdio.h>

main ()
{
    printf ("Programming is fun.\n");
    printf ("And programming in C is even more fun.\n");
    Return 0;
}
```

If we type in Program 3.2 and then compile and execute it, we can expect the following output at our terminal:

Program 3.2 OUTPUT

```
Programming is fun.
And programming in C is even more fun.
```

As you will see from the next program example, it is not necessary to make a separate call to the printf routine for each line of output. Study the program listed below in Program 3.3 and try to predict the results before examining the output (no cheating now!).

Program 3.3

```
#include <stdio.h>

main ()
{
     printf ("Testing...\n..1\n...2\n....3\n");
}
```

Program 3.3 OUTPUT

```
Testing...
..1
...2
....3
```

The printf routine is the most commonly used routine in this book. This is because it provides an easy and convenient means to display program results. Not only can simple phrases be displayed, but the values of *variables* and the results of computations can be as well. In fact, Program 3.4 uses the printf routine to display the results of adding two numbers, namely 50 and 25.

Program 3.4

```
#include <stdio.h>

main ()
{
    int sum;

    sum = 50 + 25;
    printf ("The sum of 50 and 25 is %i\n", sum);
}
```

Program 3.4 OUTPUT

```
The sum of 50 and 25 is 75
```

A bit of explanation is in order with respect to the above program. The first C program statement *declares* the *variable* sum to be of type *int*eger. C, like Pascal—and unlike FORTRAN or BASIC—requires that all program variables be declared before they are used in a program. The declaration of a variable specifies to the C compiler how a particular variable will be used by the program. This information is needed by the compiler in order to generate the correct instructions to store and retrieve values into and out of the variable. A variable declared as type int can only be used to hold integral values; that is, values without decimal places. Examples of integral values are 3, 5, -20, and 0. Numbers with decimal places, such as 3.14, 2.455, and 27.0, for example, are known as *floating point* or *real* numbers.

QUICK TIP

Remember that in C, all variables must be declared before they are used.

The integer variable sum will be used to store the result of the addition of the two integers 50 and 25. We have intentionally left a blank line following the declaration of this variable. This is done to visually separate the variable declarations of the routine from the program statements and is strictly a matter of style. Sometimes the addition of a single blank line in a program can help to make the program more readable.

The program statement

```
sum = 50 + 25;
```

reads as it would in most other programming languages: the number 50 is added (as indicated by the plus sign) to the number 25 and the result is stored (as indicated by the *assignment operator*, the equals sign) into the variable sum.

The printf routine call in Program 3.4 now has two items or *arguments* enclosed within the parentheses. These arguments are separated by a comma. The first argument to the printf routine is always the character string to be displayed. However, along with the display of the character string, we may frequently wish to have the value of certain program variables displayed as well. In our case, we would like to have the value of the variable sum displayed at the terminal after the characters

```
The sum of 50 and 25 is
```

are displayed. The percent character inside the first argument is a special character recognized by the printf function. The character that immediately follows the percent sign specifies what *type* of value is to be displayed at that point. In the above program, the letter i is recognized by the printf routine as signifying that an integer value is to be displayed.[1]

Whenever the printf routine finds the %i characters inside a character string, it will automatically display the value of the next argument to the printf routine. Since sum is the next argument to printf, its value is automatically displayed after the characters "The sum of 50 and 25 is" are displayed.

Now try to predict the output from Program 3.5.

Program 3.5

```
#include <stdio.h>

main ()
{
    int   value1, value2, sum;

    value1 = 50;
    value2 = 25;
    sum = value1 + value2;
    printf ("The sum of %i and %i is %i\n", value1, value2, sum);
}
```

---

[1]*Note that* printf *also allows you to specify* %d *format characters to display an integer. We'll stick to* %i *throughout this book.*

Program 3.5 OUTPUT

```
The sum of 50 and 25 is 75
```

The first program statement declares three variables called `value1`, `value2`, and `sum` all to be of type `int`. This statement could have equivalently been expressed using three separate declaratory statements as follows:

```
int value1;
int value2;
int sum;
```

After the three variables have been declared, the program assigns the value 50 to the variable `value1` and then 25 to `value2`. The sum of these two variables is then computed and the result assigned to the variable `sum`.

The call to the `printf` routine now contains four arguments. Once again, the first argument, commonly called the *format string*, describes to the system how the remaining arguments are to be displayed. The value of `value1` is to be displayed immediately following the display of the characters "the sum of." Similarly, the values of `value2` and `sum` are to be printed at the appropriate points as indicated by the next two occurrences of the `%i` characters in the format string.

The last program in this chapter (Program 3.6) introduces the concept of the *comment*. A comment statement is used in a program to document a program and to enhance its readability. As you will see from the following example, comments serve to tell the reader of the program—the programmer or someone else whose responsibility it is to maintain the program—just what the programmer had in mind when he or she wrote a particular program or a particular sequence of statements.

Program 3.6

```
/* This program adds two integer values and displays
   the results                                        */
#include <stdio.h>
main ()
{
    /* Declare variables */
    int  value1, value2, sum;

/* Assign values and compute the result */
    value1 = 50;
    value2 = 25;
    sum = value1 + value2;
```

continues

Program 3.6 Continued

```
    /* Display the result */
    printf ("The sum of %i and %i is %i\n", value1, value2, sum);
}
```

Program 3.6 OUTPUT

```
The sum of 50 and 25 is 75
```

A comment statement is initiated by the two characters / and *. These two characters must be written without any intervening spaces. To end a comment statement, the characters * and / are used, once again without any embedded spaces. All characters included between the opening /* and the closing */ are treated as part of the comment statement and are ignored by the C system. In Program 3.6, four separate comment statements were used. This program is otherwise identical to Program 3.5. Admittedly, this is a contrived example, since only the first comment at the head of the program is useful. (Yes, it is possible to insert so many comments into a program that the readability of the program is actually degraded instead of improved!)

The intelligent use of comment statements inside a program cannot be over-emphasized. Many times a programmer will return to a program that he coded perhaps only six months ago, only to discover to his dismay that he cannot for the life of him remember the purpose of a particular routine or of a particular group of statements. A simple comment statement judiciously inserted at that particular point in the program might have saved significant amount of time otherwise wasted on rethinking the logic of the routine or set of statements.

It is a good idea to get into the habit of inserting comment statements into the program as the program is being written or typed into the computer. There are good reasons for this. First, it is far easier to document the program while the particular program logic is still fresh in your mind than it is to go back and rethink the logic after the program has been completed. Second, by inserting comments into the program at such an early stage of the game, you to reap the benefits of the comments during the debug phase, when program logic errors are being isolated and debugged. A comment can not only help you read through the program, but it can also help point the way to the source of the logic mistake. Finally, I have yet to discover a programmer who actually enjoyed documenting a program. In fact, once you have finished debugging your program, you will probably not relish the idea of going back to the program to insert comments. Inserting comments while developing the program will make this sometimes tedious task a bit easier to swallow.

This concludes this introductory chapter on developing programs in C. By now you should have a good feel as to what is involved in writing a program in C and you should be able to develop a small program on your own. In the next chapter, we will begin to examine some of the finer intricacies of this wonderfully powerful and flexible programming language. But first, try your hand at the exercises that follow to make sure you understand the concepts presented in this chapter.

Exercises

1. If you have access to a computer facility that supports the C programming language, type in and run the six programs presented in this chapter. Compare the output produced by each program with the output presented after each program.

2. Write a program that prints the following text at the terminal.

    1. In C, lowercase letters are significant.
    2. `main` is where program execution begins.
    3. Open and closed braces enclose program statements in a routine.
    4. All program statements must be terminated by a semicolon.

3. What output would you expect from the following program?

    ```c
    #include <stdio.h>

    main ()
    {
        printf ("Testing...");
        printf ("....1");
        printf ("...2");
        printf ("..3");
        printf ("\n");
    }
    ```

4. Write a program that subtracts the value 15 from 87 and displays the result, together with an appropriate message, at the terminal.

5. Identify five syntactic errors in the following program. Then type in and run the corrected program to make sure you have correctly identified all the mistakes.

    ```c
    #include <stdio.h>
    ```

```
main ()
(
        INT  sum;
        /* COMPUTE RESULT
        sum = 25 + 37 - 19
        /* DISPLAY RESULTS */
        printf ("The answer is %i\n" sum);
}
```

6. What output might you expect from the following program?

```
#include <stdio.h>

main ()
{
   int answer, result;
   answer = 100;
   result = answer - 10;
   printf ("The result is %i\n", result + 5);
}
```

4

CHAPTER

Variables, Data Types, and Arithmetic Expressions

In this chapter, we will discuss the formation of variable names and constants, take a look at the basic data types, and describe some fundamental rules for forming arithmetic expressions in C.

Variables

Early computer programmers had the onerous task of having to write their programs in the binary language of the machine they were programming. This meant that computer instructions had to be hand-coded into binary numbers by the programmer before they could be entered into the machine. Furthermore, the programmer had to explicitly assign and reference any storage locations inside the computer's memory by a specific number or memory address.

Modern-day programming languages allow the programmer to concentrate more on solving the particular problem at hand than worrying about specific machine codes or memory locations. They enable us to assign symbolic names, known as *variable names,* for storing program computations and results. A variable name can be chosen by the programmer in a meaningful way to reflect the type of value that is to be stored in that variable.

In Chapter 3, "Writing a Program in ANSI C," we used several variables to store integer values. For example, we used the variable sum in Program 3.4 to store the result of the addition of the two integers 50 and 25.

The C language allows data types other than just integers to be stored in variables as well, provided the proper declaration for the variable is made *before* it is used in the program. Variables can be used to store floating-point numbers, characters, and even *pointers* to locations inside the computer's memory.

The rules for forming variable names are quite simple: They must begin with a letter or underscore (_) and may be followed by any combination of letters (upper- or lowercase), underscores, or the digits 0-9. The following is a list of valid variable names.

```
sum
piece_flag
i
J5x7
Number_of_moves
_sysflag
```

On the other hand, the following variable names are not valid for the stated reasons:

sum$value	$ not a valid character
piece flag	Embedded spaces not permitted
3Spencer	Can't start with a number
int	Reserved word

int cannot be used as a variable name since its use has a special meaning to the C compiler. This use is known as a *reserved name* or *reserved word*. In general, any name that has special significance to the C compiler cannot be used as a variable name. Appendix A, "ANSI C Language Summary," provides a complete list of such reserved names.

You should always remember that upper- and lowercase letters are distinct in C. Therefore, the variable names sum, Sum, and SUM each refer to a different variable.

A variable name can be up to 31 characters in length.[1]

Some systems may permit names to be even longer than that. For example, UNIX Systems (as of System V Release 2) permit variable names to be as long as desired.

QUICK TIP

When deciding on the choice of a variable name, keep one recommendation in mind—don't be lazy. Pick names that reflect the intended use of the variable. The reasons are obvious. Just as with the comment statement, meaningful variable names can dramatically increase the readability of a program and will pay off in the debug and documentation phases. In fact, the documentation task will probably be greatly reduced since the program will be more self-explanatory.

Data Types and Constants

You have already been exposed to the C basic data type `int`. As you will recall, a variable declared to be of type `int` can be used to contain integral values only—that is, values that do not contain decimal places.

The C programming language provides the user with three other basic data types: `float`, `double`, and `char`. A variable declared to be of type `float` can be used for storing floating-point numbers (values containing decimal places). The `double` type is the same as type `float`, only with roughly twice the accuracy. Finally, the `char` data type can be used to store a single character, such as the letter "a," the digit character "6," or a semicolon; more on this later.

In C, any literal number, single character, or character string is known as a *constant*. For example, the number 58 represents a constant integer value. The character string `"Programming in C is fun.\n"` is an example of a constant character string. Expressions consisting entirely of constant values are called *constant expressions*. So the expression

128 + 7 - 17

---

[1]*See Chapter 15, "Working with Larger Programs," for a discussion on external names. Your system might not allow such names to be 31 characters long.*

is a constant expression because each of the terms of the expression is a constant value. But if i were declared to be an integer variable, then the expression

```
128 + 7 - i
```

would not represent a constant expression.

It is important to understand the concept of constants in order to fully understand data types and operations in C.

Type *int*

In C, an integer constant consists of a sequence of one or more digits. A minus sign preceding the sequence indicates that the value is negative. The values 158, -10, and 0 are all valid examples of integer constants. No embedded spaces are permitted between the digits, and values larger than 999 cannot be expressed using commas. (So the value 12,000 is not a valid integer constant and must be written as 12000.)

Two special formats in C enable integer constants to be expressed in a base other than decimal (base 10). If the first digit of the integer value is a zero, then the integer is taken as expressed in *octal* notation, that is, in base 8. In that case, the remaining digits of the value must be valid base-8 digits and therefore must be from 0 through 7. So, to express the value octal 50 in C, the notation 050 is used. Similarly, the C octal constant 0177 represents the decimal value 127 (1 x 64 + 7 x 8 + 7). An integer value can be displayed at the terminal in octal notation by using the format characters %o in the format string of a printf statement. In such a case, it is noted that the value will be displayed in octal *without* a leading zero. The format character %#o *will* cause a leading zero to be displayed before an octal value.

QUICK TIP

Don't forget that any integer value preceded by a 0 is considered to be an octal number by the compiler!

If an integer constant is preceded by a 0 and the letter x (either lowercase or uppercase), then the value is taken as being expressed in hexadecimal (base 16) notation. Immediately following the letter x are the digits of the hexadecimal value, which can be composed of the digits 0 through 9 and the letters a through f (or A through F). The letters represent the values 10 through 15, respectively. So, to assign the hexadecimal value 5EB (= 16^2 x 5 + 16 x 14 + 11 = 1,515 decimal) to an integer variable called `type_mask`, the statement

```
type_mask = 0x5EB;
```

can be used. To display an integer value in hexadecimal format at the terminal, use the format characters `%x`. So the statement

```
printf ("Value = %x\n", type_mask);
```

would display the value of `type_mask` in hexadecimal format, *without* the leading `0x`. To display the value with the leading `0x`, you would use the format characters `%#x`, as in

```
printf ("Value = %#x\n", type_mask);
```

Octal and hexadecimal constants frequently find their way into systems programs and more advanced programming applications. As such, this notation will not be used again until much later in this book.

Type *float*

A variable declared to be of type `float` can be used for storing values containing decimal places. A floating-point constant is distinguished by the presence of a decimal point. It is permissible to omit digits before the decimal point, or digits after the decimal point, but obviously it is not permissible to omit both. The values `3.`, `125.8`, and `-.0001` are all valid examples of floating-point constants. To display a floating-point value at the terminal, the `printf` conversion characters `%f` are used.

Floating-point constants can also be expressed in *scientific notation*. The value `1.7e-4` is a floating-point value expressed in this notation and represents the value 1.7×10^{-4}. The value before the letter e is known as the *mantissa*, while the value that follows is called the *exponent*. This exponent, which may be preceded by an optional plus or minus sign, represents the power of 10 that the mantissa is to be multiplied by. So, in the constant `2.25e-3`, the 2.25 is the value of the mantissa and -3 is the value of the exponent. This constant represents the value 2.25^{-3}, or 0.00225. Incidentally, the letter e, which separates the mantissa from the exponent, can be written in either lower- or uppercase.

In order to display a value in scientific notation, the format characters `%e` should be specified in the `printf` format string. The `printf` format characters `%g` can be used to let `printf` decide whether to display the floating-point value in normal floating-point notation or in scientific notation. This decision will be based upon the value of the exponent: if it's less than -4 or greater than 5, `%e` (scientific notation) format will be used; otherwise, `%f` format will be used.

QUICK TIP

Use the %g format characters for displaying floating-point numbers—it produces the most aesthetically pleasing output.

Type *double*

The type `double` is very similar to type `float`. It is used whenever the accuracy provided by a `float` variable is not sufficient. Variables declared to be of type `double` can store roughly twice as many significant digits as can a variable of type `float`. The precise number of digits that can be stored in either a `float` or `double` variable depends upon the particular computer system you are using. On the DEC VAXen, a `float` variable can contain approximately seven decimal digits, while a variable of type `double` has a precision of approximately 16 decimal digits.

Unless told otherwise, all floating-point constants are taken as `double` values by the C compiler. To explicitly express a `float` constant, append either an `f` or `F` to the end of the number, as in

```
12.5f
```

To display a `double` value at the terminal, the format characters %f, %e, or %g, which are the same format characters used to display a `float` value, can be used.

Type *char*

A `char` variable can be used to store a single character. A character constant is formed by enclosing the character within a pair of *single* quote marks. So `'a'`, `';'`, and `'0'` are all valid examples of character constants. The first constant represents the letter a, the second a semicolon, and the third the *character* zero—which is not the same as the *number* zero. Do not confuse a character constant, which is a single character enclosed in single quotes, with a character string, which is any number of characters enclosed in *double* quotes. We will learn more about this distinction in Chapter 10, "Character Strings."

The character constant `'\n'`—the newline character—is a valid character constant even though it seems to contradict the rule cited above. The reason for this is that the backslash character is a special character in the C system and does not actually count as a character. In other words, the C compiler treats the character `'\n'` as a single character, even though it is actually formed by two characters. In Chapter 10, you will find that the backslash character can be used for purposes other than just for advancing to the next line. The format characters %c can be used in a `printf` call to display the value of a `char` variable at the terminal.

In Program 4.1, the basic C data types are used. Notice how a value can be assigned to a variable at the time that the variable is declared.

Program 4.1

```
#include <stdio.h>
main ()
{
    int     integer_var = 100;
    float   floating_var = 331.79;
    double  double_var =  8.44e+11;
    char    char_var = 'W';

    printf ("integer_var = %i\n", integer_var);
    printf ("floating_var = %f\n", floating_var);
    printf ("double_var = %e\n", double_var);
    printf ("double_var = %g\n", double_var);
    printf ("char_var = %c\n", char_var);
}
```

Program 4.1 OUTPUT

```
integer_var = 100
floating_var = 331.789978
double_var = 8.440000e+11
double_var = 8.44e+11
char_var = W
```

The first statement of Program 4.1 declares the variable integer_var to be an integer variable and also assigns to it an initial value of 100, as if the following two statements had been used instead:

```
int  integer_var;
integer_var = 100;
```

In the second line of the program's output, you will notice that the value of 331.79 that we assigned to floating_var is actually displayed as 331.789978. In fact, the actual value that is displayed is quite dependent on the particular computer system you are using. The reason for this inaccuracy is the particular way that numbers are internally represented inside the computer system. You have probably come across the same type of inaccuracy when dealing with numbers on your pocket calculator. If you divide 1 by 3 on your calculator, you will get the result .33333333—with perhaps some additional 3s tacked on at the end. The string of 3s is the calculator's approximation of one-third. Theoretically, there should be an infinite number of 3s. But the calculator can only hold so many digits, thus the inherent inaccuracy of the machine. The same type of inaccuracy applies to your computer system. Certain floating-point values cannot be exactly represented inside the computer's memory.

When displaying the values of `float` or `double` variables, you have the choice of three different formats. The `%f` characters are used to display values in a standard manner. Unless told otherwise, `printf` will always display a `float` or `double` value to six decimal places rounded. We will see later in this chapter how to select the number of decimal places that are displayed.

The `%e` characters are used to display the value of a `float` or `double` variable in scientific notation. Once again, six decimal places are automatically displayed by the system.

With the `%g` characters, `printf` chooses between `%f` and `%e` and also automatically removes from the display any trailing zeroes. If no digits follow the decimal point, it won't display that either.

In the last `printf` statement, the `%c` characters are used to display the single character `'W'` that we assigned to `char_var` when the variable was declared. Remember that while a character string (such as the first argument to `printf`) is enclosed within a pair of double quotes, a character constant must always be enclosed within a pair of single quotes.

Qualifiers *long, short, unsigned,* and *signed*

If the qualifier `long` is placed directly before the `int` declaration, the declared integer variable will be of extended accuracy on many computer systems. An example of a `long int` declaration might be

```
long int  factorial;
```

which would declare the variable `factorial` to be a `long` integer variable. As with `float`s and `double`s, the particular accuracy of a `long` variable depends upon the particular computer system. On the IBM PC, for example, the maximum positive value that can be stored inside a variable of type `int` is 32,767. Declaring a variable to be of type `long int` permits values up to $2^{31}-1$ or 2,147,483,647 to be stored in the variable. On the SUN SPARC Station, an `int` and a `long int` both have the same accuracy (which is the same as that for a `long int` on the IBM PC) and can therefore both be used to store integer values up to 2,147,483,647.

A constant value of type `long int` is formed by optionally appending the letter L (upper- or lowercase) to the end of an integer constant. No spaces are permitted between the number and the L. So, the declaration

```
long int  number_of_points = 131071L;
```

declares the variable `number_of_points` to be of type `long int` with an initial value of 131,071.

To display the value of a `long int` at the terminal, the letter `l` is used as a modifier before the integer format characters `i`, `o`, or `x`. This means that the format characters `%li` can be used to display the value of a `long int` in decimal format, the characters `%lo` to display the value in octal format, and the characters `%lx` to display the value in hexadecimal format.

The `long` qualifier is also allowed in front of a `double` declaration, as in

```
long double  US_deficit_2000;
```

Whether or not a `long double` gives you more precision than a `double` on your machine is uncertain, so you'll have to check your documentation.

A `long double` constant is written as a floating constant with the letter `l` or `L` immediately following, as in

```
1.234e+7L
```

To display a `long double`, the L modifier is used. So `%Lf` would display a `long double` value in floating-point notation, `%Le` would display the same value in scientific notation, and `%Lg` would tell `printf` to choose between `%Lf` and `%Le`.

The qualifier `short`, when placed in front of the `int` declaration, tells the C compiler that the particular variable being declared will be used to store fairly small integer values. The motivation for using `short` variables is primarily one of conserving the computer's memory space, which may be an issue in cases where the program needs a lot of memory and the amount available is limited.

On some machines, a `short int` will take up half the amount of storage a regular `int` variable. On the VAX-11, a `short int` can be used to store integer values in the range -32,768 to 32,767. On the IBM PC, a `short int` and an `int` take up the same amount of space: 16 bits. In any case, you are guaranteed that the amount of space allocated for a `short int` will not be less than 16 bits.

There is no way to explicitly write a constant of type `short int` in C. To display a `short int` variable, place the letter `h` in front of any of the normal integer conversion characters: `%hi`, `%ho`, `%hx`.

The final qualifier that may be placed in front of an `int` variable is used when an integer variable will be used only to store positive numbers. The declaration

```
unsigned int  counter;
```

declares to the compiler that the variable counter will be used only to contain positive values. By restricting the use of an integer variable to the exclusive storage of positive integers, the accuracy of the integer variable is extended. On the IBM PC for example, a normal int variable can assume values from -32,768 through 32,767. The same variable declared to be of type unsigned int can assume values from 0 through 65,535.

An unsigned int constant is formed by placing the letter u (or U) after the constant, as in

```
0x00ffU
```

It's possible to combine the letters u (or U) and l (or L) when writing an integer constant, so

```
20000UL
```

tells the compiler to treat the constant 20000 as unsigned long.

An integer constant that's not followed by any of the letters u, U, l, or L, and that is too large to fit into a normal-sized int, is treated as an unsigned int by the compiler. If it's too small to fit into an unsigned int, the compiler treats it as a long int. Finally, if it still can't fit inside a long int, the compiler makes it an unsigned long int.

When declaring variables to be of type long int, short int, or unsigned int, it is permissable to omit the keyword int. So the unsigned variable counter could have been equivalently declared as

```
unsigned   counter;
```

You can also declare char variables to be unsigned. The reason for using such a declaration is discussed in Chapter 14, "More on Data Types."

The signed qualifier can be used to explicitly tell the compiler that a particular variable is a signed quantity. It's use is primarily in front of the char declaration, and further discussion on this is deferred until Chapter 14.

Don't worry if the discussions of these qualifiers seem a bit esoteric to you at this point. In later sections of this book, we will illustrate the use of many of these different types with actual program examples. Chapter 14 goes into more detail about data types and conversions.

Table 4.1 summarizes the basic data types and qualifiers.

Table 4.1. Basic data types.

Type	Constant Examples	printf Chars
char	'a', '\n'	%c
short int	-	%hi, %hx, %ho
unsigned short int	-	%hu, %hx, %ho
int	12, -97, 0xFFE0, 0177	%i, %x, %o
unsigned int	12u, 100U, 0XFFu	%u, %x, %o
long int	12L, -2001, 0xffffL	%li, %lx, %lo
unsigned long int	12UL, 100ul, oxffeeUL	%lu, %lx, %lo
float	12.34f, 3.1e-5f	%f, %e, %g
double	12.34, 3.1e-5	%f, %e, %g
long double	12.341, 3.1e-5l	%Lf, %Le, %Lg

Arithmetic Expressions

In C, just as in virtually all programming languages, the plus sign (+) is used to add two values; the minus sign (-) to subtract two values; the asterisk (*) to multiply two values; and the slash (/) to divide two values. These operators are known as *binary* arithmetic operators, since they operate on *two* values or terms.

We have seen how a simple operation like addition can be performed in C. The following program further illustrates the operations of subtraction, multiplication, and division. The last two operations performed in the program introduce the notion that one operator can have a higher priority, or *precedence*, over another operator. In fact, each operator in C has a precedence associated with it. This precedence is used to determine how an expression that has more than one operator is evaluated: The operator with the higher precedence is evaluated first. Expressions containing operators of the same precedence are either evaluated from left to right or from right to left, depending upon the operator. This is known as the *associative* property of an operator. Appendix A provides a complete list of operator precedences and their rules of association.

Program 4.2

```c
/* Illustrate the use of various arithmetic operators */
#include <stdio.h>
main ()
{
    int  a = 100;
    int  b = 2;
    int  c = 25;
    int  d = 4;
    int  result;

    result = a - b;          /* subtraction */
    printf ("a - b = %i\n", result);

    result = b * c;          /* multiplication */
    printf ("b * c = %i\n", result);

    result = a / c;          /* division */
    printf ("a / c = %i\n", result);

    result = a + b * c;      /* precedence */
    printf ("a + b * c = %i\n", result);

    printf ("a * b + c * d =  %i\n", a * b + c * d);
}
```

Program 4.2 OUTPUT

```
a - b = 98
b * c = 50
a / c = 4
a + b * c = 150
a * b + c * d = 300
```

After declaring the integer variables a, b, c, d, and result, the program assigns the result of subtracting b from a to result and then proceeds to display its value with an appropriate printf call.

The next statement

```c
result = b * c;
```

has the effect of multiplying the value of b by the value of c and storing the product in result. The result of the multiplication is then displayed using a printf call that should be very familiar to you by now.

The next program statement introduces the division operator—the slash. The result of 4 as obtained by dividing 100 by 25 is displayed by the `printf` statement immediately following the division of a by c.

On most computer systems, attempting to divide a number by zero will result in abnormal termination of the program. Even if the program does not terminate abnormally, the results obtained by such a division will be meaningless. In Chapter 6, "Making Decisions," we will see how we can check for division by zero before the division operation is performed. If it is determined that the divisor is zero, then an appropriate action (such as displaying a message at the terminal) can be taken and the division operation averted.

QUICK TIP

Make sure you get into the habit of ensuring that any division in your program will not be by zero. This will prevent your programs from terminating abnormally.

The expression

```
a + b * c
```

does not produce the result of 2550 (102 * 25) as might be expected; rather, the result as displayed by the corresponding `printf` statement is shown as 150. This is because C, like most other programming languages, has rules for the order of evaluating multiple operations or terms in an expression. Evaluation of an expression generally proceeds from left to right. However, the operations of multiplication and division are given precedence over the operations of addition and subtraction. Therefore, the expression

```
a + b * c
```

is evaluated as

```
a + (b * c)
```

by the C system. (This is the same way that this expression would be evaluated if we were to apply the basic rules of algebra.)

If we wish to alter the order of evaluation of terms inside an expression, then parentheses can be used. In fact, the last expression listed above is a perfectly valid C expression. Thus the statement

```
result = a + (b * c);
```

could have been substituted in Program 4.2 to achieve identical results. However, if the expression

```
result = (a + b) * c;
```

were used instead, then the value assigned to result would be 2550, since the value of a (100) would be added to the value of b (2) *before* multiplication by the value of c (25) would take place. Parentheses may be nested, and evaluation of the expression will proceed outward from the innermost set of parentheses. Just be sure to have as many closed parentheses as there are open ones.

You will notice from the last statement in Program 4.2 that it is perfectly valid to give an expression as an argument to printf without having to first assign the result of the expression evaluation to a variable. The expression

```
a * b + c * d
```

is evaluated according to the rules stated above as

```
(a * b) + (c * d)
```

or

```
(100 * 2) + (25 * 4)
```

and the result of 300 "handed" to the printf routine.

Integer Arithmetic and the Unary Minus Operator

Program 4.3 reinforces what we have just discussed and introduces the concept of integer arithmetic.

Program 4.3

```
/* More arithmetic expressions */
#include <stdio.h>
main ()
{
    int     a = 25;
    int     b = 2;
    int     result;
    float   c = 25.0;
    float   d = 2.0;

    printf ("6 + a / 5 * b = %i\n", 6 + a / 5 * b);
    printf ("a / b * b = %i\n", a / b * b);
    printf ("c / d * d = %f\n", c / d * d);
    printf ("-a = %i\n", -a);
}
```

Program 4.3 OUTPUT

```
6 + a / 5 * b = 16
a / b * b = 24
c / d * d = 25.000000
-a = -25
```

We inserted extra blank spaces between int and the declaration of a, b, and result in the first three statements to align the declaration of each variable. This helps to make the program more readable. You also may have noticed in each program presented so far that a blank space was placed around each operator. This too is not required and is done solely for aesthetic reasons. In general, you may add extra blank spaces just about anywhere that a single blank space is allowed. A few extra presses of the spacebar will prove worthwhile if the resulting program is easier to read.

The expression in the first printf call of Program 4.3 reinforces the notion of operator precedence. Evaluation of this expression proceeds as follows:

1. Since division has higher precedence than addition, the value of a (25) is divided by 5 first. This gives the intermediate result of 5.

2. Since multiplication also has higher precedence than addition, the intermediate result of 5 is next multiplied by 2, the value of b, giving a new intermediate result of 10.

3. Finally, the addition of 6 and 10 is performed, giving a final result of 16.

The second printf statement introduces a new twist. We would expect that dividing a by b and then multiplying by b would return to us the value of a, which we have set to 25. But this does not seem to be the case, as shown by the output display of 24. Did the computer lose a bit somewhere along the way? Very unlikely. The fact of the matter is that this expression was evaluated using *integer arithmetic*.

If you glance back at the declarations for the variables a and b, you will recall that they were both declared to be of type int. Now, whenever a term to be evaluated in an expression consists of *two* integers, the C system performs the operation using integer arithmetic. In such a case, all decimal portions of numbers are lost. Therefore, when the value of a is divided by the value of b, or 25 is divided by 2, we get an intermediate result of 12 and *not* 12.5 as you might expect. Multiplying this intermediate result by 2 gives us the final result of 24, thus explaining the "lost" digit.

As can be seen from the next-to-last `printf` statement in Program 4.3, if we perform the same operation using floating-point values instead of integers, we obtain the expected result.

The decision of whether to use a `float` variable or an `int` variable should be made based upon the variable's intended use. If you don't need any decimal places, then use an integer variable. The resulting program will be more *efficient*—that is, it will execute faster on most computers. On the other hand, if you need the decimal place accuracy, then the choice is clear. The only question that you then must decide is whether to use a `float` or `double`. The answer to this question will depend upon the desired accuracy of the numbers you are dealing with, as well as their magnitude.

In the last `printf` statement, the value of the variable a is *negated* by use of the *unary minus* operator. A unary operator is one which operates on a single value, as opposed to a binary operator, which operates on two values. The minus sign actually has a dual role: As a binary operator, it is used for subtracting two values. As a unary operator, it is used to negate a value.

The unary minus operator has higher precedence than all other arithmetic operators, except for the unary plus operator (+), which has the same precedence. So the expression

```
c = -a * b;
```

will result in the multiplication of `-a` by `b`. Once again, in Appendix A you will find a table summarizing the various operators and their precedences.

The Modulus Operator

The last operator to be presented in this chapter is the *modulus* operator, which is symbolized by the percent sign (`%`). Try to determine how this operator works by analyzing the output from Program 4.4.

Program 4.4

```
/* The modulus operator */
#include <stdio.h>
main ()
{
```

```
int  a = 25, b = 5, c = 10, d = 7;

printf ("a %% b = %i\n", a % b);
printf ("a %% c = %i\n", a % c);
printf ("a %% d = %i\n", a % d);
printf ("a / d * d + a %% d = %i\n",
            a / d * d + a % d);
}
```

Program 4.4 OUTPUT

```
a % b = 0
a % c = 5
a % d = 4
a / d * d + a % d = 25
```

The first statement inside `main` declares and initializes the variables a, b, c, and d in a single statement.

In the first `printf` call, you will notice that we used *two* percent signs in the format string; yet, if you examine the program's output, you will notice that only a single percent sign was printed. The reason for this is the special significance of the % sign to the `printf` routine. As you know, `printf` uses the character that immediately follows the percent sign to determine how to print the next argument. However, if it is another percent sign that follows, then the `printf` routine takes this as an indication that you really intend to display a percent sign and inserts one at the appropriate place in the program's output.

You are correct if you concluded that the function of the modulus operator % is to give the remainder of the first value divided by the second value. In the first example, the remainder after 25 is divided by 5 is displayed as 0. If we divide 25 by 10, we get a remainder of 5, as verified by the second line of output. Dividing 25 by 7 gives a remainder of 4, as shown in the third output line.

The last line of output in Program 4.4 requires a bit of explanation. First, you will notice that the program statement has been written on two lines. This is perfectly valid in C. In fact, a program statement may be continued to the next line at any point where a blank space could be used. (An exception to this occurs when dealing with character strings—a topic discussed in Chapter 10.) At times it may not only be desirable, but perhaps even necessary to continue a program statement onto the next line. The continuation of the `printf` call in Program 4.4 is indented to visually show that it is a continuation of the preceding program statement.

Let us now turn our attention to the expression that is evaluated in this last statement. You will recall that any operations between two integer values in C are performed with integer arithmetic. Therefore, any remainder resulting from the division of two integer values will simply be discarded. Dividing 25 by 7, as indicated by the expression a / d, gives an intermediate result of 3. Multiplying this value by the value of d, which is 7, produces the intermediate result of 21. Finally, adding in the remainder of dividing a by d, as indicated by the expression a % d, leads to the final result of 25. It is no coincidence that this value is the same as the value of the variable a. In general, the expression

```
a / b * b + a % b
```

will always equal the value of a, assuming of course that a and b are both integer values. In fact, the modulus operator % is defined to work only with integer values.

As far as precedence is concerned, the modulus operator has equal precedence to the multiplication and division operators. This implies, of course, that an expression such as

```
table + value % TABLE_SIZE
```

will be evaluated as

```
table + (value % TABLE_SIZE)
```

Integer and Floating-Point Conversions

In order to effectively develop C programs, you must understand the rules that are used for the implicit conversion of floating-point and integer values in C. Program 4.5 demonstrates some of the simple conversions between numeric data types. In Chapter 14, "More on Data Types," the rules that are followed for conversion between other data types are described in detail.

Program 4.5

```
/* Basic conversions in C */
#include <stdio.h>
main ()
{
    float  f1 = 123.125, f2;
    int    i1, i2 = -150;
    char   c = 'a';

    i1 = f1;            /* floating to integer conversion */
    printf ("%f assigned to an int produces %i\n", f1, i1);
```

```
    f1 = i2;            /* integer to floating conversion */
    printf ("%i assigned to a float produces %f\n", i2, f1);

    f1 = i2 / 100;     /* integer divided by integer */
    printf ("%i divided by 100 produces %f\n", i2, f1);

    f2 = i2 / 100.0;   /* integer divided by a float */
    printf ("%i divided by 100.0 produces %f\n", i2, f2);
}
```

Program 4.5 OUTPUT

```
123.125000 assigned to an int produces 123
-150 assigned to a float produces -150.000000
-150 divided by 100 produces -1.000000
-150 divided by 100.0 produces -1.500000
```

Whenever a floating-point value is assigned to an integer variable in C, the decimal portion of the number gets *truncated*. So when the value of f1 is assigned to i1 in the above program, the number 123.125 gets truncated, which means that only its integer portion, or 123, is stored into i1. The first line of the program's output verifies that this is the case.

Assigning an integer variable to a floating variable does not cause any change in the value of the number. The value is simply converted by the system and stored into the floating variable. The second line of the program's output verifies that the value of i2, -150, was correctly converted and stored into the float variable f1.

The next two lines of the program's output illustrate two points that must be remembered when forming arithmetic expressions. The first has to do with integer arithmetic, which we have already discussed in this chapter. Whenever two operands in an expression are integers (and this applies to short, unsigned, and long integers as well), the operation is carried out under the rules of integer arithmetic. Therefore, any decimal portion resulting from a division operation will be discarded, even if the result is assigned to a floating variable (as we did in the program). So when the integer variable i2 is divided by the integer constant 100, the system performs the division as an integer division. The result of dividing -150 by 100, which is -1, is therefore the value that is stored into the float variable f1.

The next division that is performed in the above program involves an integer variable and a floating-point constant. Any operation between two values in

C will be performed as a floating-point operation if *either* value is a floating-point variable or constant. Therefore, when the value of i2 is divided by 100.0, the system treats the division as a floating-point division and produces the result of -1.5, which is assigned to the float variable f1.

We have reached the end of discussion on variables, data types, and expressions. If you are familiar with other programming languages, you may have noticed that there is no operator for raising a number to a power (exponentiation). Luckily, there is a function called pow in the program library for performing exponentiation.

Try your hand at the exercises presented on the following pages before proceeding to the next chapter, which introduces the concept of program looping.

Exercises

1. If you have access to a computer facility that supports the C programming language, type in and run the five programs presented in this chapter. Compare the output produced by each program with the output presented after each program.

2. Which of the following are invalid variable names? Why?

Int	char	6_05
calloc	Xx	alpha_beta_routine
floating	_1312	z
ReInitialize	_	A$

3. Which of the following are invalid constants? Why?

123.456	0x10.5	0X0G1
0001	0xFFFF	123L
0Xab05	0L	-597.25
123.5e2	.0001	+12
98.6F	98.7U	17777s
0996	-12E-12	07777
1234uL	1.2Fe-7	15,000
1.234L	197u	100U
0XABCDEFL	0xabcu	+123

4. Write a program that converts 27° from degrees Fahrenheit (*F*) to degrees Celsius (c) using the formula

    $$C = (F - 32)/1.8$$

5. What output would you expect from the following program?

```
main ()
{
   char  c, d;

   c = 'd';
   d = c;
   printf ("d = %c\n", d);
}
```

6. Write a program to evaluate the polynomial

$$3x^3 - 5x^2 + 6$$

for $x = 2.55$.

7. Write a program that evaluates the following expression and displays the results. (Remember to use exponential format to display the result.)

```
(3.31 x 10⁻⁸ x + 2.01 x 10⁻⁷) / (7.16 x 10⁻⁶ + 2.01 x 10⁻⁸)
```

8. To round off an integer i to the next largest even multiple of another integer j, the following formula can be used:

Next_multiple = i + j - i % j

For example, to round off 256 days to the next largest number of days evenly divisible by a week, values of $i = 256$ and $j = 7$ can be substituted into the above formula as follows:

```
Next_multiple     = 256 + 7 - 256 % 7
                  = 256 + 7 - 4
                  = 259
```

Write a program to find the next largest even multiple for the following values of i and j:

i	j
365	7
12,258	23
996	4

5

Program Looping

If we were to arrange 15 dots into the shape of a triangle, we would end up with an arrangement that might look something like this:

```
        .
      .   .
    .   .   .
  .   .   .   .
.   .   .   .   .
```

The first row of the triangle contains one dot, the second row two dots, and so on. In general, the number of dots it would take to form a triangle containing n rows would be the sum of the integers from 1 through n. This sum is known as a *triangular number*. If we start at 1, then the fourth triangular number would be the sum of the consecutive integers 1 through 4 $(1 + 2 + 3 + 4)$, or 10.

Suppose we wished to write a program that calculated and displayed the value of the eighth triangular number at the terminal. Obviously, we could easily calculate this number in our heads, but for the sake of argument, let us assume that we wanted to write a program in C to perform this task. Such a program is shown in Program 5.1.

The technique of Program 5.1 works fine for calculating relatively small triangular numbers. But what would happen if we needed to find the value of the 200th triangular number, for example? It certainly would be a bit tedious to have to modify Program 5.1 to explicitly add up all of the integers from 1 to 200. Luckily, there is an easier way.

Program 5.1

```
/* Program to calculate the eighth triangular number */
#include <stdio.h>
main ()
{
        int  triangular_number;

        triangular_number = 1 + 2 + 3 + 4 + 5 + 6 + 7 + 8;

        printf ("The eighth triangular number is %i\n",
                   triangular_number);
}
```

Program 5.1 OUTPUT

```
The eighth triangular number is 36
```

One of the fundamental properties of a computer is its ability to repetitively execute a set of statements. These *looping* capabilities enable programmers to develop concise programs containing repetitive processes that could otherwise require thousands or even millions of program statements to perform. The C programming language contains three different program statements for program looping. They are known as the for statement, the while statement, and the do statement. Each of these statements will be described in detail in this chapter.

The *for* Statement

Why don't we dive right in and take a look at a program that uses the for statement? The purpose of Program 5.2 is to calculate the 200th triangular number. See if you can determine how the for statement works.

Some explanation is owed for Program 5.2. The method employed to calculate the 200th triangular number is really the same as that used to calculate the 8th triangular number in the previous program—the integers from 1 to 200 are summed. The for statement provides the mechanism that enables us to avoid having to explicitly write out each integer from 1 to 200. In a sense, this statement is used to "generate" these numbers for us.

Program 5.2

```
/* Program to calculate the 200th triangular number */
/* Introduction of the for statement                */
#include <stdio.h>
main ()
{
    int  n, triangular_number;

    triangular_number = 0;

    for ( n = 1;  n <= 200;  n = n + 1 )
    triangular_number = triangular_number + n;

    printf ("The 200th triangular number is %i\n",
                    triangular_number);
}
```

Program 5.2 OUTPUT

```
The 200th triangular number is 20100
```

The general format of the for statement is as follows:

```
for ( init_expression; loop_condition; loop_expression )
     program statement
```

The three expressions that are enclosed within the parentheses—*init_expression*, *loop_condition*, and *loop_expression*—set up the environment for the program loop. The program statement that immediately follows (which is of course terminated by a semicolon) can be any valid C program statement and constitutes the *body of the loop*. This statement will be executed as many times as specified by the parameters set up in the for statement.

The first component of the for, labeled *init_expression*, is used to set the initial values *before* the loop begins. In Program 5.2, this portion of the for statement is used to set the initial value of n to 1. As you can see, an assignment is a valid form of an expression.

The second component of the for statement specifies the condition or conditions that are necessary *in order for the loop to continue.* In other words, looping continues *as long as* this condition is satisfied. Once again referring to Program 5.2, we find that the *loop_condition* of the for is specified by the *relational expression*

```
n <= 200
```

This expression can be read as "n less than or equal to 200." The "less than or equal to" operator (which is the less than character < followed immediately by the equals sign =) is only one of several relational operators provided in the C programming language. These operators are used to test specific conditions. The answer to the test will be "yes" or, more commonly, TRUE if the condition is satisfied and "no" or FALSE if the condition is not satisfied.

Table 5.1 lists all the relational operators that are available in C.

Table 5.1. Relational operators.

Operator	Meaning	Example
==	Equal to	count == 10
!=	Not equal to	flag != DONE
<	Less than	a < b
<=	Less than or equal to	low <= high
>	Greater than	pointer > end_of_list
>=	Greater than or equal to	j >= 0

The relational operators have lower precedence than all arithmetic operators. This means, for example, that an expression such as a

```
< b + c
```

will be evaluated as

```
a < (b + c)
```

as you would expect. It would be TRUE if the value of a were less than the value of b + c and FALSE otherwise.

Pay particular attention to the "is equal to" operator == and do not confuse its use with the assignment operator =. The expression

```
a == 2
```

tests if the value of a is equal to 2, whereas the expression

```
a = 2
```

assigns the value 2 to the variable a.

The choice of which relational operator to use will obviously depend on the particular test being made and in some instances on your particular preferences. For example, the relational expression

```
n <= 200
```

can be equivalently expressed as

```
n < 201
```

Returning to our example, the program statement that forms the body of the for loop

```
triangular_number = triangular_number + n;
```

will be repetitively executed *as long as the result of the relational test is TRUE*, or in this case, as long as the value of n is less than or equal to 200. This program statement has the effect of adding the value of triangular_number to the value of n and storing the result back into the value of triangular_number.

When the *loop_condition* is no longer satisfied, execution of the program will continue with the program statement immediately following the for loop. In our program, execution will continue with the printf statement once the loop has terminated.

The final component of the for statement contains an expression that is evaluated each time *after* the body of the loop is executed. In Program 5.2, this *loop_expression* adds 1 to the value of n. Therefore, the value of n will be incremented by 1 each time after its value has been added into the value of triangular_number and will range in value from 1 through 201.

It is worth noting that the last value that n attains, namely 201, is *not* added into the value of triangular_number since the loop is terminated *as soon as* the looping condition is no longer satisfied, or as soon as n equals 201.

In summary then, execution of the for statement proceeds as follows:

1. The initial expression is evaluated first. This expression usually sets a variable that will be used inside the loop, generally referred to as an *index* variable, to some initial value such as 0 or 1.

2. The looping condition is evaluated. If the condition is not satisfied (the expression is FALSE), then the loop is immediately terminated. Execution continues with the program statement that immediately follows the loop.

3. The program statement that constitutes the body of the loop is executed.

4. The looping expression is evaluated. This expression is generally used to change the value of the index variable, frequently by adding 1 to it or subtracting 1 from it.

5. Return to Step 2.

QUICK TIP

Remember that the looping condition is evaluated immediately on entry into the loop, before the body of the loop has even executed one time. Also, remember not to put a semicolon after the close parenthesis at the end of the loop (this will immediately end the loop).

Since Program 5.2 actually generates all of the first 200 triangular numbers on its way to its final goal, it might be nice to generate a table of these numbers. To save space, however, we will assume that we just want to print a table of the first 10 triangular numbers. Program 5.3 below performs precisely this task!

Program 5.3

```
/* Program to generate a table of triangular numbers */
#include <stdio.h>
main ()
{
    int  n, triangular_number;

    printf ("TABLE OF TRIANGULAR NUMBERS\n\n");
    printf (" n    Sum from 1 to n\n");
    printf ("---   --------------\n");

    triangular_number = 0;

    for ( n = 1;  n <= 10;  ++n )
    {
    triangular_number = triangular_number + n;
    printf (" %i           %i\n", n, triangular_number);
    }
}
```

Program 5.3 OUTPUT

```
TABLE OF TRIANGULAR NUMBERS
  n    Sum from 1 to n
 ---   ---------------
  1            1
  2            3
  3            6
  4           10
  5           15
  6           21
  7           28
  8           36
  9           45
 10           55
```

It is always a good idea to add some extra `printf` statements to a program in order to provide more meaning to the output. In Program 5.3, the purpose of the first three `printf` statements is simply to provide a general heading and to label the columns of the output. You will notice that the first `printf` statement contains two newline characters. As you would expect, this has the effect of not only advancing to the next line but also inserting an extra blank line into the display.

After the appropriate headings have been displayed, the program proceeds to calculate the first 10 triangular numbers. The variable n is used to count the current number whose "sum from 1 to n" we are computing, while the variable `triangular_number` is used to store the value of triangular number n.

Execution of the `for` statement commences by setting the value of the variable n to 1. You will recall that we mentioned earlier that the program statement immediately following the `for` statement constitutes the body of the program loop. But what happens if we wish to repetitively execute not just a single program statement but a group of program statements? This can be accomplished by enclosing all such program statements within a pair of braces. The system will then treat this group or *block* of statements as a single entity. In general, any place in a C program that a single statement is permitted, a block of statements can be used, provided that you remember to enclose the block within a pair of braces.

Therefore, in Program 5.3, both the expression that adds n into the value of `triangular_number` and the `printf` statement that immediately follows constitute the body of the program loop. Pay particular attention to the way the program statements are indented. At a quick glance, it is easy to determine which statements form part of the `for` loop. You should also note that programmers use different coding styles. Some prefer to type the loop this way:

```
for ( n = 1;  n <= 10;  ++n ) {
    triangular_number = triangular_number + n;
    printf (" %i          %i\n", n, triangular_number);
}
```

Here the opening brace is placed on the same line as the for. This is strictly a matter of taste and has no effect on the program.

The next triangular number is calculated by simply adding the value of n to the previous triangular number. The first time through the for loop, the "previous" triangular number is zero, so the new value of triangular_number when n is equal to 1 is simply the value of n, or 1. The values of n and triangular_number are then displayed, with an appropriate number of blank spaces inserted in the format string to ensure that the values of the two variables line up under the appropriate column headings.

Since the body of the loop has now been executed, the looping expression is evaluated next. The expression in this for statement appears a bit strange, however. Surely we must have made a typographical mistake and meant to insert the expression

```
n = n + 1
```

instead of the funny-looking expression

```
++n
```

The fact of the matter is that ++n is actually a perfectly valid C expression. It introduces us to a new (and rather unique) operator in the C programming language—the *increment operator*. The function of the double plus sign—or the increment operator—is to add 1 to its operand. Since addition by 1 is such a common operation in programs, a special operator was created solely for this purpose. Therefore, the expression ++n is equivalent to the expression n = n + 1. While at first glance it might appear that n = n + 1 is more readable, you will very soon get used to the function of this operator and will even learn to appreciate its succinctness.

Of course, no programming language that offered an increment operator to add 1 would be complete without a corresponding operator to subtract 1. And as you would guess, the name of this operator is the *decrement operator* and is symbolized by the double minus sign. So, an expression in C that reads

```
bean_counter = bean_counter - 1
```

can be equivalently expressed using the decrement operator as

```
--bean_counter
```

Some programmers prefer to put the ++ or -- after the variable name, as in n++ or bean_counter--. This is acceptable, and is a matter of personal preference.

QUICK TIP

One slightly disturbing thing that you may have noticed in Program 5.3's output is the fact that the 10th triangular number does not quite line up under the previous triangular numbers. This is because the number 10 takes up two print positions, whereas the previous values of n, 1 through 9, took up only one print position. Therefore, the value 55 is effectively "pushed over" one extra position in the display.

This minor annoyance can be corrected if we substitute the following `printf` statement in place of the corresponding statement from Program 5.3.

```
printf ("%2i          %i\n", n, triangular_number);
```

To verify that this change will do the trick, here is the output from the modified program (we'll call it Program 5.3A).

Program 5.3A OUTPUT

n	Sum from 1 to n
1	1
2	3
3	6
4	10
5	15
6	21
7	28
8	36
9	45
10	55

The primary change made to the `printf` statement was the inclusion of a *field width specification*. The characters `%2i` tell the `printf` routine that not only do we wish to display the value of an integer at that particular point, but also that the size of the integer to be displayed should take up two columns in the display. Any integer that would normally take up less than two columns (that is, the integers 0 through 9) will be displayed with a *leading* space. This is known as *right justification*.

Thus, by using a field width specification of `%2i` we guarantee that at least two columns will be used for displaying the value of n and, therefore, ensure that the values of `triangular_number` will be lined up.

If the value that is to be displayed requires more columns than are specified by the field width, printf simply ignores the field width specification and uses as many columns as are necessary to display the value.

Field width specifications can be used for displaying values other than integers as well. We will see some examples of this in programs that will be coming up shortly.

Program Input

Program 5.2 calculates the 200th triangular number—and nothing more. What if we wanted to calculate the 50th or the 100th triangular number instead? Well, if that were the case, then we would have to go back and change the program so that the for loop would be executed the correct number of times. We would also have to change the printf statement to display the correct message.

An easier solution might be if we could somehow have the program ask us which triangular number we wished to calculate. Then, once we had given our answer, the program could calculate the desired triangular number for us. Such a solution can be effected in C by use of a routine called scanf. The scanf routine is very similar in concept to the printf routine. Whereas the latter routine is used to display values at the terminal, the function of the former routine is to enable the programmer to type values *into* the program. Program 5.4 asks the user which triangular number should be calculated, proceeds to calculate that number, and then displays the results.

Program 5.4

```
#include <stdio.h>
main ()
{
     int   n, number, triangular_number;

     printf ("What triangular number do you want? ");
     scanf  ("%i", &number);

     triangular_number = 0;

     for ( n = 1;  n <= number;  ++n )
     triangular_number = triangular_number + n;

     printf ("Triangular number %i is %i\n", number,
     triangular_number);
}
```

In the program output that follows, the number typed in by the user (100) is set in bolder type to distinguish it from the output displayed by the program.

Program 5.4 OUTPUT

```
What triangular number do you want? 100
Triangular number 100 is 5050
```

According to the output, the number 100 was typed in by the user. The program then proceeded to calculate the 100th triangular number and displayed the result of 5050 at the terminal. The user could have just as easily typed in the number 10, or 30, if he or she desired to calculate those particular triangular numbers.

The first `printf` statement in Program 5.4 is used to prompt the user to type in a number. Of course, it is always nice to remind the user what it is you want entered. After the message is printed, the `scanf` routine is called. The first argument to `scanf` is the format string and is very similar to the format string used by `printf`. In this case, the format string doesn't tell the system what types of values are to be displayed but rather what types of values are to be read in from the terminal. Like `printf`, the `%i` characters are used to specify an integer value.

The second argument to the `scanf` routine specifies *where* the value that is typed in by the user is to be stored. The `&` character before the variable `number` is necessary in this case. Don't worry about its function here, though. We will discuss this character, which is actually an operator, in great detail in Chapter 11, "Pointers."

QUICK TIP

Don't ever forget to put the leading `&` in front of the variable name in the `scanf` function call. If you do, it will cause strange results and may cause your program to terminate abnormally.

Given the preceding discussion, we can now see that the `scanf` call from Program 5.4 specifies that an integer value is to be read from the terminal and stored into the variable `number`. This value represents the particular triangular number that the user wishes to have calculated.

Once this number has been typed in (and the "Return" key on the keyboard pressed to signal that typing of the number is completed), the program then proceeds to calculate the requested triangular number. This is done the same way as in Program 5.2, the only difference being that instead of using 200 as the limit, number is used.

After the desired triangular number has been calculated, the results are displayed, and execution of the program is then complete.

Nested *for* Loops

Program 5.4 gives the user the flexibility to have the program calculate any triangular number that is desired. But suppose the user had a list of five triangular numbers to be calculated? Well, in such a case, the user could simply execute the program five times, each time typing in the next triangular number from the list to be calculated.

Another way to accomplish the same goals, and a far more interesting method as far as learning about C is concerned, is to have the program handle the situation. This can best be accomplished by inserting a loop into the program to simply repeat the entire series of calculations five times. We know by now that the for statement can be used to set up such a loop. The following program and its associated output illustrate this technique.

Program 5.5

```
#include <stdio.h>
main ()
{
    int  n, number, triangular_number, counter;

    for ( counter = 1;   counter <= 5;   ++counter )
    {
        printf ("What triangular number do you want? ");
        scanf  ("%i", &number);

        triangular_number = 0;

        for ( n = 1;   n <= number;   ++n )
            triangular_number = triangular_number + n;

        printf ("Triangular number %i is %i\n\n",
        number, triangular_number);
    }
}
```

Program 5.5 OUTPUT

```
What triangular number do you want? 12
Triangular number 12 is 78

What triangular number do you want? 25
Triangular number 25 is 325

What triangular number do you want? 50
Triangular number 50 is 1275

What triangular number do you want? 75
Triangular number 75 is 2850

What triangular number do you want? 83
Triangular number 83 is 3486
```

The program consists of two levels of for statements. The outermost for statement

```
for ( counter = 1;   counter <= 5;   ++counter )
```

specifies that the program loop is to be executed precisely five times. This can be seen because the value of counter will be initially set to 1 and will be incremented by 1 *until* it is no longer less than or equal to 5 (in other words, until it reaches 6).

Unlike the previous program examples, the variable counter is not used anywhere else within the program. Its function is solely as a loop counter in the for statement. Nevertheless, since it *is* a variable, it must be declared in the program.

The program loop actually consists of all the remaining program statements, as indicated by the braces. It might be easier for you to comprehend the way this program operates if you conceptualize it as follows:

```
For 5 times
{
    Get the number from the user.

    Calculate the requested triangular number.

    Display the results.
}
```

The portion of the loop referred to in the preceding as *Calculate the requested triangular number* actually consists of setting the value of the variable triangular_number to 0 *plus the* for *loop that calculates the triangular number.*

Thus we see that we have a `for` statement that is actually contained *within* another `for` statement. This is perfectly valid in C, and nesting may continue even further to any desired level.

The proper use of indentation becomes even more critical when dealing with more sophisticated program constructs, such as nested `for` statements. At a quick glance you can easily determine which statements are contained within each `for` statement. (To see how unreadable a program can be if correct attention isn't paid to formatting, see Exercise 5 at the end of this chapter.)

for Loop Variants

Before leaving this discussion of the `for` loop, we should mention some of the syntactic variations that are permitted in forming this loop. It may very well be that when writing a `for` loop that you will discover that you have more than one variable that you would like to initialize before the loop begins, or perhaps more than one expression that you would like evaluated each time through the loop. We can include multiple expressions in any of the fields of the `for` loop, provided that we separate such expressions by commas. For example, in the `for` statement that begins

```
for ( i = 0, j = 0;   i < 10;   ++i )
    . . .
```

the value of `i` is set to zero *and* the value of `j` is set to zero before the loop begins. The two expressions `i = 0` and `j = 0` are separated from each other by a comma, and both expressions are considered part of the *init_expression* field of the loop. As another example, the `for` loop that starts

```
for   ( i = 0, j = 100;   i < 10;   ++i, j = j - 10 )
    . . .
```

sets up two index variables, `i` and `j`; the former initialized to 0 and the latter to 100 before the loop begins. Each time after the body of the loop is executed, the value of `i` will be incremented by 1, while the value of `j` will be decremented by 10.

Just as the need may arise to include more than one expression in a particular field of the `for` statement, the need may arise to *omit* one or more fields from the statement. This can be done simply by omitting the desired field and marking its place with a semicolon. The most common application for the omission of a field in the `for` statement occurs when there is no initial expression that needs to be evaluated. The *init_expression* field can simply be "left blank" in such a case, as long as the semicolon is still included:

```
for   (  ;   j != 100;   ++j )
    . . .
```

This statement might be used if j were already set to some initial value before the loop was entered.

A for loop that has its *looping_condition* field omitted effectively sets up an infinite loop; that is, a loop that theoretically will be executed forever. Such a loop can be used provided there is some other means used to exit from the loop (such as executing a return, break, or goto statement as discussed later in this book).

The *while* Statement

The while statement further extends the C language's repertoire of looping capabilities. The syntax of this frequently used construct is simply

```
while ( expression )
        program statement
```

The *expression* specified inside the parentheses is evaluated. If the result of *expression* evaluation is TRUE, then *program statement* that immediately follows is executed. After execution of this statement (or statements if enclosed in braces), *expression* is once again evaluated. If the result of the evaluation is TRUE, then *program statement* is once again executed. This process continues until *expression* finally evaluates FALSE, at which point the loop is terminated. Execution of the program then continues with the statement that follows *program statement*.

As an example of its use, the following program sets up a while loop, which merely counts from 1 to 5.

Program 5.6

```
/* This program introduces the while statement */
#include <stdio.h>
main ()
{
        int  count = 1;

        while ( count <= 5 )
        {
            printf ("%i\n", count);
            ++count;
        }
}
```

Program 5.6 OUTPUT

```
1
2
3
4
5
```

The program initially sets the value of count to 1. Execution of the while loop then begins. Since the value of count is less than or equal to 5, the statement that immediately follows is executed. The braces serve to define both the printf statement and the statement that increments count as the body of the while loop. From the output of the program, we can readily observe that this loop is executed precisely 5 times, or until the value of count reaches 6.

You may have realized from this program that we could have readily accomplished the same task by using a for statement. In fact, a for statement can always be translated into an equivalent while statement, and vice versa. For example, the general for statement

```
for ( init_expression;  loop_condition;  loop_expression ) program
statement
```

can be equivalently expressed in the form of a while statement as

```
init_expression;

while ( loop_condition )
{
        program statement
        loop_expression;
}
```

Once you become familiar with the use of the while statement, you will gain a better feel as to when it seems more logical to use a while and when to use a for.

QUICK TIP

In general, a loop executed a predetermined number of times is a prime candidate for implementation as a for statement. Also, if the initial expression, looping expression, and looping condition all involve the same variable, then the for statement is probably the right choice.

The next program provides another example of the use of the while statement. The program computes the *greatest common divisor* of two integer values. The greatest common divisor (we'll abbreviate it hereafter as *gcd*) of two integers is the largest integer value that evenly divides the two integers. For example, the *gcd* of 10 and 15 is 5 because 5 is the largest integer that evenly divides both 10 and 15.

There is a procedure or *algorithm* that can be followed to arrive at the *gcd* of two arbitrary integers. This algorithm is based on a procedure originally developed by Euclid around 300 B.C., and can be stated as follows:

Problem: Find the greatest common divisor of two nonnegative integers u and v.

Step 1:   If v equals 0, then we are done and the *gcd* is equal to u.

Step 2:   Calculate $temp = u \% v$, $u = v$, $v = temp$ and go back to Step 1.

Don't concern yourself with the details of how the above algorithm works—simply take it on faith. We are more concerned here with developing the program to find the greatest common divisor than in performing an analysis of how the algorithm works.

Once the solution to the problem of finding the greatest common divisor has been expressed in terms of an algorithm, it becomes a much simpler task to develop the computer program. An analysis of the steps of the algorithm reveals that Step 2 is repetitively executed as long as the value of v is not equal to 0. This realization leads to the natural implementation of this algorithm in C with the use of a while statement.

The following program will find the *gcd* of two nonnegative integer values typed in by the user.

Program 5.7

```
/* This program finds the greatest common divisor
        of two nonnegative integer values            */
#include <stdio.h>
main ()
{
    int u, v, temp;

    printf ("Please type in two nonnegative integers.\n");
    scanf ("%i%i", &u, &v);
```

continues

Program 5.7 Continued

```
while ( v != 0 )
{
     temp = u % v;
     u = v;
     v = temp;
}

printf ("Their greatest common divisor is %i\n", u);
}
```

Program 5.7 OUTPUT

```
Please type in two nonnegative integers.
150 35
Their greatest common divisor is 5
```

Program 5.7 OUTPUT (Rerun)

```
Please type in two nonnegative integers.
1026 405
Their greatest common divisor is 27
```

The double %i characters in the scanf call indicate that two integer values are to be entered from the keyboard. The first value that is entered will be stored into the integer variable u, while the second will be stored into the variable v. When the values are actually entered from the terminal, they can be separated from each other by one or more blank spaces or by a carriage return. However, they cannot be separated by a comma (BASIC programmers beware).

After the values have been entered from the keyboard and stored into the variables u and v, the program enters a while loop to calculate their greatest common divisor. After the while loop is exited, the value of u, which represents the *gcd* of v and of the original value of u, is displayed at the terminal, together with an appropriate message.

For our next program to illustrate the use of the while statement, let us consider the task of reversing the digits of an integer that is entered from the terminal. For example, if the user types in the number 1234, we would like the program to reverse the digits of this number and display the result of 4321.

To write such a program, we first must come up with an algorithm that accomplishes the stated task. Frequently, an analysis of one's own method for solving the problem will lead to the development of an algorithm. For the task of reversing the digits of a number, the method of solution can be simply stated as "successively read the digits of the number from right to left." We can have a computer program "successively read" the digits of the number by developing a procedure to successively isolate or "extract" each digit of the number, beginning with the rightmost digit. The extracted digit can be subsequently displayed at the terminal as the next digit of the reversed number.

We can extract the rightmost digit from an integer number by taking the remainder of the integer after it is divided by 10. For example, 1234 % 10 will give the value 4, which is the rightmost digit of 1234, and is also the first digit of the reversed number. (Remember the modulus operator, which gives the remainder of one integer divided by another.) We can get the next digit of the number by using the same process if we first divide the number by 10, bearing in mind the way integer division works. Thus, 1234 / 10 gives a result of 123, and 123 % 10 gives us 3, which is the next digit of our reversed number.

This procedure can be continued until the last digit has been extracted. In the general case, we know that the last digit of the number has been extracted when the result of the last integer division by 10 is 0.

Program 5.8

```
/* Program to reverse the digits of a number */
#include <stdio.h>
main ()
{
    int  number, right_digit;

    printf ("Enter your number.\n");
    scanf ("%i", &number);

    while ( number != 0 )
    {
        right_digit = number % 10;
        printf ("%i", right_digit);
        number = number / 10;
    }

    printf ("\n");
}
```

Program 5.8 OUTPUT

```
Enter your number.
13579
97531
```

Each digit is displayed as it is extracted by the program. Notice that we did not include a newline character inside the `printf` statement contained in the `while` loop. This forces each successive digit to be displayed on the same line. The final `printf` call at the end of the program contains just a newline character, which causes the cursor to advance to the start of the next line.

The *do* Statement

The two looping constructs that we have discussed thus far in this chapter both make a test of the conditions *before* the loop is executed. Therefore, the body of the loop may never be executed at all if the conditions are not satisfied. When developing programs, it sometimes becomes desirable to have the test made at the *end* of the loop rather than at the beginning. Naturally, the C language provides a special language construct to handle such a situation. This looping statement is known as the `do` statement. The syntax of this statement is

```
do
      program statement
while ( expression );
```

Execution of the do statement proceeds as follows: *program statement* is executed first. Next, the *expression* inside the parentheses is evaluated. If the result of evaluating *expression* is TRUE, the loop continues and *program statement* is once again executed. As long as evaluation of *expression* continues to be TRUE, *program statement* is repeatedly executed. When evaluation of the expression proves FALSE, the loop is terminated, and the next statement in the program is executed in the normal sequential manner.

The do statement is simply a transposition of the `while` statement, with the looping conditions placed at the end of the loop rather than at the beginning.

QUICK TIP

Remember that, unlike the `for` and `while` loops, the do statement guarantees that the body of the loop will be executed at least once.

In Program 5.8, we used a `while` statement to reverse the digits of a number. Go back to that program and try to determine what would happen if the user had typed in the number 0 instead of 13579. The fact of the matter is that the loop of the `while` statement would never be executed and we would simply end up with a blank line in our display (as a result of the display of the newline character from the second `printf` statement). If we were to use a `do` statement instead of a `while`, then we would be assured that the program loop would be executed at least once, thus guaranteeing the display of at least one digit in all cases.

Program 5.9

```
/* Program to reverse the digits of a number */
#include <stdio.h>
main ()
{
    int  number, right_digit;

    printf ("Enter your number.\n");
    scanf ("%i", &number);

    do
    {
        right_digit = number % 10;
        printf ("%i", right_digit);
        number = number / 10;
    }
    while ( number != 0 );

    printf ("\n");
}
```

Program 5.9 OUTPUT

```
Enter your number.
13579
97531
```

Program 5.9 OUTPUT (Rerun)

```
Enter your number.
0
0
```

As you can see from the program's output, when 0 is keyed into the program, the program correctly displays the digit 0.

The *break* Statement

Sometimes when executing a loop it becomes desirable to leave the loop as soon as a certain condition occurs (for instance, maybe you detect an error condition, or you reach the end of your data prematurely). The break statement can be used for this purpose. Execution of the break statement causes the program to immediately exit from the loop it is executing, whether it's a for, while, or do. Subsequent statements in the loop are skipped, and execution of the loop is terminated. Execution continues with whatever statement follows the loop.

If a break is executed from within a set of nested loops, only the innermost loop in which the break is executed is terminated.

The format of the break statement is simply the keyword break followed by a semicolon:

```
break;
```

The *continue* Statement

The continue statement is similar to the break statement except it doesn't cause the loop to terminate. Rather, as its name implies, this statement causes the loop in which it is executed to be continued. At the point that the continue statement is executed, any statements in the loop that appear *after* the continue statement are automatically skipped. Execution of the loop otherwise continues as normal.

The continue statement is most often used to bypass a group of statements inside a loop based upon some condition, but to otherwise continue execution of the loop. The format of the continue statement is simply

```
continue;
```

> **QUICK TIP**
>
> Don't use the `break` or `continue` statements until you become very familiar with writing program loops and gracefully exiting from them. These statements are too easy to abuse and can result in programs that are hard to follow.

Now that you are familiar with all the basic looping constructs provided by the C language, we are ready to discuss another class of language statements that enable you to make decisions during the execution of a program. These decision-making capabilities are described in detail in the next chapter.

Exercises

1. If you have access to a computer facility that supports the C programming language, type in and run the nine programs presented in this chapter. Compare the output produced by each program with the output presented after each program.

2. Write a program to generate and display a table of n and n^2, for integer values of n ranging from 1 through 10. Be sure to print appropriate column headings.

3. A triangular number can also be generated by the formula

   `Triangular number = n (n + 1) / 2`

   for any integer value of n. For example, the tenth triangular number, 55, can be generated by substituting the 10 as the value for n into the above formula. Write a program that generates a table of triangular numbers using the above formula. Have the program generate every fifth triangular number between 5 and 50 (that is, 5, 10, 15, ..., 50).

4. The factorial of an integer n, written $n!$, is the product of the consecutive integers 1 through n. For example, 5 factorial is calculated as

   `5! = 5 x 4 x 3 x 2 x 1 = 120`

   Write a program to generate and print a table of the first 10 factorials.

5. The following perfectly valid C program was written without much attention paid to its format. As you will observe, the program is not very readable. (And believe it or not, it is even possible to make this program significantly more unreadable!) Using the programs presented in this chapter as examples, re-format the program so that it is more readable. Then type the program into the computer and run it.

```
#include <stdio.h>
main(){
int n,two_to_the_n;
printf("TABLE OF POWERS OF TWO\n\n");
printf(" n     2 to the n\n");
printf("---     --------------\n");
two_to_the_n=1;
for(n=0;n<=10;++n){
printf("%2i       %i\n",n,two_to_the_n);
two_to_the_n=two_to_the_n*2;}
}
```

6. A minus sign placed in front of a field width specification causes the field to be displayed *left justified*. Substitute the following `printf` statement for the corresponding statement in Program 5.2, run the program, and compare the outputs produced by both programs.

   ```
   printf ("%-2i            %i\n", n, triangular_number);
   ```

7. A decimal point before the field width specification in a `printf` statement has a special purpose. Try to determine its purpose by typing in and running the following program. Experiment by typing in different values each time you are prompted.

   ```
   #include <stdio.h>
   main ()
   {
       int  dollars, cents, count;

       for ( count = 1;  count <= 10;  ++count )
       {
           printf ("Enter dollars: ");
           scanf ("%i", &dollars);
           printf ("Enter cents: ");
           scanf ("%i", &cents);
           printf ("$%i.%.2i\n\n", dollars, cents);
       }
   }
   ```

8. Program 5.5 allows the user to type in only five different numbers. Modify that program so that the user can type in the number of triangular numbers to be calculated.

9. Rewrite Programs 5.2 through 5.5, replacing all uses of the `for` statement by equivalent `while` statements. Run each program to verify that

10. What would happen if you typed a negative number into Program 5.8? Try it and see.

11. Write a program that calculates the sum of the digits of an integer. For example, the sum of the digits of the number 2155 is 2 + 1 + 5 + 5 or 13. The program should accept any arbitrary integer typed in by the user.

6

Making Decisions

In the previous chapter, we noted that one of the fundamental properties of a computer is its capability to repetitively execute a sequence of instructions. But another fundamental property lies in its capability to make decisions. We saw how these decision-making powers were used in the execution of the various looping statements to determine when to terminate the program loop. Without such capabilities, we would never be able to "get out" of a program loop and would end up executing the same sequence of statements over and over again, theoretically forever (which is why such a program loop is called an *infinite* loop).

The *if* Statement

The C programming language also provides a general decision-making capability in the form of a language construct known as the if statement. The general format of this statement is

```
if  ( expression )
      program statement
```

Imagine if you will that we could translate a statement such as "If it is not rain-ing then I will go swimming" into the C language. Using the above format for the `if` statement, this might be "written" in C as follows:

```
if ( it is not raining )
     I will go swimming
```

The `if` statement is used to stipulate execution of a program statement (or state-ments if enclosed in braces) *based upon specified conditions.* I will go swimming if it is not raining. Similarly, in the program statement

```
if ( count > COUNT_LIMIT )
     printf ("Count limit exceeded\n");
```

the `printf` statement will be executed *only* if the value of `count` is greater than the value of `COUNT_LIMIT`; otherwise, it will be ignored.

An actual program example will help drive the point home. Suppose we wish to write a program that accepts an integer typed in from the terminal and then displays the absolute value of that integer. A straightforward way to calculate the absolute value of an integer is to simply negate the number if it is less than zero. The use of the phrase "if it is less than zero" in the previous sentence sig-nals that a decision must be made by the program. This decision can be effected by the use of an `if` statement as shown in the program that follows.

Program 6.1

```
/* Calculate the absolute value of an integer */

main ()
{
    int   number;

    printf ("Type in your number: ");
    scanf ("%i", &number);

    if ( number < 0 )
        number = -number;

    printf ("The absolute value is %i\n", number);
}
```

Program 6.1 OUTPUT

```
Type in your number: -100
The absolute value is 100
```

Program 6.1 OUTPUT (Rerun)

```
Type in your number: 2000
The absolute value is 2000
```

The program was run twice to verify that it is functioning properly. Of course, it might be desirable to run the program several more times to get a higher level of confidence so that you know it is indeed working correctly, but at least we know that we have checked both possible outcomes of the decision made by the program.

After a message is displayed to the user and the integer value that is entered is stored into number, the program tests the value of number to see if it is less than zero. If it is, then the following program statement, which negates the value of number, is executed. If the value of number is not less than zero, then this program statement is automatically skipped. (If it is already positive, we don't want to negate it.) The absolute value of number is then displayed by the program, and program execution ends.

Let us now look at another program that uses the if statement. Imagine that we had a list of grades whose average we wished to compute. But in addition to computing the average, suppose that we also needed a count of the number of failing grades in the list. For the purposes of this problem, we can assume that a grade less than 65 is to be considered a failing grade.

The notion of keeping count of the number of failing grades indicates to us that we must make a decision as to whether a grade qualifies as a failing grade or not. Once again the if statement comes to the rescue.

Program 6.2

```
/* Program to calculate the average of a set of grades and to count
   the number of failing test grades      */
#include <stdio.h>
main ()
{
    int      number_of_grades, i, grade;
    int      grade_total = 0;
    int      failure_count = 0;
    float  average;

    printf ("How many grades will you be entering? ");
    scanf ("%i", &number_of_grades);
```

continues

Program 6.2 Continued

```
for ( i = 1;   i <= number_of_grades;   ++i )
{
    printf ("Enter grade #%i: ", i);
    scanf ("%i", &grade);

    grade_total = grade_total + grade;

    if ( grade < 65 )
        ++failure_count;
}

average = (float) grade_total / number_of_grades;

printf ("\nGrade average = %.2f\n", average);
printf ("Number of failures = %i\n", failure_count); }
```

Program 6.2 OUTPUT

```
How many grades will you be entering? 7
Enter grade #1: 93
Enter grade #2: 63
Enter grade #3: 87
Enter grade #4: 65
Enter grade #5: 62
Enter grade #6: 88
Enter grade #7: 76

Grade average = 76.29
Number of failures = 2
```

The variable `grade_total`, which is used to keep a cumulative total of the grades as they are typed in at the terminal, is initially set to 0. The number of failing test grades will be stored in the variable `failure_count`, whose value also is initially set to 0. The variable `average` is declared to be of type `float`, since the average of a set of integers is not necessarily an integer itself.

The program then proceeds to ask the user to enter the number of grades that will be keyed in and stores the value that is entered into the variable `number_of_grades`. A loop is then set up that will be executed for each grade. The first part of the loop prompts the user to enter in the grade. The value that is entered is stored into the variable called, appropriately enough, `grade`.

The value of grade is then added into grade_total, after which a test is made to see if it is a failing test grade. If it is, then the value of failure_count is incremented by 1. The entire loop is then repeated for the next grade in the list.

When all of the grades have been entered and totaled, the program then proceeds to calculate the grade average. On impulse, it would seem that a statement such as

```
average = grade_total / number_of_grades;
```

would do the trick. However, you will recall that if the above statement were used, then the decimal portion of the result of the division would be lost. This would be due to the fact that an integer division would be performed, since *both* the numerator and the denominator of the division operation are integers.

There are really two different solutions to this problem. One would be to declare either number_of_grades or grade_total to be of type float. This would then guarantee that the division would be carried out without the loss of the decimal places. The only problem with this approach is that the variables number_of_grades and grade_total are used by the program to store only integer values. Declaring either of them to be of type float would only obscure their use in the program and is generally not a very clean way of doing things.

The other solution, as used by the program, is to actually *convert* the value of one of the variables to a floating-point value for the purposes of the calculation. The *type cast* operator (float) has the effect of converting the value of the variable grade_total to type float for purposes of evaluation of the expression. In no way does this operator permanently affect the value of the variable grade_total; it is a unary operator that behaves like other unary operators. And, as the expression -a has no permanent effect on the value of a, neither does the expression (float) a.

The type cast operator has a higher precedence than all the arithmetic operators except the unary minus and unary plus. Of course, if necessary, parentheses can always be used in an expression to force the terms to be evaluated in any desired order.

As another example of the use of the type cast operator, the expression

```
(int) 29.55 + (int) 21.99
```

will be evaluated in C as

```
29 + 21
```

since the effect of casting a floating value to an integer is one of truncating the floating-point value. The expression

```
(float) 6 / (float) 4
```

will produce a result of 1.5, as will the expression

```
(float) 6 / 4
```

Returning to our program, since the value of grade_total is cast into a floating-point value *before* the division takes place, the C system will treat the operation as the division of a floating value by an integer. Since one of the operands is now a floating-point value, the division operation will be carried out as a floating-point operation. This means, of course, that we will get those decimal places that we want in the average.

Once the average has been calculated, it is displayed at the terminal to two decimal places of accuracy. If a decimal point followed by a number (known collectively as a *precision modifier*) is placed directly before the format character f (or e) in a printf format string, the corresponding value will be displayed to the specified number of decimal places, rounded. So in Program 6.2, the precision modifier .2 is used to cause the value of average to be displayed to two decimal places.

After the program has displayed the number of failing grades, execution of the program is complete.

The *if-else* Construct

If someone asks you whether a particular number is even or odd, you will most likely make the determination by examining the last digit of the number. If this digit is either 0, 2, 4, 6, or 8, then you will readily state that the number is even. Otherwise, you will claim that the number is odd.

An easier way for a computer to determine whether a particular number is even or odd is effected not by examining the last digit of the number to see if it is 0, 2, 4, 6, or 8, but by simply determining whether the number is evenly divisible by 2 or not. If it is, then the number is even; else it is odd.

We have already seen how the modulus operator % is used to compute the remainder of one integer divided by another. This makes it the perfect operator to use in determining whether or not an integer is evenly divisible by 2. If the remainder after division by 2 is 0, then it is even; else it is odd.

Let us now write a program that determines whether an integer value typed in by the user is even or odd and then displays an appropriate message at the terminal.

Program 6.3

```c
/* Program to determine if a number is even or odd */
#include <stdio.h>
main ()
{
    int  number_to_test, remainder;

    printf ("Enter your number to be tested.: ");
    scanf ("%i", &number_to_test);

    remainder = number_to_test % 2;

    if ( remainder == 0 )
        printf ("The number is even.\n");

    if ( remainder != 0 )
        printf ("The number is odd.\n");
}
```

Program 6.3 OUTPUT

```
Enter your number to be tested: 2455
The number is odd.
```

Program 6.3 OUTPUT (Rerun)

```
Enter your number to be tested: 1210
The number is even.
```

After the number is typed in, the remainder after division by 2 is calculated. The first if statement tests the value of this remainder to see if it is equal to 0. If it is, the message "The number is even" is displayed.

The second if statement tests the remainder to see if it's *not* equal to 0 and, if that's the case, displays a message stating that the number is odd.

The fact is that whenever the first if statement succeeds, the second one must fail, and vice versa. If you recall from our discussions of even/odd numbers at the beginning of this section, we said that if the number is evenly divisible by 2, then it is even; *else* it is odd.

When writing programs, this "else" concept is so frequently required that almost all modern programming languages provide a special construct to handle this situation. In C, this is known as the `if-else` construct and the general format is as follows:

```
if  ( expression )
     program statement 1
else
     program statement 2
```

The `if-else` is actually just an extension of the general format of the `if` statement. If the result of the evaluation of the expression is TRUE, then *program statement 1*, which immediately follows, is executed; otherwise, *program statement 2* is executed. In either case, either *program statement 1* or *program statement 2* will be executed, but *not both*.

We can incorporate the `if-else` statement into the program above, replacing the two `if` statements by a single `if-else` statement. You will see how the use of this new program construct actually helps to reduce somewhat the program's complexity and also improves its readability.

Program 6.4

```
/* Determine if a number is even or odd (Ver. 2) */
#include <stdio.h>
main ()
{
        int  number_to_test, remainder;

        printf ("Enter your number to be tested: ");
        scanf ("%i", &number_to_test);

        remainder = number_to_test % 2;

        if ( remainder == 0 )
            printf ("The number is even.\n");
        else
            printf ("The number is odd.\n");
}
```

Program 6.4 OUTPUT

```
Enter your number to be tested: 1234
The number is even.
```

Program 6.4 OUTPUT (Rerun)

```
Enter your number to be tested: 6551
The number is odd.
```

QUICK TIP

Don't forget that the double equals sign == is the equality test and the single equals sign is the assignment operator. It can lead to lots of headaches if you forget this and inadvertently use the assignment operator inside the if statement.

Compound Relational Tests

The if statements that we have used so far in this chapter set up simple relational tests between two numbers. In Program 6.1, we compared the value of number against 0, while in Program 6.2, we compared the value of grade against 65. Sometimes it becomes desirable, if not necessary, to set up more sophisticated tests. Suppose, for example, that in Program 6.2 we wished to count not the number of failing grades, but instead the number of grades that were between 70 and 79, inclusive. In such a case, we would not merely wish to compare the value of grade against one limit, but against the two limits 70 and 79 to make sure that it fell within the specified range.

The C language provides the mechanisms necessary to perform these types of compound relational tests. A *compound relational test* is simply one or more simple relational tests joined by either the *logical AND* or the *logical OR* operator. These operators are represented by the character pairs && and ¦¦ (two vertical bar characters), respectively. As an example, the C statement

```
if  ( grade >= 70  &&  grade <= 79 )
    ++grades_70_to_79;
```

will increment the value of grades_70_to_79 only if the value of grade is greater than or equal to 70 *and* less than or equal to 79. In a like manner, the statement

```
if  ( index < 0  ¦¦  index > 99 )
    printf ("Error - index out of range\n");
```

will cause execution of the printf statement if index is less than 0 *or* greater than 99.

The compound operators can be used to form extremely complex expressions in C. The C language grants the programmer ultimate flexibility in forming expressions. This flexibility is a capability that is often abused. Simpler expressions are almost always easier to read and debug.

QUICK TIP

When forming compound relational expressions, liberally use parentheses to aid readability of the expression and to avoid getting into trouble because of a mistaken assumption about the precedence of the operators in the expression. (The && operator has *lower* precedence than any arithmetic or relational operator but *higher* precedence than the ¦¦ operator.) Blank spaces also should be used to aid in the expression's readability. An extra blank space around the && and ¦¦ operators will visually set these operators apart from the expressions that are being joined by these operators.

To illustrate the use of a compound relational test in an actual program example, let us write a program that tests to see whether a year is a leap year or not. We all know that a year is a leap year if it is evenly divisible by 4. What you may not realize, however, is that a year that is divisible by 100 is *not* a leap year unless it also is divisible by 400.

Let us try to think how we would go about setting up a test for such a condition. First, we could compute the remainders of the year after division by 4, 100, and 400, and assign these values to appropriately named variables, such as rem_4, rem_100, and rem_400, respectively. Then we could proceed to test these remainders to determine if the desired criteria for a leap year were met.

If we rephrase our definition of a leap year from above, we can say that a year is a leap year if it is evenly divisible by 4 and not by 100 or if it is evenly divisible by 400. Stop for a moment to reflect on this last sentence and to verify to yourself that it is equivalent to our previously stated definition. Now that we have reformulated our definition in these terms, it becomes a relatively straightforward task to translate it into a program statement as follows:

```
if ( (rem_4 == 0  &&  rem_100 != 0) ¦¦  rem_400 == 0 )
    printf ("It's a leap year.\n");
```

The parentheses around the sub-expression

```
rem_4 == 0  &&  rem_100 != 0
```

are not required since that is how the expression will be evaluated anyway, remembering that && has higher precedence than ¦¦.

(In fact, in this particular example, the test

```
if ( rem_4 == 0  &&  ( rem_100 != 0 ¦¦  rem_400 == 0 ) )
```

would work just as well.)

If we add a few statements in front of our test to declare our variables and to enable the user to key in the year from the terminal, then we end up with a program that determines if a year is a leap year, as shown below.

Program 6.5

```
/* This program determines if a year is a leap year */
#include <stdio.h>
main ()
{
    int  year, rem_4, rem_100, rem_400;

    printf ("Enter the year to be tested: ");
    scanf ("%i", &year);

    rem_4 = year % 4;
    rem_100 = year % 100;
    rem_400 = year % 400;


    if ( (rem_4 == 0  &&  rem_100 != 0)  ¦¦  rem_400 == 0 )
        printf ("It's a leap year.\n");
    else
        printf ("Nope, it's not a leap year.\n");
}
```

Program 6.5 OUTPUT

```
Enter the year to be tested: 1955
Nope, it's not a leap year.
```

Program 6.5 OUTPUT (Rerun)

```
Enter the year to be tested: 2000
It's a leap year.
```

Program 6.5 OUTPUT (Rerun)

```
Enter the year to be tested: 1800
Nope, it's not a leap year.
```

In the above examples, we used a year that was not a leap year because it wasn't evenly divisible by 4 (1955), a year that was a leap year because it was evenly divisible by 400 (2000), and a year that wasn't a leap year because it was evenly divisible by 100 but not by 400 (1800). To complete the run of test cases, we should also try a year that is evenly divisible by 4 but not by 100. This is left as an exercise for you.

We mentioned that C gives the programmer a tremendous amount of flexibility in forming expressions. For instance, in the above program, we did not have to calculate the intermediate results `rem_4`, `rem_100`, and `rem_400`—we could have performed the calculation directly inside the `if` statement as follows:

```
if ( ( year % 4 == 0  &&  year % 100 != 0 )  ||
              year % 400 == 0 )
```

The use of blank spaces to set off the various operators still makes the above expression readable. If we decided to ignore adding blanks and removed the unnecessary set of parentheses, we could end up with an expression that looked like this:

```
if(year%4==0&&year%100!=0)||year%400==0)
```

This expression is perfectly valid and would (believe it or not) execute identically to the expression shown immediately above it. Obviously, those extra blanks go a long way toward aiding our understanding of complex expressions.

Nested *if* Statements

In discussions of the general format of the `if` statement, we indicated that if the result of evaluating the expression inside the parentheses were TRUE, then the statement that immediately followed would be executed. It is perfectly valid that this program statement be another `if` statement, as in the statement

```
if ( game_is_over == 0 )
    if ( player_to_move == YOU )
        printf ("Your Move\n");
```

If the value of `game_is_over` is 0, then the following statement will be executed, which is in turn another `if` statement. This `if` statement will compare the value of `player_to_move` against `YOU`. If the two values are equal, then the message "Your Move" will be displayed at the terminal. Therefore, the `printf` statement will be executed only if `game_is_over` equals 0 *and* `player_to_move` equals `YOU`.

In fact, this statement could have been equivalently formulated using compound relationals as

```
if ( game_is_over == 0  &&  player_to_move == YOU )
    printf ("Your Move\n");
```

A more practical example of "nested" `if` statements would be if we added an `else` clause to the above example, as shown in the following:

```
if ( game_is_over == 0 )
    if ( player_to_move == YOU )
        printf ("Your Move\n");
    else
        printf ("My Move\n");
```

Execution of this statement proceeds as described above. However, if `game_is_over` equals 0 and the value of `player_to_move` is not equal to `YOU`, then the `else` clause will be executed. This will display the message "My Move" at the terminal. If `game_is_over` does not equal 0, the entire `if` statement that follows, including its associated `else` clause, will be skipped.

Notice how the `else` clause is associated with the `if` statement that tests the value of `player_to_move`, and not with the `if` statement that tests the value of `game_is_over`. The general rule is that an `else` clause is always associated with the last `if` statement that does not contain an `else`.

We can go one step further and can add an `else` clause to the outermost `if` statement in the preceding example. This `else` clause would be executed if the value of `game_is_over` is not 0.

```
if ( game_is_over == 0 )
    if ( player_to_move == YOU )
        printf ("Your Move\n");
    else
        printf ("My Move\n");
else
    printf ("The game is over\n");
```

QUICK TIP

The proper use of indentation goes a long way toward aiding your understanding of the logic of complex statements.

Of course, even if we use indentation to indicate the way we think a statement will be interpreted in the C language, it may not always coincide with the way that the system will actually interpret the statement. For instance, removing the first `else` clause from the above example

```
if ( game_is_over == 0 )
    if ( player_to_move == YOU )
        printf ("Your Move\n");
else
    printf ("The game is over\n");
```

will *not* result in the statement's being interpreted as indicated by its format. Instead, this statement will be interpreted as

```
if ( game_is_over == 0 )
    if ( player_to_move == YOU )
        printf ("Your Move\n");
    else
        printf ("The game is over\n");
```

since the else clause is associated with the last un-elsed if. We could use braces to force a different association in those cases where an innermost if does not contain an else, but an outer if does. The braces have the effect of "closing off" the if statement. Thus,

```
if ( game_is_over == 0 )
{
    if ( player_to_move == YOU )
        printf ("Your Move\n");
}
else
    printf ("The game is over\n");
```

will achieve the desired effect, with the message "The game is over" being displayed if the value of game_is_over is not 0.

The *else if* Construct

We have seen how the else statement comes into play when we have a test against two possible conditions—either the number is even, else it is odd; either the year is a leap year, else it is not. However, programming decisions that we have to make are not always so black-and-white. Consider the task of writing a program that displayed -1 if a number typed in by a user were less than zero, 0 if the number typed in were equal to zero, and 1 if the number were greater than zero. (This is actually an implementation of what is commonly called the *sign* function.) Obviously, we must make three tests in this case—to determine if the number that is keyed in is negative, zero, or positive. Our simple if-else construct will not work. Of course, in this case, we could always resort to three separate if statements, but this solution will not always work in general—especially if the tests that are made are not mutually exclusive.

We can handle the situation just described by adding an if statement to our else clause. We mentioned that the statement that followed an else could be any valid C program statement, so why not another if? Thus, in the general case, we could write

```
if ( expression 1 )
     program statement 1
else
     if ( expression 2 )
          program statement 2
     else
program statement 3
```

which effectively extends the `if` statement from a two-valued logic decision to a three-valued logic decision. We can continue to add `if` statements to the `else` clauses, in the manner just shown, to effectively extend the decision to an *n*-valued logic decision.

The preceding construct is so frequently used that it is generally referred to as an `else if` construct and is usually formatted differently from that shown previously as

```
if ( expression 1 )
     program statement 1
else if ( expression 2 )
     program statement 2
else
     program statement 3
```

This latter method of formatting improves the readability of the statement and makes it clearer that a three-way decision is being made.

The next program illustrates the use of the `else if` construct by implementing the sign function discussed earlier.

Program 6.6

```
/* Program to implement the sign function */
#include <stdio.h>
main ()
{
    int   number, sign;

    printf ("Please type in a number: ");
    scanf ("%i", &number);

    if ( number < 0 )
        sign = -1;
    else if ( number == 0 )
        sign = 0;
    else            /* Must be positive */
        sign = 1;

    printf ("Sign = %i\n", sign);
}
```

Program 6.6 OUTPUT

```
Please type in a number: 1121
Sign = 1
```

Program 6.6 OUTPUT (Rerun)

```
Please type in a number: -158
Sign = -1
```

Program 6.6 OUTPUT (Rerun)

```
Please type in a number: 60
Sign = 0
```

If the number that is entered is less than zero, sign is assigned the value -1; if the number is equal to zero, sign is assigned the value 0; otherwise, the number must be greater than zero, so sign is assigned the value 1.

The next program analyzes a character that is typed in from the terminal and classifies it as either an alphabetic character (*a-z* or *A-Z*), a digit (*0-9*), or a special character (anything else). In order to read a single character from the terminal, the format characters %c are used in the scanf call.

Program 6.7

```
/* This program categorizes a single character
             that is entered at the terminal              */
#include <stdio.h>
main ()
{
    char  c;

    printf ("Enter a single character:\n");
    scanf ("%c", &c);

    if ( (c >= 'a'  &&  c <= 'z') || (c >= 'A'  &&  c <= 'Z') )
        printf ("It's an alphabetic character.\n");
    else if  ( c >= '0'  &&  c <= '9' )
```

```
        printf ("It's a digit.\n");
    else
        printf ("It's a special character.\n");
}
```

Program 6.7 OUTPUT

```
Enter a single character:
&
It's a special character.
```

Program 6.7 OUTPUT (Rerun)

```
Enter a single character:
8
It's a digit.
```

Program 6.7 OUTPUT (Rerun)

```
Enter a single character:
B
It's an alphabetic character.
```

The first test that is made after the character is read in determines if the char variable c is an alphabetic character or not. This is done by testing if the character is either a lowercase letter or an uppercase letter. The former test is made by the expression

```
( c >= 'a'  &&  c <= 'z' )
```

which will be TRUE if c is within the range of characters 'a' through 'z'; that is, if c is a lowercase letter. The latter test is made by the expression

```
( c >= 'A'  &&  c <= 'Z' )
```

which will be TRUE if c is within the range of characters 'A' through 'Z'; that is, if c is an uppercase letter. These tests work on all computer systems that store characters inside the machine in a format known as ASCII format. However, they do not work correctly on machines which use the EBCDIC format, since there are characters other than letters which fall within the tested ranges.

If the variable c is an alphabetic character, then the first `if` test will succeed and the message "It's an alphabetic character" will be displayed. If the test fails, then the `else if` clause will be executed. This clause determines if the character is a digit. Note that this test compares the character c against the *characters* `'0'` and `'9'` and *not* the *integers* 0 and 9. This is because a character was read in from the terminal, and the characters `'0'` to `'9'` are not the same as the numbers 0–9. In fact, on a computer system that uses the ASCII format mentioned above, the character `'0'` is actually represented internally as the number 48, the character `'1'` as the number 49, and so on.

If c is a digit character, then the phrase "It's a digit" will be displayed. Otherwise, if c is not alphabetic and is not a digit, then the final `else` clause will be executed and will display the phrase "It's a special character." Execution of the program will then be complete.

You should note that even though `scanf` is used here to read just a single character, the Return key must still be pressed after the character is typed to send the input to the program. In general, whenever you're reading data from the terminal, the program doesn't see any of the data typed on the line until the Return key is pressed.

Let us suppose for our next example that we wished to write a program that allowed the user to type in simple expressions of the form

number   operator   number

The program will evaluate the expression and display the results at the terminal, to two decimal places of accuracy. The operators that we want to have recognized are the normal operators for addition, subtraction, multiplication, and division. The following program makes use of a large `if` statement with many `else if` clauses to determine which operation is to be performed.

Program 6.8

```
/* Program to evaluate simple expressions of the form
             number   operator   number              */
#include <stdio.h>
main ()
{
    float   value1, value2;
    char    operator;

    printf ("Type in your expression.\n");
    scanf ("%f %c %f", &value1, &operator, &value2);

    if ( operator == '+' )
        printf ("%.2f\n", value1 + value2);
```

```
    else if ( operator == '-' )
        printf ("%.2f\n", value1 - value2);
    else if ( operator == '*' )
        printf ("%.2f\n", value1 * value2);
    else if ( operator == '/' )
        printf ("%.2f\n", value1 / value2);
}
```

Program 6.8 OUTPUT

```
Type in your expression.
123.5 + 59.3
182.80
```

Program 6.8 OUTPUT (Rerun)

```
Type in your expression.
198.7 / 26
7.64
```

Program 6.8 OUTPUT (Rerun)

```
Type in your expression.
89.3 * 2.5
223.25
```

The scanf call specifies that three values are to be read into the variables value1, operator, and value2. A floating value can be read in with the %f format characters, the same characters used for the output of floating values. This is the format used to read in the value of the variable value1, which is the first operand of our expression.

Next, we wish to read in the operator. Since the operator is a character ('+', '-', '*', or '/') and not a number, we read it into the character variable operator. The %c format characters tell the system to read in the next character from the terminal. The blank spaces inside the format string indicate that an arbitrary number of blank spaces are to be permitted on the input. This enables us to separate the operands from the operator with blank spaces when we type in these values. If we had specified the format string "%f%c%f" instead, then no spaces would have been permitted after typing in the first number and before typing in the operator. This is because when the scanf function is reading a character with the %c format characters, the next character on the input, *even if it is a blank space*, is the character that is read. However, it should be noted that, in general, the scanf function will *always* ignore leading spaces when it is reading in either a decimal or floating-point number. Therefore, the format string "%f %c%f" would have worked just as well in the preceding program.

After the second operand has been keyed in and stored in the variable value2, the program proceeds to test the value of operator against the four permissible operators. When a correct match is made, the corresponding printf statement is executed to display the results of the calculation. Execution of the program is then complete.

A few words about program thoroughness are in order at this point. While the preceding program does accomplish the task that we set out to perform, the program is not really complete since it does not account for mistakes made on the part of the user. For example, what would happen if the user were to type in a ? for the operator by mistake? The program would simply "fall through" the if statement and no messages would ever appear at the terminal to alert the user that he had incorrectly typed in his expression.

Another case that is overlooked is when the user types in a division operation with 0 as the divisor. We know by now that we should never attempt to divide a number by 0 in C. The program should check for this case.

Trying to predict the ways that a program can fail or produce unwanted results and then taking preventive measures to account for such situations is a necessary part of producing good, reliable programs. Running a sufficient number of test cases against a program will often point the finger to portions of the program that do not account for certain cases. But it goes further than that. It must become a matter of self-discipline while coding a program to always say "What would happen if ..." and to insert the necessary program statements to handle the situation properly.

Program 6.8A, a modified version of Program 6.8, accounts for division by 0 and the keying in of an unknown operator.

Program 6.8A

```
/* Program to evaluate simple expressions of the form
                value    operator    value                 */
#include <stdio.h>
main ()
{
```

```
      float   value1, value2;
      char    operator;

      printf ("Type in your expression.\n");
      scanf ("%f %c %f", &value1, &operator, &value2);

      if ( operator == '+' )
           printf ("%.2f\n", value1 + value2);
      else if ( operator == '-' )
           printf ("%.2f\n", value1 - value2);
      else if ( operator == '*' )
           printf ("%.2f\n", value1 * value2);
      else if ( operator == '/' )
           if ( value2 == 0 )
                printf ("Division by zero.\n");
           else
                printf ("%.2f\n", value1 / value2);
      else
           printf ("Unknown operator.\n");
}
```

Program 6.8A OUTPUT

```
Type in your expression.
123.5 + 59.3
182.80
```

Program 6.8A OUTPUT (Rerun)

```
Type in your expression.
198.7 / 0
Division by zero.
```

Program 6.8A OUTPUT (Rerun)

```
Type in your expression.
125 $ 28
Unknown operator.
```

When the operator that is typed in is the slash, for division, another test is made to determine if value2 is 0. If it is, an appropriate message is displayed at the terminal. Otherwise, the division operation is carried out and the results displayed. Pay careful attention to the nesting of the if statements and the associated else clauses in this case.

The else clause at the end of the program catches any "fall throughs." Therefore, any value of operator that does not match any of the four characters tested will cause this else clause to be executed, resulting in the display of "Unknown operator."

The *switch* Statement

The type of if-else statement chain that we encountered in the last program example—where the value of a variable is successively compared against different values—is so commonly used when developing programs that a special program statement exists in the C language for performing precisely this function. The name of the statement is the switch statement, and its general format is

```
switch ( expression )
{
    case value1:
                program statement
                program statement
                    . . .
                break;
    case value2:
                program statement
                program statement
                    . . .
                break;
        . . .
    case valuen:
                program statement
                program statement
                    . . .
                break;
    default:
                program statement
                program statement
                    . . .
                break;
}
```

The expression enclosed within parentheses is successively compared against the values value1, value2, ..., valuen, which must be simple constants or constant expressions. If a case is found whose value is equal to the value of expression, then the program statements that follow the case are executed. You will note that when more than one such program statement is included, they do *not* have to be enclosed within braces.

The break statement signals the end of a particular case and causes execution of the switch statement to be terminated.

QUICK TIP

Remember to include the break statement at the end of every case. Forgetting to do so for a particular case will cause program execution to continue into the next case whenever that case gets executed.

The special optional case called default is executed if the value of *expression* does not match any of the case values. This is conceptually equivalent to the "fall through" else that we used in the previous example. In fact, the general form of the switch statement can be equivalently expressed as an if statement as follows:

```
if  ( expression == value1 )
{
        program statement
        program statement
             . . .
}
else if ( expression == value2 )
{
        program statement
        program statement
             . . .
}
     . . .
else if ( expression == valuen )
{
        program statement
        program statement
             . . .
}
else
{
        program statement
        program statement
             . . .
}
```

Bearing the above in mind, we can translate the big if statement from Program 6.8A into an equivalent switch statement. We will call this new program Program 6.9.

Program 6.9

```
/* Program to evaluate simple expressions of the form
              value   operator   value                    */
#include <stdio.h>
main ()
{
    float   value1, value2;
    char    operator;

    printf ("Type in your expression.\n");
    scanf ("%f %c %f", &value1, &operator, &value2);

    switch ( operator )
    {
        case '+':
    printf ("%.2f\n", value1 + value2);
            break;
        case '-':
    printf ("%.2f\n", value1 - value2);
            break;
        case '*':
    printf ("%.2f\n", value1 * value2);
            break;
        case '/':
            if ( value2 == 0 )
                printf ("Division by zero.\n");
            else
        printf ("%.2f\n", value1 / value2); break;
        default:
    printf ("Unknown operator.\n");
            break;
    }
}
```

Program 6.9 OUTPUT

```
Type in your expression.
178.99 - 326.8
-147.81
```

After the expression has been read in, the value of operator is successively compared against the values as specified by each case. When a match is found, the statements contained inside the case will be executed. The break statement will then send execution out of the switch statement, where execution of the program will be complete. If none of the cases match the value of operator, the default case, which displays "Unknown operator", will be executed.

The break statement in the default case is actually unnecessary in the preceding program since no statements follow this case inside the switch. Nevertheless, it is a good programming habit to remember to include the break at the end of every case.

When writing a switch statement, you should bear in mind that no two case values may be the same. However, we can associate more than one case value with a particular set of program statements. This is done simply by listing the multiple case values (with the keyword case before the value and the colon after the value in each case) before the common statements that are to be executed. As an example, in the switch statement

```
switch  ( operator )
{
              . . .
    case '*':
    case 'x':
            printf ("%.2f\n", value1 * value2);
            break;
              . . .
}
```

the printf statement, which multiplies value1 by value2, will be executed if operator is equal to an asterisk or to the lowercase letter x.

Flags

Just about all new programmers soon find themselves with the task of having to write a program to generate a table of *prime numbers*. To refresh your memory, a positive integer p is a prime number if it not evenly divisible by any other integers, other than 1 and itself. The first prime integer is defined to be 2. The next prime is 3, since it is not evenly divisible by any integers other than 1 and 3; and 4 is *not* prime because it *is* evenly divisible by 2.

There are several approaches that we could take in order to generate a table of prime numbers. If we had the task of generating all prime numbers up to 50, for example, then the most straightforward (and simplest) algorithm to generate such a table would simply test each integer p for divisibility by all integers from 2 through p-1. If any such integer evenly divided p, then p would not be prime; otherwise, it would be a prime number.

Program 6.10

```
/* Program to generate a table of prime numbers */
#include <stdio.h>

main ()
{
        int   p, is_prime, d;

        for ( p = 2;   p <= 50;   ++p )
        {
            is_prime = 1;

            for ( d = 2;   d < p;   ++d )
                if ( p % d   ==   0 )
                    is_prime = 0;

            if ( is_prime != 0 )
                printf ("%i  ", p);
        }


        printf ("\n");
}
```

Program 6.10 OUTPUT

2 3 5 7 11 13 17 19 23 29 31 37 41 43 47

Several points are worth noting about the above program. The outermost for statement sets up a loop to cycle through the integers 2 through 50. The loop variable p represents the value we are currently testing to see if it is prime. The first statement in the loop assigns the value 1 to the variable is_prime. The use of this variable will become apparent shortly.

A second loop is set up to divide p by the integers from 2 through p-1. Inside the loop, a test is made to see if the remainder of p divided by d is 0. If it is, then we know that p cannot be prime since there exists an integer other than 1 and itself that evenly divides it. To signal that p is no longer a candidate as a prime number, the value of the variable is_prime is set equal to 0.

When the innermost loop finishes execution, the value of is_prime is tested. If its value is not equal to zero, no integer was found that evenly divided p; therefore, p must be a prime number, and its value is displayed.

You may have noticed that the variable is_prime takes on either the value 0 or 1, and no other values. Its value is 1 as long as p still qualifies as a prime number. But as soon as a single even divisor is found, its value is set to 0 to indicate that p no longer satisfies the criteria for being prime. Variables that are used in such a manner are generally referred to as Boolean variables, or more simply, as *flags*. A flag will typically assume only one of two different values. Furthermore, the value of a flag will usually be tested at least once in the program to see if it is "on" (TRUE) or "off" (FALSE) and some particular action taken based upon the results of the test.

In C, the notion of a flag being TRUE or FALSE is most naturally translated into the values 1 and 0, respectively. So in the above program, when we set the value of is_prime to 1 inside the loop, we are effectively setting it TRUE to indicate that p "is prime." If during the course of execution of the inner for loop an even divisor is found, the value of is_prime is set FALSE to indicate that p no longer "is prime."

It is no coincidence that the value 1 is typically used to represent the TRUE or "on" state and 0 to represent the FALSE or "off" state. This representation corresponds to the notion of a single bit inside a computer. When the bit is "on," its value is 1; when it is "off," its value is 0. But in C, there is an even more convincing argument in favor of these logic values. It has to do with the way the C language treats the concept of TRUE and FALSE.

When we began our discussions in this chapter, we noted that if the conditions specified inside the if statement were "satisfied," then the program statement that immediately followed would be executed. But what exactly does "satisfied" mean? In the C language, satisfied means nonzero, and nothing more. So the statement

```
if ( 100 )
    printf ("This will always be printed.\n");
```

will result in execution of the printf statement because the condition in the if statement (in this case simply the value 100) is nonzero and therefore is satisfied.

In each of the programs in this chapter, the notions of "nonzero means satisfied" and "zero means not satisfied" were used. This is because whenever a relational expression is evaluated in C, it is given the value 1 if the expression is satisfied and 0 if the expression is not satisfied. So evaluation of the statement

```
if ( number < 0 )
    number = -number;
```

actually proceeds as follows:

1. The relational expression `number < 0` is evaluated. If the condition is satisfied, that is, if `number` is less than 0, then the value of the expression is 1; otherwise, its value is 0.

2. The `if` statement tests the result of the expression evaluation. If the result is nonzero, then the statement that immediately follows is executed; otherwise, the statement is skipped.

The preceding discussion also applies to evaluation of conditions inside the `for`, `while`, and `do` statements. Evaluation of compound relational expressions such as in the statement

```
while  ( char != 'e'  &&  count != 80 )
```

also proceeds as outlined above. If both specified conditions are valid, then the result will be 1; but if either condition is not valid, then the result of the evaluation will be 0. The results of the evaluation will then be checked. If the result is 0, then the `while` loop will terminate; otherwise it will continue.

Returning to Program 6.10 and the notion of flags, it is perfectly valid in C—and even clearer—to test if the value of a flag is TRUE by an expression such as

```
if ( is_prime )
```

rather than with the equivalent expression

```
if ( is_prime != 0 )
```

To easily test if the value of a flag is FALSE, we bring into play the *logical negation* operator, `!`. In the expression

```
if ( ! is_prime )
```

the logical negation operator is used to test if the value of `is_prime` is FALSE (read this statement as "if not `is_prime`"). In general, an expression such as

```
! expression
```

negates the logical value of `expression`. So if `expression` is 0, the logical negation operator produces a 1. And if the result of the evaluation of `expression` is nonzero, the negation operator yields a 0.

The logical negation operator can be used to easily "flip" the value of a flag, such as in the expression

```
my_move = ! my_move;
```

As you might expect, this operator has the same precedence as the unary minus operator, which means that it has higher precedence than all binary arithmetic operators and all relational operators. So to test if the value of a variable x is not less than the value of a variable y, such as in

```
! ( x < y )
```

the parentheses are required to ensure proper evaluation of the expression. Of course, we could have equivalently expressed the above as

```
x >= y
```

The Conditional Operator

Perhaps the most unusual operator in the C language is one called the *conditional* operator. Unlike all other operators in C—which are either unary or binary operators—the conditional operator is a *ternary* operator; that is, it takes three operands. The two symbols that are used to denote this operator are the question mark (?) and the colon (:). The first operand is placed before the ?, the second between the ? and the :, and the third after the :.

The general format of the conditional operator is

```
condition  ?  expression1  :  expression2
```

where `condition` is an expression, usually a relational expression, that is evaluated by the C system first whenever the conditional operator is encountered. If the result of the evaluation of `condition` is TRUE (that is, nonzero), then `expression1` is evaluated and the result of the evaluation becomes the result of the operation. If `condition` evaluates FALSE (that is, zero), then `expression2` is evaluated and its result becomes the result of the operation.

The conditional operator is most often used to assign one of two values to a variable depending upon some condition. For example, suppose we have an integer variable x and another integer variable s. If we wished to assign -1 to s if x were less than 0, and the value of x^2 to s otherwise, the following statement could be written:

```
s = ( x < 0 ) ? -1 : x * x;
```

The condition x < 0 is first tested when the above statement is executed. Parentheses are generally placed around the condition expression to aid in the statement's readability. This is usually not required, since the precedence of the conditional operator is very low—lower, in fact, than all other operators but the assignment operators and the comma operator.

If the value of x is less than zero, then the expression immediately following the ? will be evaluated. This expression is simply the constant integer value -1, which will be assigned to the variable s if x is less than zero.

If the value of x is not less than zero, then the expression immediately following the : will be evaluated and assigned to s. So if x is greater than or equal to zero, the value of x * x, or x^2, will be assigned to s.

As another example of the use of the conditional operator, the following statement assigns to the variable max_value the maximum of a and b.

```
max_value = ( a > b ) ? a : b;
```

If the expression that is used after the : (the "else" part) consists of another conditional operator, then we can achieve the effects of an "else if" clause. For example, the *sign* function that was implemented in Program 6.6 can be written in one program line using two conditional operators as follows:

```
sign = ( number < 0 ) ? -1 : (( number == 0 ) ? 0 : 1);
```

If number is less than zero, then sign is assigned the value -1; else if number is equal to zero, then sign is assigned the value 0; else it is assigned the value 1. The parentheses around the "else" part of the above expression are actually unnecessary. This is because the conditional operator associates from right to left, meaning that multiple uses of this operator in a single expression, such as in

```
e1 ? e2 : e3 ? e4 : e5
```

will group from right to left and, therefore, will be evaluated as

```
e1 ? e2 : ( e3 ? e4 : e5 )
```

It is not necessary that the conditional operator be used on the right-hand side of an assignment—it can be used in any situation where an expression could be used. This means that we could display the sign of the variable number, without first assigning it to a variable, using a printf statement as shown:

```
printf ("Sign = %i\n", ( number < 0 ) ? -1
    : ( number == 0 ) ? 0 : 1);
```

The conditional operator is very handy when writing preprocessor *macros* in C. This will be seen in detail in Chapter 13, "The Preprocessor."

This concludes our discussions on making decisions. In the next chapter you will get your first look at more sophisticated data types. The *array* is a powerful concept that will find its way into many programs that you will develop in C.

Exercises

1. If you have access to a computer facility that supports the C programming language, type in and run the 10 programs presented in this chapter. Compare the output produced by each program with the

output presented after each program. Try experimenting with each program by keying in values other than those shown.

2. Write a program that asks the user to type in two integer values at the terminal. Test these two numbers to determine if the first is evenly divisible by the second, and then display an appropriate message at the terminal.

3. Write a program that accepts two integer values typed in by the user. Display the result of dividing the first integer by the second, to three-decimal-place accuracy. Remember to have the program check for division by 0.

4. Write a program that acts as a simple "printing" calculator. The program should allow the user to type in expressions of the form

   ```
   number    operator
   ```

   The following operators should be recognized by the program:

   ```
   +      -      *      /      S      E
   ```

   The S operator tells the program to set the "accumulator" to the typed-in number. The E operator tells the program that execution is to end. The arithmetic operations are performed on the contents of the accumulator with the number that was keyed in acting as the second operand. The following is a "sample run" showing how the program should operate:

   ```
   Begin Calculations
   10 S                           Set Accumulator to 10
   = 10.000000                    Contents of Accumulator
   2 /                            Divide by 2
   = 5.000000                     Contents of Accumulator
   55 -                           Subtract 55
    -50.000000
   100.25 S                       Set Accumulator to 100.25
   = 100.250000
   4 *                            Multiply by 4
   = 401.000000
   0 E                            End of program
   = 401.000000
   End of Calculations.
   ```

   Make sure that the program detects division by 0 and also checks for unknown operators.

5. We developed Program 5.9 to reverse the digits of an integer typed in from the terminal. However, this program does not function too well if we type in a negative number. Find out what happens in such a case and then modify the program so that negative numbers are correctly handled. By correctly handled, we mean that if the number -8645 were typed in, for example, then the output of the program should be 5468-.

6. Write a program that takes an integer keyed in from the terminal and extracts and displays each digit of the integer in English. So, if the user types in 932, then the program should display

   ```
   nine three two
   ```

   (Remember to display "zero" if the user types in just a 0.) Note: This exercise is a hard one!

7. Program 6.10 has several inefficiencies. One inefficiency results from checking even numbers. Since it is obvious that any even number greater than 2 cannot be prime, the program could simply skip all even numbers as possible primes *and* as possible divisors. The inner `for` loop is also inefficient because the value of `p` is *always* divided by all values of `d` from 2 through `p-1`. This inefficiency could be avoided if we added a test for the value of `is_prime` in the conditions of the `for` loop. In this manner, the `for` loop could be set up to continue as long as no divisor was found and the value of `d` was less than `p`. Modify Program 6.10 to incorporate these two changes. Then run the program to verify its operation. Note: In the next chapter, we will find even more efficient ways of generating prime numbers.

7

CHAPTER

Arrays

The C language provides a capability that enables the user to define a set of ordered data items known as an *array*. This chapter describes how arrays can be defined and manipulated in C. In later chapters, we will include further discussions on arrays to illustrate how well they work together with program functions, structures, character strings, and pointers.

Suppose we had a set of grades that we wished to read into the computer, and suppose that we wished to perform some operations on these grades, such as rank them in ascending order, compute their average, or find their median. In Program 6.2, we were able to calculate the average of a set of grades by simply adding each grade into a cumulative total as each grade was keyed in. However, if we wanted to rank the grades into ascending order, for example, then we would have to do something further. If you think about the process of ranking a set of grades, you will quickly realize that we cannot perform such an operation until each and every grade has been entered. Therefore, using the techniques we have already described, we would read in each grade and store it into a unique variable, perhaps with a sequence of statements such as

```
printf ("Enter grade 1\n");
scanf ("%i", &grade1);
```

```
printf ("Enter grade 2\n");
scanf ("%i", &grade2);
       . . .
```

Once the grades had been entered, we could then proceed to rank them. This could be done by setting up a series of if statements to compare each of the values to determine the smallest grade, the next smallest grade, and so on, until the maximum grade had been determined. If you sit down and try to write a program to perform precisely this task, you will soon realize that for any reasonably sized list of grades (where reasonably sized is probably only about 10), the resulting program will be quite large and quite complex. All is not lost, however, as this is one instance where the array comes to the rescue.

In C, we can define a variable called grades, which represents not a *single* value of a grade, but an entire *set of grades*. Each element of the set can then be referenced by means of a number called an *index* number or *subscript*. Where in mathematics a subscripted variable, x_i, refers to the ith element x in a set, in C the equivalent notation is

x[i]

So the expression

grades[5]

(read as "grades sub 5") refers to element number 5 in the array called grades. In C, array elements begin with number 0, so

grades[0]

actually refers to the first element of the array. (For this reason, it is easier to think of it as referring to element number zero, rather than as referring to the first element.)

An individual array element can be used anywhere that a normal variable could be. For example, we can assign an array value to another variable with a statement such as

g = grades[50];

This statement takes the value contained in grades[50] and assigns it to g. More generally, if i is declared to be an integer variable, then the statement

g = grades[i];

will take the value contained in element number i of the grades array and assign it to g. So if i were equal to 7 when the above statement were executed, then the value of grades[7] would get assigned to g.

A value can be stored into an element of an array simply by specifying the array element on the left side of an equals sign. In the statement

```
grades[100] = 95;
```

the value 95 is stored into element number 100 of the `grades` array. The statement

```
grades[i] = g;
```

will have the effect of storing the value of `g` into `grades[i]`.

The capability to represent a collection of related data items by a single array enables us to develop concise and efficient programs. For example, we can easily sequence through the elements in the array by varying the value of a variable that is used as a subscript into the array. So the `for` loop

```
for ( i = 0;  i < 100;  ++i )
      sum = sum + grades[i];
```

will sequence through the first 100 elements of the array `grades` (elements 0 through 99) and will add the value of each grade into `sum`. When the `for` loop is finished, the variable `sum` will then contain the total of the first 100 values of the `grades` array (assuming `sum` were set to 0 before the loop was entered).

QUICK TIP

Don't forget that the first element of an array is indexed by zero, and the last element by the number of elements in the array minus one.

In addition to integer constants, integer-valued expressions can also be used inside the brackets to reference a particular element of an array. So if `low` and `high` were defined as integer variables, then the statement

```
next_value = sorted_data[(low + high) / 2];
```

would assign to the variable `next_value` the value indexed by evaluating the expression `(low + high) / 2`. If `low` were equal to 1 and `high` were equal to 9, then the value of `sorted_data[5]` would be assigned to `next_value`. And if `low` were equal to 1 and `high` were equal to 10, then the value of `sorted_data[5]` would also be referenced, since we know that an integer division of 11 by 2 gives the result of 5.

Just as with variables, arrays must also be declared before they are used. The declaration of an array involves declaring the type of element that will be contained in the array—such as `int`, `float`, or `char`—as well as the maximum number of elements that will be stored inside the array. (The C system needs this latter information in order to determine how much of its memory space to reserve for the particular array.)

As an example, the declaration

```
int   grades[100];
```

declares grades to be an array containing 100 integer elements. Valid references to this array may be made by using subscripts from 0 through 99. But be careful to use valid subscripts, since C does not do any checking of array bounds for you. So a reference to element number 150 of array grades, as previously declared, would not necessarily cause an error but would most likely cause unwanted, if not unpredictable, program results.

To declare an array called averages that contained 200 floating-point elements, the declaration

```
float   averages[200];
```

would be used. This declaration would cause enough space inside the computer's memory to be reserved to contain 200 floating-point numbers. Similarly, the declaration

```
int   values[10];
```

would reserve enough space for an array called values that could hold up to 10 integer numbers. We could better conceptualize this reserved storage space by referring to Figure 7.1.

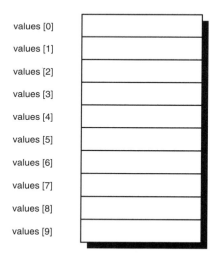

Figure 7.1. *The array* values *in memory.*

The elements of arrays declared to be of type int, float, or char may be manipulated in the same fashion as ordinary variables. We can assign values to them, display their values, add to them, subtract from them, and so on. So if the following statements were to appear in a program

```
int   values[10];

values[0] = 197;
values[2] = -100;
values[5] = 350;
values[3] = values[0] + values[5];
values[9] = values[5] / 10;
--values[2];
```

then the array `values` would contain the numbers as shown in Figure 7.2.

values [0]	197
values [1]	
values [2]	-101
values [3]	547
values [4]	
values [5]	350
values [6]	
values [7]	
values [8]	
values [9]	35

Figure 7.2. `values` *with some initialized elements.*

The first assignment statement has the effect of storing the value of 197 into `values[0]`. In a similar fashion, the second and third assignment statements store -100 and 350 into `values[2]` and `values[5]`, respectively. The next statement adds the contents of `values[0]` (which is 197) to the contents of `values[5]` (which is 350) and stores the result of 547 in `values[3]`. In the following program statement, 350—the value contained in `values[5]`—is divided by 10 and the result stored into `values[9]`. The last statement decrements the contents of `values[2]`, which has the effect of changing its value from -100 to -101.

The preceding program statements were incorporated into Program 7.1. The `for` loop sequences through each element of the array, displaying its value at the terminal in turn.

Program 7.1

```c
#include <stdio.h>
main ()
{
        int   values[10];
        int   index;

        values[0] = 197;
        values[2] = -100;
        values[5] = 350;
        values[3] = values[0] + values[5];
        values[9] =
        values[5] / 10;
        --values[2];

        for ( index = 0;  index < 10;  ++index )
                printf ("values[%i] = %i\n", index, values[index]);
}
```

Program 7.1 OUTPUT

```
values[0] = 197
values[1] = 0
values[2] = -101
values[3] = 547
values[4] = 0
values[5] = 350
values[6] = 0
values[7] = 0
values[8] = 0
values[9] = 35
```

The variable index assumes the values 0 through 9, as the last valid subscript of an array is always one less than the number of elements (due to that zeroth element). Since we never assigned values to five of the elements in the array—elements 1, 4, and 6 through 8—the values that are displayed for them are meaningless. Even though the program's output shows these values as zero, the value of any uninitialized variable or array element is simply the value that happens to be sitting around inside the computer's memory at the time that the program is executed. For this reason, no assumption should ever be made as to the value of an uninitialized variable or array element.

It is now time to consider a slightly more practical example. Suppose we took a telephone survey to discover how people felt about a particular television show and we asked each respondent to rate the show on a scale from 1 to 10, inclusive. After interviewing 5,000 people we accumulated a list of 5,000 numbers. Now we would like to analyze the results. One of the first pieces of data we would like to gather is a table showing the distribution of the ratings. In other words, we would like to know how many people rated the show a 1, how many a 2, and so on up to 10.

Although not an impossible chore, it would be a bit tedious to go through each response and manually count the number of responses in each rating category. And if we had a response which could be answered in more than ten ways (consider the task of categorizing the age of the respondent), this approach would be even more unreasonable. So we would like to develop a program to count the number of responses for each rating. The first impulse might be to set up ten different counters, called perhaps `rating_1` through `rating_10`, and then to increment the appropriate counter each time the corresponding rating was keyed in. But once again, if we considered the case where we were dealing with more than ten possible choices, this approach could become a bit tedious. And besides, an approach that uses an array provides the vehicle for implementing a much cleaner solution, even in this case.

We can set up an array of counters called `rating_counters`, for example, and then we can increment the corresponding counter as each response is keyed in. Since we don't wish to take up 100 pages in this book for the 5,000 responses to the survey, in the program that follows we assume that we are dealing with only 20 responses. Anyway, it's always good practice to get a program working on a smaller test case first before proceeding with the full set of data, since problems that are discovered in the program will be much easier to isolate and debug if the amount of test data is small.

Program 7.2

```c
#include <stdio.h>
main ()
{
        int  rating_counters[11], i, response;

        for ( i = 1;  i <= 10;  ++i )
                rating_counters[i] = 0;

        printf ("Enter your responses\n");

        for ( i = 1;  i <= 20;  ++i )
        {
                scanf ("%i", &response);

                if ( response < 1 || response > 10 )
                    printf ("Bad response: %i\n", response);
                else
                    ++rating_counters[response];
```

continues

Program 7.2 Continued

```
        }
        printf ("\n\nRating   Number of Responses\n");
        printf ("------ ------------------\n");

        for ( i = 1;  i <= 10;  ++i )
                printf ("%4d%14d\n", i, rating_counters[i]);
}
```

Program 7.2 OUTPUT

```
Enter your responses
6
5
8
3
9
6
5
7
15
Bad response: 15
5
5
1
7
4
10
5
5
6
8
9


Rating   Number of Responses
------ ------------------
1               1
2               0
3               1
4               1
5               6
6               3
7               2
8               2
9               2
10              1
```

The array `rating_counters` is defined to contain 11 elements. A valid question you might ask is, "If there are only 10 possible responses to the survey, why then is the array defined to contain 11 elements rather than 10?" The answer lies in the strategy for counting the responses in each particular rating category. Since each response can be a number from 1 to 10, the program keeps track of the responses for any one particular rating by simply incrementing the corresponding array element (after first checking to make sure that the user entered a valid response between 1 and 10). For example, if a rating of 5 is typed in, the value of `rating_counters[5]` is incremented by one. By employing this technique, the total number of respondents that rated the TV show a 5 will be contained in `rating_counters[5]`.

The reason for 11 elements versus 10 should now be clear. Since the highest rating number is a 10, we must set up our array to contain 11 elements in order to index `rating_counters[10]`, remembering that due to that zeroth element, the number of elements in an array is always one more than the highest index number. Since no response can have a value of zero, `rating_counters[0]` is never used. In fact, in the `for` loops that initialize and display the contents of the array, you will note that the variable i starts at 1, and thereby bypasses the initialization and display of `rating_counters[0]`.

As a point of discussion, it is mentioned that we could have developed our program to use an array containing precisely ten elements. Then, when each response was keyed in by the user, we could have instead incremented `rating_counters[response - 1]`. This way, `rating_counters[0]` would have contained the number of respondents that rated the show a 1, `rating_counters[1]` the number that rated the show a 2, and so on. This is a perfectly fine approach. The only reason it was not used was because storing the number of responses of value n inside `rating_counters[n]` is a slightly more straightforward approach.

Study Program 7.3, which generates a table of the first 15 *Fibonacci* numbers, and try to predict its output. What relationship exists between each number in the table?

Program 7.3

```
/* Program to generate the first 15 Fibonacci numbers */
#include <stdio.h>
main ()
{
        int  Fibonacci[15], i;

        Fibonacci[0] = 0;    /* by definition */
        Fibonacci[1] = 1;    /*    ditto     */
```

continues

Program 7.3 Continued

```
for ( i = 2;  i < 15;  ++i )
        Fibonacci[i] = Fibonacci[i-2] + Fibonacci[i-1];
for ( i = 0;  i < 15;  ++i )
        printf ("%i\n", Fibonacci[i]);
}
```

Program 7.3 OUTPUT

```
0
1
1
2
3
5
8
13
21
34
55
89
144
233
377
```

The first two Fibonacci numbers, which we will call F_0 and F_1, are defined to be 0 and 1, respectively. Thereafter, each successive Fibonacci number F_i is defined to be the sum of the two preceding Fibonacci numbers F_{i-2} and F_{i-1}. So F_2 is calculated by adding together the values of F_0 and F_1. In the preceding program, this corresponds directly to calculating Fibonacci[2] by adding the values Fibonacci[0] and Fibonacci[1]. This calculation is performed inside the for loop, which calculates the values of F_2 through F_{14} (or, equivalently, Fibonacci[2] through Fibonacci[14]).

Fibonacci numbers actually have many applications in the field of mathematics and in the study of computer algorithms. The sequence of Fibonacci numbers historically originated from the "rabbits problem": If we start with a pair of rabbits and assume that each pair of rabbits produces a new pair of rabbits each month, that each newly born pair of rabbits can produce offspring by the end of their second month, and that rabbits never die, how many pairs of rabbits will there be after the end of a year? The answer to this problem rests in the fact that at the end of the nth month, there will be a total of F_{n+2} rabbits.

Therefore, according to the table from Program 7.3's output, at the end of the twelfth month, there will be a total of 377 pairs of rabbits.

Now it's time to return to the prime number program that we developed in Chapter 6, "Making Decisions," and see how the use of an array can help us to develop a more efficient program. In Program 6.10, the criteria that we used for determining if a number was prime was to divide the prime candidate by all successive integers from two up to the number minus one. In Exercise 7 in Chapter 6, we noted two inefficiencies with this approach that could easily be corrected. But even with these changes, the approach used is still not efficient. And while such questions of efficiency may not be important when dealing with a table of prime numbers up to 50, these questions do become important, for example, when we start thinking about generating a table of prime numbers up to 100,000.

One method for generating prime numbers that is an improvement over the previous approach involves the notion that a number is prime if it is not evenly divisible by any other prime number. This stems from the fact that any nonprime integer can be expressed as a multiple of prime factors. (For example, 20 has the prime factors 2, 2, and 5.) We can use this added insight to help us to develop a more efficient prime number program. The program can test if a given integer is prime by determining if it is evenly divisible by any other previously generated prime. By now the term "previously generated" should trigger off in your mind the idea that an array must be involved here. We can use an array to store each prime number as it is generated.

As a further optimization of the prime number generator program, it can be readily demonstrated that any nonprime integer n must have as one of its factors an integer that is less than or equal to the square root of n. What this means is that it is only necessary to determine if a given integer is prime by testing it for even divisibility against all prime factors up to the square root of the integer.

Program 7.4 incorporates the above discussions into a program to generate all prime numbers up to 50. The expression

```
p / primes[i] >= primes[i]
```

is used in the innermost `for` loop as a test to ensure that the value of `primes[i]` does not exceed the square root of `p`. This test comes directly from the discussions in the last paragraph. (You might want to think about the math a bit.)

We start off by storing 2 and 3 as the first two primes into the array `primes`. This array has been defined to contain 50 elements, even though we obviously won't need that many locations for storing the prime numbers. The variable `prime_index` is initially set to 2, which is the next free slot in the `primes` array. A `for` loop is then set up to run through the odd integers from 5 to 50. After the

flag is_prime is set to TRUE, another for loop is entered. This loop will successively divide the value of p by all of the previously generated prime numbers
that are stored in the array primes. The index variable i starts at 1, since it is
not necessary to test any values of p for divisibility by primes[0] (which is 2).
This is true because our program does not even consider even numbers as
possible primes. Inside the loop, a test is made to see if the value of p is evenly
divisible by primes[i], and if it is, then is_prime is set FALSE. The for loop
continues execution so long as the value of is_prime is TRUE *and* the value of
primes[i] does not exceed the square root of p.

After exiting the for loop, a test of the is_prime flag determines whether or not
to store the value of p as the next prime number inside the primes array.

Once all values of p have been tried, the program displays each prime number
that has been stored inside the primes array. The value of the index variable i
varies from 0 through prime_index - 1, since prime_index was always set pointing to the *next* free slot in the primes array.

Program 7.4

```
#include <stdio.h>
/* Modified program to generate prime numbers */

main ()
{
        int   p, is_prime, i, primes[50], prime_index = 2;

        primes[0] = 2;
        primes[1] = 3;

        for ( p = 5;  p <= 50;  p = p + 2 )
        {
            is_prime = 1;

            for ( i = 1;  is_prime  &&
                            p / primes[i] >= primes[i]; ++i )
                if ( p % primes[i] == 0 )
                    is_prime = 0;

            if ( is_prime )
             {
                primes[prime_index] = p;
                ++prime_index;
             }
        }
}
```

```
        for ( i = 0;  i < prime_index;  ++i )
           printf ("%i  ", primes[i]);

        printf ("\n");
}
```

Program 7.4 OUTPUT

---

2 3 5 7 11 13 17 19 23 29 31 37 41 43 47

Initializing Array Elements

Just as we can assign initial values to variables when they are declared, so can we assign initial values to the elements of an array. This is done by simply listing the initial values of the array, starting from the first element. Values in the list are separated by commas and the entire list is enclosed in a pair of braces.

The statement

```
int  counters[5] = { 0, 0, 0, 0, 0 };
```

will declare an array called counters to contain 5 integer values and will initialize each of these elements to zero. In a similar fashion, the statement

```
int  integers[5] = { 0, 1, 2, 3, 4 };
```

will set the value of integers[0] to 0, integers[1] to 1, integers[2] to 2, and so on.

Arrays of characters are initialized in a similar manner; thus the statement

```
char  letters[5] = { 'a', 'b', 'c', 'd', 'e' };
```

will define the character array letters and will initialize the five elements to the characters 'a', 'b', 'c', 'd', and 'e', respectively.

It is not necessary to completely initialize an entire array. If fewer initial values are specified, only an equal number of elements will be initialized. The remaining values in the array will be set to zero. So the declaration

```
float  sample_data[500] = { 100.0, 300.0, 500.5 };
```

initializes the first three values of sample_data to 100.0, 300.0, and 500.5, and sets the remaining 497 elements to zero.

Unfortunately, C does not provide any shortcut mechanisms for initializing array elements, such as the type provided in FORTRAN, for example. There is no way to specify a repeat count, so if it were desired to initially set all 500 values of sample_data to 1, then all 500 would have to be explicitly spelled out. In such a case, it would be better to initialize the array inside the program using an appropriate for loop.

Program 7.5 illustrates the two types of array-initialization techniques.

Program 7.5

```c
#include <stdio.h>
main ()
{
    int  array_values[10] = { 0, 1, 4, 9, 16 };
    int  i;

    for ( i = 5;  i < 10;  ++i )
        array_values[i] = i * i;

     for ( i = 0;  i < 10;  ++i )
        printf ("array_values[%i] = %i\n", i, array_values[i]);
}
```

Program 7.5 OUTPUT

```
array_values[0] = 0
array_values[1] = 1
array_values[2] = 4
array_values[3] = 9
array_values[4] = 16
array_values[5] = 25
array_values[6] = 36
array_values[7] = 49
array_values[8] = 64
array_values[9] = 81
```

In the declaration of the array array_values, the first five elements of the array are initialized to the square of their element number (for example, element number 3 is set equal to 3_2 or 9). The first for loop shows how this same type of initialization can be performed inside a loop. This loop sets each of the elements 5 through 9 to the square of its element number. The second for loop simply runs through all ten elements to display their values at the terminal.

Character Arrays

The purpose of Program 7.6 is to simply illustrate how a character array can be used. However, there is one point worthy of discussion. Can you spot it?

Program 7.6

```
#include <stdio.h>
main ()
{
        char  word[] = { 'H', 'e', 'l', 'l', 'o', '!' };
        int   i;

        for ( i = 0;  i < 6;  ++i )
          printf ("%c", word[i]);

        printf ("\n");
}
```

Program 7.6 OUTPUT

```
Hello!
```

The most notable point in the preceding program is the declaration of the character array word. There is no mention of the number of elements in the array. The C language allows you to define an array without specifying the number of elements. If this is done, then the size of the array will be determined automatically based on the number of initialization elements. Since in Program 7.6 there are six initial values listed for the array word, the C language implicitly dimensions the array to six elements.

This approach works fine so long as you initialize every element in the array at the point that the array is defined. If this is not to be the case, then you must explicitly dimension the array.

The next program further illustrates the use of integer and character arrays. The task is to develop a program that converts a positive integer from its base-10 representation into its equivalent representation in another base up to base-16. As inputs to the program, we will specify the number to be converted and also the base to which we would like the number converted to. The program will then convert the keyed-in number to the appropriate base and display the result.

The first step in developing such a program is to devise an algorithm to convert a number from base 10 to another base. An algorithm to generate the digits of the converted number can be informally stated as follows: A digit of the converted number is obtained by taking the modulo of the number by the base. The number is then divided by the base, with any fractional remainder discarded, and the process is repeated until the number reaches 0.

The outlined procedure will generate the digits of the converted number starting from the rightmost digit. Why don't we pick an example and see how it works? Suppose we wanted to convert the number 10 into base 2. The following table shows the steps that would be followed to arrive at the result.

Number	Number Modulo 2	Number / 2
10	0	5
5	1	2
2	0	1
1	1	0

The result of converting 10 to base 2 is therefore seen to be 1010, reading the digits of the "Number Modulo 2" column from the bottom to the top.

In order to write a program that performs the preceding conversion process, we must take a couple of things into account. First of all, the fact that the algorithm generates the digits of the converted number in reverse order is not very nice. We certainly don't expect the user to read the result from right to left, or from the bottom of the page upward. Therefore, we must correct this problem. Rather than simply displaying each digit as it is generated, we can have the program store each digit inside an array. Then, when we have finished converting the number, we can display the contents of the array in the correct order.

The second thing that must be realized is that we specified that the program handle conversion of numbers into bases up to 16. This means that any digits of the converted number that are between 10 and 15 must be displayed using the corresponding letters, A through F. This is where our character array enters the picture.

Examine Program 7.7 to see how these two issues are handled.

The character array `base_digits` is set up to contain the 16 possible digits that will be displayed for the converted number. The array `converted_number` is defined to contain a maximum of 64 digits, which will hold the results of converting the largest possible long integer to the smallest possible base (base 2) on just about all machines. We defined the variable `number_to_convert` to be of type long int so that relatively large numbers can be converted if desired. Finally, the variables base (to contain the desired conversion base) and index (to index into the converted_number array) are both defined to be of type int.

After the user keys in the values of the number to be converted and the base—and you will note that the scanf call to read in a long integer value takes the format characters %ld—the program then enters a do loop to perform the conversion. The do was chosen so that at least one digit will appear in the converted_number array even if the user keys in the number 0 to be converted.

Inside the loop, the number_to_be_converted modulo the base is computed to determine the next digit. This digit is stored inside the converted_number array, and the index into the array incremented by 1. After dividing the number_to_be_converted by the base, the conditions of the do are checked. If the value of number_to_be_converted is 0, the loop terminates; otherwise, the loop is repeated to determine the next digit of the converted number.

Program 7.7

```
/* Program to convert a positive integer to another base */
#include <stdio.h>
main ()
{
    char  base_digits[16] =
                    { '0', '1', '2', '3', '4', '5', '6', '7',
                      '8', '9', 'A', 'B', 'C', 'D', 'E', 'F' };
    int converted_number[64];
    long int number_to_convert;
    int next_digit, base, index = 0;

    /* get the number and the base */

    printf ("Number to be converted? ");
    scanf ("%ld", &number_to_convert);
    printf ("Base? ");
    scanf ("%i", &base);

    /* convert to the indicated base */


    do
    {
       converted_number[index] = number_to_convert % base;
       ++index;
       number_to_convert = number_to_convert / base;
    }
    while  ( number_to_convert != 0 );
```

continues

Program 7.7 Continued

```
/* display the results in reverse order */

printf ("Converted number = ");

for (--index;  index >= 0;   --index )
{
        next_digit = converted_number[index];
        printf ("%c", base_digits[next_digit]);
}

printf ("\n");
}
```

Program 7.7 OUTPUT

```
Number to be converted? 10
Base? 2
Converted number = 1010
```

Program 7.7 OUTPUT (Rerun)

```
Number to be converted? 128362
Base? 16
Converted number = 1F56A
```

When the do loop is done, the value of the variable index will be the number of digits in the converted number. Since this variable will be incremented one time too many inside the do loop, its value is initially decremented by 1 in the for loop. The purpose of this for loop is to display the converted number at the terminal. The for loop sequences through the converted_number array in *reverse* sequence to display the digits in the correct order.

Each digit from the converted_number array is in turn assigned to the variable next_digit. In order that the numbers 10 through 15 be correctly displayed using the letters A through F, a lookup is then made inside the array base_digits, using the value of next_digit as the index. For the digits 0 through 9, the corresponding location in the array base_digits contains nothing more than the characters '0' through '9' (which as you will recall *are* distinct from the integers 0 through 9). Locations 10 through 15 of the array contain the characters `'A'` through `'F'`. So if the value of `next_digit` is 10, for example, then the character contained in `base_digits[10]`, or `'A'`, will be displayed. And if the value of `next_digit` is 8, then the character `'8'` as contained in `base_digits[8]` will be displayed.

When the value of `index` becomes less than 0, the `for` loop will be finished. At that point the program will display a newline character, and program execution will be terminated.

Incidentally, you might be interested in knowing that you could have easily avoided the intermediate step of assigning the value of `converted_number[index]` to `next_digit` by directly specifying this expression as the subscript of the `base_digits` array in the `printf` call. In other words, the expression

```
base_digits[ converted_number[index] ]
```

could have been supplied to the `printf` routine and the same results achieved. Of course, this expression is a bit more cryptic than the two equivalent expressions used by the program.

It should be pointed out that we were a bit sloppy in the preceding program. No check was ever made to ensure that the value of `base` was between 2 and 16. If the user had entered 0 for the value of the base, the division inside the `do` loop would have been a division by 0. That's something we should never let happen. And if the user had keyed in 1 as the value of the base, then the program would go into an infinite loop since the value of `number_to_convert` would never reach 0. If the user entered a base value that was greater than 16, there is a chance that we would have exceeded the bounds of the `base_digits` array later in the program. That's another "gotcha" that we must avoid, since the C system does not check this condition for us.

In the next chapter, "Functions," we will rewrite this program and resolve these issues. But now let's take a look at an interesting extension to the notion of an array.

Multidimensional Arrays

The types of arrays that we have been exposed to so far are all linear arrays—that is, they all dealt with a single dimension. The C language allows arrays of any dimension to be defined. In this section, we will take a look at two-dimensional arrays.

One of the most natural applications for a two-dimensional array arises in the case of a matrix. Consider the 4 x 5 matrix shown next.

```
10  5 -3  17 82
 9  0  0   8 -7
32 20  1   0 14
 0  0  8   7  6
```

In mathematics, it is quite common to refer to an element of a matrix by use of a `double` subscript. So if we called the preceding matrix M, then the notation $M_{i,j}$ would refer to the element in the ith row , jth column, where i ranges from 1 through 4, and j ranges from 1 through 5. The notation $M_{3,2}$ would refer to the value 20, which is found in the 3rd row, 2nd column of the matrix. In a similar fashion, $M_{4,5}$ would refer to the element contained in the 4th row, 5th column: the value 6.

In C, there is an analogous notation to be used when referring to elements of a two-dimensional array. However, since C likes to start numbering things at 0, the first row of the matrix is actually row 0, and the first column of the matrix is column 0. The preceding matrix would then have row and column designations as shown in the diagram below.

Row (i)	Column (j)				
	0	*1*	*2*	*3*	*4*
0	10	5	-3	17	82
1	9	0	0	8	-7
2	32	20	1	0	14
3	0	0	8	7	6

Whereas in mathematics the notation $M_{i,j}$ is used, in C the equivalent notation is

`M[i][j]`

Remember, the first index number refers to the row number, while the second index number references the column. So the statement

`sum = M[0][2] + M[2][4];`

would add the value contained in row 0, column 2—which is -3—to the value contained in row 2, column 4—which is 14—and would assign the result of 11 to the variable `sum`.

Two-dimensional arrays are declared the same way that one-dimensional arrays are; thus

`int  M[4][5];`

declares the array M to be a two-dimensional array consisting of 4 rows and 5 columns, for a total of 20 elements. Each position in the array is defined to contain an integer value.

Two-dimensional arrays may be initialized in a manner analogous to their one-dimensional counterparts. When listing elements for initialization, the values are listed by row. Brace pairs are used to separate the list of initializers for one row from the next. So to define and initialize the array M to the elements listed in the preceding table, a statement such as the following could be used.

```
int  M[4][5] = {
                    { 10,  5, -3, 17, 82 },
                    {  9,  0,  0,  8, -7 },
                    { 32, 20,  1,  0, 14 },
                    {  0,  0,  8,  7,  6 }
                };
```

Pay particular attention to the syntax of the above statement. Note that commas are required after each brace that closes off a row, except in the case of the last row. The use of the inner pairs of braces is actually optional. If not supplied, then initialization proceeds by row. Thus the above statement could also have been written as

```
int  M[4][5] = { 10, 5, -3, 17, 82, 9, 0, 0, 8, -7, 32,
                 20, 1, 0, 14, 0, 0, 8, 7, 6 };
```

As with one-dimensional arrays, it is not required that the entire array be initialized. A statement such as

```
int  M[4][5] = {
                    { 10,  5, -3 },
                    {  9,  0,  0 },
                    { 32, 20,  1 },
                    {  0,  0,  8 }
                };
```

would only initialize the first three elements of each row of the matrix to the indicated values. The remaining values will be set to 0. Note that, in this case, the inner pairs of braces *are required* to force the correct initialization. Without them, the first two rows and the first two elements of the third row would have been initialized instead. (Verify to yourself that this would be the case.)

Exercises

A program example showing the use of multidimensional arrays is deferred to the next chapter, where we will begin our detailed discussion of one of the most important concepts in the C language—the program *function*. Before proceeding to that chapter, however, try to work the exercises that follow.

1. If you have access to a computer facility that supports the C programming language, type in and run the seven programs presented in this chapter. Compare the output produced by each program with the output presented after each program.

2. Modify Program 7.1 so that the elements of the array `values` are initially set to 0. Use a `for` loop to perform the initialization.

3. Program 7.2 permits only 20 responses to be entered. Modify that program so that any number of responses may be keyed in. So that the user does not have to count the number of responses in the list, set up the program so that the value 999 can be keyed in by the user to indicate that the last response has been entered. (Hint: you can use the `break` statement here if you want to exit your loop.)

4. Write a program that calculates the average of an array of ten floating-point values.

5. What output would you expect from the following program?

```c
#include <stdio.h>
main ()
{
    int  numbers[10] =
            { 1, 0, 0, 0, 0, 0, 0, 0, 0, 0 };
    int  i, j;

    for ( j = 0;  j < 10;  ++j )
        for ( i = 0;  i < j;  ++i )
            numbers[j]  =  numbers[j] + numbers[i];
    for ( j = 0;  j < 10;  ++j )
        printf ("%i ", numbers[j]);

    printf ("\n");
}
```

6. Prime numbers may also be generated by an algorithm known as the *Sieve of Erastosthenes*. The algorithm for this procedure is presented here. Write a program that implements this algorithm. Have the program find all prime numbers up to 150. What can you say about this algorithm as compared to the ones used in the text for calculating prime numbers?

Sieve of Erastosthenes Algorithm
To Display All Prime Numbers Between 1 and n

Step 1:	Define an array of integers P. Set all elements P_i to 0, $2 <= i <=$ n.
Step 2:	Set i to 2.
Step 3:	If $i > n$, the algorithm terminates.
Step 4:	If P_i is zero, then i is prime.
Step 5:	For all positive integer values of j, such that $i \times j < n$, set P_{ixj} to 1.
Step 6:	Add 1 to i and go to Step 3.

8

Functions

Behind all well-written programs in the C programming language lies the same fundamental element—the *function*. We have used functions in every program that we have encountered thus far. The printf and scanf routine are examples of functions. Indeed, each and every program also used a function called main. So you may ask, what is all the fuss about? The truth is that the program function provides the mechanism for producing programs that are easy to write, read, understand, debug, modify, and maintain. Obviously, anything that can accomplish all of these things is worthy of a bit of fanfare.

Let us first understand what a function is, and then proceed to show how it can be most effectively used in the development of programs. Let's go back to the very first program that we wrote (Program 3.1), which displayed the phrase "Programming is fun" at the terminal:

```
#include <stdio.h>
main ()
{
    printf ("Programming is fun.\n");
}
```

Here is a function called `print_message` that does the same thing:

```
void print_message (void)
{
    printf ("Programming is fun.\n");
}
```

The only difference between `print_message` and the function `main` from Program 3.1 is in the first line. The first line of a function definition tells the compiler four things about the function:

1. Its name.

2. The *type* of value it *returns*.

3. The arguments it takes.

4. Who can call it (discussed in Chapter 15, "Working with Larger Programs").

The first line of the `print_message` function definition tells the compiler that `print_message` is the name of the function, that it returns no value (the first use of the keyword `void`), and that it takes no arguments (the second use of the keyword `void`). We'll go into more details about the `void` keyword shortly.

QUICK TIP

Choosing meaningful function names is just as important as choosing meaningful variable names—the choice of names greatly affects the program's readability.

In our discussions of Program 3.1 we mentioned that `main` was a specially recognized name in the C system that always indicated where the program was to begin execution. There *always* must be a `main`. We can add a `main` function to the preceding code to end up with a complete program, as shown next.

Program 8.1

```
#include <stdio.h>
void print_message (void)
{
    printf ("Programming is fun.\n");
}

main ()
{
    print_message ();
}
```

Program 8.1 OUTPUT

```
Programming is fun.
```

Program 8.1 consists of *two* functions: `print_message` and `main`. Program execution always begins with `main`. Inside that function, the statement

```
print_message ();
```

appears. This statement indicates that the function `print_message` is to be executed. The open and closed parentheses are used to tell the compiler that `print_message` is a function and that no arguments or values are to be passed to this function (which is consistent with the way we defined the function in the program). When a function call is executed, program execution is transferred directly to the indicated function. Inside the `print_message` function, the `printf` statement will be executed to display the message "Programming is fun" at the terminal. After the message has been displayed, the `print_message` routine will be finished (as signalled by the closed brace) and the program will *return* to the `main` routine, where program execution will continue at the point where the function call was executed.

As mentioned previously, the idea of calling a function is not new. The `printf` and `scanf` routines are both program functions. The main distinction here is that these routines did not have to be written by us since they are a part of the C program library. Whenever we used the `printf` function to display a message or program results, execution was transferred to the `printf` function, which performed the required tasks and then returned back to the program. In each case, execution was returned to the program statement that immediately followed the call to the function.

Now try to predict the output from the following program.

Program 8.2

```
#include <stdio.h>
void print_message (void)
{
    printf ("Programming is fun.\n");
}

main ()
{
    print_message ();
    print_message ();
}
```

Program 8.2 OUTPUT

```
Programming is fun.
Programming is fun.
```

Execution of the preceding program starts at main, which contains two calls to the print_message function. When the first call to the function is executed, control is sent directly to the print_message function, which displays the message "Programming is fun" at the terminal and then returns to the main routine. Upon return, another call to the print_message routine is encountered, which results in the execution of the same function a second time. After the return is made from the print_message function, execution is terminated.

As a final example of the print_message function, try to guess the output from the following program.

Program 8.3

```c
#include <stdio.h>
void print_message (void)
{
    printf ("Programming is fun.\n");
}

main ()
{
    int  i;

    for ( i = 1;  i <= 5;  ++i )
        print_message ();
}
```

Program 8.3 OUTPUT

```
Programming is fun.
Programming is fun.
Programming is fun.
Programming is fun.
Programming is fun.
```

Arguments and Local Variables

When the printf function is called, we always supply one or more values to the function, the first value being the format string and the remaining values the specific program results to be displayed. These values, called *arguments*, greatly increase the usefulness and flexibility of a function. Unlike our print_message routine, which will display the same message each time it is called, the printf function will display whatever you tell it to display.

We can define a function that accepts arguments. In Chapter 5, "Program Looping," we developed an assortment of programs for calculating triangular numbers. Here we'll define a function to generate a triangular number. We'll call it, appropriately enough, calculate_triangular_number. As an argument to the function, we will specify which triangular number to calculate. The function will then calculate the desired number and display the results at the terminal. Here then is the function to accomplish the task and a main routine to try it out.

Program 8.4

```
/* Function to calculate the nth triangular number */
#include <stdio.h>
void calculate_triangular_number (int n)
{
    int  i, triangular_number = 0;

    for ( i = 1;  i <= n;  ++i )
        triangular_number = triangular_number + i;

    printf ("Triangular number %i is %i\n", n, triangular_number);
}

main ()
{
    calculate_triangular_number (10);
    calculate_triangular_number (20);
    calculate_triangular_number (50);
}
```

Program 8.4 OUTPUT

```
Triangular number 10 is 55
Triangular number 20 is 210
Triangular number 50 is 1275
```

The function `calculate_triangular_number` requires a bit of explanation. The first line of the function:

```
void calculate_triangular_number (int n)
```

is called the *function prototype declaration*. It tells the compiler that `calculate_triangular_number` is a function that returns no value (the keyword `void`) and that takes a single argument, called `n`, which is an `int`. The name that is chosen for an argument, called its *formal parameter name*, as well as the name of the function itself, can be any valid name formed by observing the rules outlined in Chapter 4, "Variables, Data Types, and Arthmetic Expressions," for forming variable names. For obvious reasons, you should choose meaning-ful names.

Once the formal parameter name has been defined, it can be used to refer to the argument anywhere inside the body of the function.

The beginning of the function's definition is indicated by the opening curly brace. Since we wish to calculate the nth triangular number, we have to set up a variable to store the value of the triangular number as it is being calculated. We also need a variable to act as our loop index. The variables `triangular_number` and `i` are defined for these purposes and are declared to be of type `int`. These variables are defined and initialized in the same manner that we defined and initialized our variables inside the `main` routine in previous programs.

QUICK TIP

If an initial value is given to a variable inside a function, that initial value will be assigned to the variable *each* time the function is called.

Variables defined inside a function are known as *automatic local* variables, since they are automatically "created" each time the function is called, and since their values are local to the function.

QUICK TIP

The value of a local variable can only be accessed by the function in which the variable is defined. Its value cannot be accessed by any other function.

When defining a local variable inside a function, it is more precise in C to use the keyword `auto` before the definition of the variable. An example of this would be the following:

```
auto int  i, triangular_number = 0;
```

Since the C compiler assumes by default that any variable defined inside a function is an automatic local variable, the keyword auto is seldom used, and for this reason it will not be used in this book.

Returning to our program example, after the local variables have been defined, the function calculates the triangular number and displays the results at the terminal. The closed brace then defines the end of the function.

Inside the main routine, the value 10 is passed as the argument in the first call to calculate_triangular_number. Execution is then transferred directly to the function where the value 10 *becomes the value of the formal parameter n* inside the function. The function then proceeds to calculate the value of the tenth triangular number and display the result.

The next time that calculate_triangular_number is called, the argument 20 is passed. In a similar process, as described earlier, this value becomes the value of n inside the function. The function then proceeds to calculate the value of the twentieth triangular number and display the answer at the terminal.

For an example of a function that takes more than one argument, let us rewrite the greatest common divisor program (Program 5.7) in function form. The two arguments to the function will be the two numbers whose greatest common divisor (*gcd*) we wish to calculate.

Program 8.5

```c
/* This function finds the greatest common divisor
       of two nonnegative integer values             */
#include <stdio.h>

void gcd (int u, int v)
{
    int  temp;

    printf ("The gcd of %i and %i is ", u, v);

    while ( v != 0 )
    {
        temp = u % v;
        u = v;
        v = temp;
    }

    printf ("%i\n", u);
}
```

continues

Program 8.5 Continued

```
main ()
{
    gcd (150, 35);
    gcd (1026, 405);
    gcd (83, 240);
}
```

Program 8.5 OUTPUT

```
The gcd of 150 and 35 is 5
The gcd of 1026 and 405 is 27
The gcd of 83 and 240 is 1
```

The function gcd is defined to take two integer arguments. The function will refer to these arguments through their formal parameter names u and v. After declaring the variable temp to be of type int, the program displays the values of the arguments u and v, together with an appropriate message at the terminal. The function then calculates and displays the greatest common divisor of the two integers .

You may be wondering why we have two printf statements inside the function gcd. We must display the values of u and v *before* we enter the while loop, since their values are changed inside the loop. If we waited until after the loop had finished, the values displayed for u and v would not at all resemble the original values that were passed to the routine. Another solution to this problem would have been to assign the values of u and v to two variables before entering the while loop. The values of these two variables could have then been displayed together with the value of u (the greatest common divisor) using a single printf statement after the while loop was completed.

Returning Function Results

The functions in Programs 8.4 and 8.5 perform some straightforward calculations and then display the results of the calculations at the terminal. However, we may not always wish to have the results of our calculations displayed. The C language provides us with a convenient mechanism whereby the results of a function may be *returned* to the calling routine. The syntax of this construct is straightforward enough:

```
return (expression);
```

This statement indicates that the function is to return the value of *expression* to the calling routine. The parentheses around *expression* are actually optional, but seem to be used by many programmers.

However, an appropriate return statement is not enough. When the function declaration is made, we must also declare the *type of value the function returns*. This declaration is placed immediately *before* the function's name. Each of the previous examples in this chapter defined functions that did not return a value, that's why we placed the keyword void directly before the function name. On the other hand, a function declaration that started like this:

```
float  kmh_to_mph (float  km_speed)
```

would begin the definition of a function kmh_to_mph, which takes one float argument called km_speed and which *returns* a floating-point value. Similarly,

```
int  gcd (int  u, int  v)
```

defines a function gcd with integer arguments u and v that returns an integer value. In fact, let us modify Program 8.5 so that the greatest common divisor is not displayed by the function gcd but is instead returned to the main routine.

Program 8.6

```
/* This function finds the greatest common divisor of two
     nonnegative integer values and returns the result    */
#include <stdio.h>
int  gcd (int u, int v)
{
    int  temp;

    while ( v != 0 )
    {
        temp = u % v;
        u = v;
        v = temp;
    }

    return (u);
}

main ()
{
    int  result;

    result = gcd (150, 35);
    printf ("The gcd of 150 and 35 is %i\n", result);

    result = gcd (1026, 405);
```

continues

Program 8.6 Continued

```
    printf ("The gcd of 1026 and 405 is %i\n", result);

    printf ("The gcd of 83 and 240 is %i\n", gcd (83, 240));
}
```

Program 8.6 OUTPUT

```
The gcd of 150 and 35 is 5
The gcd of 1026 and 405 is 27
The gcd of 83 and 240 is 1
```

Once the value of the greatest common divisor has been calculated by the gcd function, the statement

```
return (u);
```

is executed. This has the effect of returning the value of u, which is the value of the greatest common divisor, back to the calling routine.

You might be wondering what we can do with the value that is returned to the calling routine. As you can see from the main routine, in the first two cases, the value that is returned is stored in the variable result. More precisely, the statement

```
result = gcd (150, 35);
```

says to call the function gcd with the arguments 150 and 35 and to store the value that is returned by this function into the variable result.

The result that is returned by a function does not have to be assigned to a variable, as you will observe by the last statement in the main routine. In this case, the result returned by the call

```
gcd (83, 240)
```

is passed directly to the printf function, where its value is displayed.

A C function can only return a single value in the manner that we have just described. Unlike FORTRAN or Pascal, C makes no distinction between subroutines (procedures) and functions. In C, there is only the function, which can optionally return a value. If the declaration of the type returned by a function is omitted, the C compiler assumes that the function will return an integer—if it returns a value at all. Many C programmers take advantage of this fact and omit the return type declaration on functions that return integers. This is a bad programming habit that should be avoided.

QUICK TIP

Whenever a function returns a value, make sure you declare the type of value returned in the function's header, if only for the sake of improving the program's readability. In this manner, you will always be able to tell from the function header not only the function's name and the number and type of its arguments, but also if it returns a value and what the type of the returned value is.

As noted earlier, a function declaration that is preceded by the keyword `void` explicitly informs the compiler that the function does not return a value. A subsequent attempt at using the function in an expression, as if a value were returned, will result in a compiler error message. For example, since the `calculate_triangular_number` function of Program 8.4 did not return a value, we placed the keyword `void` before its name when defining the function. Subsequently attempting to use this function as if it returned a value, as in

```
number = calculate_triangular_number (20);
```

would result in a compiler error.

In a sense, the `void` data type is actually defining the *absence* of a data type. Therefore, a function declared to be of type `void` has no value and cannot be used as if it does in an expression.

In Chapter 6, "Making Decisions," we wrote a program to calculate and display the absolute value of a number. Let us now write a function that takes the absolute value of its argument and then returns the result. Instead of using integer values as we did in Program 6.1, we'll write this function to take a floating value as an argument and to also return the answer as type `float`.

Program 8.7

```
/* Function to calculate the absolute value */
#include <stdio.h>
float  absolute_value (float x)
{
    if ( x < 0 )
      x = -x;
```

continues

Program 8.7 Continued

```
    return (x);
}

main ()
{
    float  f1 = -15.5, f2 = 20.0, f3 = -5.0;
    int    i1 = -716;
    float  result;

    result = absolute_value (f1);
    printf ("result = %.2f\n", result);
    printf ("f1 = %.2f\n", f1);

    result = absolute_value (f2) + absolute_value (f3);
    printf ("result = %.2f\n", result);

    result = absolute_value ( (float) i1 );
    printf ("result = %.2f\n", result);

    result = absolute_value (i1);
    printf ("result = %.2f\n", result);

    printf ("%.2f\n", absolute_value (-6.0) / 4 );
}
```

Program 8.7 OUTPUT

```
result = 15.50
f1 = -15.50
result = 25.00
result = 716.00
result = 716.00
1.50
```

The absolute_value function is relatively straightforward. The formal parameter called x is tested against 0. If it is less than 0, the value is negated to take its absolute value. The result is then returned back to the calling routine with an appropriate return statement.

There are some interesting points with respect to the main routine that tests out the absolute_value function. In the first call to the function, the value of the variable f1, initially set to -15.5, is passed. Inside the function itself, this value is assigned to the variable x. Since the result of the if test will be TRUE, the statement that negates the value of x will be executed, thereby setting the value of x to 15.5. In the next statement, the value of x is returned to the main routine where it is assigned to the variable result and then displayed.

When the value of x is changed inside the absolute_value function, this in no way affects the value of the variable f1. When f1 was passed to the absolute_value function, its *value was automatically copied* into the formal parameter x by the system. Therefore, any changes made to the value of x inside the function affect only the value of x and not the value of f1. This is verified by the second printf call, which displays the unchanged value of f1 at the terminal.

QUICK TIP

It's not possible for a function to directly change the value of any of its arguments—it can only change copies of them.

The next two calls to the absolute_value function illustrate how the result returned by a function can be used in an arithmetic expression. The absolute value of f2 is added to the absolute value of f3 and the sum is assigned to the variable result.

The fourth call to the absolute_value function introduces the notion that the type of argument that is passed to a function should agree with the type of the argument as declared inside the function. Since the function absolute_value expects a floating value as its argument, we first cast our integer variable i1 to type float before the call is made. If you omit the cast operation, the compiler will do it for you anyway, since it knows the absolute_value function is expecting a floating argument. (This is verified by the fifth call to the absolute_value function.) However, it's clearer what's going on if you do the casting yourself rather than relying on the compiler to do the conversion for you.

The final call to the absolute_value function shows that the rules for evaluation of arithmetic expressions also pertain to values returned by functions. Since the value returned by the absolute_value function is declared to be of type float, the compiler treats the division operation as the division of a floating-point number by an integer. As you will recall, if one operand of a term is of type float, then the operation is performed using floating arithmetic. In accordance with this rule, the division of the absolute value of -6.0 by 4 produces a result of 1.5.

Now that we have defined a function that computes the absolute value of a number, we can use it in any future programs where we might need such a calculation performed. In fact, the next program is just such an example.

Functions Calling Functions Calling ...

With today's pocket calculators as commonplace as wristwatches, it is usually no big deal to find the square root of a particular number should the need arise. But years ago, students were taught manual techniques that could be used to arrive at an approximation of the square root of a number. One such approximation method that lends itself most readily to solution by a computer is known as the *Newton-Raphson Iteration Technique*. In the next program, we'll write a square root function that uses this technique to arrive at an approximation of the square root of a number.

The Newton-Raphson method may be easily described as follows. We begin by selecting a "guess" at the square root of the number. The closer that this guess is to the actual square root, the fewer the number of calculations that will have to be performed to arrive at the square root. For the sake of argument, however, we will assume that we are not very good at guessing and will therefore always make an initial guess of 1.

The number whose square root we wish to obtain is divided by the initial guess and is then added to the value of guess. This intermediate result is then divided by 2. The result of this division becomes the new guess for another go-around with the formula. That is, the number whose square root we are calculating is divided by this new guess, added into this new guess, and then divided by 2. This result then becomes the new guess and another iteration is performed.

Since we don't wish to continue this iterative process forever, we need some way of knowing when to stop. Since the successive guesses that are derived by repeated evaluation of the formula get closer and closer to the true value of the square root, we can set a limit that we can use for deciding when to terminate the process. The difference between the square of the guess and the number itself can then be compared against this limit—usually called epsilon (ϵ). If the difference is less than ϵ, then the desired accuracy for the square root will have been obtained and the iterative process can be terminated.

This procedure can be expressed in terms of an algorithm as shown.

Newton-Raphson Method to Compute the Square Root of x

Step 1:	Set the value of guess to 1.
Step 2:	If $|\text{guess}^2 - x| < \varepsilon$, proceed to Step 4.
Step 3:	Set the value of guess to $(x / \text{guess} + \text{guess}) / 2$ and return to Step 2.
Step 4:	guess is the approximation of the square root.

It is necessary to test the *absolute* difference of guess^2 and x against ε in Step 2, since the value of guess can approach the square root of x from either side.

Now that we have an algorithm for finding the square root at our disposal, it once again becomes a relatively straightforward task to develop a function to calculate the square root. For the value of ε in the following function, the value .00001 was arbitrarily chosen.

Program 8.8

```
/* Function to calculate the absolute value of a number */
#include <stdio.h>
float  absolute_value (float x)
{
    if ( x < 0 )
        x = -x;
    return (x);
}


/* Function to compute the square root of a number */

float  square_root (float x)
{
    float  epsilon = .00001;
    float  guess   = 1.0;

    while ( absolute_value (guess * guess - x) >= epsilon )
      guess = ( x / guess + guess ) / 2.0;

    return (guess);
}


main ()
{
```

continues

Program 8.8 Continued

```
    printf ("square_root (2.0) = %f\n", square_root (2.0));
    printf ("square_root (144.0) = %f\n", square_root (144.0));
    printf ("square_root (17.5) = %f\n", square_root (17.5));
}
```

Program 8.8 OUTPUT

```
square_root (2.0) = 1.414216
square_root (144.0) = 12.000000
square_root (17.5) = 4.183300
```

(The actual values that are displayed by running this program on your computer system may differ slightly in the less significant digits.)

The above program requires a detailed analysis. The `absolute_value` function is defined first. This is the same function that was used in Program 8.7.

Next we find the `square_root` function. This function takes one argument called x and returns a value of type `float`. Inside the body of the function, two local variables called `epsilon` and `guess` are defined. The value of `epsilon`, which is used to determine when to end the iteration process, is set to .00001. The value of our `guess` at the square root of the number is initially set to 1.0. These initial values are assigned to these two variables each time that the function is called.

After the local variables have been declared, a `while` loop is set up to perform the iterative calculations. The statement that immediately follows the `while` condition will be repetitively executed as long as the absolute difference between $guess^2$ and x is greater than or equal to `epsilon`. The expression

```
guess * guess - x
```

is evaluated and the result of the evaluation is passed to the `absolute_value` function. The result returned by the `absolute_value` function is then compared against the value of `epsilon`. If the value is greater than or equal to `epsilon`, then the desired accuracy of the square root has not yet been obtained. In that case, another iteration of the loop is performed to calculate the next value of `guess`.

Eventually the value of `guess` will be close enough to the true value of the square root and the `while` loop will terminate. At that point, the value of `guess` will be returned to the calling program. Inside the `main` function, this returned value is passed to the `printf` function, where it is displayed.

You may have noticed that *both* the `absolute_value` function and the `square_root` function have formal parameters named x. The C compiler doesn't get confused, however, and keeps these two values distinct.

In fact, a function always has its own set of formal parameters. So the formal parameter x used inside the `absolute_value` function is distinct from the formal parameter x used inside the `square_root` function.

The same is true for local variables. We can declare local variables with the same name inside as many functions as we desire. The C compiler will not confuse the usage of these variables, since a local variable can only be accessed from within the function where it is defined. Another way of saying this is that the *scope* of a local variable is the function in which it is defined. (As you will see in Chapter 11, "Pointers," C does provide a mechanism for indirectly accessing a local variable from outside of a function.)

Based upon this discussion, you can understand that when the value of guess^2 - x is passed to the `absolute_value` function and assigned to the formal parameter x, this assignment has absolutely *no* effect on the value of x inside the `square_root` function.

Declaring Return Types and Argument Types

We mentioned earlier that the C compiler assumes that a function returns a value of type `int` as the default case. More specifically, whenever a call is made to a function, the compiler will assume that the function returns a value of type `int` unless either of the following has occurred:

1. The function has been defined in the program before the function call is encountered.

2. The value returned by the function has been *declared* before the function call is encountered.

In Program 8.8, the `absolute_value` function is defined before the compiler encounters a call to this function from within the `square_root` function. The compiler will know, therefore, that when this call is encountered, that the `absolute_value` function will return a value of type `float`. Had the `absolute_value` function been defined *after* the `square_root` function, then upon encountering the call to the `absolute_value` function the compiler would have assumed that this function returned an integer value. Most C compilers will catch this error and generate an appropriate diagnostic message.

In order to be able to define the `absolute_value` function *after* the `square_root` function (or even in another file—see Chapter 15), we must *declare* the type of the result returned by the `absolute_value` function *before* the function is called. The declaration can be made inside the `square_root` function itself, or outside of any function. In the latter case, the declaration is usually made at the beginning of the program.

Not only is the function declaration used to declare the function's return type, but it is also used to tell the compiler how many arguments the function takes and what their types are.

To declare `absolute_value` as a function that returns a value of type `float` and that takes a single argument, also of type `float`, the following declaration would be used:

```
float  absolute_value (float);
```

As you can see, you just have to specify the argument type inside the parentheses, and not its name. You can optionally specify a "dummy" name after the type if you like:

```
float  absolute_value (float  x);
```

This name doesn't have to be the same as the one used in the function definition—the compiler ignores it anyway.

QUICK TIP

A foolproof way to write a function declaration is to simply use your text editor to make a copy of the first line from the actual definition of the function. Remember to place a semicolon at the end.

If the function doesn't take an argument, use the keyword `void` between the parentheses. If the function doesn't return a value, this fact can also be declared to thwart any attempts at using the function as if it does:

```
void  calculate_triangular_number (int  n);
```

If the function takes a variable number of arguments (such as is the case with `printf` and `scanf`), the compiler must be informed. The declaration

```
int printf (char *format, ...);
```

tells the compiler that `printf` takes a character *pointer* as its first argument (more on that later), and is followed by any number of additional arguments (the use of the . . .). `printf` and `scanf` are declared in the special file `stdio.h`. This is why you have been placing the following line at the start of each of your programs:

```
#include <stdio.h>
```

Without this line, the compiler can assume `printf` and `scanf` take a fixed number of arguments, which may result in incorrect code being generated.

The compiler will automatically convert your arguments to the appropriate types when a function is called, but only if you have placed the function's definition or have declared the function and its argument types before the call.

Here are some reminders and suggestions about functions:

1. Remember that, by default, the compiler assumes that a function returns an `int`.

2. When defining a function that returns an `int`, define it as such.

3. When defining a function that doesn't return a value, define it as `void`.

4. The compiler will convert your arguments to agree with the ones the function expects only if you have previously defined or declared the function.

QUICK TIP

To play it safe, declare all functions in your program, even if they are defined before they are called. (You may decide later to move them someplace else in your file or even to another file.)

Note that ANSI C also supports an alternate older format for defining and declaring functions. This format is described in Appendix A and will not be used in this text. Whenever we talk about defining or declaring a function, we are referring to the newer *prototyping* format as described in this chapter.

Checking Function Arguments

The square root of a negative number takes us away from the realm of real numbers and into the area of imaginary numbers. So what would happen if we were to pass a negative number to our `square_root` function? The fact is, the Newton-Raphson process would never converge; that is, the value of `guess` would not get closer to the correct value of the square root with each iteration of the loop. Therefore, the criteria set up for termination of the `while` loop would *never* be satisfied, and the program would go into an infinite loop. Execution of the program would have to be abnormally terminated by typing in some command or hitting a special key at the terminal (such as the *Delete* key under UNIX or *CTRL-C* under MS-DOS).

Obviously, modifying the program to correctly account for this situation is called for in this case. We could put the burden on the calling routine and mandate that it never pass a negative argument to the square_root function. While this approach might seem reasonable, it does have its drawbacks. Eventually, we would develop a program that used the square_root function but which forgot to check the argument before calling the function. If a negative number were then passed to the function, the program would go into an infinite loop as described and would have to be aborted. Not very nice!

A much wiser and safer solution to the problem is to place the onus of checking the value of the argument on the square_root function itself. In that way, the function would be "protected" from *any* program that used it. A reasonable approach to take would be to check the value of the argument x inside the function and then (optionally) display a message if the argument were negative. The function could then immediately return without performing its calculations. As an indication to the calling routine that the square_root function did not work as expected, a value not normally returned by the function could be returned.

The following is a modified square_root function, which tests the value of its argument and which also includes a prototype declaration for the absolute_value function as described in the previous section.

```
/* Function to compute the square root of a number.
   If a negative argument is passed, then a message
   is displayed and -1.0 is returned.                   */

float  square_root (float x)
{
    float  epsilon = .00001;
    float  guess   = 1.0;
    float  absolute_value (float  x);

    if ( x < 0 )
    {
        printf ("Negative argument to square_root.\n");
        return (-1.0);
    }

    while ( absolute_value (guess * guess - x) >= epsilon )
            guess = ( x / guess + guess ) / 2.0;

    return (guess);
}
```

If a negative argument is passed to the above function, an appropriate message is displayed, and the value -1.0 is immediately returned to the calling routine. If the argument is not negative, then calculation of the square root proceeds as previously described.

As you can see from the modified `square_root` function, we can have more than one `return` statement in a function. Whenever a `return` is executed, control is immediately sent back to the calling function; any program statements in the function that appear after the `return` are not executed. This fact also makes the `return` statement ideal for use by a function that does not return a value. In such a case, the `return` statement takes the simpler form

```
return;
```

since no value is to be returned. Obviously, if the function *is* supposed to return a value, then this form cannot be used to return from the function.

Top-Down Programming

The notion of functions that call functions that in turn call functions, and so on, forms the basis for producing good structured programs. In the `main` routine of Program 8.8, the `square_root` function is called several times. All the details concerned with the actual calculation of the square root are contained within the `square_root` function itself, and not within `main`. Thus, we can write a call to this function before we even write the instructions of the function itself, as long as we specify the arguments that the function takes and the value that it returns.

Later, when proceeding to write the code for the `square_root` function, this same type of *top-down programming* technique can be applied: We can write a call to the `absolute_value` function without concerning ourselves at that time with the details of operation of that function. All we need to know is that we *can* develop a function to take the absolute value of a number.

The same programming technique that makes programs easier to write also makes them easier to read. Thus the reader of Program 8.8 can easily determine upon examination of the `main` routine that the program is simply calculating and displaying the square root of three numbers. He or she need not sift through all of the details of how the square root is actually calculated in order to glean this information. If the reader wishes to get more involved in details, then the specific code associated with the `square_root` function can be studied. Inside that function, the same discussion applies to the `absolute_value` function. The reader need not know how the absolute value of a number is calculated in order to understand the operation of the `square_root` function. Such details are relegated to the `absolute_value` function itself, which can be studied if a more detailed knowledge of its operation is desired.

Functions and Arrays

As with ordinary variables and values, it is also possible to pass the value of an array element and even an entire array as an argument to a function. To pass a single array element to a function (which is what we were doing in Chapter 7, "Arrays," when we used the `printf` function to display the elements of an array), the array element is specified as an argument to the function in the normal fashion. So, to take the square root of `averages[i]` and assign the result to a variable called `sq_root_result`, a statement such as

```
sq_root_result = square_root (averages[i]);
```

would do the trick.

Inside the `square_root` function itself, nothing special has to be done to handle single array elements passed as arguments. In the same manner as with a simple variable, the value of the array element will be copied into the value of the corresponding formal parameter when the function is called.

Passing an entire array to a function is an entirely new ball game. To pass an array to a function, it is only necessary to list the name of the array, *without any subscripts*, inside the call to the function. As an example, if we assume that `grade_scores` has been declared as an array containing 100 elements, then the expression

```
minimum (grade_scores)
```

will in effect pass the entire 100 elements contained in the array `grade_scores` to the function called `minimum`. Naturally, on the other side of the coin, the `minimum` function must be expecting an entire array to be passed as an argument and must make the appropriate formal parameter declaration. So the `minimum` function might look something like this:

```
int  minimum (int  values[100])
{
    ...
    return (minimum_value);
}
```

The declaration defines the function `minimum` as returning a value of type `int` and as taking as its argument an array containing 100 integer elements. References made to the formal parameter array `values` will reference the appropriate elements inside the array that was passed to the function. Based upon the function call previously shown and the corresponding function declaration, a reference made to `values[4]`, for example, would actually reference the value of `grade_scores[4]`.

Program 8.9

```c
/* Function to find the minimum in an array */
#include <stdio.h>
int  minimum (int  values[10])
{
    int  minimum_value, i;

    minimum_value = values[0];

    for ( i = 1;   i < 10;   ++i )
        if ( values[i] < minimum_value )
            minimum_value = values[i];

    return (minimum_value);
}

main ()
{
    int  scores[10], i, minimum_score;
    int  minimum (int  values[10]);

    printf ("Enter 10 scores\n");

    for ( i = 0;   i < 10;   ++i )
        scanf ("%i", &scores[i]);

    minimum_score = minimum (scores);
    printf ("\nMinimum score is %i\n", minimum_score);
}
```

Program 8.9 OUTPUT

```
Enter 10 scores
69
97
65
87
69
86
78
67
92
90

Minimum score is 65
```

For our first program that illustrates a function that takes an array as an argument, let's write a function minimum to find the minimum value in an array of ten integers. This function, together with a main routine to set up the initial values in the array, is shown in Program 8.9.

The first thing that will catch your eye inside main is the prototype declaration for the minimum function. This tells the compiler that minimum returns an int and takes an array of ten ints. Remember, it's not really necessary to make this declaration here, since the minimum function is defined before it's called from inside main. However, we're going to play it safe throughout the rest of this text and declare all functions that are used.

After the array scores is defined, the user is prompted to enter ten values. The scanf call places each number as it is keyed in into scores[i], where i ranges from 0 through 9. After all the values have been entered, the minimum function is called with the array scores as an argument.

The formal parameter name values is used to reference the elements of the array inside the function. It is declared to be an array of ten integer values. The local variable minimum_value is used to store the minimum value in the array and is initially set to values[0], the first value in the array. The for loop sequences through the remaining elements of the array, comparing each element in turn against the value of minimum_value. If the value of values[i] is less than minimum_value, then a new minimum in the array has been found. In such a case, the value of minimum_value is reassigned to this new minimum value and the scan through the array continues.

When the for loop has completed execution, minimum_value is returned to the calling routine, where it is assigned to the variable minimum_score and is then displayed to the user.

With our general-purpose minimum function in hand, we can use it to find the minimum of *any* array containing ten integers. If we had five different arrays containing ten integers each, we could simply call the minimum function five separate times to find the minimum value of each array. And we can just as easily define other functions to perform tasks, such as finding the maximum value, the median value, the mean (average) value, and so on.

By defining small, independent functions that perform well-defined tasks, we can build upon these functions to accomplish more sophisticated tasks and also make use of them for other related programming applications. For example, we could define a function statistics, which takes an array as an argument and perhaps, in turn, calls a mean function, a standard_deviation function, and so on, to accumulate statistics about an array. This type of program methodology is the key to the development of programs that are easy to write, understand, modify, and maintain.

Of course, our general-purpose `minimum` function is not so general purpose in the sense that it only works on an array of precisely ten elements. But this problem is relatively easy to rectify. We can extend the versatility of this function by having it take the number of elements in the array as an argument. In the function declaration, we can then omit the specification of the number of elements contained in the formal parameter array. The C compiler actually ignores this part of the declaration anyway; all the compiler is concerned with is the fact that an array is expected as an argument to the function and not how many elements are in it.

Program 8.10 is a revised version of Program 8.9 in which the `minimum` function finds the minimum value in an integer array of arbitrary length.

Program 8.10

```
/* Function to find the minimum in an array */
#include <stdio.h>
int  minimum (int  values[], int  number_of_elements)
{
    int  minimum_value, i;

    minimum_value = values[0];

    for ( i = 1;  i < number_of_elements;  ++i )
        if ( values[i] < minimum_value )
            minimum_value = values[i];

    return (minimum_value);
}

main ()
{
    int  array1[5] = { 157, -28, -37, 26, 10 };
    int  array2[7] = { 12, 45, 1, 10, 5, 3, 22 };
    int  minimum (int  values[], int  number_of_elements);

    printf ("array1 minimum: %i\n", minimum (array1, 5));
    printf ("array2 minimum: %i\n", minimum (array2, 7));
}
```

Program 8.10 OUTPUT

```
array1 minimum: -37
array2 minimum: 1
```

This time the function minimum is defined to take two arguments: first, the array whose minimum we wish to find; and second, the number of elements in the array. The open and closed brackets that immediately follow values in the function header serve to inform the C compiler that values is an array of integers. As was stated, the compiler really doesn't need to know how large it is.

The formal parameter number_of_elements replaces the constant 10 as the upper limit inside the for statement. So the for statement sequences through the array from values[1] through the last element of the array, which is values[number_of_elements - 1].

In the main routine, two arrays called array1 and array2 are defined to contain five and seven elements, respectively.

Inside the first printf call, a call is made to the minimum function with the arguments array1 and 5. This second argument specifies the number of elements contained in array1. The minimum function finds the minimum value in the array and the returned result of -37 is then displayed at the terminal. The second time the minimum function is called, array2 is passed, together with the number of elements in that array. The result of 1 as returned by the function is then passed to the printf function to be displayed.

Assignment Operators

Study the following program and try to guess the output *before* looking at the actual program results.

Program 8.11

```c
#include <stdio.h>
void  multiply_by_two (float  array[], int  n)
{
    int  i;

    for ( i = 0;  i < n;  ++i )
        array[i] *= 2;
}

main ()
{

    float  float_values[4] = { 1.2, -3.7, 6.2, 8.55 };
    int    i;
    void   multiply_by_two (float  array[], int  n);

    multiply_by_two (float_values, 4);

    for ( i = 0;  i < 4;  ++i )
```

```
        printf ("%.2f   ", float_values[i]);

    printf ("\n");
}
```

Program 8.11 OUTPUT

```
2.40   -7.40   12.40   17.10
```

When you were examining Program 8.11, your attention surely must have been drawn to the statement

```
array[i] *= 2;
```

Hopefully, based upon the name of the function, you were able to determine what this statement is actually doing. This is certainly one of the primary reasons why meaningful function names should always be chosen. The effect of the so-called "times equals" operator (*=) is to multiply the expression on the left side of the operator by the expression on the right side of the operator and *to store the result back into the variable on the left side of the operator.* So the previous expression is equivalent to the statement

```
array[i] = array[i] * 2;
```

The "times equals" operator saves us from having to repeat what appears on the left side of the operator on the right side.

As you might have guessed, there are analagous operators for all binary arithmetic operators in C. These operators are called *assignment operators* and are formed by listing the normal binary operator immediately followed by the assignment operator =. So the expression

```
counter += 5
```

uses the "plus equals" assignment operator to add 5 to the value of counter and is equivalent to the expression

```
counter = counter + 5
```

A slightly more involved expression,

```
a /= b + c
```

divides a by whatever appears to the right of the equals sign—or by the sum of b and c—and stores the result back into a. The addition is performed first because the addition operator has higher precedence than the assignment operator. In fact, all operators except the comma operator have higher precedence than the assignment operators, which all have the same precedence.

In this case, this expression is identical to

```
a = a / (b + c)
```

The motivation for using assignment operators is threefold. First, the program statement becomes easier to write, since what appears on the left side of the operator does not have to be repeated on the right side. Second, the resulting expression is usually easier to read. Third, the use of these operators can result in programs that execute faster on the computer.

As an example of an expression that is both easier to write and to read, consider the following program statement, which subtracts 10 from the value contained in `Board[row + col - 5]`:

```
Board[row + col - 5]  =  Board[row + col - 5] - 10;
```

With the use of the `-=` assignment operator, this statement could be written as

```
Board [row + col - 5] -= 10;
```

In the latter case, it is far easier to see that 10 is being subtracted from the indicated element in the `Board` array, since in the former case, a visual comparison must be made between the element on the left side of the equals sign and the element on the right side to determine that the same element of the `Board` array is being referenced.

Getting back to the main point to be made about the preceding program, you may have realized by now that the function `multiply_by_two` actually *changes* values inside the `float_values` array. Isn't this a contradiction to what we have stated before about a function not being able to change the value of its arguments? Not really.

This program example points out one major distinction that must always be kept in mind when dealing with array arguments.

QUICK TIP

If a function changes the value of an array element, then that change will be made to the original array that was passed to the function. This change remains in effect even after the function has completed execution and has returned to the calling routine.

The reason an array behaves differently from a simple variable or an array element—whose value *cannot* be changed by a function—is worthy of explanation. We stated that when a function is called, the values that are passed as arguments to the function are copied into the corresponding formal parameters. This statement is still valid. However, when dealing with arrays, the entire contents of the array are *not* copied into the formal parameter array. Instead, the function gets passed information describing *where* in the computer's memory the array is located. Any changes made to the formal parameter array by the function are actually made to the original array passed to the function, and not to a copy of the array. Therefore, when the function returns, these changes still remain in effect.

Remember, the preceding discussion applies only to entire arrays that are passed as arguments, and not to individual elements, whose values are copied into the corresponding formal parameters and therefore cannot be permanently changed by the function. Chapter 11, "Pointers," discusses these concepts in greater detail.

To further illustrate the idea that a function can change values in an array passed as an argument, we will develop a function to sort (rank) an array of integers. The process of sorting has always received much attention by computer scientists, probably because sorting is an operation that is so commonly performed. Many sophisticated algorithms have been developed in order to sort a set of information in the least amount of time, using as little of the computer's memory as possible. Since the purpose of this book is not to teach such sophisticated algorithms, we will develop a sort function that uses a fairly straightforward algorithm to sort an array into *ascending order*. Sorting an array into ascending order means rearranging the values in the array so that the elements progressively increase in value from the smallest to the largest. By the end of such a sort, the minimum value will be contained in the first location of the array, while the maximum value will be found in the last location of the array, with values that progressively increase in between.

If we wanted to sort an array of *n* elements into ascending order, we could do so by performing a successive comparison of each of the elements of the array. We could begin by comparing the first element in the array against the second. If the first element were greater in value than the second, then we could simply "swap" the two values in the array; that is, exchange the values contained in these two locations.

Next, we could compare the first element in the array (which we now know is less than the second) against the third element in the array. Once again, if the first value were greater than the third, we would exchange these two values. Otherwise, we would leave them alone. Now we would have the smallest of the first three elements contained in the first location of the array.

If we repeated the above process for the remaining elements in the array—comparing the first element against each successive element and exchanging their values if the former were larger than the latter—then the smallest value of the entire array would be contained in the first location of the array by the end of the process.

If we now did the same thing with the second element of the array, that is, compared it against the third element, then against the fourth, and so on; and if we exchanged any values that were out of order, we would then end up with the next smallest value contained in the second location of the array when the process was completed.

It should now be clear how we can go about sorting the array by performing these successive comparisons and exchanges as needed. The process will stop after we have compared the next-to-last element of the array against the last and have interchanged their values if required. At that point, the entire array will have been sorted into ascending order.

The following algorithm gives a more concise description of the above sorting process. We assume here that we are sorting an array a of n elements.

Simple Exchange Sort Algorithm

Step 1:	Set i to 0.
Step 2:	Set j to $i + 1$.
Step 3:	If $a[i] > a[j]$, exchange their values.
Step 4:	Set j to $j + 1$. If $j < n$, go to Step 3.
Step 5:	Set i to $i + 1$. If $i < n - 1$, go to Step 2.
Step 6:	a is now sorted in ascending order.

Program 8.12 implements the above algorithm in a function called `sort`, which takes two arguments: the array to be sorted and the number of elements in the array.

The `sort` function implements the algorithm as a set of nested `for` loops. The outermost loop sequences through the array from the first element to the next-to-last element (`a[n-2]`). For each such element, a second `for` loop is entered, which starts from the element after the one currently selected by the outer loop and ranges through the last element of the array.

If the elements are out of order (that is, if `a[i]` is greater than `a[j]`), then the elements are switched. The variable `temp` is used as a temporary storage place while the switch is being made.

When both `for` loops are finished, the array will have been sorted into ascending order. Execution of the function is then complete.

In the `main` routine, `array` is defined and initialized to 16 integer values. The program then displays the values of the array at the terminal and proceeds to call the `sort` function, passing as arguments `array` and 16, the number of elements in `array`. After the function returns, the program once again displays the values contained in `array`. As you can see from the output, the function successfully sorted the array into ascending order.

The `sort` function shown in Program 8.12 is fairly simple. The price that must be paid for such a simplistic approach is one of execution time. If we had to sort an extremely large array of values (arrays containing thousands of elements, perhaps), then the sort routine as we have implemented it here could take a considerable amount of execution time. If this happened, then we would have to resort to one of the more sophisticated algorithms that we alluded to in our discussions. *The Art of Computer Programming, Volume 3, Sorting and Searching* (Donald E. Knuth, Addison-Wesley) is probably the best reference source for such algorithms.

Program 8.12

```
/* Sort an array of integers into ascending order */
#include <stdio.h>
void  sort (int  a[], int  n)
{
    int  i, j, temp;

    for ( i = 0;  i < n - 1;  ++i )
        for ( j = i + 1;  j < n;  ++j )
            if ( a[i] > a[j] )
            {
                temp = a[i];
                a[i] = a[j];
                a[j] = temp;
            }
}

main ()
{
    int  i;
    int  array[16] = { 34, -5, 6, 0, 12, 100, 56, 22,
                       44, -3, -9, 12, 17, 22, 6, 11 };
    void sort (int  a[], int  n);

    printf ("The array before the sort:\n");
```

continues

Program 8.12 Continued

```
    for ( i = 0;  i < 16;  ++i )
        printf ("%i ", array[i]);

    sort (array, 16);

    printf ("\n\nThe array after the sort:\n");

    for ( i = 0;  i < 16;  ++i )
        printf ("%i ", array[i]);

    printf ("\n");
}
```

Program 8.12 OUTPUT

```
The array before the sort:
34 -5 6 0 12 100 56 22 44 -3 -9 12 17 22 6 11

The array after the sort:
-9 -5 -3 0 6 6 11 12 12 17 22 22 34 44 56 100
```

Multidimensional Arrays

A multidimensional array element may be passed to a function just as any ordinary variable or single-dimensional array element can. So the statement

```
square_root (matrix[i][j]);
```

will call the square_root function, passing the value contained in matrix[i][j] as the argument.

An entire multidimensional array can be passed to a function the same way that a single-dimensional array can: You simply list the name of the array. For example, if the matrix measured_values is declared to be a two-dimensional array of integers, the C statement

```
scalar_multiply (measured_values, constant);
```

could be used to invoke a function that multiplies each element in the matrix by the value of constant. This implies, of course, that the function itself may change the values contained inside the measured_values array. The discussion of this topic for single-dimensional arrays also applies here: An assignment made to any element of the formal parameter array inside the function makes a permanent change to the array that was passed to the function.

When declaring a single-dimensional array as a formal parameter inside a function, it was stated that the actual dimension of the array was not needed; simply use a pair of empty brackets to inform the C compiler that the parameter is in fact an array. This does not totally apply in the case of multi-dimensional arrays. For a two-dimensional array, the number of rows in the array may be omitted, but the declaration *must* contain the number of columns in the array. So the declarations

```
int   array_values[100][50]
```

and

```
int   array_values[][50]
```

are both valid declarations for a formal parameter array called `array_values` containing 100 rows by 50 columns; but the declarations

```
int   array_values[100][]
```

and

```
int   array_values[][]
```

are not, since the number of columns in the array *must* be specified.

In the next program, we define a function `scalar_multiply`, which multiplies a two-dimensional integer array by a scalar integer value. We will assume for purposes of this example that the array is dimensioned 3 x 5. The `main` routine will call the `scalar_multiply` routine twice. After each call, the array will be passed to the `display_matrix` routine to display the contents of the array. Pay careful attention to the nested `for` loops that are used in both `scalar_mutiply` and `display_matrix` to sequence through each element of the two-dimensional array.

Program 8.13

```
#include <stdio.h>
main ()
{
    void   scalar_multiply (int  matrix[3][5], int  scalar);
    void   display_matrix (int  matrix[3][5]);
```

continues

Program 8.13 Continued

```c
    {
        {  7, 16, 55, 13, 12 },
        { 12, 10, 52,  0,  7 },
        { -2,  1,  2,  4,  9 }
    };

    printf ("Original matrix:\n");
    display_matrix (sample_matrix);

    scalar_multiply (sample_matrix, 2);

    printf ("\nMultiplied by 2:\n");
    display_matrix (sample_matrix);

    scalar_multiply (sample_matrix, -1);

    printf ("\nThen multiplied by -1:\n");
    display_matrix (sample_matrix);
}

/* Function to multiply a 3 x 5 array by a scalar */

void  scalar_multiply (int  matrix[3][5], int  scalar)
{
    int  row, column;

    for ( row = 0;  row < 3;  ++row )
        for ( column = 0;  column < 5;  ++column )
            matrix[row][column]  *=  scalar;
}


void  display_matrix (int  matrix[3][5])
{
    int   row, column;

    for ( row = 0;  row < 3;  ++row)
    {

        for ( column = 0;  column < 5;  ++column )
            printf ("%5i", matrix[row][column]);

        printf ("\n");
    }
}
```

Program 8.13 OUTPUT

```
Original matrix:
    7   16   55   13   12
   12   10   52    0    7
   -2    1    2    4    9

Multiplied by 2:
   14   32  110   26   24
   24   20  104    0   14
   -4    2    4    8   18

Then multiplied by -1:
  -14  -32 -110  -26  -24
  -24  -20 -104    0  -14
    4   -2   -4   -8  -18
```

The `main` routine defines the matrix `sample_values` and then calls the `display_matrix` function to display its initial values at the terminal. Inside the `display_matrix` routine, you will notice the nested `for` statements. The first or outermost `for` statement sequences through each row in the matrix, so the value of the variable `row` varies from 0 through 2. For each value of `row`, the innermost `for` statement is executed. This `for` statement sequences through each column of the particular row, so the value of the variable `column` ranges from 0 through 4.

The `printf` statement displays the value contained in the specified row and column using the format characters `%5i` to ensure that the elements line up in the display. After the innermost `for` loop has finished execution—meaning that an entire row of the matrix has been displayed—a newline character is displayed so that the next row of the matrix is displayed on the next line of the terminal.

The first call to the `scalar_mutiply` function specifies that the `sample_matrix` array is to be multiplied by 2. Inside the function, a simple set of nested `for` loops is set up to sequence through each element in the array. The element contained in `matrix[row][column]` is multiplied by the value of `scalar` in accordance with the use of the assignment operator `*=`. After the function returns to the `main` routine, the `display_matrix` function is once again called to display the contents of the `sample_matrix` array. The program's output verifies that each element in the array has in fact been multiplied by 2.

The `scalar_multiply` function is called a second time to multiply the now modified elements of the `sample_matrix` array by -1. The modified array is then displayed by a final call to the `display_matrix` function, and program execution is then complete.

Global Variables

We are now ready to tie together many of the principles that we have learned in this chapter, as well as learn some new ones. What we would like to do now is take Program 7.7, which converted a positive integer to another base, and rewrite it in function form. In order to do this, we must conceptually divide the program into logical segments. If you glance back at that program you will see that this is readily accomplished simply by looking at the three comment statements inside `main`. They suggest the three primary functions that the program is performing: getting the number and base from the user, converting the number to the desired base, and then displaying the results.

We can define three functions to perform an analogous task. The first function we will call `get_number_and_base`. This function will prompt the user to enter the number to be converted and the base and will read these values in from the terminal. Here we will make a slight improvement over what was done in Program 7.7. If the user types in a value of base that is less than 2 or greater than 16, then the program will display an appropriate message at the terminal and set the value of the base to 10. In this manner, the program will end up redisplaying the original number to the user. (Another approach might be to let the user re-enter a new value for the base, but this is left as an exercise.)

The second function we will call `convert_number`. This function will take the value as typed in by the user and convert it to the desired base, storing the digits resulting from the conversion process inside the `converted_number` array.

The third and final function we will call `display_converted_number`. This function will take the digits contained inside the `converted_number` array and display them to the user in the correct order. For each digit to be displayed, a lookup will be made inside the `base_digits` array so that the correct character is displayed for the corresponding digit.

The three functions that we will define will communicate with each other by means of *global variables*. It has been previously noted that one of the fundamental properties of a local variable is that its value can be accessed only by the function in which the variable is defined. As you might expect, this restriction does not apply to global variables. That is, a global variable's value can be accessed by *any* function in the program.

The distinguishing quality of a global variable declaration versus a local variable declaration is that the former is made *outside* of any function. This indicates its global nature—it does not belong to any particular function. *Any* function in the program can then access the value of that variable and can also change its value if desired.

In Program 8.14, four global variables are defined. Each of these variables is used by at least two functions in the program. Since the base_digits array and the variable next_digit are used exclusively by the function display_converted_number, they are *not* defined as global variables. Instead, these variables are locally defined within the function display_converted_number.

The global variables are defined first in the program. Since they are not defined within any particular function, the C system classifies these variables as global variables, which means, as we have mentioned, that they can now be referenced by any function in the program.

Program 8.14

```
/* Program to convert a positive integer to another base */
#include <stdio.h>
int         converted_number[64];
long int    number_to_convert;
int         base;
int         index = 0;

void  get_number_and_base (void)
{
    printf ("Number to be converted? ");
    scanf ("%li", &number_to_convert);

    printf ("Base? ");
    scanf ("%i", &base);

    if ( base < 2  ||  base > 16 )
    {
        printf ("Bad base - must be between 2 and 16\n");
        base = 10;
    }
}
void  convert_number (void)
{
    do
    {
        converted_number[index] = number_to_convert % base;
        ++index;
        number_to_convert /= base;
    }
    while  ( number_to_convert != 0 );
}

void  display_converted_number (void)
{
```

continues

Program 8.14 Continued

```c
char  base_digits[16] =
       { '0', '1', '2', '3', '4', '5', '6', '7',
         '8', '9', 'A', 'B', 'C', 'D', 'E', 'F' };
int   next_digit;

printf ("Converted number = ");

for (--index;  index >= 0; --index )
{
    next_digit = converted_number[index];
    printf ("%c", base_digits[next_digit]);
}

printf ("\n");
}

main ()
{
    void  get_number_and_base (void), convert_number (void),
          display_converted_number (void);

    get_number_and_base ();
    convert_number ();
    display_converted_number ();
}
```

Program 8.14 OUTPUT

```
Number to be converted? 100
Base? 8
Converted number = 144
```

Program 8.14 OUTPUT (Rerun)

```
Number to be converted? 1983
Base? 0
Bad base - must be between 2 and 16
Converted number = 1983
```

You will notice how the wise choice of function names makes the operation of Program 8.14 clear. Spelled out directly in the main routine is the function of the program: to get a number and a base, convert the number, and then display the converted number. The much improved readability of this program over the equivalent one from Chapter 7 is a direct result of the structuring of the program into separate functions that perform small, well-defined tasks. Note that we do not even need comment statements inside the `main` routine to describe what the program is doing—the function names speak for themselves.

The primary use of global variables is in programs in which many functions must access the value of the same variable. Rather than having to pass the value of the variable to each individual function as an argument, the function can explicitly reference the variable instead. There is a drawback with this approach. Because the function explicitly references a particular global variable, the generality of the function is somewhat reduced. So, every time that function is to be used, we must make sure that the global variable exists, by its particular name.

For example, the `convert_number` function of Program 8.14 will succeed in converting only a number that is stored in the variable `number_to_convert` to a base as specified by the value of the variable `base`. Furthermore, the variable `index` and the array `converted_number` must be defined. A far more flexible version of this function would allow the arguments to be passed to the function.

QUICK TIP

While the use of global variables may reduce the number of arguments that need to be passed to a function, the price that must be paid is reduced function generality and, in some cases, reduced program readability. This issue of program readability stems from the fact that if you use global variables, the variables that are used by a particular function are not evident simply by examining the function's header. Also, a call to the particular function does not indicate to the reader what types of parameters the function needs as inputs or produces as outputs.

One final thing about global variables. They do have default initial values: zero. So in the global declaration

```
int  data[100] = { 1, 2, 3, 4, 5 };
```

the first five values of `data` are set as shown, with the remaining 95 elements set to zero.

QUICK TIP

Global variables have default initial values of zero; local variables have no
default initial value and so must be explicitly initialized by the program.

Automatic and Static Variables

When we normally declare a local variable inside a function, as in the declaration of the variables guess and epsilon in our square_root function:

```
float  square_root (float  x)
{
    float  epsilon = .00001;
    float  guess   =  1.0;
        . . .
}
```

we are declaring *automatic* local variables. As you will recall, the keyword auto may in fact precede the declaration of such variables, but is optional, since it is the default case. An automatic variable is, in a sense, actually created each time the function is called. In the preceding example, the local variables epsilon and guess are created whenever the square_root function is called. As soon as the square_root function is finished, these local variables "disappear." This process happens automatically, hence the name automatic variables.

Automatic local variables may be given initial values, as is done with the values of epsilon and guess, above. In fact, any valid C expression can be specified as the initial value for a simple automatic variable. The value of the expression will be calculated and assigned to the automatic local variable *each* time the function is called. And since an automatic variable disappears once the function has completed execution, the value of that variable disappears along with it. In other words, the value an automatic variable has when a function finishes execution is *guaranteed* not to exist the next time the function is called.

If we stick the word static in front of a variable declaration, then we are in an entirely new ball game. The word static in C refers not to an electric charge but rather to the notion of something that has no movement. This is the key to the concept of a static variable—it does *not* come and go as the function is called and returns. This implies that the value a static variable has upon leaving a function will be the same value that variable will have the next time the function is called.

Static variables also differ with respect to their initialization. A static local variable is initialized only *once* at the start of overall program execution and not each time that the function is called. Furthermore, the initial value specified for a static variable *must* be a simple constant or constant expression. Static variables also have default initial values of zero, unlike automatic variables, which have no default initial value.

In the function `auto_static`, which is defined as follows:

```
void auto_static (void)
{
    static int  static_variable = 100;
            .
            .
            .
}
```

the value of `static_variable` will be initialized to 100 only once when program execution begins. In order to set its value to 100 each time the function is executed, an explicit assignment statement is needed, as in

```
void auto_static (void)
{
    static int  static_variable;

    static_variable = 100;
            .
            .
            .
}
```

The following program should help make the concepts of automatic and static variables a bit clearer.

Program 8.15

```
/* Illustrate static and automatic variables */
#include <stdio.h>
void  auto_static (void)
{
    int         auto_variable = 1;
    static int  static_variable = 1;

    printf ("automatic = %i, static = %i\n",
            auto_variable, static_variable);

    ++auto_variable;
    ++static_variable;
}
```

continues

Program 8.15 Continued

```
main ()
{
    int    i;
    void   auto_static (void);

    for ( i = 0;   i < 5;   ++i )
        auto_static ();
}
```

Program 8.15 OUTPUT

```
automatic = 1, static = 1
automatic = 1, static = 2
automatic = 1, static = 3
automatic = 1, static = 4
automatic = 1, static = 5
```

Inside the auto_static function, two local variables are declared. The first variable, called auto_variable, is an automatic variable of type int with an initial value of 1. The second variable, called static_variable, is a static variable, also of type int and also with an initial value of 1. The function calls the printf routine to display the values of these two variables. After this, the variables are each incremented by 1, and execution of the function is then complete.

The main routine sets up a loop to call the auto_static function five times. The output from Program 8.15 points out the difference between the two variable types. The value of the automatic variable is listed as 1 for each line of the display. This is because its value is set to 1 each time the function is called. On the other hand, the output shows the value of the static variable steadily increasing from 1 through 5. This is because its value is set equal to 1 only once—when program execution begins—and because its value is retained from one function call to the next.

The choice of whether to use a static variable or automatic variable depends upon the intended use of the variable. If you want the variable to retain its value from one function call to the next (for example, consider a function that counts the number of times that it is called), then use a static variable. Also, if your function uses a variable whose value is set once and then never changes, you may want to declare the variable static, as it saves the inefficiency of having the variable reinitialized each time that the function is called. This efficiency consideration is even more important when dealing with arrays.

From the other direction, if the value of a local variable must be initialized at the beginning of each function call, an automatic variable seems the logical choice.

Recursive Functions

The C language supports a capability known as *recursive* function. Recursive functions can be effectively used to succinctly and efficiently solve problems. They are commonly used in applications in which the solution to a problem can be expressed in terms of successively applying the same solution to subsets of the problem. One example might be in the evaluation of expressions containing nested sets of parenthesized expressions. Other common applications involve the searching and sorting of data structures called *trees* and *lists*.

Recursive functions are most commonly illustrated by an example that calculates the factorial of a number. As you will recall, the factorial of a positive integer n, written $n!$, is simply the product of the successive integers 1 through n. The factorial of 0 is a special case and is defined equal to 1. So 5! is calculated as follows:

```
5!    =  5 x 4 x 3 x 2 x 1
      =  120
```

and

```
6!    =  6 x 5 x 4 x 3 x 2 x 1
      =  720
```

Comparing the calculation of 6! to the calculation of 5!, you will observe that the former is equal to 6 times the latter; that is, 6! = 6 x 5!. In the general case, the factorial of any positive integer n greater than 0 is equal to n multiplied by the factorial of $n - 1$:

```
n! = n x (n - 1)!
```

The expression of the value of $n!$ in terms of the value of $(n-1)!$ is called a *recursive* definition, since the definition of the value of a factorial is based on the value of another factorial. In fact, we can develop a function that calculates the factorial of an integer n according to this recursive definition. Such a function is illustrated in the following program.

Program 8.16

```c
#include <stdio.h>
main ()
{
    int   j;
    long int  factorial (int  n);
    for ( j = 0;   j < 11;   ++j )
        printf ("%2i! = %li\n", j, factorial (j));
}

/* Recursive function to calculate the factorial
          of a positive integer                 */

long int  factorial (int  n)
{
    long int   result;

    if  ( n == 0 )
        result = 1;
    else
        result = n * factorial (n - 1);

    return (result);
}
```

Program 8.16 OUTPUT

```
 0! = 1
 1! = 1
 2! = 2
 3! = 6
 4! = 24
 5! = 120
 6! = 720
 7! = 5040
 8! = 40320
 9! = 362880
10! = 3628800
```

The fact that the `factorial` function includes a call to itself makes this function recursive. When the function is called to calculate the factorial of 3, the value of the formal parameter n will be set to 3. Since this value is not 0, the following program statement

```c
result = n * factorial (n - 1);
```

will be executed, which, given the value of n, will be evaluated as

```
result = 3 * factorial (2);
```

This expression specifies that the `factorial` function is to be called, this time to calculate the factorial of 2. Therefore, the multiplication of 3 by this value will be left pending while `factorial (2)` is calculated.

Even though we are again calling the same function, we should conceptualize this as a call to a separate function. Each time any function is called in C—be it recursive or not—the function gets its own set of local variables and formal parameters to work with. Therefore, the local variable `result` and the formal parameter n that exist when the `factorial` function is called to calculate the factorial of 3 are distinct from the variable `result` and the parameter n when the function is called to calculate the factorial of 2.

With the value of n equal to 2, the `factorial` function will execute the statement

```
result = n * factorial (n - 1);
```

which will be evaluated as

```
result = 2 * factorial (1);
```

Once again, the multiplication of 2 by the factorial of 1 will be left pending while the `factorial` function is called to calculate the factorial of 1.

With the value of n equal to 1, the `factorial` function will once again execute the statement

```
result = n * factorial (n - 1);
```

which will be evaluated as

```
result = 1 * factorial (0);
```

When the `factorial` function is called to calculate the factorial of 0, the function will set the value of `result` to 1 and *return*, thus initiating the evaluation of all of the pending expressions. So the value of `factorial (0)`, or 1, will be returned to the calling function (which happened to be the `factorial` function), multiplied by 1, and assigned to `result`. This value of 1, which represents the value of `factorial (1)`, will then be returned back to the calling function (once again the `factorial` function) where it will be multiplied by 2, stored into re-sult, and returned as the value of `factorial (2)`. Finally, the returned value of 2 will be multiplied by 3, thus completing the pending calculation of `facto-rial (3)`. The resulting value of 6 will be returned as the final result of the call to the `factorial` function, to be displayed by the `printf` function.

In summary, the sequence of operations that is performed in the evaluation of `factorial (3)` can be conceptualized as follows:

```
factorial (3) = 3 * factorial (2)
              = 3 * 2 * factorial (1)
              = 3 * 2 * 1 * factorial (0)
              = 3 * 2 * 1 * 1
              = 6
```

It might be a good idea for you to trace through the operation of the `factorial` function with a pencil and paper. Assume that the function is initially called to calculate the factorial of 4. List the values of n and `result` at each call to the `factorial` function.

This discussion concludes this chapter on functions and variables. The program function is a powerful tool in the C programming language. Enough cannot be said about the critical importance of structuring a program in terms of small, well-defined functions. Functions will be used heavily throughout the remainder of this book. At this point, you should review any topics covered in this chapter that still may seem unclear. Working through the following exercises will also help reinforce the topics that have been discussed.

Exercises

1. If you have access to a computer facility that supports the C programming language, type in and run the 16 programs presented in this chapter. Compare the output produced by each program with the output presented after each program.

2. Modify Program 8.4 so the value of `triangular_number` is returned by the function. Then go back to Program 5.5 and change that program so that it calls the new version of the `calculate_triangular_number` function.

3. Modify Program 8.8 so that the value of `epsilon` is passed as an argument to the function. Try experimenting with different values of `epsilon` to see the effect that it has on the value of the square root.

4. Modify Program 8.8 so that the value of `guess` is printed each time through the `while` loop. Notice how quickly the value of `guess` converges to the square root. What conclusions can you reach about the number of iterations through the loop, the number whose square root is being calculated, and the value of the initial guess?

5. The criteria used for termination of the loop in the `square_root` function of Program 8.8 is not suitable for use when computing the square root of very large or very small numbers. Rather than comparing the *difference* between the value of x and the value of $guess^2$, the program

should compare the *ratio* of the two values to 1. The closer this ratio gets to 1, the more accurate the approximation of the square root.

Modify Program 8.8 so this new termination criteria is used.

6. Modify Program 8.8 so that the square_root function accepts a double precision argument and returns the result as a double precision value. Be sure to change the value of the variable epsilon to reflect the fact that double precision variables are now being used.

7. Write a function that raises an integer to a positive integer power. Call the function x_to_the_n taking two integer arguments x and n. Have the function return a long int, which represents the results of calculating x^n.

8. An equation of the form

$$ax^2 + bx + c = 0$$

is known as a *quadratic* equation. The values of *a*, *b*, and *c* in the above example represent constant values. So

$$4x^2 - 17x - 15 = 0$$

represents a quadratic equation where $a = 4$, $b = -17$, and $c = -15$. The values of *x* that satisfy a particular quadratic equation, known as the *roots* of the equation, may be calculated by substituting the values of *a*, *b*, and *c* into the following two formulas:

$$x_1 = \frac{-b + \sqrt{b^2 - 4ac}}{2a}$$

$$x_2 = \frac{-b - \sqrt{b^2 - 4ac}}{2a}$$

If the value of $b^2 - 4ac$, called the *discriminant*, is less than 0, then the roots of the equation, x_1 and x_2, are imaginary numbers.

Write a program to solve a quadratic equation. The program should allow the user to enter the values for *a*, *b*, and *c*. If the discriminant is less than 0, then a message should be displayed that the roots are imaginary; otherwise, the program should then proceed to calculate and display the two roots of the equation. (Note: Be sure to make use of the square_root function that we developed in this chapter.)

9. The least common multiple (*lcm*) of two positive integers u and v is the smallest positive integer that is evenly divisible by both u and v. Thus, the *lcm* of 15 and 10, written *lcm* (15, 10), is 30 since 30 is the smallest integer divisible by both 15 and 10. Write a function `lcm` that takes two integer arguments and returns their *lcm*. The `lcm` function should calculate the least common multiple by calling the `gcd` function from Program 8.6 in accordance with the following identity:

$$lcm\ (u, v) = uv\ /\ gcd\ (u, v) \qquad u, v >= 0$$

10. Write a function `prime` that returns 1 if its argument is a prime number and returns 0 otherwise.

11. Write a function called `array_sum` that takes two arguments: an integer array and the number of elements in the array. Have the function return as its result the sum of the elements in the array.

12. A matrix M with i rows, j columns can be *transposed* into a matrix N having j rows and i columns by simply setting the value of $N_{a,b}$ equal to the value of $M_{b,a}$ for all relevant values of a and b.

    Write a function *transpose_matrix* that takes as an argument a 4 x 5 matrix and a 5 x 4 matrix. Have the function transpose the 4 x 5 matrix and store the results into the 5 x 4 matrix. Also write a `main` routine to test the function.

13. Modify the `sort` function of Program 8.12 to take a third argument indicating whether the array is to be sorted into ascending or descending order. Then modify the sort algorithm to correctly sort the array into the indicated order.

14. Rewrite the functions developed in the last four exercises to use global variables instead of arguments. For example, the last exercise should now transpose a globally defined 4 x 5 matrix, storing the results of the transposition into another globally defined 5 x 4 matrix.

15. Modify Program 8.14 so that the user is re-asked to type in the value of the base if an invalid base is entered. The modified program should continue to ask for the value of the base until a valid response is given.

16. Modify Program 8.14 so that the user can convert any number of integers. Make provision for the program to terminate when a 0 is typed in as the value of the number to be converted.

9

Structures

Chapter 7, "Arrays," introduced the array that permits us to group elements of the same type into a single logical entity. To reference an element in the array, all that was necessary was that the name of the array be given together with the appropriate subscript.

The C language provides another tool for grouping elements together. This falls under the name of *structures* and forms the basis for the discussions in this chapter. As you will see, the structure is a powerful concept that you will use in many C programs that you develop.

Suppose we wished to store today's date—which is 7/18/93—inside a program, perhaps to be used for the heading of some program output, or even for computational purposes. A natural method for storing the date would be to simply assign the month to an integer variable called `month`, the day to an integer variable `day`, and the year to an integer variable `year`. So the statements

```
int  month = 7, day = 18, year = 1993;
```

would work just fine. This is a totally acceptable approach. But what if our program also needed to store the date of purchase of a particular item, for example? We could go about the same procedure of defining three more variables such as `month_of_purchase`, day_of_purchase, and year_of_purchase. Whenever we needed to use the purchase date, these three variables could then be explicitly accessed.

Using this method, we must keep track of three separate variables for each date that we use in the program—variables that are logically related. It would be much better if we could somehow group these sets of three variables together. This is precisely what the structure in C allows us to do.

We can define a structure called date in the C language that consists of three components that represent the month, day, and year. The syntax for such a definition is rather straightforward, as shown by the following:

```
struct  date
{
    int   month;
    int   day;
    int   year;
};
```

The date structure just defined contains three integer *members* called month, day, and year. The definition of date in a sense defines a new type in the language in that variables may subsequently be declared to be of type struct date, as in the declaration

```
struct date   today;
```

We can also declare a variable purchase_date to be of the same type by a separate declaration, such as

```
struct date   purchase_date;
```

or we can simply include the two declarations on the same line, as in

```
struct date   today, purchase_date;
```

Unlike variables of type int, float, or char, a special syntax is needed when dealing with structure variables. A member of a structure is accessed by specifying the variable name, followed by a period, and then the member name. For example, to set the value of the day in the variable today to 21, you write

```
today.day = 21;
```

Note that there are no spaces permitted between the variable name, the period, and the member name. To set the year in today to 1993, the expression

```
today.year = 1993;
```

can be used. Finally, to test the value of month to see if it is equal to 12, a statement such as

```
if  ( today.month == 12 )
   next_month = 1;
```

will do the trick.

What do you think would be the effect of the following statement?

```
if  ( today.month == 1  &&  today.day == 1 )
  printf ("Happy New Year!!!\n");
```

The following incorporates the preceding discussions into an actual C program.

Program 9.1

```
/* Program to illustrate a structure */
#include <stdio.h>
main ()
{
    struct  date
    {
        int  month;
        int  day;
        int  year;
    };

    struct date  today;

    today.month = 9;
    today.day = 25;
    today.year = 1993;

    printf ("Today's date is %i/%i/%i.\n", today.month,
            today.day, today.year % 100);
}
```

Program 9.1 OUTPUT

```
Today's date is 9/25/93.
```

The first statement inside main defines the structure called date to consist of three integer members called month, day, and year. In the second statement, the variable today is declared to be of type struct date. So the first statement simply defines what a date structure looks like to the C compiler and causes no storage to be reserved inside the computer. The second statement declares a variable to be of type struct date and therefore *does* cause memory to be reserved for storing the three integer values of the variable today.

QUICK TIP

Be sure you understand the difference between defining a structure and declaring variables of the particular structure type.

After `today` has been declared, the program then proceeds to assign values to each of the three members of `today`, as depicted in Figure 9.1.

Figure 9.1. *Assigning values to a structure variable.*

After the assignments have been made, the values contained inside the structure are displayed by an appropriate `printf` call. The remainder of `today.year` divided by 100 is calculated prior to being passed to the `printf` function so that just 93 is displayed for the year.

When it comes to the evaluation of expressions, structure members follow the same rules as ordinary variables do in the C language. So division of an integer structure member by another integer would be performed as an integer division, as in

```
century = today.year / 100 + 1;
```

Suppose we wanted to write a simple program that accepted today's date as input and displayed tomorrow's date to the user? Now, at first glance, this seems a perfectly simple task to perform. We can ask the user to enter today's date and then proceed to calculate tomorrow's date by a series of statements, such as

```
tomorrow.month = today.month;
tomorrow.day   = today.day + 1;
tomorrow.year  = today.year;
```

Of course, the above statements would work just fine for the majority of dates, but the following two cases would not be properly handled:

1. If today's date fell at the end of a month.

2. If today's date fell at the end of a year (that is, if today's date were December 31).

One way to determine easily if today's date falls at the end of a month is to set up an array of integers that corresponds to the number of days in each month. A lookup inside the array for a particular month will then give the number of days in that month. So the statement

```
int  days_per_month[12] =
   { 31, 28, 31, 30, 31, 30, 31, 31, 30, 31, 30, 31 };
```

defines an array called `days_per_month` containing 12 integer elements. For each month `i`, the value contained in `days_per_month[i - 1]` corresponds to the number of days in that particular month. Therefore, the number of days in April, which is the fourth month of the year, is given by `days_per_month[3]`, which is equal to 30. (We could have defined the array to contain 13 elements, with `days_per_month[i]` corresponding to the number of days in month `i`. Access into the array could then have been made directly based on the month number, rather than on the month number minus 1. The decision of whether to use 12 or 13 elements in this case is strictly a matter of personal preference.)

If it is determined that today's date falls at the end of the month, then we can calculate tomorrow's date by simply adding 1 to the month number and setting the value of the day equal to 1.

In order to solve the second problem mentioned earlier, we must determine if today's date is at the end of a month and if the month is 12. If this is the case, then tomorrow's day and month must be set equal to 1 and the year appropriately incremented by 1.

Program 9.2 asks the user to enter today's date, calculates tomorrow's date, and displays the results.

If you look at the program's output, you will quickly notice that we seemed to have made a mistake somewhere: The day after February 28, 1992 is listed as March 1, 1992 and *not* as February 29, 1992. I think our program forgot about leap years! But we'll return to this problem shortly. First, let's discuss the program and its logic.

After the `date` structure is defined, two variables of type `struct date`, `today` and `tomorrow`, are declared. The program then asks the user to enter today's date. The three integer values that are entered are stored into `today.month`, `today.day`, and `today.year`, respectively.

Program 9.2

```c
/* Program to determine tomorrow's date */
#include <stdio.h>
main ()
{
    struct  date
    {
        int  month;
        int  day;
        int  year;
    };

    struct date  today, tomorrow;

    int  days_per_month[12] =
      { 31, 28, 31, 30, 31, 30, 31, 31, 30, 31, 30, 31 };

    printf ("Enter today's date (mm dd yyyy): ");
    scanf ("%i%i%i", &today.month, &today.day, &today.year);

    if ( today.day != days_per_month[today.month - 1] )
    {
        tomorrow.day = today.day + 1;
        tomorrow.month = today.month;
        tomorrow.year = today.year;
    }
    else if ( today.month == 12 )       /* end of year */
    {
        tomorrow.day = 1;
        tomorrow.month = 1;
        tomorrow.year = today.year + 1;
    }
    else
    {                                        /* end of month */
        tomorrow.day = 1;
        tomorrow.month = today.month + 1;
        tomorrow.year = today.year;
    }

    printf ("Tomorrow's date is %i/%i/%i.\n",tomorrow.month,
            tomorrow.day, tomorrow.year % 100);
}
```

Program 9.2 OUTPUT

```
Enter today's date (mm dd yyyy): 7 16 1993
Tomorrow's date is 7/17/93.
```

Program 9.2 OUTPUT (Rerun)

```
Enter today's date (mm dd yyyy): 12 31 1992
Tomorrow's date is 1/1/93.
```

Program 9.2 OUTPUT (Rerun)

```
Enter today's date (mm dd yyyy): 2 28 1992
Tomorrow's date is 3/1/92.
```

Next, a test is made to determine if the day is at the end of the month, by comparing `today.day` to `days_per_month[today.month - 1]`. If it is not the end of the month, then tomorrow's date is calculated by simply adding one to the day and setting tomorrow's month and year equal to today's month and year.

If today's date does fall at the end of the month, then another test is made to determine if we are at the end of the year. If the month equals 12, meaning that today's date is December 31, then tomorrow's date is set equal to January 1 of the next year. If the month does not equal 12, then tomorrow's date is set to the first day of the following month (of the same year).

After tomorrow's date has been calculated, the values are displayed to the user with an appropriate `printf` statement call, and program execution is complete.

Functions and Structures

Now let's return to the problem that was discovered in the previous program. Our program thinks that February always has 28 days, so naturally when we ask it for the day after February 28, it will always display March 1 as the answer. What we need to do is to make a special test for the case of a leap year. If the year is a leap year, and the month is February, then the number of days in that month is 29. Otherwise, the normal lookup inside the days_per_month array can be made.

A good way to incorporate the required changes into Program 9.2 would be to develop a function called `number_of_days` to determine the number of days in a month. The function would perform the leap year test and the lookup inside the days_per_month array as required. Inside the `main` routine all that would have to be changed would be the `if` statement, which compares the value of `today.day` to `days_per_month[today.month - 1]`. Instead, we could now compare the value of `today.day` to the value returned by our `number_of_days` function.

Study the following program carefully. What is being passed to the number_of_days function as an argument?

Program 9.3

```c
/* Program to determine tomorrow's date */
#include <stdio.h>
struct  date
{
    int   month;
    int   day;
    int   year;
};

main ()
{
    struct date  today, tomorrow;
    int  number_of_days (struct date d);

    printf ("Enter today's date (mm dd yyyy): ");
    scanf ("%i%i%i", &today.month, &today.day, &today.year);

    if  ( today.day != number_of_days (today) )
    {
        tomorrow.day = today.day + 1;
        tomorrow.month = today.month;
        tomorrow.year = today.year;
    }
    else if ( today.month == 12 )     /* end of year */
    {
        tomorrow.day = 1;
        tomorrow.month = 1;
        tomorrow.year = today.year + 1;
    }
    else
    {                               /* end of month */
        tomorrow.day = 1;
        tomorrow.month = today.month + 1;
        tomorrow.year = today.year;
    }

    printf ("Tomorrow's date is %i/%i/%i.\n",tomorrow.month,
                tomorrow.day, tomorrow.year % 100);
}
/* Function to find the number of days in a month */

int  number_of_days  (struct date  d)
{
    int  answer, is_leap_year (struct date  d);
    int  days_per_month[12] =
```

```
        { 31, 28, 31, 30, 31, 30, 31, 31, 30, 31, 30, 31 };
    if ( is_leap_year (d) &&  d.month == 2 )
        answer = 29;
    else
        answer = days_per_month[d.month - 1];

    return (answer);
}

/* Function to determine if it's a leap year */

int  is_leap_year (struct date  d)
{
    int  leap_year_flag;

    if ( (d.year % 4 == 0  &&  d.year % 100 != 0)  ||
                d.year % 400 == 0 )
        leap_year_flag = 1;    /* It's a leap year */
    else
        leap_year_flag = 0;    /* Not a leap year  */

    return (leap_year_flag);
}
```

Program 9.3 OUTPUT

```
Enter today's date (mm dd yyyy): 2 28 1992
Tomorrow's date is 2/29/92.
```

Program 9.3 Output (Rerun)

```
Enter today's date (mm dd yyyy): 2 28 1993
Tomorrow's date is 3/1/93.
```

The first thing that will catch your eye in the preceding program is the fact that the definition of the date structure appears first and outside of any function. This is because structure definitions behave very much like variables—if a structure is defined within a particular function, then only that function knows of its existence. This is a *local* structure definition. If we define the structure outside of any function, then that definition is *global*. A global structure definition allows any variables that are subsequently defined in the program (either inside or outside of a function) to be declared to be of that structure type.

Inside the `main` routine, the prototype declaration

```
int  number_of_days (struct date d);
```

informs the C compiler that the `number_of_days` function returns an integer value and takes a single argument of type `struct date`.

Instead of comparing the value of `today.day` against the value `days_per_month[today.month - 1]`, as was done in the preceding example, the statement

```
if  ( today.day != number_of_days (today) )
```

is used. As you can see from the function call, we are specifying that the structure `today` is to be passed as an argument. Inside the `number_of_days` function, the appropriate declaration must be made to inform the system that a structure is expected as an argument:

```
int  number_of_days  (struct date  d)
```

QUICK TIP

As with ordinary variables, and unlike arrays, any changes made by the function to the values contained in a structure argument have no effect on the original structure. They affect only the copy of the structure that is created when the function is called.

The `number_of_days` function begins by determining if it is a leap year and if the month is February. The former determination is made by calling another function called `is_leap_year`. We will discuss this function shortly. From reading the `if` statement

```
if ( is_leap_year  && d.month == 2 )
```

we can assume that the `is_leap_year` function will return nonzero (TRUE) if it is a leap year and will return 0 (FALSE) if it is not a leap year. This is directly in line with our discussions of flags back in Chapter 6, "Making Decisions."

An interesting point to be made about the above `if` statement concerns the choice of the function name `is_leap_year`. This name makes the `if` statement extremely readable and implies that the function is returning some kind of yes/no answer.

Getting back to our program, if the determination is made that we are in February of a leap year, then the value of the variable `answer` is set to 29; otherwise, the value of `answer` is found by indexing the `days_per_month` array with the appropriate month. The value of answer is then returned to the main routine, where execution is continued as in Program 9.2.

The is_leap_year function is straightforward enough—it simply tests the year contained in the date structure given as its argument and returns 1 if it is a leap year and 0 if it is not.

As an exercise in producing a better structured program, let's take the entire process of determining tomorrow's date and relegate it to a separate function. We can call the new function date_update and have it take as its argument today's date. The function will then calculate tomorrow's date and *return* the new date back to us. Can this be done in C? But of course.

Program 9.4

```
/* Program to determine tomorrow's date */
#include <stdio.h>
struct  date
{
    int  month;
    int  day;
    int  year;
};

/* Function to calculate tomorrow's date */

struct date  date_update (struct date  today)
{
    struct date  tomorrow;
    int  number_of_days (struct date  d);

    if ( today.day != number_of_days (today) )
    {
        tomorrow.day = today.day + 1;
        tomorrow.month = today.month;
        tomorrow.year = today.year;
    }
    else if ( today.month == 12 )      /* end of year */
    {
        tomorrow.day = 1;
        tomorrow.month = 1;
        tomorrow.year = today.year + 1;
    }
    else
    {                                  /* end of month */
        tomorrow.day = 1;
        tomorrow.month = today.month + 1;
```

continues

Program 9.4 Continued

```c
        tomorrow.year = today.year;
    }

    return (tomorrow);
}
/* Function to find the number of days in a month */

int  number_of_days  (struct date  d)
{
    int  answer, is_leap_year (struct date  d);
    int  days_per_month[12] =
      { 31, 28, 31, 30, 31, 30, 31, 31, 30, 31, 30, 31 };

    if ( is_leap_year   &&  d.month == 2 )
        answer = 29;
    else
        answer = days_per_month[d.month - 1];

    return (answer);
}


/* Function to determine if it's a leap year */

int  is_leap_year (struct date  d)
{
    int  leap_year_flag;

    if ( (d.year % 4 == 0  &&  d.year % 100 != 0)  ||
                d.year % 400 == 0 )
        leap_year_flag = 1;    /* It's a leap year */
    else
        leap_year_flag = 0;    /* Not a leap year  */

    return (leap_year_flag);
}

main ()
{
    struct date  date_update (struct date  today);
    struct date  this_day, next_day;

    printf ("Enter today's date (mm dd yyyy): ");
    scanf ("%i%i%i", &this_day.month, &this_day.day,
            &this_day.year);

    next_day = date_update (this_day);

    printf ("Tomorrow's date is %i/%i/%i.\n",next_day.month,
            next_day.day, next_day.year % 100);
}
```

Program 9.4 OUTPUT

```
Enter today's date (mm dd yyyy): 2 28 1992
Tomorrow's date is 2/29/92.
```

Program 9.4 OUTPUT (Rerun)

```
Enter today's date (mm dd yyyy): 10 2 1993
Tomorrow's date is 10/3/93.
```

Inside main, the statement

```
next_date = date_update (this_day);
```

illustrates the ability to pass a structure to a function and to return one as well. The date_update function has the appropriate declaration to indicate that the function returns a value of type struct date. Inside the function is the same code that was included in the main routine of Program 9.3. The functions number_of_days and is_leap_year remain unchanged from that program.

Make sure that you understand the hierarchy of function calls in the above program: The main function calls date_update, which in turn calls number_of_days, which itself calls the function is_leap_year.

A Structure for Storing the Time

Suppose we had the need to store values inside a program that represented various times expressed as hours, minutes, and seconds. Since we have seen how useful our date structure has been in helping us to logically group the day, month, and year, it seems only natural to use a structure that we could call appropriately enough, time, to group the hours, minutes, and seconds. The structure definition would be straightforward enough, as shown:

```
struct time
{
    int    hour;
    int    minutes;
    int    seconds;
};
```

Most computer installations choose to express the time in terms of a 24-hour clock, known as military time. This representation avoids the hassle of having to qualify a time with a.m. or p.m. The hour begins with 0 at 12 midnight and increases by 1 until it reaches 23, which represents 11:00 p.m. So, for example,

4:30 means 4:30 a.m., while 16:30 represents 4:30 p.m.; and 12:00 represents noon, while 00:01 represents 1 minute after midnight.

Most computer systems have a clock contained within the system that is always running. This clock is used for such diversified purposes as informing the user as to the current time, causing certain events to occur or programs to be executed at specific times, or for recording the time that a particular event occurs. There are one or more computer programs that are usually associated with the clock. One of these programs might be executed every second, for example, to update the current time that is stored somewhere in the computer's memory.

Suppose we wished to mimic the function of the program described above—namely develop a program that updates the time by one second. If you think about this for a second (pun intentional), you will realize that this problem is quite analagous to the problem of updating the date by one day.

Just as finding the next day had some special requirements, so does the process of updating the time. In particular, these special cases must be handled:

1. If the number of seconds reaches 60, the seconds must be reset to 0 and the minutes increased by 1.

2. If the number of minutes reaches 60, the minutes must be reset to 0 and the hour increased by 1.

3. If the number of hours reaches 24, the hours, minutes, and seconds must be reset to 0.

The following program uses a function called time_update, which takes as its argument the current time and returns a time that is one second later.

Program 9.5

```
/* Program to update the time by one second */
#include <stdio.h>
struct   time
{
    int   hour;
    int   minutes;
    int   seconds;
};

main ()
{
    struct time   time_update (struct time   now);
    struct time   current_time, next_time;
```

```
    printf ("Enter the time (hh:mm:ss): ");
    scanf ("%i:%i:%i", &current_time.hour,
            &current_time.minutes, &current_time.seconds);

    next_time = time_update (current_time);

    printf ("Updated time is %.2i:%.2i:%.2i\n", next_time.hour,
            next_time.minutes, next_time.seconds );
}
/* Function to update the time by one second */

struct time  time_update (struct time  now)
{
    ++now.seconds;

    if ( now.seconds == 60 )
    {                                      /* next minute */
        now.seconds = 0;
        ++now.minutes;

        if ( now.minutes == 60 )
        {                                  /* next hour */
            now.minutes = 0;
            ++now.hour;

            if ( now.hour == 24 )
                now.hour = 0;   /* midnight */
        }
    }

    return (now);
}
```

Program 9.5 OUTPUT

```
Enter the time (hh:mm:ss): 12:23:55
Updated time is 12:23:56
```

Program 9.5 OUTPUT (Rerun)

```
Enter the time (hh:mm:ss): 16:12:59
Updated time is 16:13:00
```

Program 9.5 OUTPUT (Rerun)

```
Enter the time (hh:mm:ss): 23:59:59
Updated time is 00:00:00
```

The `main` routine asks the user to enter in the time. The `scanf` call uses the format string

`"%i:%i:%i"`

to read the data. Specifying a nonformat character, such as `':'`, in a format string signals to the `scanf` function that the particular character is expected as input. Therefore, the format string listed in Program 9.5 specifies that three integer values are to be input, the first separated from the second by a colon, and the second from the third by a colon. We will see in a later chapter how the `scanf` function returns a value that may be tested to determine if the values were entered in the correct format.

After the time has been entered, the program calls the `time_update` function, passing along the `current_time` as the argument. The result returned by the function is assigned to the `struct time` variable `next_time`, which is then displayed with an appropriate `printf` call. You will recall that the format characters `%.2i` are used to specify that two integer digits are to be displayed with zero fill. This ensures that we get the proper display for times such as `00:00:00`.

The `time_update` function begins execution by "bumping" the time in `now` by one second. A test is then made to determine if the number of seconds has reached 60. If it has, then the seconds are reset to 0 and the minutes are bumped by 1. Another test is then made to see if the number of minutes has now reached 60, and if it has, the minutes are reset to 0 and the hour is increased by 1. Finally, if the two preceding conditions are satisfied, a test is then made to see if the hour is equal to 24; that is, if it is precisely midnight. If it is, then the hour is reset to 0. The function then returns the value of `now`, which contains the updated time, back to the calling routine.

Initializing Structures

Initializing structures is similar to initializing arrays—the elements are simply listed inside a pair of braces, with each element separated by a comma.

To initialize the `date` structure variable `today` to July 2, 1988, the statement

`struct date  today = { 7, 2, 1988 };`

can be used. The statement

```
struct time  this_time = { 3, 29, 55 };
```

defines the struct time variable this_time and sets its value to 3:29:55 a.m. As with other variables, if this_time is a local structure variable, it will be initialized each time the function is entered. If the structure variable is made static (by placing the keyword static in front of it), it will only be initialized once at the start of program execution. In either case, the initial values listed inside the curly braces must be constant expressions.

As with the initialization of an array, fewer values may be listed than are contained in the structure. So the statement

```
struct time  time1 = { 12, 10 };
```

sets time1.hour to 12 and time1.minutes to 10 but gives no initial value to time1.seconds. In such a case, its default initial value is undefined.

Arrays of Structures

We have seen how useful the structure is in enabling us to logically group related elements together. With the time structure, for instance, it is only necessary to keep track of one variable, instead of three, for each time that it is used by the program. So to handle ten different times in a program, we would only have to keep track of ten different variables, instead of 30.

An even better method for handling the ten different times involves the combination of two powerful features of the C programming language: structures and arrays. C does not limit the programmer to the storing of simple data types inside an array; it is perfectly valid to define an *array of structures*. For example,

```
struct time  experiments[10];
```

defines an array called experiments, which consists of ten elements. Each element inside the array is defined to be of type struct time. Similarly, the definition

```
struct date  birthdays[15];
```

defines the array birthdays to contain 15 elements of type struct date. Referencing a particular structure element inside the array is quite natural. To set the second birthday inside the birthdays array to February 4, 1955, the sequence of statements

```
birthdays[1].month = 2;
birthdays[1].day   = 4;
birthdays[1].year  = 1955;
```

will work just fine. To pass the entire `time` structure contained in `experiments[4]` to a function called `check_time`, the array element is specified:

```
check_time (experiments[4]);
```

As is to be expected, the `check_time` function declaration must specify that an argument of type `struct time` is expected:

```
void check_time (struct time  t0)
{
      .
      .
      .
}
```

Initialization of arrays containing structures is similar to initialization of multidimensional arrays. So the statement

```
struct time  run_time [5] =
    {  {12, 0, 0},  {12, 30, 0},  {13, 15, 0} };
```

sets the first three times in the array `run_time` to 12:00:00, 12:30:00, and 13:15:00. The inner pairs of braces are optional, meaning that the above statement could be equivalently expressed as

```
struct time  run_time[5] =
    { 12, 0, 0,  12, 30, 0, 13, 15, 0 };
```

Program 9.6 sets up an array of time structures called `test_times`. The program then calls our `time_update` function from Program 9.5. To conserve space, the `time_update` function was not included in the program listing . However, a comment statement was inserted to indicate where in the program the function could be included.

In the program, an array called `test_times` is defined to contain five different times. The elements in this array are assigned initial values that represent the times 11:59:59, 12:00:00, 1:29:59, 23:59:59, and 19:12:27, respectively. Figure 9.2 can help you to understand what the `test_times` array actually looks like inside the computer's memory. A particular `time` structure stored in the `test_times` array is accessed by using the appropriate index number 0-4. A particular member (`hour`, `minutes`, or `seconds`) is then accessed by appending a period followed by the member name.

For each element in the `test_times` array, Program 9.6 displays the time as represented by that element, calls the `time_update` function, and then displays the updated time.

Program 9.6

```c
/* Program to illustrate arrays of structures */
#include <stdio.h>
struct  time
{
    int  hour;
    int  minutes;
    int  seconds;
};

main ()
{
    struct time  time_update (struct time  now);
    struct time  test_times[5] =
        {  { 11, 59, 59 }, { 12, 0, 0 }, { 1, 29, 59 },
           { 23, 59, 59 }, { 19, 12, 27 }};
    int  i;

    for ( i = 0;  i < 5;  ++i )
    {
        printf ("Time is %.2i:%.2i:%.2i", test_times[i].hour,
            test_times[i].minutes, test_times[i].seconds);

        test_times[i] = time_update (test_times[i]);

        printf (" ...one second later it's %.2i:%.2i:%.2i\n",
            test_times[i].hour, test_times[i].minutes,
            test_times[i].seconds);
    }
}

/*** Include the time_update function here ***/
```

Program 9.6 OUTPUT

```
Time is 11:59:59 ...one second later it's 12:00:00
Time is 12:00:00 ...one second later it's 12:00:01
Time is 01:29:59 ...one second later it's 01:30:00
Time is 23:59:59 ...one second later it's 00:00:00
Time is 19:12:27 ...one second later it's 19:12:28
```

The concept of an array of structures is a very powerful and important one in C. Make sure you understand it fully before you go on.

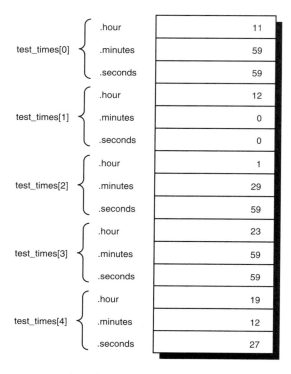

Figure 9.2. *The array* `test_times` *in memory.*

Structures Within Structures

C provides you with an enormous amount of flexibility in defining structures. For instance, you can define a structure that itself contains other structures as one or more of its members, or define structures that contain arrays.

We have seen how it is possible to logically group the month, day, and year into a structure called `date` and how to group the hour, minutes, and seconds into a structure called `time`. It is quite possible that in some applications the need might arise to logically group both a date and a time together. For example, we might need to set up a list of events that are to occur at a particular date and time.

What the above discussion implies is that we would like to have a convenient means for associating *both* the date and the time together. We can do this in C by defining a new structure, called, perhaps, `date_and_time`, which contains as its members two elements: the date and the time.

```
struct date_and_time
{
    struct date    sdate;
    struct time    stime;
};
```

The first member of this structure is of type `struct date` and is called `sdate`. The second member of the `date_and_time` structure is of type `struct time` and is called `stime`. This definition of a `date_and_time` structure requires that a `date` structure and a `time` structure have been previously defined to the compiler.

Variables can now be defined to be of type `struct date_and_time`, as in

```
struct date_and_time   event;
```

To reference the `date` structure of the variable `event`, the syntax is the same:

```
event.sdate
```

So we could call our `date_update` function with this date as the argument and assign the result back to the same place by a statement such as

```
event.sdate = date_update (event.sdate);
```

We can do the same type of thing with the `time` structure contained within our `date_and_time` structure:

```
event.stime = time_update (event.stime);
```

To reference a particular member *inside* one of these structures, a period followed by the member name is tacked onto the end:

```
event.sdate.month = 10;
```

This statement sets the `month` of the `date` structure contained within `event` to October, and the statement

```
++event.stime.seconds;
```

adds one to the `seconds` contained within the `time` structure.

The event variable can be initialized in the expected manner:

```
struct date_and_time   event =
        { { 2, 1, 1993 }, { 3, 30, 0 } };
```

This sets the date in the variable `event` to February 1, 1993 and sets the time to 3:30:00.

Naturally, it is possible to set up an array of `date_and_time` structures, as is done with the following declaration:

```
struct date_and_time   events[100];
```

The array `events` is declared to contain 100 elements of type `struct date_and_time`. The fourth `date_and_time` contained within the array is referenced in the usual way as `events[3]`, and the 25th date in the array can be sent to our `date_update` function as follows:

```
events[24].sdate = date_update (events[24].sdate);
```

To set the first time in the array to noon, the series of statements

```
events[0].stime.hour    = 12;
events[0].stime.minutes = 0;
events[0].stime.seconds = 0;
```

can be used.

Structures Containing Arrays

As the heading of this section implies, it is possible to define structures that contain arrays as members. One of the most common applications of this type is in setting up an array of characters inside a structure. For example, suppose we wanted to define a structure called `month` that contained as its members the number of days in the month as well as a three-character abbreviation for the name of the month. The following definition would do the job:

```
struct  month
{
    int     number_of_days;
    char    name[3];
};
```

This sets up a `month` structure that contains an integer member called `number_of_days` and a character member called `name`. The member `name` is actually an array of three characters. We can now define a variable to be of type `struct month` in the normal fashion:

```
struct month  a_month;
```

We can set the proper fields inside a_month for January with the following sequence of statements:

```
a_month.number_of_days = 31;
a_month.name[0] = 'J';
a_month.name[1] = 'a';
a_month.name[2] = 'n';
```

Or we can initialize this variable to the same values with the following statement:

```
struct month  a_month = { 31, { 'J', 'a', 'n' } };
```

And to go one step further, we can set up 12 month structures inside an array to represent each month of the year:

```
struct month  months[12];
```

Program 9.7 illustrates the months array. Its purpose is simply to set up the initial values inside the array and then display these values at the terminal.

It might be easier for you to conceptualize the notation that is used to reference particular elements of the months array as defined in the program by examining Figure 9.3.

Program 9.7

```
/* Program to illustrate structures and arrays */
#include <stdio.h>
main ()
{
    int  i;

    struct  month
    {
        int     number_of_days;
        char    name[3];
    };

    struct month  months[12] =
        { { 31, {'J', 'a', 'n'} },  { 28, {'F', 'e', 'b'} },
          { 31, {'M', 'a', 'r'} },  { 30, {'A', 'p', 'r'} },
          { 31, {'M', 'a', 'y'} },  { 30, {'J', 'u', 'n'} },
          { 31, {'J', 'u', 'l'} },  { 31, {'A', 'u', 'g'} },
          { 30, {'S', 'e', 'p'} },  { 31, {'O', 'c', 't'} },
          { 30, {'N', 'o', 'v'} },  { 31, {'D', 'e', 'c'} } };

    printf ("Month    Number of Days\n");
    printf ("----     --------------\n");

    for ( i = 0;  i < 12;  ++i )
        printf (" %c%c%c            %i\n",
            months[i].name[0], months[i].name[1],
            months[i].name[2], months[i].number_of_days);
}
```

Program 9.7 OUTPUT

```
Month    Number of Days
----     --------------
 Jan          31
 Feb          28
 Mar          31
 Apr          30
 May          31
 Jun          30
 Jul          31
 Aug          31
 Sep          30
 Oct          31
 Nov          30
 Dec          31
```

As you can see in Figure 9.3, the notation

```
months[0]
```

refers to the *entire* month structure contained in the first location of the months array. The type of this expression is struct month. Therefore, when passing months[0] to a function as an argument, the corresponding formal parameter inside the function must be declared to be of type struct month.

Going one step further, the expression

```
months[0].number_of_days
```

refers to the number_of_days member of the month structure contained in months[0]. The type of this expression is int. The expression

```
months[0].name
```

references the three-character array called name inside the month structure of months[0]. If passing this expression as an argument to a function, then the corresponding formal parameter would be declared to be an array of type char.

Finally, the expression

```
months[0].name[0]
```

references the first character of the name array contained in months[0] (the character 'J').

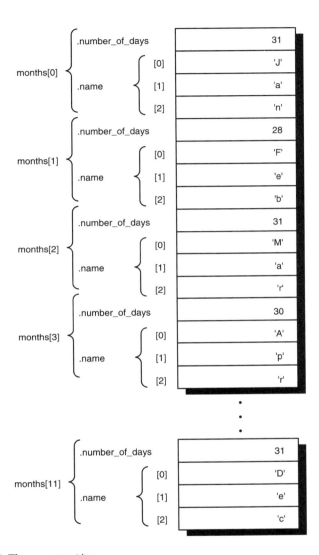

Figure 9.3. *The array* months.

Structure Variants

There is some flexibility in defining a structure that we should mention here. First, it is valid to declare a variable to be of a particular structure type at the same time that the structure is defined. This is done simply by including the variable name (or names) before the terminating semicolon of the structure definition. For example, the statement

```
struct  date
{
    int  month;
    int  day;
    int  year;
} todays_date, purchase_date;
```

defines the structure date *and* also declares the variables todays_date and purchase_date to be of this type. We can also assign initial values to the variables in the normal fashion. Thus,

```
struct  date
{
    int  month;
    int  day;
    int  year;
} todays_date = { 9, 25, 1988 };
```

defines the structure date and the variable todays_date with initial values as indicated.

If all of the variables of a particular structure type are defined when the structure is defined, the structure name can be omitted. So the statement

```
struct
{
    int  month;
    int  day;
    int  year;
}  dates[100];
```

defines an array called dates to consist of 100 elements. Each element is a structure containing three integer members: month, day, and year. Since we did not supply a name to the structure, the only way to subsequently declare variables of the same type would be by explicitly defining the structure again.

Exercises

1. If you have access to a computer facility that supports the C programming language, type in and run the seven programs presented in this chapter. Compare the output produced by each program with the output presented after each program.

2. In certain applications, particularly in the financial area, it is often necessary to calculate the number of elapsed days between two dates. For example, the number of days between July 2, 1983, and July 16, 1983, is obviously 14. But how many days are there between February 3, 1979, and June 21, 1980? This calculation requires a bit more thought.

Luckily, there is a formula that can be used to calculate the number of days between two dates. This is effected by computing the value of N for each of the two dates and then taking the difference, where N is calculated as follows:

```
N = 1461 x f(year, month) / 4 + 153 x g(month) / 5  + day
```

where:

```
f(year, month)    =    year - 1       if  month <= 2
                       year           otherwise



    g(month)  =        month + 13     if month <= 2
                       month + 1      otherwise
```

As an example of applying the formula, to calculate the number of days between February 3, 1979, and June 21, 1980, we can calculate the values of N_1 and N_2 by substituting the appropriate values into the above formula as shown:

```
N₁    = 1461 x f(1979, 2) / 4  +  153 x g(2) / 5  +  3
        = (1461 x 1978) / 4  +  (153 x 15) / 5  +  3
        = 2,889,858 / 4  +  2295 / 5  +  3
        = 722,464 + 459 + 3
        = 722,926


N₂    = 1461 x f(1980, 6) / 4  +  153 x g(6) / 5  +  21
        = (1461 x 1980) / 4  +  (153 x 7) / 5  +  21
        = 2,892,780 / 4  +  1071 / 5  +  21
        = 723,195 + 214 + 21
        = 723,430
```

Number of elapsed days $= N_2 - N_1$

$$= 723{,}430 - 722{,}926$$

$$= 504$$

So the number of days between the two dates is shown to be 504. The above formula is applicable for any dates after March 1, 1900 (1 must be added to N for dates from March 1, 1800, to February 28, 1900, and 2 must be added for dates between March 1, 1700, and February 28, 1800).

3. Write a program that permits the user to type in two dates and then calculates the number of elapsed days between the two dates. Try to structure the program logically into separate functions. For example, you should have a function that accepts as an argument a date structure and returns the value of *N* computed as above. This function can then be called twice, once for each date, and the difference taken to determine the number of elapsed days. One word of advice: Be careful about the calculation of *N*, as you will be dealing with very large numbers. Use long int variables and make sure that the necessary calculations are performed with long integer arithmetic.

4. Write a function elapsed_time that takes as its arguments two time structures and returns a time structure that represents the elapsed time (in hours, minutes, and seconds) between the two times. So the call

   ```
   elapsed_time (time1, time2)
   ```

   where time1 represents 3:45:15 and time2 represents 9:44:03, should return a time structure that represents 5 hours, 58 minutes, and 48 seconds. Be careful with times that cross midnight.

5. If we take the value of *N* as computed in Exercise 2, subtract 621,049 from it, and then take that result modulo 7, we get a number from 0 to 6 that represents the day of the week (Sunday through Saturday, respectively) that the particular day falls on. For example, the value of *N* computed for February 3, 1979, is 722,926 as derived above. 722,926 − 621,049 gives 101,877, and 101,877 % 7 gives 6, indicating that this date fell on a Saturday.

6. Use the functions developed in the previous exercise to develop a program that displays the day of the week that a particular date falls on. Make sure that the program displays the day of the week in English (such as "Monday").

7. Write a function called clock_keeper that takes as its argument a date_and_time structure as defined in this chapter. The function should call the time_update function, and if the time reaches midnight, the function should call the date_update function to switch over to the next day. Have the function return the updated date_and_time structure.

10

Character Strings

Now we are ready to take a look at character strings in more detail. You were first introduced to character strings in Chapter 3, "Writing a Program in ANSI C," when we wrote our first C program. In the statement

```
printf ("Programming in C is fun.\n");
```

the argument that is passed to the `printf` function is the character string

```
"Programming in C is fun.\n"
```

The double quote signs are used to delimit the character string, which can contain any combinations of letters, numbers, or special characters, other than a double quote sign. But as we shall see shortly, it is even possible to include a double quote sign inside a character string.

When we introduced the data type `char`, we mentioned that a variable that was declared to be of this type could contain only a *single* character. To assign a single character to such a variable, the character was enclosed within a pair of single quote marks. Thus the assignment

```
plus_sign = '+';
```

would have the effect of assigning the character '+' to the variable plus_sign, which we assume has been appropriately declared. We also pointed out that there *is* a distinction made between the single quote and double quote marks, and that if plus_sign were declared to be of type char, then the statement

```
plus_sign = "+";
```

would be incorrect. Make sure you remember that single quotes and double quotes are used to create two different types of constants in C.

We would like to be able to deal with variables that can hold more than a single character, and this is precisely where the array of characters comes into play.

In Program 7.6, we defined an array of characters called word as follows

```
static char  word [] = { 'H', 'e', 'l', 'l', 'o', '!' };
```

Remembering that in the absence of a particular array size, the C system automatically computes the number of elements in the array based upon the number of initializers, this statement would reserve space in memory for exactly six characters, as shown in Figure 10.1.

word[0]	'H'
word[1]	'e'
word[2]	'l'
word[3]	'l'
word[4]	'o'
word[5]	'!'

Figure 10.1. *The array* word *in memory.*

In order to print out the contents of the array word, we ran through each element in the array and displayed it using the %c format characters.

With this technique, we can begin to build an assortment of useful functions for dealing with character strings. Some of the more commonly performed operations on character strings include combining two character strings together (concatenation), copying one character string to another, extracting a portion of a character string (substring), and determining if two character strings are equal (that is, contain the same characters). Why don't we take the first mentioned operation, concatenation, and develop a function to perform this task. We can define a call to our concat function as follows:

```
concat (result, str1, n1, str2, n2);
```

where str1 and str2 represent the two character arrays that are to be concatenated and n1 and n2 represent the number of characters in the respective arrays. This makes the function flexible enough so that we can concatenate two
character arrays of arbitrary length. The argument result represents the character array that is to be the destination of the concatenated character arrays str1
followed by str2.

Program 10.1

```
/* Function to concatenate two character arrays */
#include <stdio.h>
void  concat (char  result[], char  str1[], int  n1,
                            char  str2[], int  n2)
{
    int  i, j;

    /* copy str1 to result */

    for ( i = 0;  i < n1;  ++i )
        result[i] = str1[i];

    /* copy str2 to result */

    for ( j = 0;  j < n2;  ++j )
        result[n1 + j] = str2[j];
}

main ()
{
    void    concat (char  result[], char  str1[], int  n1,
                                char  str2[], int  n2);
    char    s1[5] = { 'T', 'e', 's', 't', ' '};
    char    s2[6] = { 'w', 'o', 'r', 'k', 's', '.' };
    char    s3[11];
    int     i;

    concat (s3, s1, 5, s2, 6);

    for ( i = 0;  i < 11;  ++i )
        printf ("%c", s3[i]);

    printf ("\n");
}
```

Program 10.1 OUTPUT

```
Test works.
```

The first for loop inside the concat function copies the characters from the str1 array into the result array. This loop is executed n1 times, which is the number of characters contained inside the str1 array.

The second for loop copies str2 into the result array. Since str1 was n1 characters long, copying into result begins at result[n1]—the position immediately following the one occupied by the last character of str1. After this for loop is done, the result array will contain the n1+n2 characters of str2 concatenated to the end of str1.

Inside the main routine, two character arrays, s1 and s2, are defined. The first array is initialized to the characters 'T', 'e', 's', 't', and ' '. This last character represents a blank space and is a perfectly valid character constant. The second array is initially set to the characters 'w', 'o', 'r', 'k', 's', and '.'. A third character array, s3, is defined with enough space to hold s1 concatenated to s2—11 characters. It is not declared to be static because there are no initial values assigned to it. Of course, it would have made no difference if it had been declared static.

The function call

```
concat (s3, s1, 5, s2, 6);
```

calls the concat function to concatenate the character arrays s1 and s2, with the destination array s3. The arguments 5 and 6 are passed to the function to indicate the number of characters in s1 and s2, respectively.

After the concat function has completed execution and returns to the main routine, a for loop is set up to display the results of the function call. The 11 elements of s3 are displayed at the terminal, and as can be seen from the program's output, the concat function seems to be working properly. In the preceding program example we assume the user will ensure that the first argument to the concat function—the result array—contains enough space to hold the resulting concatenated character arrays. Failure to do so can produce unpredictable results when the program is run.

Variable Length Character Strings

We can adopt a similar approach to that used by the concat function for defining other functions to deal with character arrays. That is, we can develop a set of routines, each of which has as its arguments one or more character arrays plus the number of characters contained in each such array. Unfortunately, after working with these functions for a while, you will find that it gets a bit tedious trying to keep track of the number of characters contained in each character array that you are using in the program—especially if you are using your arrays to store character strings of varying sizes. What we need is a method for dealing with character arrays without having to worry about precisely how many characters we have stored in them.

There is such a method, and it is based upon the idea of placing a special character at the end of every character string. In this manner, the function can then determine for itself when it has reached the end of a character string once it encounters this special character. By developing all of our functions to deal with character strings in this fashion, we can thus eliminate the need to specify the number of characters that are contained inside a character string.

In the C language, the special character that is used to signal the end of a string is known as the *null* character and is written as '\0'. So the statement

```
char  word [] = { 'H', 'e', 'l', 'l', 'o', '!', '\0' };
```

defines a character array called word that contains *seven* characters, the last of which is the null character. (You will recall that the backslash character (\) is a special character in the C language and does not count as a separate character; therefore, '\0' represents a single character in C.) The array word is depicted in Figure 10.2.

word[0]	'H'
word[1]	'e'
word[2]	'l'
word[3]	'l'
word[4]	'o'
word[5]	'!'
word[6]	'\0'

Figure 10.2. The array word *with terminating null character.*

To begin with an illustration of how these *variable length* character strings are used, let us write a function that counts the number of characters in a character string. We will call our function `string_length` and have it take as its argument a character array that is terminated by the null character. The function will determine the number of characters in the array and will return this value back to the calling routine. We will define the number of characters in the array as the number of characters up to, but not including, the terminating null character. So the function call

```
string_length (character_string)
```

should return the value 3 if `character_string` was defined as follows:

```
char  character_string[] = { 'c', 'a', 't', '\0' };
```

Program 10.2

```
/* Function to count the number of characters in a string */
#include <stdio.h>
int  string_length (char  string[])
{
    int  count = 0;

    while ( string[count] != '\0' )
        ++count;

    return (count);
}

main ()
{
    int    string_length (char  string[]);
    char   word1[] = { 'a', 's', 't', 'e', 'r', '\0' };
    char   word2[] = { 'a', 't', '\0' };
    char   word3[] = { 'a', 'w', 'e', '\0' };

    printf ("%i   %i   %i\n", string_length (word1),
            string_length (word2), string_length (word3));
}
```

Program 10.2 OUTPUT

```
5    2    3
```

Inside the `string_length` function, the variable `count` is defined and its value set to 0. The program then enters a `while` loop to sequence through the `string` array until the null character is reached. When the function finally hits upon this character, signaling the end of the character string, the `while` loop is exited and the value of `count` returned. This value represents the number of characters in the string, excluding the null character. You might want to trace through the operation of this loop on a small character array to verify that the value of `count` when the loop is exited is in fact equal to the number of characters in the array, excluding the null character.

In the `main` routine, three character arrays, `word1`, `word2`, and `word3`, are defined. The `printf` function call displays the results of calling the `string_length` function for each of these three character arrays.

Initializing and Displaying Character Strings

Now it is time to go back to the `concat` function developed in Program 10.1 and rewrite it to work with variable-length character strings. Obviously, the function must be changed somewhat since we no longer wish to pass as arguments the number of characters in the two arrays. The function will now take only three arguments: the two character arrays to be concatenated and the character array to place the result into.

Before presenting this program, now would be a good time to discuss two of the nice features that C provides for dealing with character strings.

The first feature involves the initialization of character arrays. C permits a character array to be initialized by simply specifying a constant character string rather than a list of individual characters. So, for example, the statement

```
char  word[] = { "Hello!" };
```

can be used to set up an array of characters called `word` with the initial characters `'H'`, `'e'`, `'l'`, `i\&'l'`, `'o'`, and `'\0'`, respectively. This statement is equivalent to the statement

```
char  word[] = { 'H', 'e', 'l', 'l', 'o', '!', '\0' };
```

If you're explicitly specifying the size of the array, make sure you leave enough space for the terminating null character. So in

```
char  word[7] = { "Hello!" };
```

the compiler has enough room in the array to place the terminating null. However, in

```
char  word[6] = { "Hello!" };
```

the compiler can't fit a terminating null at the end of the array, and so won't put one there.

In general, character-string constants in the C language are automatically terminated by the null character. This fact helps functions such as printf determine when the end of a character string has been reached. So in the call

```
printf ("Programming in C is fun.\n");
```

the null character is automatically placed after the newline character in the character string, thereby enabling the printf function to determine when it has reached the end of the format string.

The other feature to be mentioned here involves the display of character strings. The special format characters %s inside a printf format string can be used to display an array of characters that is terminated by the the null character. So if word is a null-terminated array of characters, the printf call

```
printf ("%s\n", word);
```

can be used to display the entire contents of the word array at the terminal. The printf function assumes when it encounters the %s format characters that the corresponding argument is a character string that is terminated by a null character.

The two features just described were incorporated into the main routine of the following program, which illustrates our revised concat function. Since we are no longer passing the number of characters in each string as arguments to the function, the function must determine when the end of each string is reached by testing for the null character. Also, when str1 is copied into the result array, we want to be sure *not* to also copy the null character, since this would end the string in the result array right there. We do need, however, to place a null character into the result array *after* str2 has been copied so as to signal the end of the newly created string.

Program 10.3

```
#include <stdio.h>
main ()
{
    void  concat (char  result[], char  str1[], char  str2[]);
    char  s1[] = { "Test " };
    char  s2[] = { "works." };
    char  s3[20];

    concat (s3, s1, s2);

    printf ("%s\n", s3);
}
```

```
/* Function to concatenate two character strings */

void concat (char  result[], char  str1[], char  str2[])
{
    int  i, j;

    /* copy str1 to result */

    for ( i = 0;  str1[i] != '\0';  ++i )
        result[i] = str1[i];

    /* copy str2 to result */

    for ( j = 0;  str2[j] != '\0';  ++j )
        result[i + j] = str2[j];

    /* Terminate the concatenated string with a null */

    result [i + j] = '\0';
}
```

Program 10.3 OUTPUT

```
Test works.
```

In the first for loop of the concat function, the characters contained inside str1 are copied into the result array until the null character is reached. Since the for loop will terminate as soon as the null character is matched, it will not get copied into the result array.

In the second loop, the characters from str2 are copied into the result array directly after the last character from str1. This loop makes use of the fact that when the previous for loop finished execution, the value of i was equal to the number of characters in str1, excluding the null character. Therefore, the assignment statement

```
result[i + j] = str2[j];
```

is used to copy the characters from str2 into the proper locations of result.

After the second loop is completed, the concat function puts a null character at the end of the string. Study the function to make sure that you understand the use of i and j. Many program errors when dealing with character strings involve the use of an index number that is off by 1 in either direction.

QUICK TIP

Remember, to reference the first character of an array, an index number of 0 is used. And if a character array `string` contains n characters, excluding the null byte, then `string[n - 1]` references the last (nonnull) character in the string while `string[n]` references the null. Furthermore, `string` must be defined to contain at least n + 1 characters, bearing in mind that the null character occupies a location in the array.

Returning to our program, the `main` routine defines two `char` arrays, `s1` and `s2`, and sets their values using the new initialization technique previously described. The array `s3` is defined to contain 20 characters, thus ensuring that sufficient space is reserved for the concatenated character string and also saving us from the trouble of having to precisely calculate its size.

The `concat` function is then called with the three strings `s1`, `s2`, and `s3` passed as arguments. The final result, as contained in `s3` after the `concat` function returns, is displayed using the `%s` format characters. Although `s3` is defined to contain 20 characters, the `printf` function only displays characters from the array up to the null character.

Testing Two Character Strings for Equality

We cannot directly test two strings to see if they are equal with a statement in C such as

```
if ( string1 == string2 )
    . . .
```

since the equality operator can only be applied to simple variable types such as `floats`, `ints`, or `chars` and not to more sophisticated types such as structures or arrays.

In order to determine if two strings are equal, we therefore must explicitly compare the two character strings character by character. If we reach the end of both character strings at the same time, and if all of the characters up to that point are identical, then the two strings are equal; otherwise, they are not.

It might be a good idea to develop a function that could be used to compare two character strings for us. We can call the function `equal_strings` and have it take as arguments the two character strings to be compared. Since we are only interested in determining if the two character strings are equal or not, we can have the function return 1 (TRUE) if the two strings are identical, and 0 (FALSE) if they are not. In this way, the function can be used directly inside test statements, such as in

```
if  ( equal_strings (string1, string2) )
    ...
```

Program 10.4

```
/* Function to determine if two strings are equal */
#include <stdio.h>
int  equal_strings (char  s1[], char  s2[])
{
    int  i = 0, answer;

    while ( s1[i] == s2 [i]  &&
               s1[i] != '\0' &&  s2[i] != '\0' )
        ++i;

    if ( s1[i] == '\0'  &&  s2[i] == '\0' )
        answer = 1;       /* strings equal */
    else
        answer = 0;       /* not equal     */

    return (answer);
}


main ()
{
    int   equal_strings (char  s1[], char  s2[]);
    char  stra[] = "string compare test";
    char  strb[] = "string";

    printf ("%i\n", equal_strings (stra, strb));
    printf ("%i\n", equal_strings (stra, stra));
    printf ("%i\n", equal_strings (strb, "string"));
}
```

Program 10.4 OUTPUT

```
0
1
1
```

The equal_strings function uses a while loop to sequence through the character strings s1 and s2. The loop will be executed so long as the two character strings are equal (s1[i] == s2[i]) and so long as the end of either string is not reached (s1[i] != '\0' && s2[i] != '\0'). The variable i, which is used as the index number for both arrays, is incremented each time through the while loop.

The `if` statement that is executed after the `while` loop has terminated determines if we have simultaneously reached the end of both strings s1 and s2. Why could we have used the statement

```
if ( s1[i] == s2[i] )
        ...
```

instead to achieve the same results? If we *are* at the end of both strings, then the strings must be identical, in which case answer is set to 1 and returned to the calling routine. Otherwise, the strings are not identical and answer is set to 0 and returned.

In `main`, two character arrays `stra` and `strb` are set up and assigned the indicated initial values. The first call to the `equal_strings` function passes these two character arrays as arguments. Since these two strings are not equal, the function correctly returns the value 0.

The second call to the `equal_strings` function passes the string `stra` twice. The function correctly returns the value 1 to indicate that the two strings are equal, as verified by the program's output.

The third call to the `equal_strings` function is a bit more interesting. As you can see from this example, we can pass a constant character string to a function that is expecting an array of characters as an argument. In the next chapter, which deals with pointers, you will see how this works. The `equal_strings` function compares the character string contained in `strb` to the character string `"string"` and returns 1 to indicate that the two strings are equal.

Inputting Character Strings

By now you are used to the idea of displaying a character string using the `%s` format characters. But what about reading in a character string from the terminal? Well, on your particular system, there are probably several library functions that you can use to input character strings. The `scanf` function can be used with the `%s` format characters to read in a string of characters up to a blank space, tab character, or the end of the line, whichever occurs first. So the statements

```
char  string[81];
```

```
scanf ("%s", string);
```

will have the effect of reading in a character string from the terminal and storing it inside the character array `string`. Note that unlike previous `scanf` calls, in the case of reading strings, the `&` is *not* placed before the array name (the reason for this will also be explained in the next chapter).

If the preceding `scanf` call were executed, and the following characters typed in at the terminal:

```
Shawshank
```

then the string `"Shawshank"` would be read in by the `scanf` function and stored inside the `string` array. If the following line of text were typed instead:

scanf test

then just the string `"scanf"` would be stored inside the `string` array, since the blank space after the word `scanf` would terminate the string. If the `scanf` call were executed again, this time the string `"test"` would be stored inside the `string` array, as the `scanf` function always continues scanning from the last character that was read in.

The `scanf` function automatically terminates the string that is read in with a null character. So execution of the preceding `scanf` call with the line of text

abcdefghijklmnopqrstuvwxyz

would cause the entire lowercase alphabet to be stored in the first 26 locations of the `string` array, with `string[26]` automatically set to the null character.

If `s1`, `s2`, and `s3` were defined to be character arrays of appropriate sizes, the execution of the statement

scanf ("%s%s%s", s1, s2, s3);

with the line of text

micro computer system

would result in the assignment of the string `"micro"` to `s1`, `"computer"` to `s2`, and `"system"` to `s3`. If the following line of text were typed instead:

system expansion

it would result in the assignment of the string `"system"` to `s1`, and `"expansion"` to `s2`. Since no further characters appear on the line, the `scanf` function would then wait for more input to be entered from the terminal.

Program 10.5

```
/* Program to illustrate the %s scanf format characters */
#include <stdio.h>
main ()
{
    char  s1[81], s2[81], s3[81];

    printf ("Enter text:\n");
    scanf ("%s%s%s", s1, s2, s3);
    printf ("\ns1 = %s\ns2 = %s\ns3 = %s\n", s1, s2, s3);

}
```

Program 10.5 OUTPUT

```
Enter text:
system expansion
bus

s1 = system
s2 = expansion
s3 = bus
```

The scanf function was called to read in three character strings: s1, s2, and s3. Since the first line of text contained only two character strings—whereas the definition of a character string to scanf is a sequence of characters up to a space, tab, or the end of the line—the program waited for more text to be entered. After this was done, the printf call was used to verify that the strings "system", "expansion", and "bus" were correctly stored inside the string arrays s1, s2, and s3, respectively.

If the user types in more than 80 consecutive characters to the above program without pressing the spacebar, the tab key, or the RETURN key, scanf will overflow one of the character arrays. This might cause the program to terminate abnormally or unpredictable things to happen. Unfortunately, scanf has no way of knowing how large your character arrays are. When handed a %s format, it will simply continue to read and store characters until one of the noted terminator characters is reached.

If you place a number after the % in the scanf format string, this will tell scanf the maximum number of characters to read. So, if you used the following scanf call:

```
scanf ("%80s%80s%80s", s1, s2, s3);
```

instead of the one shown in Program 10.5, scanf would know that no more than 80 characters are to be read and stored into either s1, s2, or s3. (We still have to leave room for the terminating null character that scanf stores at the end of the array. That's why %80s is used instead of %81s.)

QUICK TIP

Always remember to insert a null character at the end of your character strings. Also, always remember to leave room in your character arrays for them to be stored there.

Single-Character Input

The Standard C Library provides several functions for the express purposes of reading and writing single characters and entire character strings. A function called getchar can be used to read in a single character from the terminal. Repeated calls to the getchar function will return successive single characters from the input. When the end of the line has been reached, the function will return the newline character '\n'. So if the characters "abc" are typed at the terminal, followed immediately by the Return key, then the first call to the getchar function will return the character 'a', the second call the character 'b', the third call 'c', and the fourth call the newline character '\n'. A fifth call to this function will cause the program to wait for more input to be entered from the terminal.

You may be wondering why we need the getchar function when we already know how to read in a single character with the %c format characters of the scanf function. The fact of the matter is that using the scanf function for this purpose is a perfectly valid approach. However, the getchar function is a more direct approach, as its sole purpose is for reading in single characters and therefore does not require any arguments. The function returns a single character that may be assigned to a variable or used as desired by the program.

In many text-processing applications, we need to read in an entire line of text from the terminal. This line of text is frequently stored in a single place—generally called a "buffer"—where it will be processed further. Using the scanf call with the %s format characters will not work in this case because the string is terminated as soon as a space is encountered in the input.

Also available from the function library is a function called gets. The sole purpose of this function—you guessed it—is to read in a single line of text from the terminal. As an interesting program exercise, we will show how a function similar to the gets function—we will call it read_line here—can be developed using the getchar function. The function will take a single argument: a character array where the line of text is to be stored. Characters read from the terminal up to, but not including, the newline character will be stored into this array by the function.

In order to use the getchar function, you must include the line

```
#include <stdio.h>
```

at the beginning of your program. Hopefully, you have been doing this all along anyway. In Chapter 13, "The Preprocessor," we will describe what this line does in detail.

Program 10.6

```
#include <stdio.h>

main ()
{
    int    i;
    char   line[81];
    void   read_line (char   buffer[]);

    for ( i = 0; i < 3; ++i )
    {
        read_line (line);
        printf ("%s\n\n", line);
    }
}

/* Function to read a line of text from the terminal */

void   read_line (char   buffer[])
{
    char   character;
    int    i = 0;

    do
    {
        character = getchar ();
        buffer[i] = character;
        ++i;
    }
    while ( character != '\n' );

    buffer[i - 1] = '\0';
}
```

Program 10.6 OUTPUT

```
This is a sample line of text.
This is a sample line of text.

abcdefghijklmnopqrstuvwxyz
abcdefghijklmnopqrstuvwxyz

runtime library routines
runtime library routines
```

The do loop in the read_line function is used to build up the input line inside the character array buffer. Each character that is returned by the getchar function is stored into the next location of the array. When the newline character is reached—signaling the end of the line—the loop is exited. The null character is then stored inside the array to terminate the character string, replacing the newline character that was stored there the last time that the loop was executed. The index number i - 1 indexes the correct position in the array, since the index number was incremented one extra time inside the loop the last time it was executed.

The main routine defines a character array called line with enough space reserved to hold 81 characters. This will ensure that an entire line from most terminals (80 characters + the null character) can be stored inside the array. However, even on terminals that have 80 characters per line, we are still in danger of overflowing the array if we continue typing past the end of the line without pressing the Return key on the keyboard. It would be a good idea to extend the read_line function to accept as a second argument the size of the buffer. In this way, the function can ensure that the capacity of the buffer is not exceeded.

The program then enters a for loop, which simply calls the read_line function three times. Each time that this function is called, a new line of text is read from the terminal. This line is simply echoed back at the terminal in order to verify proper operation of the function. After the third line of text has been displayed, execution of Program 10.6 is then complete.

For our next program example, let us consider a practical text-processing application: counting the number of words in a portion of text. We will develop a function called count_words, which will take as its argument a character string and which will return the number of words contained in that string. For the sake of simplicity, we will assume here that a word will be defined as a sequence of one or more alphabetic characters. The function can scan the character string for the occurrence of the first alphabetic character and will consider all subsequent characters up to the first nonalphabetic character as part of the same word. Then the function can continue scanning the string for the next alphabetic character, which identifies the start of a new word.

Program 10.7

```
/* Function to determine if a character is alphabetic */
#include <stdio.h>
int   alphabetic (char  c)
{
    if ( (c >= 'a'  && c <= 'z') || (c >= 'A'  && c <= 'Z') )
        return (1);
```

continues

Program 10.7 Continued

```
        else
            return (0);
}

/* Function to count the number of words in a string */

int  count_words (char  string[])
{
    int  i, looking_for_word = 1, word_count = 0;
    int  alphabetic (char  c);

    for ( i = 0;  string[i] != '\0';  ++i )
        if ( alphabetic(string[i]) )
        {
            if ( looking_for_word )
            {
                ++word_count;
                looking_for_word = 0;
            }
        }
        else
            looking_for_word = 1;

    return (word_count);
}

main ()
{
    char  text1[] = "Well, here goes.";
    char  text2[] = "And here we go... again.";
    int   count_words (char  string[]);

    printf ("%s — words = %i\n", text1, count_words (text1));
    printf ("%s — words = %i\n", text2, count_words (text2));
}
```

Program 10.7 OUTPUT

```
Well, here goes. — words = 3
And here we go... again. — words = 5
```

The `alphabetic` function is straightforward enough—it simply tests the value of the character passed to it to determine if it is either a lowercase or uppercase letter. If it is either, the function returns 1, indicating that the character is alphabetic; otherwise, the function returns 0.

The count_words function is not as straightforward. The integer variable i is used as an index number to sequence through each character in the string. The integer variable looking_for_word is used as a flag to indicate whether we are currently in the process of looking for the start of a new word. At the beginning of the execution of the function, we obviously *are* looking for the start of a new word, so this flag is set to 1. The local variable word_count is used for the obvious purpose of counting the number of words in the character string.

For each character inside the character string, a call to the alphabetic function is made to determine if the character is alphabetic or not. If the character is alphabetic, then the looking_for_word flag is tested to determine if we are in the process of looking for a new word. If we are, then the value of word_count is incremented by 1, and the looking_for_word flag is set to FALSE, indicating that we are no longer looking for the start of a new word.

If the character is alphabetic and the looking_for_word flag is FALSE, this means that we are currently scanning *inside* a word. In such a case, the for loop is continued with the next character in the string.

If the character is not alphabetic—meaning either that we have reached the end of a word or that we have still not found the beginning of the next word—then the flag looking_for_word is set to TRUE (even though it may already be TRUE).

When all of the characters inside the character string have been examined, the function returns the value of word_count to indicate the number of words that were found in the character string.

It would be helpful to present a table of the values of the various variables in the count_words function to see how the algorithm works. Table 10.1 shows such a table, with the first call to the count_words function from the above program as an example. The first line of Table 10.1 shows the initial value of the variables word_count and looking_for_word before the for loop is entered. Subsequent lines depict the values of the indicated variables each time through the for loop. So the second line of the table shows that the value of word_count has been set to 1 and the looking_for_word flag set to FALSE (0) after the first time through the loop (after the 'W' has been processed). The last line of the table shows the final values of the variables when the end of the string is reached. You should spend some time studying this table, verifying the values of the indicated variables against the logic of the count_words function. Once this has been accomplished, you should then feel comfortable with the algorithm that is used by the function to count the number of words in a string.

Table 10.1. Execution of the `count_words` function.

i	string[i]	word_count	looking_for_word
		0	1
0	'W'	1	0
1	'e'	1	0
2	'l'	1	0
3	'l'	1	0
4	','	1	1
5	' '	1	1
6	'h'	2	0
7	'e'	2	0
8	'r'	2	0
9	'e'	2	0
10	' '	2	1
11	'g'	3	0
12	'o'	3	0
13	'e'	3	0
14	's'	3	0
15	'.'	3	1
16	'\0'	3	1

The Null String

Now let us see a slightly more practical example of the use of the `count_words` function. This time we will make use of our `read_line` function to allow the user to type in multiple lines of text at the terminal. The program will then count the total number of words in the text and display the result.

In order to make the program more flexible, we would rather not have to limit or specify the number of lines of text that are entered. Therefore, we must have a way for the user to "tell" the program when he or she is done entering text. One way to do this is to have the user simply press the Return key an extra time after the last line of text has been entered. When the `read_line` function is called to read-in such a line, the function will immediately encounter the newline character and, as a result, will store the null character as the first (and only) character in the buffer. Our program can check for this special case and can know that the last line of text has been entered once a line containing no characters has been read.

A character string that contains no characters other than the null character has a special name in the C language; it is called the *null string*. When you think about it, the use of the null string is still perfectly consistent with all of the functions that we have defined so far in this chapter. The string_length function will correctly return 0 as the size of the null string; our concat function will also properly concatenate "nothing" onto the end of another string; even our equal_strings function will work correctly if either string is null or if both strings are null (and in the latter case, the function will correctly call these strings equal).

Always remember that the null string does in fact have a character in it, albeit a null one.

Sometimes it becomes desirable to set the value of a character string to the null string. In C, the null string is denoted by an adjacent pair of double quotes. So the statement

```
char  buffer[100] = "";
```

defines a character array called buffer and sets its value to the null string. Note the fact that the character string "" is *not* the same as the character string " ", since the second string contains a single blank character. (If you are doubtful, send both strings to the equal_strings function and see what result comes back.)

The following program uses the read_line, alphabetic, and count_words functions from previous programs. They have not been shown in the program listing to conserve space.

Program 10.8

```
#include <stdio.h>

/*****  Insert alphabetic function here    *****/

/*****  Insert read_line function here     *****/

/*****  Insert count_words function here   *****/

main ()
{
    char   text[81];
    int    end_of_text = 0, total_words = 0;
    int    count_words (char   string[]);
    void   read_line (char   buffer[]);
```

continues

Program 10.8 Continued

```
    printf ("Type in your text.\n");
    printf ("When you are done, press `RETURN'.\n\n");

    while ( ! end_of_text )
    {
        read_line (text);

        if ( text[0] == '\0' )
            end_of_text = 1;
        else
            total_words += count_words (text);
    }

    printf ("\nThere are %i words in the above text.\n",
                total_words);
}
```

Program 10.8 OUTPUT

```
Type in your text.
When you are done, press 'RETURN'.

Wendy glanced up at the ceiling where the mound of lasagna loomed like
a mottled mountain range. Within seconds, she was crowned with ricotta
ringlets and a tomato sauce tiara. Bits of beef formed meaty moles on
her forehead. After the second thud, her culinary coronation was
complete.
Return
There are 48 words in the above text.
```

The line labeled *Return* indicates the pressing of the Return or Enter key at the terminal.

The end_of_text variable is used as a flag to indicate when the end of the input text has been reached. The while loop will be executed as long as this flag is FALSE. Inside this loop, the program calls the read_line function to read a line of text from the terminal. The if statement then tests the input line that is stored inside the text array to see if just the Return key was pressed. If so, then the buffer will contain the null string, in which case the end_of_text flag will be set TRUE to signal that all of the text has been entered.

If the buffer does contain some text, then the count_words function is called to count the number of words in the text array. The value that is returned by this function is added into the value of `total_words`, which contains the cumulative number of words from all lines of text entered thus far.

After the `while` loop is exited, the program displays the value of `total_words`, along with some informative text, at the terminal.

It might seem that the preceding program does not help to reduce our work efforts much because we still have to manually enter all of the text at the terminal. But as we will see in a later chapter, this same program can also be used to count the number of words contained in a file stored on a disk, for example. So an author using a computer system for the preparation of a manuscript might find this program extremely valuable as it could be used to quickly determine the number of words contained in the manuscript.

Escape Characters

We have alluded to the fact that the backslash character has a special significance that extends beyond its use in forming the newline and null characters. Just as the backslash and the letter n, when used in combination, cause subsequent printing to begin on a new line, so can other characters be combined with the backslash character to perform special functions. These various backslash characters, often referred to as *escape characters*, are summarized in Table 10.2.

Table 10.2. Escape Characters.

Escape Character	Name
\a	audible alert
\b	backspace
\f	form feed
\n	newline
\r	carriage return
\t	horizontal tab
\v	vertical tab
\\	backslash
\"	double quote
\'	single quote
\?	question mark
\nnn	octal character value *nnn*
\xnn	hexadecimal character value *nn*

The first seven characters listed in Table 10.2 will perform the indicated function on most video terminals when they are displayed. The *audible alert* character, \a will sound a bell on most terminals. So the `printf` call

```
printf ("\aSYSTEM SHUT DOWN IN 5 MINUTES!!\n");
```

will sound an alert at the terminal and display the indicated message.

Including the backspace character ' \b ' inside a character string will cause the terminal to backspace one character at the point where the character appears in the string, provided that the terminal has the appropriate capabilities for performing this function. Similarly, the function call

```
printf ("%i\t%i\t%i\n", a, b, c);
```

will display the value of a, space over to the next tab setting (typically set to every eight columns on many terminals), display the value of b, space over to the next tab setting, and then display the value of c. The horizontal tab character is particularly useful for lining up data in columns.

In order to include the backslash character itself inside a character string, two backslash characters are necessary, so the `printf` call

```
printf ("\\t is the horizontal tab character.\n");
```

will display the following at the terminal:

```
\t is the horizontal tab character.
```

(Note that since the \\ is encountered first in the string, a tab is not displayed in this case.)

In order to include a double quote character inside a character string, it must be preceded by a backslash. So the `printf` call

```
printf ("\"Hello\", he said.\n");
```

will result in the display of the message

```
"Hello", he said.
```

To assign a single quote character to a character variable, the backslash character must be placed before the quote. If c was declared to be a variable of type char, then the statement

```
c = '\'';
```

would assign a single quote character to c.

The backslash character, followed immediately by a ?, is used to represent a ? character. This is sometimes necessary when dealing with *trigraphs* in non-ASCII character sets. For more details, consult Appendix A, "ANSI C Language Summary."

The last two entries in the table of escape characters (Table 10.2) enable *any* character to be included in a character string. In the escape character '\nnn', *nnn* is a one- to three-digit *octal* number. In the escape character '\xnn', nn is a hexadecimal number. These numbers represent the internal *code* of the character. This enables characters that may not be directly available from the keyboard to be coded into a character string. For example, to include an ASCII escape code, which has the value octal 33, you could include the sequence \033 or \x1b inside your string.

The null character '\0' is a special case of the above. It represents the character that has a value of 0. In fact, since the value of the null character *is* 0, this knowledge is frequently used by programmers in tests and loops dealing with variable-length character strings. For example, the loop to count the length of a character string in the function string_length from Program 10.2 can also be equivalently coded as follows:

```
while ( string[count] )
    ++count;
```

The value of string[count] will be nonzero until the null character is reached, at which point the while loop will be exited.

It should once again be pointed out that these escape characters are only considered a single character inside a string. So the character string "\033\"Hello\"\n" actually consists of nine characters: the character '\033', the double quote character '\"', the five characters in the word Hello, the double quote character once again, and the newline character. Try passing the preceding character string to the string_length function to verify that nine is indeed the number of characters in the string.

More on Constant Strings

If you put a backslash character at the very end of the line and follow it immediately by a carriage return, it will tell the C compiler to ignore the end of the line. This line continuation technique is used primarily for continuing long constant character strings onto the next line and, as we will see in Chapter 13, "The Preprocessor," for continuing a *macro* definition onto the next line.

Without the line continuation character, your C compiler will generate an error message if you attempt to initialize a character string across multiple lines; for example:

```
    char  letters[] =
        { "abcdefghijklmnopqrstuvwxyz
ABCDEFGHIJKLMNOPQRSTUVWXYZ" };
```

By placing a backslash character at the end of each line to be continued, a character string constant can be written over mutiple lines:

```
char  letters[] =
      { "abcdefghijklmnopqrstuvwxyz\
ABCDEFGHIJKLMNOPQRSTUVWXYZ" };
```

It is necessary to begin the continuation of the character string constant at the *beginning* of the next line because, otherwise, the leading blank spaces on the line would get stored into the character string. The preceding statement would therefore have the net result of defining the character array `letters` and of initializing its elements to the character string

```
"abcdefghijklmnopqrstuvwxyzABCDEFGHIJKLMNOPQRSTUVWXYZ"
```

An even easier way of breaking up long character strings is to divide them into two or more adjacent strings. Adjacent strings are constant strings separated by zero or more spaces, tabs, or newlines. The compiler automatically concatenates adjacent strings together. Therefore, writing the strings

```
"one"  "two"  "three"
```

is syntactically equivalent to writing the single string

```
"onetwothree"
```

So, the `letters` array can be set to all the letters of the alphabet by writing

```
char  letters[] =
      { "abcdefghijklmnopqrstuvwxyz"
        "ABCDEFGHIJKLMNOPQRSTUVWXYZ" };
```

Finally, the three `printf` calls

```
printf ("Programming in C is fun\n");
printf ("Programming"  " in C is fun\n");
printf ("Programming"  " in C"  " is fun\n");
```

all pass a *single* argument to `printf`, since the compiler concatentates the strings together in the second and third calls.

Character Strings, Structures, and Arrays

There are many ways to combine the basic elements of the C programming language to form very powerful programming constructs. In the previous chapter, for example, we saw how we could easily define an array of structures. The next program example further illustrates the notion of arrays of structures, combined with the variable-length character string.

Suppose we wanted to write a computer program that acted as a dictionary. If we had such a program, we could then use it whenever we came across a word whose meaning was not clear. We could type the word into the program, and the program could then automatically "look up" the word inside the dictionary and tell us the definition of the word.

If we were to contemplate developing such a program, one of the first thoughts that would come to mind would be the representation of the word and its definition inside the computer. Obviously, since the word and its definition are logically related, the notion of a structure comes immediately to mind. We can define a structure called `entry`, for example, to hold the word and its definition:

```
struct   entry
{
    char   word[10];
    char   definition[50];
};
```

In the above structure definition, we have defined enough space for a nine-letter word (remember, we are dealing with variable-length character strings, so we need to leave room for the null character) plus a 49-character definition. The following would be an example of a variable defined to be of type `struct entry` that is initialized to contain the word "blob" and its definition.

```
struct entry   word1 =
                    { "blob", "an amorphous mass" };
```

Since we would like to provide for many words inside our dictionary, it seems logical to define an array of `entry` structures, such as in

```
struct entry   dictionary[100];
```

which would allow for a dictionary of 100 words. Obviously, this is far from sufficient if we are interested in setting up an English language dictionary, which would require at least 50,000 entries to be of any value. In that case, it would not be very practical to define such a dictionary with a statement such as

```
struct entry English_dictionary[50000];
```

as this would impose severe storage requirements on the computer. (Each character occupies one storage unit known as a *byte* inside most computer systems; 50,000 multiplied by 60 bytes—10 for the word plus 50 for the definition— equals 3,000,000 bytes, a very large amount of storage.) So the above approach would really not work if we were interested in such a large dictionary. We would need to adopt a more sophisticated approach, one that would involve storing the dictionary on the computer's disk, as opposed to storing it in memory.

Despite the preceding objections, we will proceed with this example, since it is quite illustrative and can still be used for smaller-sized dictionaries—a specialized technical dictionary, for example.

Having defined the structure of our dictionary, we should now think a bit about its organization. Most dictionaries are organized alphabetically. Does it make much sense to organize ours the same way? The answer to this question is "yes." For now, let us assume that the reason for this is that it makes the dictionary easier to read. Later we will see the real motivation for such an organization.

Now it is time to think about the development of the program. It would be convenient to define a function to look up a word inside the dictionary. If the word were found, then the function could return the entry number of the word inside the dictionary; otherwise, the function could return -1 to indicate that the word was not found in the dictionary. So a typical call to this function, which we can call lookup, might appear as follows:

```
entry_number = lookup (dictionary, word, entries);
```

In this case, the lookup function would search dictionary for the word as contained in the character string word. The third argument, entries, represents the number of entries in the dictionary. The function would search the dictionary for the specified word and would return the entry number in the dictionary if the word were found, or -1 if the word were not found.

In the program that follows, the lookup function will use the equal_strings function defined in Program 10.4 to determine when the specified word matches an entry in the dictionary.

Program 10.9

```
/* Dictionary lookup program */
#include <stdio.h>
struct  entry
{
    char    word[10];
    char    definition[50];
};

/***** Insert equal_strings function here *****/

/* function to lookup a word inside a dictionary */

int  lookup (struct entry  dictionary[], char  search[],
             int  entries)
{
```

```
    int  i, equal_strings (char s1[], char s2[]);

    for ( i = 0;  i < entries;  ++i )
        if ( equal_strings (search, dictionary[i].word) )
            return (i);

    return (-1);
}

main ()
{
    struct entry  dictionary[100] =
      { { "aardvark", "a burrowing African mammal"        },
        { "abyss",    "a bottomless pit"                  },
        { "acumen",   "mentally sharp; keen"              },
        { "addle",    "to become confused"                },
        { "aerie",    "a high nest"                       },
        { "affix",    "to append; attach"                 },
        { "agar",     "a jelly made from seaweed"         },
        { "ahoy",     "a nautical call of greeting"       },
        { "aigrette", "an ornamental cluster of feathers" },
        { "ajar",     "partially opened"                  } };

    char  word[10];
    int   entries = 10;
    int   entry_number;
    int   lookup (struct entry  dictionary[], char  search[],
                  int  entries);

    printf ("Enter word: ");
    scanf ("%9s", word);
    entry_number = lookup (dictionary, word, entries);

    if ( entry_number != -1 )
        printf ("%s\n", dictionary[entry_number].definition);
    else
        printf ("Sorry, that word is not in my dictionary.\n");
}
```

Program 10.9 OUTPUT

```
Enter word: agar
a jelly made from seaweed
```

Program 10.9 OUTPUT (Rerun)

```
Enter word: accede
Sorry, that word is not in my dictionary.
```

The `lookup` function sequences through each entry in the dictionary. For each such entry, the function calls the `equal_strings` function to determine if the character string `search` matches the `word` member of the particular dictionary entry. If it does match, then the function returns the value of the variable i, which is the entry number of the word that was found in the dictionary. The function is exited immediately upon execution of the `return` statement, despite the fact that the function is in the middle of executing a `for` loop.

If the `lookup` function exhausts all the entries in the dictionary without finding a match, the `return` statement after the `for` loop will be executed to return the "not found" indication (-1) back to the caller.

A Better Search Method

The method used by the `lookup` function to search for a particular word in the dictionary was straightforward enough; the function simply performed a sequential search through all the entries in the dictionary until either a match was made or the end of the dictionary was reached. For a small-sized dictionary like the one in our program, this approach is perfectly fine. However, if we start dealing with large dictionaries containing hundreds or perhaps even thousands of entries, this approach is no longer sufficient because of the time it takes to sequentially search through all of the entries. The time required can be considerable—considerable in this case could mean several seconds. One of the prime considerations that must be given to any sort of information retrieval program is that of speed. And since the searching process is one that is so frequently used in computer applications, much attention has been given by computer scientists to developing efficient algorithms for searching (almost as much attention as has been given to the process of sorting).

We can make use of the fact that our dictionary is in alphabetical order to develop a more efficient `lookup` function. The first obvious optimization that comes to mind is in the case that the word that we are looking for does not exist in the dictionary. We can make our `lookup` function "intelligent" enough to recognize when it has gone too far in its search. For example, if we were looking up the word "active" in the dictionary defined in Program 10.9, then as soon as we reached the word "acumen," we could conclude that "active" is not there because, if it were, it would have appeared in the dictionary *before* the word "acumen."

As was mentioned, the above optimization strategy does help to reduce our search time somewhat, but only when a particular word is *not* present in the dictionary. What we are really looking for is an algorithm that reduces the search time in most cases, not just in one particular case. Such an algorithm exists under the name of the *binary search*.

The strategy behind the binary search is relatively simple to understand. To illustrate how this algorithm works, let's take an analogous situation of a simple guessing game. Suppose I pick a number from 1 to 99 and then tell you to try to guess the number in the fewest number of guesses. For each guess that you make, I can tell you if you are too low, too high, or if your guess is correct. After a few tries at the game, you will probably realize that a good way to narrow in on the answer is by using a halving process. For example, if you take 50 as your first guess, then an answer of either "too high" or "too low" will narrow the possibilities down from 100 to 49. If the answer was "too high," then the number must be from 1 to 49, inclusive; if the answer was "too low," then the number must be from 51 to 99, inclusive.

We can now repeat the halving process with the remaining 49 numbers. So if the first answer was "too low," then the next guess should be halfway between 51 and 99, which is 75. This process can be continued until we finally narrow in on the answer. On the average, this procedure will take far less time to arrive at the answer than any other search method.

The preceding discussion describes precisely how the binary search algorithm works. The following provides a formal description of the algorithm. In this algorithm, we are looking for an element x inside an array M, which contains n elements. The algorithm assumes that the array M is sorted in ascending order.

Binary Search Algorithm

Step 1:	Set *low* to 0, *high* to $n - 1$.
Step 2:	If *low* > *high*, x does not exist in M and the algorithm terminates.
Step 3:	Set *mid* to (*low* + *high*) / 2.
Step 4:	If M[*mid*] < x, set *low* to *mid* + 1 and go to Step 2.
Step 5:	If M[*mid*] > x, set *high* to *mid* - 1 and go to Step 2.
Step 6:	M[*mid*] equals x and the algorithm terminates.

The division performed in Step 3 is an integer division, so if *low* were 0 and *high* were 49, the value of *mid* would be 24.

Now that we have the algorithm for performing a binary search, we can rewrite our `lookup` function to use this new search strategy. Since the binary search must be able to determine if one value is less than, greater than, or equal to another value, we might want to replace our `equal_strings` function with another function that makes this type of determination for two character strings. We'll call the function `compare_strings` and have it return the value -1 if the first string is lexicographically less than the second string, 0 if the two strings are equal, and 1 if the first string is lexicographically greater than the second string. So the function call

```
compare_strings ("alpha", "altered")
```

would return the value -1 since the first string is lexicographically less than the second string (think of this to mean that the first string would occur *before* the second string in a dictionary). And the function call

```
compare_strings ("zioty", "yucca");
```

would return the value 1 since "zioty" is lexicographically greater than "yucca."

In Program 10.10, the new `compare_strings` function is presented. The `lookup` function now uses the binary search method to scan through the dictionary. The `main` routine remains unchanged from the previous program.

The `compare_strings` function is identical to the `equal_strings` function up through the end of the `while` loop. When the `while` loop is exited, the function analyzes the two characters that resulted in the termination of the `while` loop. If `s1[i]` is less than `s2[i]`, `s1` must be lexicographically less than `s2`. In such a case, -1 is returned. If `s1[i]` is equal to `s2[i]`, the two strings are equal so 0 is returned. If neither is true, `s1` must be lexicographically greater than `s2`, in which case the 1 is returned.

The `lookup` function defines `int` variables `low` and `high` and assigns them initial values defined by the binary search algorithm. The `while` loop executes as long as `low` does not exceed `high`. Inside the loop, the value `mid` is calculated by adding `low` and `high` and dividing the result by 2. The `compare_strings` function is then called with the word contained in `dictionary[mid]` and the word we are searching for as arguments. The returned value is assigned to the variable `result`.

If `compare_strings` returns a value of -1—indicating that `dictionary[mid].word` is less than `search`—then `lookup` sets the value of `low` to `mid + 1`. If `compare_strings` returns a 1—indicating that `dictionary[mid].search` is greater than `search`—then `lookup` sets the value of `high` to `mid - 1`. If neither -1 nor 1 is returned, the two strings must be equal, and, in that case, `lookup` returns the value of `mid`, which is the entry number of the word in the dictionary.

If `low` eventually exceeds `high`, the word is not in the dictionary. In that case, `lookup` returns -1 to indicate this "not found" condition.

Program 10.10

```
/* Dictionary lookup program */
#include <stdio.h>
struct  entry
{
    char  word[10];
    char  definition[50];
};

/* Function to compare two character strings */

int  compare_strings (char  s1[], char  s2[])
{
    int  i = 0, answer;

    while ( s1[i] == s2[i] && s1[i] != '\0'&& s2[i] != '\0' )
        ++i;

    if ( s1[i] < s2[i] )
        answer = -1;                    /* s1 < s2   */
    else if ( s1[i] == s2[i] )
        answer = 0;                     /* s1 == s2 */
    else
        answer = 1;                     /* s1 > s2   */

    return (answer);
}

/* Function to lookup a word inside a dictionary */

int  lookup (struct entry  dictionary[], char  search[],
             int  entries)
{
    int  low = 0;
    int  high = entries - 1;
    int  mid, result;
    int  compare_strings (char  s1[], char  s2[]);

    while  ( low <= high )
    {
        mid = (low + high) / 2;
        result = compare_strings (dictionary[mid].word, search);

        if ( result == -1 )
            low = mid + 1;
        else if ( result == 1 )
            high = mid - 1;
        else
            return (mid);    /* found it */
    }
```

continues

Program 10.10 Continued

```
    return (-1);              /* not found */
}

main ()
{
    struct entry  dictionary[100] =
        { { "aardvark", "a burrowing African mammal"      },
          { "abyss",    "a bottomless pit"                },
          { "acumen",   "mentally sharp; keen"            },
          { "addle",    "to become confused"              },
          { "aerie",    "a high nest"                     },
          { "affix",    "to append; attach"               },
          { "agar",     "a jelly made from seaweed"       },
          { "ahoy",     "a nautical call of greeting"     },
          { "aigrette", "an ornamental cluster of feathers" },
          { "ajar",     "partially opened"                } };

    int    entries = 10;
    char   word[10];
    int    entry_number;
    int    lookup (struct entry  dictionary[], char  search[],
                   int  entries);

    printf ("Enter word: ");
    scanf ("%9s", word);

    entry_number = lookup (dictionary, word, entries);

    if ( entry_number != -1 )
        printf ("%s\n", dictionary[entry_number].definition);
    else
        printf ("Sorry, that word is not in my dictionary.\n");
}
```

Program 10.10 OUTPUT

```
Enter word: aigrette
an ornamental cluster of feathers
```

Program 10.10 OUTPUT (Rerun)

```
Enter word: acerb
Sorry, that word is not in my dictionary.
```

Character Operations

Character variables and constants are frequently used in relational and arithmetic expressions. In order to properly use characters in such situations, it is necessary for you to understand how they are handled by the C compiler.

Whenever a character constant or variable is used in an expression in C, it is automatically converted to, and subsequently treated as, an integer value.

In Chapter 6, "Making Decisions," we saw how the expression

```
c >= 'a'  &&  c <= 'z'
```

could be used to determine if the character variable c contained a lowercase letter. We mentioned there that such an expression could be used on systems that used an ASCII character representation since the lowercase letters are represented sequentially in ASCII, with no other characters in between. The first part of the preceding expression, which compares the value of c against the value of the character constant 'a', is actually comparing the value of c against the internal representation of the character \&'a'. In ASCII, the character 'a' has the value 97, the character 'b' the value 98, and so on. Therefore, the expression c >= 'a' will be TRUE (nonzero) for any lowercase character contained in c, since it will have a value that is greater than or equal to 97. However, since there are characters other than the lowercase letters whose ASCII values are greater than 97 (such as the open and closed braces), the test must be bounded on the other end to ensure that the result of the expression is TRUE for lowercase characters only. For this reason, c is compared against the character 'z', which, in ASCII, has the value 122.

Since comparing the value of c against the characters 'a' and 'z' in the preceding expression actually compares c to the numerical representations of 'a' and 'z', the expression

```
c >= 97  &&  c <= 122
```

could be equivalently used to determine if c was a lowercase letter. The first expression is preferred, however, because it does not require the knowledge of the specific numerical values of the characters 'a' and 'z', and because its intentions are less obscure.

The printf call

```
printf ("%i\n", c);
```

can be used to print out the value that is used to internally represent the character stored inside c. If your machine uses ASCII, the statement

```
printf ("%i\n", 'a');
```

will result in the display of 97 at the terminal, for example.

What do you think the following two statements would produce?

```
c = 'a' + 1;
printf ("%c\n", c);
```

Since the value of 'a' is 97 in ASCII, the effect of the first statement would be to assign the value 98 to the character variable c. Since this value represents the character 'b' in ASCII, this is the character that would be displayed by the printf call.

While adding one to a character constant hardly seems practical, the preceding example gives way to an important technique that is used to convert the characters '0' through \&'9' into their corresponding numerical values 0 through 9. You will recall that we stressed the fact that the character '0' is not the same as the integer 0, the character '1' is not the same as the integer 1, and so on. In fact, the character '0' has the numerical value 48 in ASCII, which is what would be displayed by the following printf call:

```
printf ("%i\n", '0');
```

Suppose the character variable c contained one of the characters '0' through '9' and that we wished to convert this value into the corresponding integer 0 through 9. Since the digits of virtually all character sets are represented by sequential integer values, we can easily convert c into its integer equivalent by subtracting the character constant '0' from it. Therefore, if i is defined as an integer variable, the statement

```
i = c - '0';
```

will have the effect of converting the character digit contained in c into its equivalent integer value. Suppose c contained the character '5', which, in ASCII, is the number 53. The ASCII value of '0' is 48, so execution of the above statement would result in the integer subtraction of 48 from 53, which would result in the integer value 5 being assigned to i. On a machine that used a character set other than ASCII, the same result would most likely be obtained, even though the internal representations of '5' and '0' might differ.

The above technique can be extended to convert a character string consisting of digits into its equivalent numerical representation. This has been done in the following program in which a function called string_to_integer is presented to convert the character string passed as its argument into an integer value. The function ends its scan of the character string once a nondigit character is encountered and returns the result back to the calling routine. It is assumed that an int variable is large enough to hold the value of the converted number.

Program 10.11

```c
/* Function to convert a string to an integer */
#include <stdio.h>
int  string_to_integer (char  string[])
{
    int  i, integer_value, result = 0;

    for ( i = 0; string[i] >= '0' && string[i] <= '9'; ++i )
    {
        integer_value = string[i] - '0';
        result = result * 10 + integer_value;
    }

    return (result);
}

main ()
{
    int  string_to_integer (char  string[]);

    printf ("%i\n", string_to_integer("245"));
    printf ("%i\n", string_to_integer("100") + 25);
    printf ("%i\n", string_to_integer("13x5"));
}
```

Program 10.11 OUTPUT

```
245
125
13
```

The `for` loop is executed as long as the character contained in `string[i]` is a digit character. Each time through the loop, the character contained in `string[i]` is converted into its equivalent integer value and is then added into the value of `result` multiplied by 10. To see how this technique works, consider execution of this loop when the function is called with the character string `"245"` as an argument: The first time through the loop, `integer_value` will be assigned the value of `string[0]` - `'0'`. Since `string[0]` will contain the character `'2'`, this will result in the value 2 being assigned to `integer_value`. Since the value of `result` is 0 the first time through the loop, multiplying it by 10 will produce 0, which will be added to `integer_value` and stored back into `result`. So by the end of the first pass through the loop, `result` will contain the value 2.

The second time through the loop, integer_value will be set equal to 4, as calculated by subtracting '0' from \&'4'. Multiplying result by 10 will produce 20, which will be added to the value of integer_value, producing 24 as the value stored into result.

The third time through the loop, integer_value will be equal to '5' - '0', or 5, which will be added into the value of result multiplied by 10 (240). Thus, the value 245 will be the value of result after the loop has been executed for the third time.

Upon encountering the terminating null character, the for loop will be exited and the value of result, 245, will be returned to the calling routine.

The string_to_integer function could be improved in two ways. First, it doesn't handle negative numbers. Second, it doesn't let you know whether or not the string contained *any* valid digit characters at all. For example, string_to_integer ("xxx") returns 0. These improvements are left as an exercise.

This discussion concludes this chapter on character strings. As you can see, C provides capabilities that enable character strings to be efficiently and easily manipulated. The library actually contains a wide variety of library functions for performing operations on strings. For example, it offers the function strlen to calculate the length of a character string, strcmp to compare two strings, strcat to concatenate two strings, strcpy to copy one string to another, atoi to convert a string to an integer, and isupper, islower, isalpha, and isdigit to test whether a character is uppercase, lowercase, alphabetic, or a digit. A good exercise is to rewrite the examples from this chapter to make use of these routines. Consult Appendix B, "The Standard C Library," which lists many of the functions available from the library.

Exercises

1. If you have access to a computer facility that supports the C programming language, type in and run the 11 programs presented in this chapter. Compare the output produced by each program with the output presented after each program.

2. Why could we have replaced the while statement of the equal_strings function of Program 10.4 with the statement

   ```
   while ( s1[i] == s2[i]  &&  s1[i] != '\0' )
   ```

   to achieve the same results?

3. The count_words function from Programs 10.7 and 10.8 will incorrectly count a word that contains an apostrophe as two separate words. Modify this function to correctly handle this situation. Also, extend the

function to count a sequence of positive or negative numbers, including any embedded commas and periods, as a single word.

4. Write a function called `substring` to extract a portion of a character string. The function should be called as follows:

```
substring (source, start, count, result);
```

where `source` is the character string from which we are extracting the substring, `start` is an index number into `source` indicating the first character of the `substring`, `count` is the number of characters to be extracted from the `source` string, and `result` is an array of characters that is to contain the extracted substring. For example, the call

```
substring ("character", 4, 3, result_array);
```

will extract the substring `"act"` (three characters starting with character number 4) from the string `"character"` and will place the result in `result_array`.

Make sure the function inserts a null character at the end of the substring in the result array. Also, have the function check that the requested number of characters does in fact exist in the string. If this is not the case, have the function end the substring when it reaches the end of the source string. So, for example, a call such as

substring ("two words", 4, 20, result);

should just place the string "words" inside the result array, even though 20 characters were requested by the call.

5. Write a function called `find_string` to determine if one character string exists inside another string. The first argument to the function should be the character string that is to be searched and the second argument is the string we are interested in finding. If the function finds the specified string, then have it return the location in the source string where the string was found. If the function does not find the string, then have it return -1. So, for example, the call

```
index = find_string ("a chatterbox", "hat");
```

will search the string `"a chatterbox"` for the string `"hat"`. Since `"hat"` does exist inside the source string, the function will return 3 to indicate the starting position inside the source string where `"hat"` was found.

6. Write a function called `remove_string` to remove a specified number of characters from a character string. The function should take three arguments: the source string, the starting index number in the source

string, and the number of characters to remove. So if the character array `text` contained the string `"the wrong son"` then the call

```
remove_string (text, 4, 6);
```

would have the effect of removing the characters "wrong " (the word "wrong" plus the space that follows) from the array `text`. The resulting string inside `text` would then be `"the son"`.

7. Write a function called `insert_string` to insert one character string into another string. The arguments to the function should consist of the source string, the string to be inserted, and the position in the source string where the string is to be inserted. So the call

```
insert_string (text, "per", 10);
```

with `text` as originally defined in the previous exercise, would result in the character string `"per"` being inserted inside `text`, beginning at `text[10]`. Therefore, the character string `"the wrong person"` would be stored inside the `text` array after the function returned.

8. Using the `find_string`, `remove_string`, and `insert_string` functions from preceding exercises, write a function called `replace_string` that takes three character string arguments as follows

```
replace_string (source, s1, s2);
```

and that will replace s1 inside source with the character string s2. The function should call the find_string function to locate s1 inside source, then call the remove_string function to remove s1 from source, and finally call the insert_string function to insert s2 into source at the proper location.

So the function call

replace_string (text, "1", "one");

will replace the first occurrence of the character string "1" inside the character string text, if it exists, with the string "one". Similarly, the function call

replace_string (text, "*", "");

will have the effect of removing the first asterisk inside the text array, since the replacement string is the null string.

9. We can extend even further the usefulness of the `replace_string` function from the preceding exercise if we have it return a value that indicates whether the replacement succeeded, where succeeded means that the string to be replaced was found inside the source string. So if

the function returns 1 if the replacement succeeds and 0 if it does not, then the loop

```
do
    still_found = replace_string (text, " ", "");
while  ( still_found );
```

could be used to remove *all* blank spaces from text, for example.

Incorporate this change into the replace_strings function and try it with various character strings to make sure that it works properly.

10. Write a function called `dictionary_sort` that sorts a dictionary, as defined in Programs 10.9 and 10.10, into alphabetical order.

11. Extend the `string_to_integer` function from Program 10.11 so that if the first character of the string is a minus sign, then the value that follows is taken as a negative number.

12. Write a function called `string_to_float` that will convert a character string into a floating point value. Have the function accept an optional leading minus sign. So the call

```
string_to_float ("-867.6921");
```

should return the value -867.6921.

13. If c is a lowercase character, then the expression

```
c - 'a' + 'A'
```

will produce the uppercase equivalent of c, assuming an ASCII character set.

14. Write a function called `uppercase` that converts all lowercase characters in a string into their uppercase equivalents. Write a function called `integer_to_string` that will convert an integer value into a character string. Make sure the function handles negative integers properly.

11

Pointers

In this chapter, we will examine one of the most sophisticated features of the C programming language: *pointers*. In fact, the power and flexibility that C provides in dealing with pointers serve to set it apart from other programming languages such as Pascal. Pointers enable you to effectively represent complex data structures, to change values passed as arguments to functions, to work with memory that has been allocated "dynamically" (see Chapter 17, "Miscellaneous and Advanced Features"), and to more concisely and efficiently deal with arrays.

To understand the way in which pointers operate, it is first necessary to understand the concept of *indirection*. We are used to this concept in our everyday life. For example, suppose that I needed to buy a new ribbon for my printer. In the company that I work for, all purchases are handled by the purchasing department. So I would call Jim in purchasing and ask him to order the new ribbon for me. Jim, in turn, would call the local supply store to order the ribbon. The approach that I would take in obtaining my new ribbon would actually be an indirect one, since I would not be ordering the ribbon directly from the supply store myself.

This same notion of indirection applies to the way pointers work in C. A pointer provides an indirect means of accessing the value of a particular data item. And just as there are reasons why it makes sense to go through the purchasing department to order new ribbons (I don't have to know which particular store the ribbons are being ordered from, for example), so are there good reasons why, at times, it makes sense to use pointers in C.

But enough talk—it's time to see how pointers actually work. Suppose we define a variable called count as follows:

```
int   count = 10;
```

We can define another variable, called int_pointer, that will enable us to indirectly access the value of count by the declaration

```
int   *int_pointer;
```

The asterisk defines to the C system that the variable int_pointer is of type *pointer to int*. This means that int_pointer will be used in the program to indirectly access the value of one or more integer variables.

We have seen how the & operator was used in the scanf calls of previous programs. This unary operator, known as the *address* operator, is used to make a pointer to an object in C. So if x is a variable of a particular type, then the expression &x is a pointer to that variable. The expression &x can be assigned to any pointer variable, if desired, that has been declared to be a pointer to the same type as x.

Therefore, with the definitions of count and int_pointer as given, we can write a statement such as

```
int_pointer = &count;
```

to set up the indirect reference between int_pointer and count. The address operator has the effect of assigning to the variable int_pointer, not the value of count, but a *pointer* to the variable count. The link that has been made between int_pointer and count is conceptualized in Figure 11.1. The directed line illustrates the idea that int_pointer does not directly contain the value of count, but a pointer to the variable count.

Figure 11.1. *Pointer to an integer.*

In order to reference the contents of count through the pointer variable int_pointer, we use the *indirection* operator, which is the asterisk *. So if x were defined to be of type int, then the statement

```
x = *int_pointer;
```

would assign the value that is indirectly referenced through int_pointer to the variable x. Since int_pointer was previously set pointing to count, this statement would have the effect of assigning the value contained in the variable count—which is 10—to the variable x.

The previous statements have been incorporated into the following program, which illustrates the two fundamental pointer operators: the address operator, &, and the indirection operator, *.

Program 11.1

```
/* Program to illustrate pointers */
#include <stdio.h>
main ()
{
    int    count = 10, x;
    int    *int_pointer;

    int_pointer = &count;
    x = *int_pointer;

    printf ("count = %i, x = %i\n", count, x);
}
```

Program 11.1 OUTPUT

```
count = 10, x = 10
```

The variables count and x are declared to be integer variables in the normal fashion. On the next line, the variable int_pointer is declared to be of type "pointer to int." Note that the two lines of declarations could have been combined into the single line

```
int  count = 10, x, *int_pointer;
```

Next, the address operator is applied to the variable count. This has the effect of creating a pointer to this variable, which is then assigned by the program to the variable int_pointer.

Execution of the next statement in the program,

```
x = *int_pointer;
```

proceeds as follows: The indirection operator tells the C system to treat the variable int_pointer as containing a pointer to another data item. This pointer is then used to access the desired data item, whose type is specified by the declaration of the pointer variable. Since we told the compiler that int_pointer points to integers when we declared the variable, the compiler knows that the value referenced by the expression *int_pointer is an integer. And since we set int_pointer to point to the integer variable count in the previous program statement, it is the value of count that is indirectly accessed by this expression.

It should be realized that the program we have just presented is a manufactured example of the use of pointers and does not show a practical use for them in a program. Such motivation will be presented shortly, after you have become familiar with the basic ways in which pointers may be defined and manipulated in a program.

Program 11.2 illustrates some interesting properties of pointer variables. Here a pointer to a character is used.

Program 11.2

```
/* Further examples of pointers */
#include <stdio.h>
main ()
{
    char   c = 'Q';
    char   *char_pointer = &c;

    printf ("%c %c\n", c, *char_pointer);

    c = '/';
    printf ("%c %c\n", c, *char_pointer);

    *char_pointer = '(';
    printf ("%c %c\n", c, *char_pointer);
}
```

Program 11.2 OUTPUT

```
Q Q
/ /
( (
```

The character variable c is defined and initialized to the character 'Q'. In the next line of the program, the variable char_pointer is defined to be of type "pointer to char," meaning that whatever value is stored inside this variable should be treated as an indirect reference (pointer) to a character. You will notice that we can assign an initial value to this variable in the normal fashion. The value that we assign to char_pointer in the program is a pointer to the variable c, which is obtained by applying the address operator to the variable c. (Note that this initialization would have generated a compiler error had c been defined *after* this statement, since a variable must always be declared *before* its value may be referenced in an expression.)

The declaration of the variable char_pointer and the assignment of its initial value could have been equivalently expressed in two separate statements as

```
char  *char_pointer;
char_pointer = &c;
```

(and *not* by the statements

```
char  *char_pointer;
*char_pointer = &c;
```

as may be implied from the single line declaration).

Always remember, that the value of a pointer in C is meaningless until it is set pointing to something.

The first printf call simply displays the contents of the variable c and the contents of the variable that is referenced by char_pointer. Since we set char_pointer to point to the variable c, the value that is displayed is the contents of c, as verified by the first line of the program's output.

In the next line of the program, the character '/' is assigned to the character variable c. Since char_pointer still points to the variable c, displaying the value of *char_pointer in the subsequent printf call correctly displays this new value of c at the terminal. This is an important concept. Unless the value of char_pointer is changed, the expression *char_pointer will *always* access the value of c. So as the value of c changes, so does the value of *char_pointer.

The previous discussion can help you to understand how the program statement that appears next in the program works. We mentioned that unless char_pointer were changed, the expression *char_pointer would always reference the value of c. Therefore, in the expression

```
*char_pointer = '(';
```

we are assigning the left parenthesis character to c. More formally, the character '(' is assigned to the variable that is pointed to by char_pointer. We know that this variable is c, since we placed a pointer to c in char_pointer at the beginning of the program.

The above concepts are the key to your understanding of the operation of pointers. Please review them at this point if they still seem a bit unclear.

In the next program, two integer pointers, p1 and p2, are defined. Notice how the value referenced by a pointer can be used in an arithmetic expression. If p1 is defined to be of type "pointer to integer," what conclusion do you think can be made about the use of *p1 in an expression?

Program 11.3

```
/* More on pointers */
#include <stdio.h>
main ()
{
     int  i1, i2;
     int  *p1, *p2;

     i1 = 5;
     p1 = &i1;
     i2 = *p1 / 2 + 10;
     p2 = p1;

     printf ("i1 = %i, i2 = %i, *p1 = %i, *p2 = %i\n",
          i1, i2, *p1, *p2);
}
```

Program 11.3 OUTPUT

```
i1 = 5, i2 = 12, *p1 = 5, *p2 = 5
```

After defining the integer variables i1 and i2 and the integer pointer variables p1 and p2, the program then assigns the value 5 to i1 and stores a pointer to i1 inside p1. Next, the value of i2 is calculated with the following expression:

```
i2 = *p1 / 2 + 10;
```

We implied from our discussions of Program 11.2 that if a pointer px points to a variable x, and px has been defined to be a pointer to the same data type as is x, then use of *px in an expression is, in all respects, identical to the use of x in the same expression.

Since in Program 11.3 the variable p1 is defined to be an integer pointer, the preceding expression is evaluated using the rules of integer arithmetic. And since the value of *p1 is 5 (p1 points to i1), the final result of the evaluation of the preceding expression is 12, which is the value that is assigned to i2. (As you would expect, the pointer reference operator * has higher precedence than the arithmetic operation of division. In fact, this operator, as well as the address operator &, has higher precedence than *all* binary operators in C.)

In the next statement, the value of the pointer p1 is assigned to p2. This assignment is perfectly valid and has the effect of setting p2 to point to the same data item that p1 points to. Since p1 points to i1, after the assignment statement has been executed, p2 will *also* point to i1 (and we can have as many pointers to the same item as we desire in C).

The printf call verifies that the values of i1, *p1, and *p2 are all the same (5) and that the value of i2 was set to 12 by the program.

Pointers and Structures

We have seen how a pointer can be defined to point to a basic data type such as an int or a char. But pointers can also be defined to point to structures as well. In Chapter 9, "Structures," we defined our date structure as follows:

```
struct date
{
    int   month;
    int   day;
    int   year;
};
```

Just as we defined variables to be of type struct date, as in

```
struct date    todays_date;
```

so can we define a variable to be a pointer to a struct date variable:

```
struct date   *date_pointer;
```

The variable date_pointer, as just defined, then can be used in the expected fashion. For example, we can set it to point to todays_date with the assignment statement

```
date_pointer = &todays_date;
```

Once such an assignment has been made, we then can indirectly access any of the members of the date structure pointed to by date_pointer in the following way:

```
(*date_pointer).day = 21;
```

This statement will have the effect of setting the day of the date structure pointed to by date_pointer to 21. The parentheses are required since the structure member operator . has higher precedence than the indirection operator *.

To test the value of month stored in the date structure pointed to by date_pointer, a statement such as

```
if  ( (*date_pointer).month == 12  )
        . . .
```

can be used.

Pointers to structures are so often used in C that a special operator exists in the language. The structure pointer operator ->, which is the dash followed by the greater than sign, permits expressions that would otherwise be written as

```
(*x).y
```

to be more clearly expressed as

```
x->y
```

So the if statement from above can be conveniently written as

```
if  ( date_pointer->month == 12 )
        . . .
```

Program 9.1, which was the first program that illustrated structures, was rewritten using the concept of structure pointers. This program is presented below.

Program 11.4

```
/* Program to illustrate structure pointers */
#include <stdio.h>
main ()
{
    struct date
    {
        int  month;
        int  day;
        int  year;
    };

    struct date  today, *date_pointer;

    date_pointer = &today;
    date_pointer->month = 9;
    date_pointer->day = 25;
    date_pointer->year = 1988;

    printf ("Today's date is %i/%i/%i.\n",
        date_pointer->month, date_pointer->day, date_pointer->year % 100);
}
```

Program 11.4 OUTPUT

```
Today's date is 9/25/88.
```

Figure 11.2 depicts how the variables `today` and `date_pointer` would look after all of the assignment statements from the preceding program have been executed.

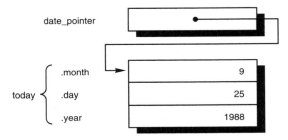

Figure 11.2. *Pointer to a structure.*

Once again, it should be pointed out that there is no real motivation shown here as to why we should even bother using a structure pointer when it seems as though we can get along just fine without it (as we did in Program 9.1). We will get to the motivation shortly.

QUICK TIP

It's important to understand how structure pointers work. They are used in most complex C programs.

Structures Containing Pointers

Naturally, a pointer also can be a member of a structure. In the structure definition

```
struct  int_pointers
{
    int  *p1;
    int  *p2;
};
```

a structure called `int_pointers` is defined to contain two integer pointers, the first one called p1 and the second one p2. We can define a variable of type `struct int_pointers` in the usual way:

```
struct int_pointers  pointers;
```

The variable `pointers` can now be used in the normal fashion, remembering that `pointers` itself is *not* a pointer, but a structure variable that has two pointers as its members.

The following program shows how the `int_pointers` structure can be handled in a C program.

Program 11.5

```
/* Structures containing pointers */
#include <stdio.h>
main ()
{
    struct  int_pointers
    {
        int  *p1;
        int  *p2;
    };

    struct int_pointers  pointers;
    int  i1 = 100, i2;

    pointers.p1 = &i1;
    pointers.p2 = &i2;
    *pointers.p2 = -97;

printf ("i1 = %i, *pointers.p1 = %i\n", i1, *pointers.p1);
printf ("i2 = %i, *pointers.p2 = %i\n", i2, *pointers.p2);
}
```

Program 11.5 OUTPUT

```
i1 = 100, *pointers.p1 = 100
i2 = -97, *pointers.p2 = -97
```

After the variables have been defined, the assignment statement

```
pointers.p1 = &i1;
```

sets the p1 member of pointers pointing to the integer variable i1, while the next statement

```
pointers.p2 = &i2;
```

sets the p2 member pointing to i2. Next, -97 is assigned to the variable that is pointed to by pointers.p2. Since we just set this to point to i2, -97 is stored in i2. No parentheses are needed in this assignment statement since, as we mentioned previously, the structure member operator . has higher precedence than the indirection operator. Therefore, the pointer is correctly referenced from the structure *before* the indirection operator is applied. Of course, parentheses could have been used just to play it safe, as at times it can be difficult to try to remember which of two operators has higher precedence.

The two printf calls that follow in the preceding program verify that the correct assignments were made.

Figure 11.3 has been provided to help you understand the relationship between the variables i1, i2, and pointers after the assignment statements from Program 11.5 have been executed. As you can see in Figure 11.3, the p1 member points to the variable i1, which contains the value 100, while the p2 member points to the variable i2, which contains the value -97.

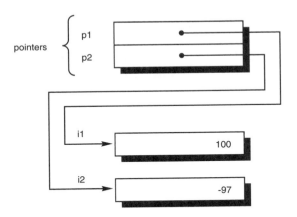

Figure 11.3. *Structure containing pointers.*

Linked Lists

The concepts of pointers to structures and structures containing pointers are very powerful ones in C, for they enable us to create sophisticated data structures, such as *linked lists*, *doubly linked lists*, and *trees*.

Suppose we define a structure as follows:

```
struct entry
{
    int           value;
    struct entry  *next;
};
```

This defines a structure called `entry`, which contains two members. The first member of the structure is a simple integer called `value`. The second member of the structure is a member called `next`, which is a *pointer to an entry structure*. Think about this for a moment. Contained inside an `entry` structure is a pointer to another `entry` structure. This is a perfectly valid concept in the C language. Now suppose we define two variables to be of type `struct entry` as follows:

```
struct entry  n1, n2;
```

We set the next pointer of structure n1 to point to structure n2 by executing the statement

```
n1.next = &n2;
```

This statement effectively makes a link between n1 and n2, as depicted in Figure 11.4.

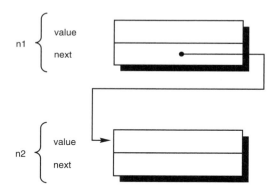

Figure 11.4. *Linked structures.*

Assuming a variable n3 were also defined to be of type `struct entry`, then we could add another link with the statement

```
n2.next = &n3;
```

This resulting chain of linked entries, known more formally as a *linked list*, is illustrated in Figure 11.5. Program 11.6 illustrates this linked list.

The structures n1, n2, and n3 are defined to be of type `struct entry`, which consists of an integer member called `value` and a pointer to an `entry` structure called `next`. The program then assigns the values 100, 200, and 300 to the value members of n1, n2, and n3, respectively.

The next two statements in the program

```
n1.next = &n2;
n2.next = &n3;
```

set up the linked list, with the `next` member of n1 pointing to n2 and the `next` member of n2 pointing to n3.

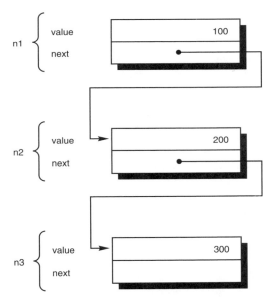

Figure 11.5. *A linked list.*

Program 11.6

```
/* Linked Lists */
#include <stdio.h>
main ()
{
     struct   entry
     {
```

continues

Program 11.6 Continued

```
        int             value;
        struct entry    *next;
    };

    struct entry n1, n2, n3;
    int             i;

    n1.value = 100;
    n2.value = 200;
    n3.value = 300;

    n1.next = &n2;
    n2.next = &n3;

    i = n1.next->value;
    printf ("%i  ", i);

    printf ("%i\n", n2.next->value);
}
```

Program 11.6 OUTPUT

```
200  300
```

Execution of the statement

```
i = n1.next->value;
```

proceeds as follows: The value member of the entry structure pointed to by n1.next is accessed and assigned to the integer variable i. Since we set n1.next to point to n2, the value member of n2 is accessed by this statement. Therefore, this statement has the net result of assigning 200 to i, as verified by the printf call that follows in the program. You may want to verify that the expression n1.next->value is the correct one to use and not n1.next.value, since the n1.next field contains a pointer to a structure, and not the structure itself. This distinction is important and can quickly lead to programming errors if it is not fully understood.

The structure member operator . and the structure pointer operator -> have the same precedence in the C language. In expressions such as the preceding one, where both operators are used, the operators are evaluated from left to right. Therefore, the expression is evaluated as

```
i = (n1.next)->value;
```

which is what was intended.

The second `printf` call in Program 11.6 displays the `value` member that is pointed to by n2.next. Since we set n2.next to point to n3, the contents of n3.value are displayed by the program.

As mentioned, the concept of a linked list is a very powerful one in programming. Linked lists greatly simplify operations such as the insertion and removal of elements from large lists of sorted items.

For example, if n1, n2, and n3 are as defined above, then we can easily remove n2 from the list simply by setting the next field of n1 to point to whatever n2 is pointing to:

```
n1.next = n2.next;
```

This statement has the effect of copying the pointer contained in n2.next into n1.next, and, since n2.next was set to point to n3, n1.next will now be pointing to n3. Furthermore, since n1 no longer points to n2, we have effectively removed it from our list. Figure 11.6 depicts this situation after the above statement is executed. Of course, we could have set n1 pointing to n3 directly with the statement

```
n1.next = &n3;
```

but this latter statement is not as general, since we must know in advance that n2 was pointing to n3.

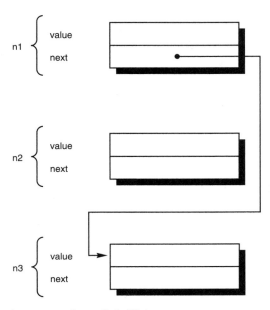

Figure 11.6. *Removing an entry from a linked list.*

Inserting an element into a list is just as straightforward. If we wanted to insert a `struct entry` called n2_3 after n2 in the list, we could simply set n2_3.next to point to whatever n2.next was pointing to, and then set n2.next to point to n2_3. So the sequence of statements

```
n2_3.next = n2.next;
n2.next = &n2_3;
```

would insert n2_3 into the list, immediately after entry n2. Note that the sequence of the above statements is important, since executing the second statement first would overwrite the pointer stored in n2.next before it had a chance to be assigned to n2_3.next. The inserted element n2_3 is depicted in Figure 11.7. You will notice that we did not show n2_3 between n1 and n3. This is to emphasize that n2_3 can be anywhere in the computer's memory and does not have to physically occur after n1 and before n3. This is one of the main motivations for the use of a linked list approach for storing information: Entries of the list do not have to be stored sequentially in memory, as *is* the case with elements contained in an array.

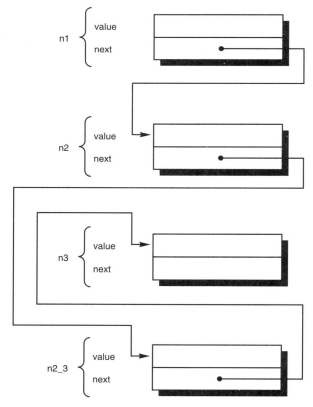

Figure 11.7. *Inserting an element into a linked list.*

Before we start developing some functions to work with linked lists, two more issues must be discussed. Usually associated with a linked list is at least one pointer to the list. Often, a pointer to the start of the list is kept. So, for our original three-element list, which consisted of n1, n2, and n3, we can define a variable called `list_pointer` and set it to point to the beginning of the list with the statement

```
struct entry *list_pointer = &n1;
```

(assuming here that n1 has been previously defined). A pointer to a list is useful for sequencing through the entries in the list, as we will see shortly.

The second issue to be discussed involves the idea of having some way of identifying the end of the list. This is needed so that a procedure that searches through the list, for example, can tell when it has reached the last element in the list. By convention, a constant value of 0 is used for such a purpose and is known as the *null* pointer. We can use the null pointer to mark the end of a list by storing this value in the pointer field of the last entry of the list.[1]

In our three-entry list, we can mark its end by storing the null pointer into n3.next:

```
n3.next =  0;
```

(We will see in Chapter 13, "The Preprocessor," how this assignment statement can be made a bit more readable.)

Figure 11.8 depicts the linked list from Program 11.6, with a `struct entry` pointer called `list_pointer` pointing to the start of the list and the n3.next field set to the null pointer.

Program 11.7 incorporates the concepts we have just described. The program uses a `for` loop to sequence through the list and display the `value` member of each entry in the list.

---

[1]*A null pointer is not necessarily internally represented as the value 0. However, the compiler must recognize assignment of the constant 0 to a pointer as assigning the null pointer. This also applies to comparing a pointer against the constant 0: The compiler interprets it as a test to see if the pointer is null.*

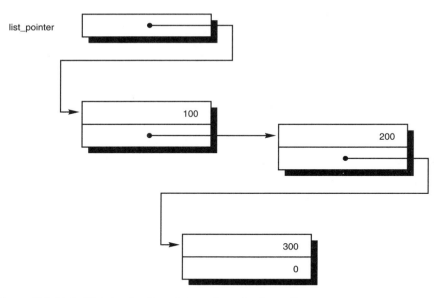

Figure 11.8. *Linked list showing list pointer and terminating null.*

Program 11.7

```
/* List traversal */
#include <stdio.h>
main ()
{
    struct entry
    {
        int          value;
        struct entry  *next;
    };

    struct entry   n1, n2, n3;
    struct entry   *list_pointer = &n1;

    n1.value = 100;
    n1.next  = &n2;

    n2.value = 200;
    n2.next  = &n3;

    n3.value = 300;
    n3.next  = 0;
```

```
        while ( list_pointer != 0 )
        {
            printf ("%i\n", list_pointer->value);
        list_pointer = list_pointer->next;
        }
}
```

Program 11.7 OUTPUT
100
200
300

The program defines the variables n1, n2, and n3 and the pointer variable list_pointer, which is initially set to point to n1, the first entry in the list. The next program statements link together the three elements of the list, with the next member of n3 set to the null pointer to mark the end of the list.

A while loop is then set up to sequence through each element of the list. This loop will be executed as long as the value of list_pointer is not equal to the null pointer. The printf call inside the while loop displays the value member of the entry currently pointed to by list_pointer.

The statement that follows the printf call,

```
list_pointer = list_pointer->next;
```

has the effect of taking the pointer from the next member of the structure pointed to by list_pointer and assigning it to list_pointer. So the first time through the loop, this statement takes the pointer contained in n1.next (remember, list_pointer was initially set pointing to n1) and assigns it to list_pointer. Since this value is not null—it's a pointer to the entry structure n2—the while loop is repeated.

The second time through the while loop results in the display of n2.value, which is 200. The next member of n2 is then copied into list_pointer, and since we set this value to point to n3, list_pointer will point to n3 by the end of the second pass through the loop.

When the while loop is executed for the third time, the printf call displays the value of 300 as contained in n3.value. At that point, list_pointer->next (which is actually n3.next) is copied into list_pointer, and, since we set this member to the null pointer, the while loop will terminate after it has been executed three times.

Trace through the operation of the `while` loop just discussed, using a pencil and paper, if necessary, to keep track of the values of the various variables. Understanding the operation of this loop is the key to your understanding the operation of pointers in C. Incidentally, it should be noted that this same `while` loop can be used to sequence through the elements of a list of any size, provided the end of the list is marked by the null pointer.

Pointers and Functions

Pointers and functions get along quite well together. That is, we can pass a pointer as an argument to a function in the normal fashion, and we can also have a function return a pointer as its result.

The first case cited above, passing pointer arguments, is straightforward enough: The pointer is simply included in the list of arguments to the function in the normal fashion. So to pass the pointer `list_pointer` from the previous program to a function called `print_list`, you can write

```
print_list (list_pointer);
```

Inside the `print_list` routine, the formal parameter must be declared to be a pointer to the appropriate type:

```
void  print_list  (struct entry  *pointer)
{
    . . .
}
```

The formal parameter `pointer` can then be used in the same way as a normal pointer variable. One thing worth remembering when dealing with pointers that are sent to functions as arguments: The value of the pointer is copied into the formal parameter when the function is called. Therefore, any change made to the formal parameter by the function will *not* affect the pointer that was passed to the function. But here's the catch: While the pointer cannot be changed by the function, the data elements that the pointer references *can* be changed! The next program example will help clarify this point.

Program 11.8

```
/* pointers and functions */
#include <stdio.h>
void test (int  *int_pointer)
{
    *int_pointer = 100;
}
```

```
main ()
{
        void test (int  *int_pointer);
        int  i = 50, *p = &i;

        printf ("i before the call to test = %i\n", i);

        test (p);
        printf ("i after the call to test = %i\n", i);
}
```

Program 11.8 OUTPUT

```
i before the call to test = 50
i after the call to test = 100
```

The function test is defined to take as its argument a pointer to an integer. Inside the function, a single statement is executed to set the integer pointed to by int_pointer to the value 100.

The main routine defines an integer variable i with an initial value of 50 and a pointer to an integer called p that is set to point to i. The program then displays the value of i and calls the test function, passing the pointer p as the argument. As you can see from the second line of the program's output, the test function did in fact change the value of i to 100.

QUICK TIP

Remember that you can pass a pointer to a variable as an argument to a function if you need to change that variable from inside the function.

Now consider the following program.

Program 11.9

```
/* More on pointers and functions */
#include <stdio.h>
void  exchange (int *pint1, int *pint2)
{
```

continues

Program 11.9 Continued

```
    int   temp;

    temp = *pint1;
    *pint1 = *pint2;
    *pint2 = temp;
}

main ()
{
    void  exchange (int *pint1, int *pint2);
    int   i1 = -5, i2 = 66, *p1 = &i1, *p2 = &i2;

    printf ("i1 = %i, i2 = %i\n", i1, i2);

    exchange (p1, p2);
    printf ("i1 = %i, i2 = %i\n", i1, i2);

    exchange (&i1, &i2);
    printf ("i1 = %i, i2 = %i\n", i1, i2);
}
```

Program 11.9 OUTPUT

```
i1 = -5, i2 = 66
i1 = 66, i2 = -5
i1 = -5, i2 = 66
```

The purpose of the `exchange` function is to interchange the two integer values pointed to by its two arguments. The local integer variable `temp` is used to hold one of the integer values while the exchange is made. Its value is set equal to the integer that is pointed to by `pint1`. The integer pointed to by `pint2` is then copied into the integer pointed to by `pint1`, and the value of `temp` is then stored into the integer pointed to by `pint2`, thus making the exchange complete.

The `main` routine defines integers `i1` and `i2` with values of -5 and 66, respectively. Two integer pointers, `p1` and `p2`, are then defined and are set to point to `i1` and `i2`, respectively. The program then displays the values of `i1` and `i2` and calls the `exchange` function, passing the two pointers, `p1` and `p2`, as arguments. The `exchange` function exchanges the value contained in the integer pointed to by `p1` with the value contained in the integer pointed to by `p2`. Since `p1` points to `i1`, and `p2` to `i2`, the values of `i1` and `i2` end up getting exchanged by the function. The output from the second `printf` call verifies that the exchange worked properly.

The second call to exchange is a bit more interesting. This time, the arguments that are passed to the function are pointers to i1 and i2 that are manufactured right on the spot by applying the address operator to these two variables. Since the expression &i1 produces a pointer to the integer variable i1, this is right in line with the type of argument that our function expects for the first argument (a pointer to an integer). The same applies for the second argument as well. And as can be seen from the program's output, the exchange function did its job and switched the values of i1 and i2 back to their original values.

You should realize that without the use of pointers we could not have written our exchange function to exchange the value of two integers, since we are limited to returning only a single value from a function and since a function cannot permanently change the value of its arguments.

QUICK TIP

Study the last program example in detail. It illustrates with a small example the key concepts to be understood when dealing with pointers in C.

The next program example shows how a function can return a pointer. The program defines a function called find_entry whose purpose is to search through a linked list to find a specified value. When the specified value has been found, the program returns a pointer to the entry in the list. If the desired value is not found, then the program returns the null pointer.

Program 11.10

```
#include <stdio.h>
struct entry
{
    int  value;
    struct entry    *next;
};

struct entry  *find_entry (struct entry  *lptr, int match)
{
    while  ( lptr != 0 )
        if ( lptr->value == match )
            return (lptr);
        else
            lptr = lptr->next;

    return (0);
}
```

continues

Program 11.10 Continued

```
main ()
{
    struct entry  *find_entry (struct entry  *lptr, int match);
    struct entry  n1, n2, n3;
    struct entry  *lptr, *list_start = &n1;
    int i, search;

    n1.value = 100;
    n1.next =  &n2;

    n2.value = 200;
    n2.next =  &n3;

    n3.value = 300;
    n3.next =  0;

    printf ("Enter value to locate: ");
    scanf ("%i", &search);

    lptr = find_entry (list_start, search);

    if ( lptr != 0 )
        printf ("Found %i.\n", lptr->value);
    else
        printf ("Not found.\n");
}
```

Program 11.10 OUTPUT

```
Enter value to locate: 200
Found 200.
```

Program 11.10 OUTPUT (Rerun)

```
Enter value to locate: 400
Not found.
```

Program 11.10 OUTPUT (Rerun)

```
Enter value to locate: 300
Found 300.
```

The function header

```
struct entry  *find_entry (struct entry  *lptr, int match)
```

specifies that the function find_entry will return a pointer to an entry structure and that it takes such a pointer as its first argument and an integer as its second. The function begins by entering a while loop to sequence through the elements of the list. This loop is executed until either match is found equal to one of the value entries in the list (in which case the value of lptr is immediately returned) or until the null pointer is reached (in which case the while loop will be exited and a null pointer will be returned).

After setting up the list as in previous programs, the main routine asks the user for a value to locate in the list and then calls the find_entry function with a pointer to the start of the list (list_start) and the value entered by the user (search) as arguments. The pointer that is returned by find_entry is assigned to the struct entry pointer variable lptr. If lptr is not null, the value member pointed to by lptr is displayed. This should be the same as the value entered by the user. If lptr is null, then a "Not found" message is displayed.

The program's output verifies that the values 200 and 300 were correctly located in the list, and the value 400 was properly not found.

The pointer that is returned by the find_entry function in the program does not seem to serve any useful purpose. However, in more practical situations, this pointer might be used to access other elements contained in the particular entry of the list. For example, we could have a linked list of our dictionary entries from the previous chapter. Then, we could call the find_entry function (or rename it lookup as it was called in that chapter) to search the linked list of dictionary entries for the given word. The pointer returned by the lookup function could then be used to access the definition member of the entry.

Organizing the dictionary as a linked list has several advantages. Inserting a new word into the dictionary is easy: Once it has been determined where in the list the new entry is to be inserted, it can be done so by simply adjusting some pointers, as illustrated earlier in this chapter. Removing an entry from the dictionary is also simple. Finally, as you will learn in Chapter 17, this approach also provides the framework that enables us to dynamically expand the size of the dictionary.

However, the linked list approach for the organization of the dictionary does suffer from one major drawback: We can not apply our fast binary search algorithm to such a list. This algorithm only works with an array of elements that can be directly indexed. Unfortunately, there is no faster way to search our linked list other than by a straight sequential search, since each entry in the list can only be accessed from the previous one.

One way to glean the benefits of easy insertion and removal of elements, as well as fast search time, is by using a different type of data structure known as a *tree*. The reader is respectfully referred elsewhere—such as to *The Art of Computer Programming, Volume 1, Fundamental Algorithms* (Donald E. Knuth, Addison-Wesley)—for a discussion of this type of data structure, which can be easily implemented in C with the techniques we have already described.

Pointers and Arrays

One of the most common uses of pointers in C is as pointers to arrays. The main reasons for using pointers to arrays are ones of notational convenience and of program efficiency. Pointers to arrays generally result in code that uses less memory space and executes faster. The reason this is so will become apparent through our discussions in this section.

If we have an array of 100 integers called `values`, then we can define a pointer called `values_pointer`, which can be used to access the integers contained in this array with the statement

```
int    *values_pointer;
```

When we define a pointer that will be used to point to the elements of an array, we don't designate the pointer as type "pointer to array"; rather we designate the pointer as pointing to the type of element that is contained in the array.

If we had an array of characters called `text`, then we could similarly define a pointer to be used to point to elements in `text` with the statement

```
char    *text_pointer;
```

In order to set `values_pointer` to point to the first element in the `values` array, we simply write

```
values_pointer = values;
```

The address operator is not used in this case since the C compiler treats the occurrence of an array name without a subscript as a pointer to the array. Therefore, simply specifying `values` without a subscript has the effect of producing a pointer to the first element of values (see Figure 11.9).

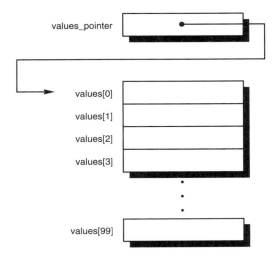

Figure 11.9. *Pointer to an array element.*

An equivalent way of producing a pointer to the start of values is to apply the address operator to the first element of the array. Thus the statement

```
values_pointer = &values[0];
```

can be used to serve the same purpose of placing a pointer to the first element of values in the pointer variable values_pointer.

To set text_pointer to point to the first character inside the text array, either the statement

```
text_pointer = text;
```

or

```
text_pointer = &text[0];
```

can be used. Whichever statement you choose to use is strictly a matter of taste.

The real power of using pointers to arrays comes into play when we wish to sequence through the elements of an array. If values_pointer is defined as above and is set pointing to the first element of values, then the expression

```
*values_pointer
```

can be used to access the first integer of the values array, i.e., values[0]. To reference values[3] through the values_pointer variable, we can add 3 to values_pointer and then apply the indirection operator:

```
*(values_pointer + 3)
```

In general, the expression

```
*(values_pointer + i)
```

can be used to access the value contained in `values[i]`.

So, to set `values[10]` to 27, we could obviously write the expression

```
values[10] = 27;
```

or, using `values_pointer`, we could write

```
*(values_pointer + 10) = 27;
```

To set `values_pointer` to point to the second element of the `values` array, we can apply the address operator to `values[1]` and assign the result to `values_pointer`:

```
values_pointer = &values[1];
```

If `values_pointer` points to `values[0]`, then we can set it to point to `values[1]` by simply adding 1 to the value of `values_pointer`:

```
values_pointer += 1;
```

This is a perfectly valid expression in C and can be used for pointers to *any* data type.

So, in general, if a is an array of elements of type x, px is of type "pointer to x," and i and n are integer constants of variables, then the statement

```
px = a;
```

will set px to point to the first element of a, and the expression

```
*(px + i)
```

will subsequently reference the value contained in a[i]. Furthermore, the statement

```
px += n;
```

will set px to point n elements further in the array, *no matter what type of element is contained in the array.*

The increment and decrement operators ++ and -- are particularly handy when dealing with pointers. Applying the increment operator to a pointer has the same effect as adding one to the pointer, while applying the decrement operator has the same effect as subtracting one from the pointer. So if `text_pointer` were defined as a char pointer and were set pointing to the beginning of an array of chars called text, the statement

```
++text_pointer;
```

would set `text_pointer` pointing to the next character in `text`, which is text[1]. In a similar fashion, the statement

```
—text_pointer;
```

would set `text_pointer` pointing to the previous character in `text`, assuming, of course, that `text_pointer` was not pointing to the beginning of `text` prior to the execution of this statement.

It is perfectly valid to compare two pointer variables in C. This is particularly useful when comparing two pointers into the same array. For example, we could test the pointer `values_pointer` to see if it points past the end of an array containing 100 elements by comparing it to a pointer to the last element in the array. So the expression

```
values_pointer > &values[99]
```

would be TRUE (nonzero) if `values_pointer` was pointing past the last element in the `values` array, and would be FALSE (zero) otherwise. From our previous discussions, we can replace the above expression with its equivalent

```
values_pointer > values + 99
```

since `values` used without a subscript is a pointer to the beginning of the `values` array. (Remember, it's the same as writing `&values[0]`.)

The next program illustrates pointers to arrays. The `array_sum` function calculates the sum of the elements contained in an array of integers.

Program 11.11

```
/* Function to sum the elements of an integer array */
#include <stdio.h>
int  array_sum (int  array[], int  n)
{
    int  sum = 0, *ptr;
    int  *array_end = array + n;

    for (  ptr = array;  ptr < array_end;  ++ptr )
        sum += *ptr;

    return (sum);
}

main ()
{
    int  array_sum (int  array[], int  n);
    int  values[10] = { 3, 7, -9, 3, 6, -1, 7, 9, 1, -5 };

    printf ("The sum is %i\n", array_sum (values, 10));
}
```

Program 11.11 OUTPUT
`The sum is 21`

Inside the `array_sum` function, the integer pointer `array_end` is defined and set pointing immediately after the last element of `array`. A `for` loop is then set up to sequence through the elements of `array`. The value of `ptr` is set to point to the beginning of `array` when the loop is entered. Each time through the loop, the element of `array` pointed to by `ptr` is added into `sum`. The value of `ptr` is then incremented by the `for` loop to set it pointing to the next element in `array`. When `ptr` points past the end of `array`, the `for` loop is exited, and the value of `sum` is returned to the calling routine.

A Slight Digression About Program Optimization

It is pointed out that the local variable `array_end` was not actually needed by the function, as we could have explicitly compared the value of `ptr` to the end of the array inside the `for` loop:

```
for ( ...; pointer <= array + n; ... )
```

The sole motivation for using `array_end` was one of optimization. Each time through the `for` loop, the looping conditions are evaluated. Since the expression `array + n` is never changed from within the loop, its value is constant throughout the execution of the `for` loop. By evaluating it once *before* the loop is entered, we save the time that would otherwise be spent reevaluating this expression each time through the loop. While there is virtually no savings in time for a 10-element array, especially if the `array_sum` function is called only once by the program, there could be a more substantial savings if this function were heavily used by a program for summing large-sized arrays, for example.

The other issue to be discussed about program optimization concerns the very use of pointers themselves in a program. In the `array_sum` function discussed earlier, the expression `*ptr` is used inside the `for` loop to access the elements in the array. Conventionally, we would have written our `array_sum` function with a `for` loop that used an index variable, such as `i`, and then would have added the value of `array[i]` into `sum` inside the loop. In general, the process of indexing an array takes more time to execute than does the process of accessing the contents of a pointer. In fact, this is one of the main reasons why pointers are used to access the elements of an array—the code that is generated is generally more efficient. Of course, if access to the array is not generally sequential, then pointers accomplish nothing, as far as this issue is concerned, since the expression `*(pointer + j)` will take just as long to execute as will the expression `array[j]`.

Is It an Array or Is It a Pointer?

You will recall that in order to pass an array to a function, we simply specify the name of the array, as we did previously with the call to the array_sum function. But we also mentioned in this section that in order to produce a pointer to an array that we need only specify the name of the array. This implies that in the call to the array_sum function, what was passed to the function was actually a *pointer* to the array values. This is precisely the case and explains why we are able to change the elements of an array from within a function.

But if it is indeed the case that a pointer to the array is passed to the function, then why isn't the formal parameter inside the function declared to be a pointer? In other words, in the declaration of array in the array_sum function, why isn't the declaration

```
int   *array;
```

used? Shouldn't all references to an array from within a function be made using pointer variables?

To answer these questions, we must first reiterate what we have said before about pointers and arrays. We mentioned that if values_pointer points to the same type of element as contained in an array called values, then the expression *(values_pointer + i) is in all ways equivalent to the expression values[i], assuming that values_pointer has been set to point to the beginning of values. What follows from this is that we also can use the expression *(values + i) to reference the ith element of the array values, and, in general, if x is an array of any type, then the expression x[i] can always be equivalently expressed in C as *(x + i).

As you can see, pointers and arrays are intimately related in C, and this is why we can declare array to be of type "array of ints" inside the array_sum function *or* to be of type "pointer to int." Either declaration works just fine in the preceding program—try it and see.

If you are going to be using index numbers to reference the elements of an array that is passed to a function, then declare the corresponding formal parameter to be an array. This will more correctly reflect the usage of the array by the function. Similarly, if you will be using the argument as a pointer to the array, then declare it to be of type pointer.

Realizing now that we could have declared array to be an int pointer in the last program example, and then could have subsequently used it as such, we can eliminate the variable ptr from the function and use array instead. We have done just this in the program that follows.

Program 11.12

```
/* Function to sum the elements of an integer array
Version 2                              */
#include <stdio.h>
int   array_sum (int   *array, int   n)
{
    int   sum = 0;
    int   *array_end = array + n;

    for (   ; array < array_end;   ++array )
        sum += *array;

    return (sum);
}



main ()
{
    int   array_sum (int   *array, int   n);
    int   values[10] = { 3, 7, -9, 3, 6, -1, 7, 9, 1, -5 };

    printf ("The sum is %i\n", array_sum (values, 10));
}
```

Program 11.12 OUTPUT

```
The sum is 21
```

The program is fairly self-explanatory. The first expression inside the for loop was omitted because no value had to be initialized before the loop was started. One point worth repeating is that when the array_sum function is called, a pointer to the values array is passed, where it is called array inside the function. Changes to the value of array (as opposed to the values referenced by array) do not in any way affect the contents of the values array. So the increment operator that is applied to array is just incrementing a pointer to the array values, and not affecting its contents. (Of course, we know that we *can* change values in the array if we want to, simply by assigning values to the element referenced by the pointer.)

Pointers to Character Strings

One of the most common applications of using a pointer to an array is as a pointer to a character string. The reasons are ones of notational convenience and efficiency. To show how easily pointers to character strings can be used, let's write a function called `copy_string` to copy one string into another. If we were writing this function using our normal array indexing methods, then the function might be coded as follows:

```
void copy_string (char  to[], char  from[])
{
    int  i;

    for ( i = 0;  from[i] != '\0';  ++i )
        to[i] = from[i];

    to[i] = '\0';
}
```

The `for` loop is exited before the null character is copied into the `to` array, thus explaining the need for the last statement in the function.

If we write `copy_string` using pointers, then we no longer need the index variable `i`. A pointer version is shown in the following program.

Program 11.13

```
#include <stdio.h>
void copy_string (char  *to, char  *from)
{
    for (  ;  *from != '\0';  ++from, ++to )
        *to = *from;

    *to = '\0';
}

main ()
{
    void  copy_string (char  *to, char  *from);
    char  string1[] = "A string to be copied."; char  string2[50];

    copy_string (string2, string1);
    printf ("%s\n", string2);

    copy_string (string2, "So is this."); printf ("%s\n", string2);
}
```

Program 11.13 OUTPUT

```
A string to be copied.
So is this.
```

The `copy_string` function defines the two formal parameters `to` and `from` as character pointers and not as character arrays as was done in the previous version of `copy_string`. This reflects how these two variables will be used by the function.

A `for` loop is then entered (with no initial conditions) to copy the string pointed to by `from` into the string pointed to by `to`. Each time through the loop, the `from` and `to` pointers are each incremented by one. This sets the `from` pointer pointing to the next character that is to be copied from the source string and sets the `to` pointer pointing to the location in the destination string where the next character is to be stored.

When the `from` pointer points to the null character, the `for` loop is exited. The function then places the null character at the end of the destination string.

In the `main` routine, the `copy_string` function is called twice, the first time to copy the contents of `string1` into `string2`, and the second time to copy the contents of the constant character string `"So is this."` into `string2`.

Constant Character Strings and Pointers

The fact that the call

```
copy_string (string2, "So is this.");
```

works in the previous program implies that when a constant character string is passed as an argument to a function, what is actually passed is a pointer to that character string. Not only is this true in this case, but it also can be generalized by saying that *whenever* a constant character string is used in C, it is a pointer to that character string that is produced. So if `text_pointer` is declared to be a character pointer, as in

```
char  *text_pointer;
```

then the statement

```
text_pointer = "A character string.";
```

will assign to `text_pointer` a *pointer* to the constant character string `"A character string."` Be careful to make the distinction here between character pointers and character arrays, as the type of assignment shown above is *not* valid with a character array. So, for example, if `text` were defined instead to be an array of `char`s, with a statement such as

```
char  text[80];
```

then we *could not* write a statement such as

```
text = "This is not valid.";
```

The *only* time that C lets you get away with performing this type of assignment to a character array is when initializing it, as in

```
char  text[80] =  "This is okay.";
```

Initializing the text array in this manner does not have the effect of storing a pointer to the character string "This is okay." inside text, but rather the actual characters themselves inside corresponding elements of the text array.

If text were a character pointer, initializing text with the statement

```
char  *text =  "This is okay.";
```

would assign to it a pointer to the character string "This is okay."

As another example of the distinction between character strings and character string pointers, the following sets up an array called days, which contains *pointers* to the names of the days of the week.

```
char *days[] =
     { "Sunday", "Monday", "Tuesday", "Wednesday",
       "Thursday", "Friday", "Saturday" };
```

The array days is defined to contain seven entries, each a pointer to a character string. So days[0] contains a pointer to the character string "Sunday", days[1] a pointer to the string "Monday", and so on (see Figure 11.10). We could display the name of the third weekday, for example, with the following statement:

```
printf ("%s\n", days[3]);
```

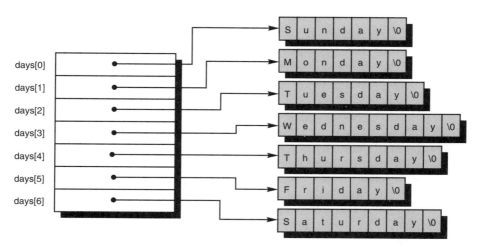

Figure 11.10. Array of pointers.

The Increment and Decrement Operators Revisited

Up to this point, whenever we used the increment or decrement operator it was the only operator that appeared in the expression. When we write the expression ++x, we know that this has the effect of adding 1 to the value of the variable x. And as we have just seen, if x is a pointer to an array, then this has the effect of setting x to point to the next element of the array.

The increment and decrement operators can be used in expressions in which other operators also appear. In such cases, it becomes important to know more precisely how these operators work.

Whenever we used the increment and decrement operators, we always placed them *before* the variables that were being incremented or decremented. So, to increment a variable i, we simply wrote

```
++i;
```

Actually, it also is perfectly valid to place the increment operator *after* the variable, as in

```
i++;
```

Both expressions are perfectly valid and both achieve the same result—namely, of incrementing the value of i. In the first case, where the ++ is placed before its operand, the increment operation is more precisely identified as a *pre-increment*. In the second case, where the ++ is placed after its operand, the operation is identified as a *post-increment*.

The same discussion applies to the decrement operator. So the statement

```
--i;
```

technically performs a *pre-decrement* of i, whereas the statement

```
i--;
```

performs a *post-decrement* of i. Both have the same net result of subtracting 1 from the value of i.

It is when the increment and decrement operators are used in more complex expressions that the distinction between the *pre-* and *post-* nature of these operators is realized.

Suppose we have two integers called i and j. If we set the value of i to 0 and then write the statement

```
j = ++i;
```

the value that gets assigned to j is 1, and not 0 as you might expect. In the case of the pre-increment operator, the variable is incremented *before* its value is used in an expression. So in the above expression, the value of i is first incremented from 0 to 1 and then its value is assigned to j, as if the following two statements had been written instead:

```
++i;
j = i;
```

If we use the post-increment operator in the statement

```
j = i++;
```

then i will be incremented *after* its value has been assigned to j. So if i were 0 before the above statement were executed, 0 would be assigned to j and *then* i would be incremented by 1, as if the statements

```
j = i;
++i;
```

were used instead.

As another example, if i is equal to 1, then the statement

```
x = a[--i];
```

has the effect of assigning the value of a[0] to x, since the variable i will be decremented before its value is used to index into a. The statement

```
x = a[i--];
```

used instead would have the effect of assigning the value of a[1] to x, since i would be decremented after its value had been used to index into a.

As a third example of the distinction between the pre- and post- increment and decrement operators, the function call

```
printf ("%i\n", ++i);
```

will increment i and then send its value to the printf function, while the call

```
printf ("%i\n", i++);
```

will increment i after its value has been sent to the function. So if i were equal to 100, then the first printf call would display 101 at the terminal, whereas the second printf call would display 100. In either case, the value of i would be equal to 101 after the statement had been executed.

As a final example on this topic before we present a program, if text_pointer is a character pointer, then the expression

```
*(++text_pointer)
```

first increments text_pointer and then fetches the character it points to, whereas the expression

```
*(text_pointer++)
```

fetches the character pointed to by text_pointer before its value is incremented. In either case, the parentheses are not required, since the * and ++ operators have equal precedence but associate from right to left.

Now let's go back to the copy_string function from Program 11.13 and rewrite it to incorporate the increment operations directly into the assignment statement.

Since the to and from pointers are incremented each time after the assignment statement inside the for loop is executed, they should be incorporated into the assignment statement as post-increment operations. The revised for loop of Program 11.13 then becomes

```
for (  ;  *from != '\0';  )
     *to++ = *from++;
```

Execution of the assignment statement inside the loop would proceed as follows. The character pointed to by from would be retrieved and then from would be incremented to point to the next character in the source string. The referenced character would then be stored inside the location pointed to by to, and then to would be incremented to point to the next location in the destination string.

QUICK TIP

Study the preceding assignment statement until you fully understand its operation. Statements of this type are so commonly used in C programs, it's important that you understand the preceding one completely before continuing.

The for statement above hardly seems worthwhile, since it has no initial expression and no looping expression. In fact, the logic would be better served when expressed in the form of a while loop. This has been done in Program 11.14. This program presents our new version of the copy_string function. The while loop uses the fact that the null character is equal to the value 0, as is commonly done by experienced C programmers.

Program 11.14

```
/* Function to copy one string to another
         pointer version 2                    */
#include <stdio.h>
void  copy_string (char  *to, char  *from)
{
     while ( *from )
          *to++ = *from++;
```

```
        *to = '\0';
}


main ()
{
        void  copy_string (char  *to, char  *from);
        char  string1[] = "A string to be copied.";
        char  string2[50];

        copy_string (string2, string1);
        printf ("%s\n", string2);

        copy_string (string2, "So is this.");
        printf ("%s\n", string2);
}
```

Program 11.14 OUTPUT

```
A string to be copied.
So is this.
```

Operations on Pointers

As we have seen in this chapter, we can add or subtract integer values from pointers. Furthermore, we can compare two pointers to see if they are equal or not, or if one pointer is less than or greater than another pointer. The only other operation that is permitted on pointers is the subtraction of two pointers of the same type. The result of subtracting two pointers in C is the number of elements contained between the two pointers. So if a points to an array of elements of any type and b points to another element somewhere farther along in the same array, then the expression b - a represents the number of elements between these two pointers. For example, if p points to some element in an array x, then the statement

```
n = p - x;
```

will have the effect of assigning tox the variable n (assumed here to be an integer variable) the index number of the element inside x that p points to. Therefore, if p had been set pointing to the hundredth element in x by a statement such as

```
p = &x[99];
```

then the value of n after the above subtraction was performed would be 99.

As a practical application of this newly learned fact about pointer subtraction, let us present a new version of the string_length function from Chapter 10, "Character Strings."

In Program 11.15, the character pointer cptr is used to sequence through the characters pointed to by string until the null character is reached. At that point, string is subtracted from cptr to obtain the number of elements (characters) contained in the string. The program's output verifies that the function is working correctly.

Program 11.15

```
/* Function to count the characters in a string
              pointer version                         */
#include <stdio.h>
int  string_length (char  *string)
{
    char  *cptr = string;

    while ( *cptr )
         ++cptr;
    return ( cptr - string );
}
main ()
{
    int  string_length (char  *string);
    printf ("%i  ", string_length ("string_length test"));
    printf ("%i  ", string_length (""));
    printf ("%i\n", string_length ("complete"));
}
```

Program 11.15 OUTPUT

18 0 8

Pointers to Functions

Of a slightly more advanced nature, but presented here for the sake of completeness, is the notion of a pointer to a function. When working with pointers to functions, the C compiler needs to know not only that the pointer variable points to a function, but also the type of value returned by that function as well as the number and types of its arguments. To declare a variable fn_pointer to be of type "pointer to function that returns an `int` and that takes no arguments," the declaration

```
int   (*fn_pointer) (void);
```

can be written. The parentheses around `*fn_pointer` are required, as otherwise the C compiler would treat the preceding statement as the declaration of a function called `fn_pointer` that returns a pointer to an `int` (because the functional call operator `()` has higher precedence than the pointer indirection operator `*`).

In order to set our function pointer pointing to a specific function, we simply assign the name of the function to it. So if `lookup` were a function that returned an `int` and that took no arguments, the statement

```
fn_pointer = lookup;
```

would store a pointer to this function inside the function pointer variable `fn_pointer`. Writing a function name without a subsequent set of parentheses is treated in an analogous way to writing an array name without a subscript. The C compiler automatically produces a pointer to the specified function. An ampersand is permitted in front of the function name, but it's not required.

If the `lookup` function has not been previously defined in the program, it will be necessary to declare the function before the above assignment can be made. So a statement such as

```
int   lookup (void);
```

would be needed before a pointer to this function could be assigned to the variable `fn_pointer`.

We can call the function that is indirectly referenced through a pointer variable by applying the function call operator to the pointer, listing any arguments to the function inside the parentheses. For example,

```
entry = fn_pointer ();
```

would call the function pointed to by `fn_pointer`, storing the returned value inside the variable `entry`.

One common application for pointers to functions is in passing them as arguments to other functions. The Standard C Library uses this, for example, in the function `qsort`, which performs a "quicksort" on an array of data elements. This function takes as one of its arguments a pointer to a function that is called whenever `qsort` needs to compare two elements in the array being sorted. In this manner, `qsort` can be used to sort arrays of any type, as the actual comparison of any two elements in the array is made by a user-supplied function, and not by the `qsort` function itself. Appendix B, "The Standard C Library," goes into more detail about `qsort` and contains an actual example of its use.

Another common application for function pointers is to create what is known as *dispatch* tables. You can't store functions themselves inside the elements of an array. However, it is valid to store function *pointers* inside an array. Given this, you can create tables that contain pointers to functions to be called. For example, you might create a table for processing different commands that will be entered by a user. Each entry in the table could contain both the command name and a pointer to a function to call to process that particular command. Now, whenever the user entered a command, you could lookup the command inside the table and invoke the corresponding function to handle it. This technique is presented in detail in the book *Topics in C Programming, Revised Edition* (Kochan & Wood, John Wiley & Sons, Inc., 1991).

Pointers and Memory Addresses

Before we end this discussion of pointers in C, we should point out the details of how they are actually implemented. A computer's memory can be conceptualized as a sequential collection of storage cells. Each cell of the computer's memory has a number, called an *address*, associated with it. Typically, the first address of a computer's memory is numbered 0. On most computer systems, a "cell" is called a *byte*.

The computer uses memory for storing the instructions of your computer program, and also for storing the values of the variables that are associated with a program. So, if we declare a variable called count to be of type int, then the system would assign location(s) in memory to hold the value of count while the program is executing. This location might be at address 500, for example, inside the computer's memory.

Luckily, one of the advantages of higher-level programming languages such as C is that we don't need to concern ourselves with the particular memory addresses that are assigned to variables—they are automatically handled by the system. However, the knowledge that a unique memory address is asociated with each variable will help you to understand the way pointers operate.

Whenever we apply the address operator to a variable in C, the value that is generated is the actual address of that variable inside the computer's memory. (Obviously, this is where the address operator gets its name.) So the statement

```
int_pointer = &count;
```

will assign to int_pointer the address in the computer's memory that has been assigned to the variable count. So if count were located at address 500, then this statement would assign the value 500 to int_pointer.

Applying the indirection operator to a pointer variable, as in the expression

```
*int_pointer
```

has the effect of treating the value contained in the pointer variable as a memory address. The value stored at that memory address is then fetched and interpreted in accordance with the type declared for the pointer variable. So if int_pointer were of type pointer to int, then the value stored in the memory address given by *int_pointer would be interpreted as an integer by the system.

At times, system's programmers must access particular locations inside the computer's memory. In such cases, this knowledge of the way that pointer variables operate will prove helpful.

As you can see from this chapter, the pointer is a very powerful construct in C. The flexibility in defining pointer variables extends beyond those illustrated in this chapter. For example, you can define a pointer to a pointer, and even a pointer to a pointer to a pointer. These types of constructs are beyond the scope of this book, although they are simply logical extensions of everything you've learned about pointers in this chapter.

The topic of pointers is probably the hardest for novices to grasp. You should reread any sections of this chapter that still seem unclear before proceeding. Solving the exercises that follow also will help you to understand the material.

Exercises

1. If you have access to a computer facility that supports the C programming language, type in and run the 15 programs presented in this chapter. Compare the output produced by each program with the output presented after each program.

2. Write a function called insert_entry to insert a new entry into a linked list. Have the procedure take as arguments a pointer to the list entry to be inserted (of type struct entry as defined in this chapter), and a pointer to an element in the list *after* which the new entry is to be inserted.

3. The function developed in the previous exercise only inserts an element after an existing element in the list, thereby preventing us from inserting a new entry at the front of the list. How can we use this same function and yet overcome this problem? (Hint: think about setting up a special structure to point to the beginning of the list.)

4. Write a function called `remove_entry` to remove an `entry` from a linked list. The sole argument to the procedure should be a pointer into the list. Have the function remove the entry *after* the one pointed to by the argument. (Why can't we remove the entry pointed to by the argument?) You will need to use the special structure you set up in the previous exercise to handle the special case of removing the first element from the list.

5. A *doubly linked list* is a list in which each entry contains a pointer to the preceding entry in the list as well as a pointer to the next entry in the list. Define the appropriate structure definition for a doubly linked list entry and then write a small program that implements a small doubly linked list and prints out the elements of the list.

6. Develop `insert_entry` and `remove_entry` functions for a doubly linked list that are similar in function to those developed in previous exercises for a singly linked list. Why can our `remove_entry` function now take as its argument a direct pointer to the entry to be removed from the list?

7. Write a pointer version of the `sort` function from Chapter 8. Make sure that pointers are exclusively used by the function, including as index variables in the loops.

8. Write a function called `sort3` to sort three integers into ascending order. (This function is not to be implemented with arrays.)

9. Rewrite the `read_line` function from Chapter 10 so that it uses a character pointer rather than an array.

10. Rewrite the `compare_strings` function from Chapter 10 to use character pointers instead of arrays.

11. Given the definition of a `date` structure as defined in this chapter, write a function called `date_update` that takes a pointer to a `date` structure as its argument and that updates the structure to the following day (see Program 9.4).

12. Given the following declarations:

```
char   *message = "Programming in C is fun\n";
char   message2[] = "You said it\n";
char   *format  = "x = %i\n";
int    x = 100;
```

determine whether or not each `printf` call from the following sets is valid and produces the same output as other calls from the set.

```
/*** set 1 ***/
printf ("Programming in C is fun\n");
printf ("%s", "Programming in C is fun\n");
printf ("%s", message);
printf (message);

/*** set 2 ***/
printf ("You said it\n");
printf ("%s", message2);
printf (message2);
printf ("%s", &message2[0]);

/*** set 3 ***/
printf ("said it\n");
printf (message2 + 4);
printf ("%s", message2 + 4);
printf ("%s", &message2[4]);

/*** set 4 ***/
printf ("x = %i\n", x);
printf (format, x);
```

12

C H A P T E R

Operations on Bits

On several occasions, we have remarked that the C language was developed with systems programming applications in mind. Pointers are the perfect case in point, since they give the programmer an enormous amount of control over and access into the computer's memory. Along these same lines, systems programmers frequently must get in and "twiddle with the bits" of particular computer words. In this area, C once again shines above other programming languages, such as Pascal, because it provides a host of operators specifically designed for performing operations on individual bits.

In our discussions in the previous chapter, we talked about the concept of a *byte*. On most computer systems, a byte consists of eight smaller units called *bits*. A bit can assume either of two values: 1 or 0. So a byte stored at address 1000 in a computer's memory, for example, might be conceptualized as a string of eight binary digits as shown:

```
01100100
```

The rightmost bit of a byte is known as the *least significant* or *low-order* bit, while the leftmost bit is known as the *most significant* or *high-order* bit. If we treat the string of bits as an integer, then the rightmost bit of the above byte represents 2^0 or 1, the bit immediately to its left represents 2^1 or 2, the next bit 2^2 or 4, and so on. Therefore, the preceding binary number represents the value $2^2 + 2^5 + 2^6 = 4 + 32 + 64 = 100$ decimal.

The representation of negative numbers is handled slightly differently. Most computers represent such numbers using a so-called "twos complement" notation. Using this notation, the leftmost bit represents the *sign* bit. If this bit is 1, the number is negative; otherwise, the bit is 0 and the number is positive. The remaining bits represent the value of the number. In twos complement notation, the value -1 is represented by all bits being equal to 1:

`11111111`

A convenient way to convert a negative number from decimal to binary is to first add 1 to the value, express the absolute value of the result in binary, and then "complement" all the bits; that is, change all 1s to 0s and 0s to 1s. So, for example, to convert -5 to binary, 1 is added, which gives -4; 4 expressed in binary is 00000100, and complementing the bits produces 11111011.

To convert a negative number from binary back to decimal, first complement all of the bits, convert the result to decimal, change the sign of the result, and then subtract 1.

Given the above discussion about twos complement representation, the largest positive number that can be stored into n bits is $2^{n-1}-1$. So in eight bits, we can store a value up to $2^7 - 1$, or 127. Similarly, the smallest negative number that can be stored into n bits is -2^{n-1}, which in an eight-bit byte comes to -128. (Can you figure out why the largest positive and smallest negative values are not of the same magnitude?)

On the IBM PC, integers occupy two contiguous bytes, or 16 bits, in the computer's memory. The largest positive value that can therefore be stored into such an integer is $2^{15}-1$ or 32,767, while the smallest negative number that can be stored is -32,768.

In Chapter 4, "Variables, Data Types, and Arithmetic Expressions," we introduced the `unsigned` modifier and mentioned that it could be used to effectively increase the accuracy of a variable. This is because the leftmost bit is no longer needed to store the sign of the number, since we are only dealing with positive integers. This "extra" bit is used to increase the magnitude of the value stored in that variable by a factor of 2. More precisely, n bits can now be used to store values up to 2^n-1. On a machine that stores integers in 16 bits, this means that unsigned integers can range in value from 0 through 65,535.

Bit Operators

Now that we have completed some preliminaries, it is time to discuss the various bit operators that are available. The operators that C provides for manipulating bits are presented in Table 12.1.

Table 12.1. Bit operators.

Symbol	Operation
&	Bitwise AND
|	Bitwise Inclusive-OR
^	Bitwise-OR
~	Ones Complement
<<	Left Shift
>>	Right Shift

All the operators listed in Table 12.1, with the exception of the ones complement operator ~, are binary operators and as such take two operands. Bit operations can be performed on any type of integer value in C—be it short or long, signed or unsigned—and on characters, but cannot be performed on floating-point values.

The Bitwise AND Operator

When two values are ANDed in C, the binary representations of the values are compared bit by bit. Each corresponding bit that is a 1 in the first value *and* a 1 in the second value produces a 1 in the corresponding bit position of the result; anything else produces a 0. If *b1* and *b2* represent corresponding bits of the two operands, then the following table, called a *truth table*, shows the result of *b1* ANDed with *b2* for all possible values of *b1* and *b2*.

b1	b2	b1 & b2
0	0	0
0	1	0
1	0	0
1	1	1

So, for example, if w1 and w2 are defined as ints, and w1 is set equal to 25 and w2 is set equal to 77, then the C statement

```
w3 = w1 & w2;
```

will assign the value 9 to w3. This can be more easily seen by treating the values of w1, w2, and w3 as binary numbers. Here we will assume that we are dealing with an `int` size of 16 bits.

```
w1      0000000000011001      25
w2      0000000001001101    & 77
        - - - - - - - - - - - - - - - - - - - - - - - - -
w3      0000000000001001       9
```

If you think about the way the logical AND operator && works (TRUE only if both operands are TRUE), you will be able to more easily remember the way the bitwise AND operator works. Incidentally, make sure that you don't get these two operators confused! The logical AND operator && is used in logical expressions for producing a TRUE/FALSE result; it does not perform a bitwise AND.

Bitwise ANDing is frequently used for masking operations. That is, this operator can be used to easily set specific bits of a data item to 0. For example, the statement

```
w3 = w1 & 3;
```

will assign to w3 the value of w1 bitwise ANDed with the constant 3. This has the effect of setting all of the bits in w3, other than the rightmost two bits, to 0, and of preserving the rightmost two bits from w1.

As with all binary arithmetic operators in C, the binary bit operators can also be used as assignment operators by tacking on an equal sign. So the statement

```
word &= 15;
```

will perform the same function as

```
word = word & 15;
```

and will have the effect of setting all but the rightmost four bits of word to 0.

When using constants in performing bitwise operations, it is usually more convenient to express the constants in either octal or hexadecimal notation. The choice as to which to use is usually influenced by the size of the data that you are dealing with. For example, when dealing with 16-bit computers, hexadecimal notation is often used, since 16 is an even multiple of 4 (the number of bits in a hexadecimal digit).

The following program is presented to illustrate the bitwise AND operator. Since we are dealing with only positive values in this program, we have declared all integers as `unsigned int` variables.

Program 12.1

```
/* Demonstration of the bitwise AND operator */
#include <stdio.h>
main ()
{
    unsigned int  word1 = 077u, word2 = 0150u,
                  word3 = 0210u;

    printf ("%o  ", word1 & word2);
    printf ("%o  ", word1 & word1);
    printf ("%o  ", word1 & word2 & word3);
    printf ("%o\n", word1 & 1);
}
```

Program 12.1 OUTPUT

```
50  77  10  1
```

You will recall that if an integer constant has a leading 0 it represents an octal (base 8) constant in C. Therefore, the three unsigned ints, word1, word2, and word3, are given initial *octal* values of 077, 0150, and 0210, respectively. Recall also from Chapter 4, "Variables, Data Types, and Arithmetic Expressions," that if a u or U follows an integer constant, it is treated as unsigned.

The first printf call displays octal 50 as the result of bitwise ANDing word1 with word2. The following depicts how this value was calculated:

```
word1    ... 000 111 111      077
word2    ... 001 101 000   & 0150
         -------------------------
         ... 000 101 000      050
```

We have shown only the rightmost nine bits of the above values, since all bits to the left are 0. The binary numbers have been arranged in groups of three bits to make it easier to translate back and forth between binary and octal.

The second printf call results in the display of octal 77, which is the result of ANDing word1 with itself. By definition, any quantity x, when ANDed with itself, will produce x.

The third printf call displays the result of ANDing word1, word2, and word3 together. The operation of bitwise ANDing is such that it makes no difference whether an expression such as a & b & c is evaluated as (a & b) & c or as a &

(b & c), but for the record, evaluation proceeds from left to right. It is left as an exercise to you to verify that the displayed result of octal 10 is the correct result of ANDing word1 with word2 with word3.

The final printf call has the effect of extracting the rightmost bit of word1. This is actually another way of testing if an integer is even or odd, since that rightmost bit of any odd integer is 1 and of any even integer is 0. Therefore when the if statement

```
if  ( word1 & 1 )
    . . .
```

gets executed, the expression will be TRUE if word1 is odd (since the result of the AND operation will be 1) and FALSE if it is even (since the result of the AND operation will be 0). (Note: On machines that use a ones complement representation for numbers, this will not work for negative integers.)

The Bitwise Inclusive-OR Operator

When two values are bitwise Inclusive-ORed in C, the binary representation of the two values are once again compared bit by bit. This time, each bit that is a 1 in the first value *or* a 1 in the second value will produce a 1 in the corresponding bit of the result. The truth table for the Inclusive-OR operator is shown next.

$b1$	$b2$	$b1 \mid b2$
0	0	0
0	1	1
1	0	1
1	1	1

So if w1 is an unsigned int equal to octal 0431 and w2 is an unsigned int equal to octal 0152, then a bitwise Inclusive-OR of w1 and w2 will produce a result of octal 0573 as shown:

```
w1    ... 100  011  001       0431
w2    ... 001  101  010   |   0152
      - - - - - - - - - - - - - - - - - - - - - - -
      ... 101  111  011       0573
```

As was pointed out with the bitwise AND operator, be sure not to confuse the operation of bitwise ORing (|) with that of logical ORing (||), the latter operation being used to determine if either of two logical values is TRUE.

Bitwise Inclusive-ORing, frequently called just bitwise ORing, is used to set some specified bits of a word to 1. For example, the statement

```
w1 = w1 | 07;
```

will set the three rightmost bits of w1 to 1, regardless of the state of these bits before the operation was performed. Of course, we could have used a special assignment operator in the statement, as in

```
w1 |= 07;
```

We will defer presentation of a program example illustrating the use of the Inclusive-OR operator until later.

The Bitwise Exclusive-OR Operator

The bitwise Exclusive-OR operator, which is often called the XOR operator, works as follows: For corresponding bits of the two operands, if either bit is a 1—but not both—the corresponding bit of the result is a 1; otherwise it is a 0. The truth table for this operator is as shown.

$b1$	$b2$	$b1 \wedge b2$
0	0	0
0	1	1
1	0	1
1	1	0

If w1 and w2, were set equal to octal 0536 and octal 0266, respectively, then the result of w1 Exclusive-ORed with w2 would be octal 0750, as illustrated:

```
w1      ...  101  011  110      0536
w2      ...  010  110  110    ^ 0266
- - - - - - - - - - - - - - - - - - - - - - - - - - -
        ...  111  101  000      0750
```

One interesting property of the Exclusive-OR operator is that any value Exclusive-ORed with itself produces 0. This trick is frequently used by assembly language programmers as a fast way to set a value to 0 or to compare two values to see if they are equal. This method is not recommended for use in C programs, however, as it won't save any time and will most likely make the program more obscure.

Another interesting application of the Exclusive-OR operator is that it can be used to effectively exchange two values without the need for an extra memory location. We all know that normally we would interchange two integers called i1 and i2 with a sequence of statements such as

```
temp = i1;
i1 = i2;
i2 = temp;
```

(We assume in the above sequence of statements that temp has been appropriately declared.) Using the Exclusive-OR operator, we can exchange values without the need of the temporary storage location:

```
i1 ^= i2;
i2 ^= i1;
i1 ^= i2;
```

It is left as an exercise to you to verify that the above statements do in fact succeed in interchanging the values of i1 and i2.

The Ones Complement Operator

The ones complement operator is a unary operator, and its effect is to simply "flip" the bits of its operand. Each bit of the operand that is a 1 is changed to a 0, and each bit that is a 0 is changed to a 1. The truth table is provided below simply for the sake of completeness.

$b1$	$\sim b1$
0	1
1	0

If w1 is an int 16 bits long, and is set equal to octal 0122457, then taking the ones complement of this value will produce a result of octal 0055320.

```
w1   0   010   010   100   101   111      0122457
w2   0   101   101   011   010   000      0055320
```

The ones complement operator (~) should not be confused with the arithmetic minus operator (-) or with the logical negation operator (!). So if w1 is defined as an int, and set equal to 0, then -w1 still results in 0. If we apply the ones complement operator to w1, we end up with w1 being set to all ones, which is -1 when treated as a signed value in twos complement notation. Finally, applying the logical negation operator to w1 produces the result TRUE (1), since w1 is FALSE (0).

The ones complement operator is useful when we don't know the precise bit size of the quantity that we are dealing with in an operation. Its use can help make a program more portable—in other words, less dependent on the particular computer that the program is running on and therefore easier to get running on a different machine. For example, in order to set the low-order bit of an int called w1 to 0, we can AND w1 with an int consisting of all 1s except for a single 0 in the rightmost bit. So a statement in C such as

```
w1 &= 0177776;
```

will work fine on machines in which an integer is represented by 16 bits. However, on machines that represent integers using more than 16 bits, this statement will not produce the desired results.

If we replace the preceding statement with

```
w1 &= ~1;
```

then w1 will get ANDed with the correct value on any machine, since the ones complement of 1 will be calculated and will consist of as many leftmost one bits as are necessary to fill the size of an int (15 leftmost bits on a 16-bit integer machine, and 31 leftmost bits on a 32-bit integer machine).

Now it's time to present a program that summarizes the various bitwise operators presented thus far. Before proceeding, however, we should mention the precedences of the various operators. The AND, OR, and Exclusive-OR operators each have lower precedence than any of the arithmetic or relational operators, but higher precedence than the logical AND and logical OR operators. The bitwise AND is higher in precedence than the bitwise Exclusive OR, which in turn is higher in precedence than the bitwise OR. The unary ones complement operator has higher precedence than *any* binary operator. For a summary of these operator precedences, see Appendix A, "ANSI C Language Summary."

Program 12.2

```
/* Bitwise operators illustrated */
#include <stdio.h>
main ()
{
    unsigned int   w1 = 0525u, w2 = 0707u, w3 = 0122u;

    printf ("%o\t%o\t%o\n", w1 & w2, w1 ¦ w2, w1 ^ w2);
    printf ("%o\t%o\t%o\n", ~w1, ~w2, ~w3);
    printf ("%o\t%o\t%o\n", w1 ^ w1, w1 & ~w2, w1 ¦ w2 ¦ w3);
    printf ("%o\t%o\n", w1 ¦ w2 & w3, w1 ¦ w2 & ~w3);
    printf ("%o\t%o\n", ~(~w1 & ~w2), ~(~w1 ¦ ~w2));

    w1 ^= w2;
    w2 ^= w1;
    w1 ^= w2;
    printf ("w1 = %o, w2 = %o\n", w1, w2);
}
```

Program 12.2 OUTPUT

```
505     727     222
177252 177070  177655
0       20      727
527     725
727     505
w1 = 707, w2 = 525
```

(We used the tab character `'\t'` in the display of the program's results to help make the output more readable.)

You should work out each of the operations from Program 12.2 with a paper and pencil to verify that you understand how the results were obtained. The program was run on a computer that uses 16 bits to represent an `int`.

In the fourth `printf` call, it is important to remember that the bitwise AND operator has higher precedence than the bitwise OR, because this fact influences the resulting value of the expression.

The fifth `printf` call illustrates DeMorgan's rule, namely that `~(~a & ~b)` is equal to `a | b`, and that `~(~a | ~b)` is equal to `a & b`. The sequence of statements that follow next in the program verifies that the exchange operation works as discussed in the section on the Exclusive-OR operator.

The Left Shift Operator

When a left shift operation is performed on a value, the bits contained in the value are literally shifted to the left. Associated with this operation is the number of places (bits) that the value is to be shifted. Bits that are shifted out through the high-order bit of the data item are lost, and 0s are always shifted in through the low-order bit of the value. So if `w1` is equal to 3, then the expression

```
w1 = w1 << 1;
```

which can also be expressed as

```
w1 <<= 1;
```

will result in 3 being shifted 1 place to the left, which will result in 6 being assigned to `w1`:

```
w1           ... 000 011     03
w1 << 1   ... 000 110     06
```

The operand on the left of the `<<` operator is the value to be shifted, while the operand on the right is the number of bit positions the value is to be shifted by. If we were to shift `w1` one more place to the left, we would end up with octal 014 as the value of `w1`:

```
w1           ... 000 110     06
w1 << 1   ... 001 100     014
```

Left shifting actually has the effect of multiplying the value that is shifted by two. In fact, some C compilers will automatically perform multiplication by a power of two by left shifting the value the appropriate number of places, since shifting is a much faster operation than multiplication on most computers.

A program example illustrating the left shift operator will be presented after the right shift operator has been described.

The Right Shift Operator

As implied from its name, the right shift operator >> shifts the bits of a value to the right. Bits shifted out of the low order bit of the value are lost. Right shifting an unsigned value will always result in 0s being shifted in on the left; that is, through the high-order bits. What is shifted in on the left for signed values depends on the sign of the value that is being shifted and also on how this operation is implemented on your computer system. If the sign bit is 0 (meaning the value is positive), 0s will be shifted in no matter what machine we are talking about. However, if the sign bit is 1, on some machines 1s will be shifted in, and on others 0s will be shifted in. This former type of operation is known as an *arithmetic* right shift, while the latter is known as a *logical* right shift.

QUICK TIP

Never make any assumptions about whether a system implements an arithmetic or a logical right shift. A program that shifts signed values right may work correctly on one system and then fail on another due to this type of assumption.

If w1 is an unsigned int, which is represented in 16 bits, and w1 is set equal to octal 0155667, then shifting w1 one place to the right with the statement

```
w1 >>= 1;
```

will set w1 equal to octal 0066733:

```
w1          1   101 101 110 110 111     0155667
w1 >> 1     0   110 110 111 011 011     0066733
```

If w1 were declared to be a (signed) int, then the same result would be produced on some computers; on others, the result would be 0166733 if the operation were performed as an arithmetic right shift.

It should be noted that the ANSI C language does not produce a defined result if an attempt is made to shift a value to the left or right by an amount that is greater than or equal to the number of bits in the size of the data item. So on a machine that represents integers in 32 bits, for example, shifting an integer to the left or right by 32 or more bits is not guaranteed to produce a defined result in your program. You should also note that if you shift a value by a negative amount, the result is also undefined.

Now it is time to put the left and right shift operators to work in an actual program example. Some computers have a single machine instruction to shift a value to the left if the shift count is positive and to the right if the shift count is negative. Let us now write a function in C to mimic this type of operation. We can have the function take two arguments: the value to be shifted and the shift count. If the shift count is positive, the value will be shifted left the designated number of places; otherwise, the value will be shifted right the number of places as specified by the absolute value of the shift count.

Program 12.3

```
/* Function to shift an unsigned int left if
   the count is positive, and right if negative */
#include <stdio.h>
unsigned int  shift (unsigned int  value, int  n)
{
    if ( n > 0 )       /* left shift */
        value <<= n;
    else               /* right shift */
        value >>= -n;

    return (value);
}

main ()
{
    unsigned int  w1 = 0177777u, w2 = 0444u;
    unsigned int  shift (unsigned int  value, int  n);

    printf ("%o\t%o\n", shift (w1, 5), w1 << 5);
    printf ("%o\t%o\n", shift (w1, -6), w1 >> 6);
    printf ("%o\t%o\n", shift (w2, 0), w2 >> 0);
    printf ("%o\n", shift (shift (w1, -3), 3));
}
```

Program 12.3 OUTPUT

```
177740 177740
1777    1777
444     444
177770
```

The shift function shown in Program 12.3 declares the type of the argument value to be unsigned int, thus ensuring that a right shift of value will be zero filled; in other words, performed as a logical right shift.

If the value of n, which is the shift count, is greater than zero, the function shifts value left n bits. If n is negative (or zero), the function performs a right shift, where the number of places that the value is shifted is obtained by negating the value of n.

The first call to the shift function from the main routine specifies that the value of w1 is to be left shifted five bits. The printf call that displays the result of the call to the shift function also displays the result of directly shifting w1 left five places so that these values can be compared.

The second call to the shift function has the effect of shifting w1 six places to the right. The result returned by the function is identical to the result obtained by directly shifting w1 to the right six places, as verified by the program's output.

In the third call to shift, a shift count of 0 is specified. In this case, the shift function will perform a right shift of value by 0 bits, which, as you can see from the program's output, has no effect on the value.

The last printf call illustrates nested function calls to the shift function. The innermost call to shift is executed first. This call specifies that w1 is to be shifted right three places. The result of this function call, which is 0017777, is then passed to the shift function to be shifted to the left three places. As you can see from the program's output, this has the net effect of setting the low-order three bits of w1 to 0. (Of course, we know by now that this could also have been done by simply ANDing w1 with ~7.)

For the next program example, which ties together some of the bit operations we have presented in this chapter, we will develop a function to rotate a value to the left or right. The process of rotation is similar to shifting, except that when a value is rotated to the left, the bits that are shifted out of the high-order bits are shifted back into the low-order bits. When a value is rotated to the right, the bits that are shifted out of the low-order bits of the value are shifted back into the high-order bits. So, if we are dealing with 16-bit unsigned integers, the value octal 0100000 rotated to the left by one bit would produce octal 0000001, since the 1 from the sign bit that would normally be lost by a left shift of one bit would be brought around and shifted back into the low-order bit.

We will have our function take two arguments: the first, the value to be rotated, and the second, the number of bits the object is to be rotated by. If this second argument is positive, then we will rotate the value to the left; otherwise, we will rotate the value to the right.

We can adopt a fairly straightforward approach to implementing our rotate function. For example, in order to compute the result of rotating x to the left by n bits, where x is of type int and n ranges from 0 to the number of bits in an int minus 1, we can extract the leftmost n bits of x, shift x to the left by n bits, and then put the extracted bits back into *x* at the right. A similar algorithm also can be used to implement the right rotate function.

The program that follows implements the rotate function using the algorithm described previously. This function makes the assumption that an int uses 16 bits on the computer. Exercises at the end of the chapter show one way to write this function so that this assumption does not have to be made.

Program 12.4

```
/* Rotation of integers */
#include <stdio.h>
main ()
{
    unsigned int  w1 = 0xa1b5u, w2 = 0xff22u;
    unsigned int  rotate (unsigned int  value, int  n);

    printf ("%x\n", rotate (w1, 4));
    printf ("%x\n", rotate (w1, -4));
    printf ("%x\n", rotate (w2, 8));
    printf ("%x\n", rotate (w2, -2));
    printf ("%x\n", rotate (w1, 0));
    printf ("%x\n", rotate (w1, 20));
}

/* Function to rotate an unsigned int left or right */

unsigned int  rotate (unsigned int  value, int  n)
{
    unsigned int  result, bits;

    /* scale down the shift count to a defined range */

    if  ( n > 0 )
        n = n % 16;
    else
        n = -(-n % 16);

    if  ( n == 0 )
        result = value;
    else if ( n > 0 )      /* left rotate */
    {
        bits = value >> (16 - n);
        result = value << n  ¦  bits;
    }
    else                    /* right rotate */
    {
        n = -n;
        bits = value << (16 - n);
        result = value >> n  ¦  bits;
```

```
    }

    return (result);
}
```

Program 12.4 OUTPUT

```
1b5a
5a1b
22ff
bfc8
a1b5
1b5a
```

The function first ensures that the shift count, n, is valid. The code

```
if  ( n > 0 )
    n = n % 16;
else
    n = -(-n % 16);
```

checks first to see if n is positive. If it is, the value of n modulo the size of an int (assumed to be 16 in this example) is calculated and stored back inside n. This places the shift count in the range of 0 through 15. If n is negative, its value is negated before the modulus operator is applied. This is done because ANSI C does not define what the sign of the result of applying the modulus operator to a negative value is. Your machine can produce either a positive or negative result. By negating the value first, we ensure the result is positive. We then apply the unary minus operator to the result to turn it negative again; that is, within the range of values -15 through 0.

If the adjusted shift count is 0, the function simply assigns value to result. Otherwise, it proceeds with the rotation.

An n-bit rotation to the left is divided into three steps by the function. First, the n leftmost bits of value are extracted and shifted to the right. This is done by shifting value to the right by the size of an int (in our case, 16) minus n. Next, value is shifted n bits to the left, and finally, the extracted bits are ORed back in. A similar procedure is followed to rotate value to the right.

In the main routine, we resorted to the use of hexadecimal notation for a change. The first call to the rotate function specifies that the value of w1 is to be rotated four bits to the left. As can be seen from the program's output, the hexadecimal value 1b5a is returned by the rotate function, which is in fact a1b5 rotated to the left four bits (which conveniently happens to be the number of bits in a hexadecimal digit).

The second call to the `rotate` function has the effect of rotating the value of w1 four bits to the right; and as you can see from the program's output, the 5 that was in the low-order four bits of w1 was correctly rotated around into the high-order four bits.

The next two calls to the `rotate` function do similar things with the value of w2 and are fairly self-explanatory. The next-to-last call to `rotate` specifies a rotate count of 0. The program's output verifies that in such a case the function simply returns the value unchanged.

The last call to `rotate` specifies a left rotate 20 places. This has the net effect of rotating the value left four bits (20% of 16 is 4).

Bit Fields

With the bit operators discussed, we can proceed to perform all sorts of sophisticated operations on bits. Bit operations are frequently performed on data items that contain packed information. Just as a `short int` can be used to conserve memory space on some computers, so can we pack information into the bits of a byte or word if we do not need to use the entire byte or word to represent the data. For example, flags that are used for a Boolean TRUE or FALSE condition can be represented in a single bit on a computer. Declaring a `char` variable that will be used as a flag will use eight bits (one byte) on most computer systems. And if we needed to store many flags inside a large table, then the amount of memory that would be wasted could become significant.

There are two methods in C that can be used to pack information together to make better use of memory. One way is to simply represent the data inside a normal `int`, for example, and then access the desired bits of the `int` using the bit operators we have just described. Another way is to define a structure of packed information using a C construct known as a *bit field*.

To illustrate how the first method can be used, suppose we needed to pack five data values into a single word because we had to maintain a very large table of these values in memory. Assume that three of these data values are flags, which we will call *f1*, *f2*, and *f3*; the fourth value is an integer called *type*, which ranges from 1 through 12; and the final value an integer called *index*, which ranges from 0 to 500.

In order to store the values of the flags *f1*, *f2*, and *f3*, we would only require three bits of storage, one bit for the TRUE/FALSE value of each flag. To store the value of the integer *type*, which ranges from 1 to 12, would require four bits of storage. Finally, to store the value of the integer *index*, which can assume a value from 0 to 500, we would need nine bits. Therefore, the total amount of storage needed to store the five data values *f1*, *f2*, *f3*, *type*, and *index*, would (conveniently) be 16 bits. We could define an integer variable that could be used to contain all five of these values, as in

```
unsigned int  packed_data;
```

and could then arbitrarily assign specific bits or *fields* inside `packed_data` to be used to store the five data values. One such assignment is depicted in Figure 12.1, which assumes that the size of `packed_data` is 16 bits. If it were larger than 16 bits, then we could still conceptualize these field assignments as occupying the 16 rightmost bits of the integer.

Figure 12.1. *Bit field assignments in* `packed_data`.

We can now apply the correct sequence of bit operations to `packed_data` to set and retrieve values to and from the various fields of the integer. For example, we can set the *type* field of `packed_data` to 7 by shifting the value 7 the appropriate number of places to the left and then ORing it into `packed_data`:

```
packed_data |= 7 << 9;
```

or we can set the *type* field to the value n, where n is between 0 and 15, by the statement

```
packed_data |= n << 9;
```

(To ensure that n is between 0 and 15, we can AND it with 0xf before it is shifted.)

Of course, the preceding statements will work only if we know that the *type* field is zero; otherwise, we must zero it first by ANDing it with a value (frequently called a mask) that consists of 0s in the four bit locations of the *type* field and 1s everywhere else:

```
packed_data &= 0xe1ffu;
```

To save us the bother of having to explicitly calculate the preceding mask, and also to make the operation independent of the size of an integer, the following statement could be used instead to set the type field to zero:

```
packed_data &= ~(0xf << 9);
```

Combining the statements described above, we can set the *type* field of `packed_data` to the value contained in the four low-order bits of n, irrespective of any value previously stored in this field, with the statement

```
packed_data = (packed_data & ~(0xf << 9)) ¦ ((n & 0xf) << 9); .ps +1
```

(Some of the parentheses are superfluous but were added to aid readability.)

You can see how complex the above expression is for accomplishing the relatively simple task of setting the bits in the *type* field to a specified value. Extracting a value from one of these fields is not as bad: The field can be shifted into the low-order bits of the word and then ANDed with a mask of the appropriate bit length. So, to extract the *type* field of packed_data and assign it to n, the statement

```
n = (packed_data >> 9) & 0xf;
```

will do the trick.

The C language does provide a more convenient way of dealing with bit fields. This method uses a special syntax in the structure definition that allows you to define a field of bits and assign a name to that field. Whenever the term "bit fields" is applied to C, it is this approach that is referenced.

In order to define the bit field assignments previously mentioned, we can define a structure called packed_struct, for example, as follows:

```
struct   packed_struct
{
    unsigned int   f1:1;
    unsigned int   f2:1;
    unsigned int   f3:1;
    unsigned int   type:4;
    unsigned int   index:9;
};
```

The structure packed_struct is defined to contain five members. The first member, called f1, is an unsigned int. The :1 that immediately follows the member name specifies that this member is to be stored in one bit. The flags f2 and f3 are similarly defined as being a single bit in length. The member type is defined to occupy four bits, while the member index is defined as being nine bits long.

The C compiler automatically packs the preceding bit field definitions together. The nice thing about this approach is that the fields of a variable defined to be of type packed_struct can now be referenced in the same convenient way normal structure members are referenced. So, if we were to declare a variable called packed_data as follows:

```
struct packed_struct   packed_data;
```

then we could easily set the type field of packed_data to 7 with the simple statement

```
packed_data.type = 7;
```

or we could set this field to the value of n with the similar statement

```
packed_data.type = n;
```

In this last case, we needn't worry about whether the value of n is too large to fit into the type field; only the low-order four bits of n will be assigned to packed_data.type.

Extraction of the value from a bit field is also automatically handled, so the statement

```
n = packed_data.type;
```

will extract the type field from packed_data (automatically shifting it into the low-order bits as required) and assign it to n.

Bit fields can be used in normal expressions and are automatically converted to integers. So the statement

```
i = packed_data.index / 5 + 1;
```

is perfectly valid, as is

```
if  ( packed_data.f2 )
   . . .
```

which tests if flag f2 is TRUE or FALSE. One thing worth noting about bit fields is that there is no guarantee whether the fields are internally assigned from left to right or from right to left. So, if bit fields are assigned from right to left, this would mean that f1 would be in the low-order bit position, f2 in the bit position immediately to the left of f1, and so on. This should not present a problem unless you are dealing with data that was created by a different program or by a different machine. In such cases, you must know how the bit fields are assigned and make the declarations appropriately. We could have defined the structure packed_struct as

```
struct  packed_struct
{
    unsigned int  index:9;
    unsigned int  type:4;
    unsigned int  f3:1;
    unsigned int  f2:1;
    unsigned int  f1:1;
};
```

to achieve the same representation on a machine that assigns fields from right to left as depicted in Figure 12.1. Never make any assumptions about how structure members—whether they contain bit field members or not—are stored.

We can also include normal data types within a structure that contains bit fields. So if we wanted to define a structure that contained an int, a char, and two one-bit flags, the following definition would be valid:

```
struct  table_entry
{
    int          count;
    char         c;
    unsigned int f1:1;
    unsigned int f2:1;
};
```

Certain points are worth mentioning with respect to bit fields. They can only be declared to be of integer type. If just int is used in the declaration, it's implementation dependent whether this is interpreted as a signed or unsigned value. To play it safe, use the explicit declarations signed int or unsigned int. A bit field cannot be dimensioned; that is, we cannot have an array of fields, such as flag:1[5]. Finally, we cannot take the address of a bit field, and therefore, there is obviously no such thing as a type "pointer to bit field."

Bit fields are packed into *units* as they appear in the structure definition, where the size of a *unit* is defined by the implementation and is most likely a word.

The C compiler will *not* rearrange the bit field definitions to try to optimize storage space.

A bit field that has no name can be specified to cause bits inside a word to be skipped. So the definition

```
struct  x_entry
{
    unsigned int  type:4;
    unsigned int  :3;
    unsigned int  count:9;
};
```

would define a structure x_entry that contained a four-bit field called type and a nine-bit field called count. The unnamed field specifies that three bits separate the type from the count field.

A final point concerning the specification of fields concerns the special case of an unnamed field of length 0. This may be used to force alignment of the next field in the structure at the start of a unit boundary.

This concludes our discussion of bit operations in C. You can see how much power and flexibility the C language provides for the efficient manipulation of bits.

See Chapter 14, "More on Data Types," for a discussion on what happens when you perform bitwise operations between two values of differing integral types, for example between an unsigned long int and a short int.

In the next chapter, we will see how another powerful feature known as the *preprocessor* can be used to effectively customize the C language to one's particular tastes and to enable programs to be developed that are easier to write and to read.

Exercises

1. If you have access to a computer facility that supports the C programming language, type in and run the four programs presented in this chapter. Compare the output produced by each program with the output presented after each program.

2. Write a program that determines whether your particular computer performs an arithmetic or a logical right shift.

3. Given that the expression ~0 produces an integer that contains all 1s, write a function called `int_size` that returns the number of bits contained in an `int` on your particular machine.

4. Using the result obtained in Exercise 3, modify the `rotate` function from Program 12.4 so that it no longer makes any assumptions about the size of an `int`.

5. Write a function called `bit_test` that takes two arguments: an `unsigned int` and a bit number n. Have the function return 1 bit number n if it is on inside the word, and 0 if it is off. Assume that bit number 0 references the leftmost bit inside the integer. Also write a corresponding function called `bit_set` that takes two arguments: an `unsigned int` and a bit number n. Have the function return the result of turning bit n on inside the integer.

6. Write a function called `bitpat_search` that looks for the occurrence of a specified pattern of bits inside an `unsigned int`. The function should take three arguments and should be called as shown:

```
bitpat_search (source, pattern, n)
```

The function will search the integer `source`, starting at the leftmost bit, to see if the rightmost n bits of `pattern` occur in `source`. If the pattern is found, then have the function return the number of the bit that the pattern begins at, where the leftmost bit is bit number 0. If the pattern is not found, then have the function return -1. So, for example, the call

```
index = bitpat_search (0xe1f4, 0x5, 3);
```

will cause the `bitpat_search` function to search the number 0xe1f4 (= 1110 0001 1111 0100 binary) for the occurrence of the three-bit pattern 0x5 (= 101 binary). The function would return 11 to indicate that the pattern was found in the source beginning with bit number 11.

Make sure that the function makes no assumptions about the size of an `int` (see Exercise 3, this chapter).

7. Write a function called `bitpat_get` to extract a specified set of bits. Have it take three arguments: the first an `unsigned int`, the second an integer starting bit number, and the third a bit count. Using the convention that bit numbering starts at 0 with the leftmost bit, extract the specified number of bits from the first argument and return the result. So the call

    ```
    bitpat_get (x, 0, 3)
    ```

    would extract the three leftmost bits from x. The call

    ```
    bitpat_get (x, 3, 5)
    ```

    would extract five bits starting with the fourth bit in from the left.

8. Write a function called `bitpat_set` to set a specified set of bits to a particular value. The function should take four arguments: a pointer to an `unsigned int` in which the specified bits are to be set; another `unsigned int` containing the value that the specified bits are to be set to, right adjusted in the `unsigned int`; a third `int` that specifies the starting bit number (with the leftmost bit numbered 0); and a fourth `int` specifying the size of the field. So the call

    ```
    bitpat_set (&x, 0, 2, 5);
    ```

    would have the effect of setting the five bits contained in x, beginning with the third bit from the left (bit number 2), to 0. Similarly, the call

    ```
    bitpat_set (&x, 0x55u, 0, 8);
    ```

    would set the eight leftmost bits of x to hexadecimal 55.

    Make no assumptions about the particular size of an `int` (refer to Exercise 3, this chapter).

13

CHAPTER

The Preprocessor

This chapter describes yet another unique feature of the C language that is not found in most other higher-level programming languages. The C preprocessor provides the tools that enable the programmer to develop programs that are easier to develop, easier to read, easier to modify, and easier to transport to a different computer system. The programmer can also use the preprocessor to literally customize the C language to suit a particular programming application or to satisfy one's own programming style. If you have ever had any dealings with a macro processor, you will be one step ahead in our discussions of the C preprocessor.

The preprocessor is a part of the C compilation process that recognizes special statements that may be interspersed throughout a C program. As its name implies, the preprocessor actually analyzes these statements *before* analysis of the C program itself takes place. Preprocessor statements are identified by the presence of a pound sign, `#`, which must be the first nonspace character on the line. As you will see, preprocessor statements have a syntax that is slightly different from that of normal C statements. We will begin by examining the `#define` statement.

The *#define* Statement

One of the primary uses of the #define statement is to assign symbolic names to program constants. The preprocessor statement

```
#define    TRUE    1
```

defines the name TRUE and makes it equivalent to the value 1. The name TRUE can subsequently be used anywhere in the program where the constant 1 could be used. Whenever this name appears, its defined value of 1 will be automatically substituted into the program by the preprocessor. For example, we might have the following C statement that uses the defined name TRUE:

```
game_over = TRUE;
```

This statement would assign the value of TRUE to game_over. We don't need to concern ourselves with the actual value that we defined for TRUE, but since we do know that we defined it to be 1, the preceding statement would have the effect of assigning 1 to game_over. The preprocessor statement

```
#define    FALSE    0
```

would define the name FALSE and would make its subsequent use in the program equivalent to specifying the value 0. Therefore, the statement

```
game_over = FALSE;
```

would assign the value of FALSE to game_over, and the statement

```
if ( game_over == FALSE )
   ...
```

would compare the value of game_over against the defined value of FALSE. Just about the only place that we *cannot* used a defined name is inside a character string; so the statement

```
char   *char_pointer = "TRUE";
```

sets char_pointer pointing to the string "TRUE" and not to the string "1".

A defined name is *not* a variable. Therefore, we cannot assign a value to it, unless the result of substituting the defined value is in fact a variable. Whenever a defined name is used in a program, whatever appears to the right of the defined name in the #define statement gets automatically substituted into the program by the preprocessor.

You will notice that the #define statement has a special syntax: There is no equal sign used to assign the value 1 to TRUE. Furthermore, a semicolon does *not* appear at the end of the statement. Soon you will understand why this special syntax exists. But first, let's take a look at a small program that uses the TRUE and FALSE defines as previously illustrated. The function is_even in the following program simply returns TRUE if its argument is even and FALSE if its argument is odd.

Program 13.1

```
#include <stdio.h>
#define    TRUE     1
#define    FALSE    0

/* Function to determine if an integer is even */
int  is_even (int  number)
{
    int  answer;

    if ( number % 2 == 0 )
        answer = TRUE;
    else
        answer = FALSE;

    return (answer);
}

main ()
{
    int  is_even (int  number);

    if ( is_even (17) == TRUE )
        printf ("yes ");
    else
        printf ("no ");

    if ( is_even (20) == TRUE )
        printf ("yes\n");
    else
        printf ("no\n");
}
```

Program 13.1 OUTPUT

```
no yes
```

The #define statements appear first in the program. This is not required; they can appear *anywhere* in the program. What is required is that a name be defined before it is referenced by the program. Defined names do not behave like variables: There is no such thing as a local define. Once a name has been defined in a program, either inside or outside a function, it can subsequently be used anywhere in the program. Most programmers group their defines at the beginning of the program (or inside an *include* file[1]) where they may be quickly referenced.

The defined name NULL is frequently used by programmers to represent the null pointer.[2]

By including a definition such as

```
#define   NULL   0
```

in a program, we can then write more readable statements, such as

```
while ( list_pointer != NULL )
   ...
```

to set up a while loop that will execute as long as the value of list_pointer is not equal to the null pointer.

As another example of the use of a defined name, suppose we wanted to write three functions to find the area of a circle, the circumference of a circle, and the volume of a sphere of a given radius. Since all of these functions need to use the constant π, which is not a particularly easy constant to remember, it would make sense to define the value of this constant once at the start of the program and then use this value where needed in each function.

Program 13.2

```
/* Function to calculate the area and circumference of a
   circle, and the volume of a sphere of a given radius   */
#include <stdio.h>
#define  PI        3.141592654

double  area (double  r)
{
    return ( PI * r * r );
}
```

---

[1]*Read on to learn how defines can be set up inside special files that you can include in your program.*

[2]*NULL is already defined on your system inside a file named stddef.h. Again, we'll talk more about include files shortly.*

```
double  circumference (double  r)
{
    return ( 2.0 * PI * r );
}

double  volume (double r)
{
    return ( 4.0 / 3.0  *  PI * r * r * r );
}

main ()
{
    double  area (double  r), circumference (double  r),
            volume (double r);

    printf ("radius = 1: %.4f   %.4f   %.4f\n",
        area(1.0), circumference(1.0), volume(1.0));

    printf ("radius = 4.98: %.4f   %.4f   %.4f\n",
        area(4.98), circumference(4.98), volume(4.98));
}
```

Program 13.2 OUTPUT

```
radius = 1: 3.1416   6.2832   4.1888
radius = 4.98: 77.9128   31.2903   517.3403
```

The symbolic name PI is defined as the value 3.141592654 at the beginning of the program. Subsequent use of the name PI inside the area, circumference, and volume functions has the effect of causing its defined value to be automatically substituted at the appropriate point.

Assignment of a constant to a symbolic name frees us from having to remember the particular constant value every time we wish to use it in a program. Furthermore, if we ever needed to change the value of the constant (if perhaps we found out that we were using the wrong value, for example), then we would only have to change the value in one place in the program: in the `#define` statement. Without this approach, we would have to otherwise search throughout the program and explicitly change the value of the constant whenever it was used.

You may have realized that all the defines we have shown so far (`TRUE`, `FALSE`, `NULL`, and `PI`) have been written in capital letters. The reason this is done is to visually distinguish a defined value from a variable. By adopting the convention that all defined names be capitalized, it then becomes easy to determine when a name represents a variable and when it represents a defined name.

QUICK TIP

Write all your preprocessor definitions in capital letters. Even though it's not required, it's conventional among C programmers.

Program Extendability

Using a defined name for a constant value helps to make programs more readily extendable. For example, we know that when we define an array, we must specify the number of elements in the array—either explicitly or implicitly (by specifying a list of initializers). Subsequent program statements will likely use the knowledge of the number of elements contained inside the array. For example, if the array `data_values` were defined in a program as follows:

```
float   data_values[1000];
```

then there is a good chance that we would see statements in the program that used the fact that `data_values` contains 1,000 elements. For instance, in a `for` loop

```
for ( i = 0;  i < 1000;  ++i )
   . . .
```

we would use the value 1000 as an upper bound for sequencing through the elements of the array. A statement such as

```
if ( index  > 999 )
   . . .
```

might also be used in the program to test if an index value exceeded the maximum size of the array.

Now suppose that we had to increase the size of the `data_values` array from 1,000 to 2,000 elements. This would necessitate changing all statements which used the fact that `data_values` contained 1,000 elements.

A better way of dealing with array bounds, which makes programs easier to extend, is to define a name for the upper array bound. So, if we define a name such as `MAXIMUM_DATA_VALUES` with an appropriate `#define` statement:

```
#define  MAXIMUM_DATA_VALUES   1000
```

then we can subsequently define the `data_values` array to contain `MAXIMUM_DATA_VALUES` elements with the following program line:

```
float  data_values[MAXIMUM_DATA_VALUES];
```

Statements that use the upper array bound can also make use of this defined name. To sequence through the elements in `data_values`, for example, the `for` statement

```
for ( i = 0;  i < MAXIMUM_DATA_VALUES;  ++i )
   ...
```

could be used. To test if an index value were greater than the upper bound of the array, we could write

```
if  ( index > MAXIMUM_DATA_VALUES - 1 )
   ...
```

and so on. The nicest thing about the preceding approach is that we can now easily change the size of the `data_values` array to 2,000 elements by simply changing the definition:

```
#define  MAXIMUM_DATA_VALUES   2000
```

And if the program was written to use `MAXIMUM_DATA_VALUES` in all cases where the size of the array was used, the preceding definition would probably be *the only statement in the program that would have to be changed.*

Program Portability

Another nice use of the define is that it helps to make programs more portable from one computer system to another. At times, it may be necessary to use constant values that are related to the particular computer that the program is running on. This might have to do with the use of a particular computer memory address, a file name, or the number of bits contained in a computer word, for example. You will recall that our `rotate` function from Program 12.4 used the knowledge that an `int` contained 16 bits on the machine that the program was executed on.

If we wanted to execute this program on a different machine, such as on a VAX-11 or on an 80386, where an int contains 32 bits, the rotate function would not work correctly.[3] Study the following code. In cases where the program *must* be written to make use of machine dependent values, it makes sense to isolate such dependencies from the program as much as possible. The #define statement can help significantly in this respect. The new version of the rotate function would be easier to port to another machine, even though it is a rather simple case in point.

```c
#include <stdio.h>
#define  INT_SIZE  32    /*** machine dependent !!! ***/

/* Function to rotate an unsigned int left or right */

unsigned int  rotate (unsigned int  value, int  n)
{
    unsigned int  result, bits;

    /* scale down the shift count to a defined range */

    if  ( n > 0 )
        n = n % INT_SIZE;
    else
        n = -(-n % INT_SIZE);

    if  ( n == 0 )
        result = value;
    else if ( n > 0 )      /* left rotate */
    {
        bits = value >> (INT_SIZE - n);
        result = value << n  | bits;
    }
    else                   /* right rotate */
    {
        n = -n;
        bits = value << (INT_SIZE - n) ;
        result = value >> n  | bits;
    }

    return (result);
}
```

---

[3] *Of course, we can write the* rotate *function so that it determines the number of bits in an* int *by itself and therefore is completely machine independent. Refer back to Exercises 3 and 4 at the end of Chapter 12, "Operations on Bits."*

More Advanced Types of Definitions

A definition for a name can include more than a simple constant value. It can include an expression, and, as we will see shortly, just about anything else!

The following defines the name TWO_PI as the product of 2.0 and 3.141592654:

```
#define  TWO_PI    2.0 * 3.141592654
```

We can subsequently use this defined name anywhere in a program where the expression 2.0 * 3.141592654 would be valid. So we could have replaced the return statement of the circumference function from the previous program with the following statement, for example:

```
return ( TWO_PI * r );
```

Whenever a defined name is encountered in a C program, *everything* that appears to the right of the defined name in the #define statement is literally substituted for the name at that point in the program. So, when the C preprocessor encounters the name TWO_PI in the return statement shown on the previous page, it substitutes for this name whatever appeared in the #define statement for this name. Therefore, 2.0 * 3.141592654 is literally substituted by the preprocessor whenever the defined name TWO_PI occurs in the program.

The fact that the preprocessor performs a literal text substitution whenever the defined name occurs explains why you don't usually want to end your #define statement with a semicolon. If you did, then the semicolon would also be substituted into the program wherever the defined name appeared. If we had defined PI as

```
#define  PI        3.141592654;
```

and then written

```
return ( 2.0 * PI * r );
```

the preprocessor would replace the occurrence of the defined name PI by 3.141592654;. The compiler would therefore see this statement as

```
return ( 2.0 * 3.141592654; * r );
```

after the preprocessor had made its substitution, which would result in a syntax error.

QUICK TIP

Remember not to put a semicolon at the end of your define statements unless you're really sure you want one there.

A preprocessor definition does not have to be a valid C expression in its own right—just so long as wherever it is used the resulting expression is valid. For instance, the definition

```
#define  LEFT_SHIFT_8    << 8
```

is legitimate, even though what appears after LEFT_SHIFT_8 is not a syntactically valid expression. We can use our definition of LEFT_SHIFT_8 in a statement such as

```
x = y  LEFT_SHIFT_8;
```

to shift the contents of y to the left eight bits and assign the result to x. Of a much more practical nature, we can set up the definitions

```
#define  AND        &&
#define  OR         ||
```

and then write expressions such as

```
if ( x > 0  AND  x < 10 )
    ...
```

and

```
if ( y == 0  OR  y == value )
    ...
```

We can even include a define for the equality test:

```
#define  EQUALS    ==
```

and then write the statement

```
if  ( y  EQUALS 0  OR  y EQUALS value )
    ...
```

thus removing the very real possibility of mistakenly using a single equals sign for the equality test, as well as improving the statement's readability.

To make things even more interesting, a defined value can itself reference another defined value. So the two defines

```
#define  PI       3.141592654
#define  TWO_PI    2.0 * PI
```

are perfectly valid. The name TWO_PI is defined in terms of the previously defined name PI, thus obviating the need to spell out the value 3.141592654 again.

Reversing the order of the defines, as in

```
#define  TWO_PI    2.0 * PI
#define  PI        3.141592654
```

is also valid. The rule is that you can reference other defined values in your definitions provided everything is defined at the time the defined name is *used* in the program.

Good use of defines will often reduce the need for comments within the program. Consider the following statement:

```
if ( year % 4 == 0  &&  year % 100 != 0  ||  year % 400 == 0 )
   ...
```

We know from previous programs in this book that the above expression tests if the variable year is a leap year or not. Now consider the following define and the subsequent if statement:

```
#define  IS_LEAP_YEAR    year % 4 == 0  &&  year % 100 != 0 \
                    || year % 400 == 0

   ...
if  ( IS_LEAP_YEAR )
   ...
```

Normally, the preprocessor assumes that a definition is contained on a single line of the program. If a second line is needed, then the last character on the line must be a backslash character. This character signals a continuation to the preprocessor and is otherwise ignored. The same holds true for more than one continuation line; each line to be continued must be ended with a backslash character.

The preceding if statement is far easier to understand than the one shown directly before it. There is no need for a comment as the statement is self-explanatory. The purpose that the define IS_LEAP_YEAR serves is analogous to that served by a function. We could have used a call to a function named is_leap_year to achieve the same degree of readability. The choice of which to use in this case is completely subjective. Of course, the is_leap_year function could be made more general than the above define, since it could be written to take an argument. This would enable us to test if the value of any variable were a leap year and not just the variable year as the IS_LEAP_YEAR define restricts us to. Actually, we *can* write a definition to take one or more arguments, which leads us to our next point of discussion.

IS_LEAP_YEAR can be defined to take an argument called y as follows:

```
#define  IS_LEAP_YEAR(y)    y % 4 == 0  &&  y % 100 != 0  \
                    || y % 400 == 0
```

Unlike a function, we do not define the type of the argument y here, since we are merely performing a literal text substitution and not invoking a function.

QUICK TIP

Note that no spaces are permitted between the defined name and the left
parenthesis of the argument list.

With the above definition, we can write a statement such as

```
if ( IS_LEAP_YEAR (year) )
    ...
```

to test if the value of year were a leap year or not, or

```
if ( IS_LEAP_YEAR (next_year) )
    ...
```

to test if the value of next_year were a leap year or not. In the preceding statement, the definition for IS_LEAP_YEAR would be directly substituted inside the
if statement, with the argument next_year replacing y wherever it appeared
in the definition. So the if statement would actually be seen by the compiler
as

```
if ( next_year % 4 == 0  &&  next_year % 100 != 0
        || next_year % 400 == 0 )
    ...
```

In C, definitions are frequently called *macros*. This terminology is more often
applied to definitions that take one or more arguments. An advantage of implementing something in C as a macro, as opposed to as a function, is that in the
former case the type of the argument is not important. For example, consider
a macro called SQUARE that simply squares its argument. The definition

```
#define  SQUARE(x)   x * x
```

enables us to subsequently write statements, such as

```
y = SQUARE (v);
```

to assign the value of v^2 to y. The point to be made here is that v can be of type
int, or of type long, or of type float, for example, and the *same* macro can be
used. If SQUARE were implemented as a function that took an int argument, for
example, we couldn't use it to calculate the square of a double value. One thing
to bear in mind about macro definitions: Since they are directly substituted into
the program by the preprocessor, they will inevitbly use more memory space
than an equivalently defined function. On the other hand, since a function takes
time to call and to return, this overhead is avoided when a macro definition is
used instead.

While the macro definition for SQUARE is straightforward, there is an interesting pitfall that you must be careful to avoid when defining macros. As we have described, the statement

```
y = SQUARE (v);
```

will assign the value of v^2 to y. What do you think would happen in the case of the statement

```
y = SQUARE (v + 1);
```

This statement will *not* assign the value of $(v + 1)^2$ to y as you would expect. Since the preprocessor performs a literal text substitution of the argument into the macro definition, the preceding expression would actually be evaluated as

```
y = v + 1 * v + 1;
```

which would obviously not produce the expected results. In order to handle this situation properly, parentheses are needed in the definition of the SQUARE macro:

```
#define  SQUARE(x)   (x) * (x)
```

While the above definition might look strange, remember that it is the entire expression as given to the SQUARE macro that will be literally substituted wherever x appears in the definition. With our new macro definition for SQUARE, the statement

```
y = SQUARE (v + 1);
```

will then be correctly evaluated as

```
y = (v + 1) * (v + 1);
```

The conditional expression operator can be particularly handy when defining macros. The following defines a macro called MAX that gives the maximum of two values:

```
#define  MAX(a,b)   ( ((a) > (b)) ? (a) : (b) )
```

This macro enables us to subsequently write statements such as

```
limit = MAX (x + y, min_value);
```

which would assign to limit the maximum of x + y and min_value. Parentheses were placed around the entire MAX definition to ensure that an expression such as

```
MAX (x, y) * 100
```

gets evaluated properly; and parentheses were individually placed around each argument to ensure that expressions such as

```
MAX (x & y, z)
```

get correctly evaluated.

The following macro tests if a character is a lowercase letter:

```
#define  IS_LOWER_CASE(x)  ( ((x) >= 'a') && ((x) <= 'z') )
```

and thereby permits expressions such as

```
if ( IS_LOWER_CASE (c)  )
    ...
```

to be written. We can even use this macro in a subsequent macro definition to convert a character from lowercase to uppercase, leaving any non-lowercase character unchanged:

```
#define  TO_UPPER(x) ( IS_LOWER_CASE (x) ? (x) - 'a' + 'A' : (x) )
```

The program loop

```
while ( *string  != '\0' )
{
    *string = TO_UPPER (*string);
    ++string;
}
```

would sequence through the characters pointed to by string, converting any lowercase characters in the string to uppercase.[4]

The # Operator

If you place a # in front of a parameter in a macro definition, the preprocessor will create a constant string out of the macro argument when the macro is invoked. For example, the definition

```
#define  str(x)   # x
```

will cause the subsequent invocation

```
str (testing)
```

to be expanded into

```
"testing"
```

---

[4]*There is a host of functions in the library for doing character tests and conversion. For example,* islower *and* toupper *serve the same purpose as our macros* IS_LOWER_CASE *and* TO_UPPER. *For more details, consult Appendix B, "The Standard C Library."*

by the preprocessor. The `printf` call

```
printf (str (Programming in C is fun.\n));
```

is therefore equivalent to

```
printf ("Programming in C is fun.\n");
```

The preprocessor literally inserts double quotes around the actual macro argument. Any double quotes or backslashes in the argument are preserved by the preprocessor. So

```
str ("hello")
```

produces

```
"\"hello\""
```

A more practical example of the use of the # operator might be in the following macro definition:

```
#define  printint(var)    printf (# var " = %i\n", var)
```

This macro is used to display the value of an integer variable. If `count` is an integer variable with a value of 100, the statement

```
printint (count);
```

will be expanded into

```
printf ("count" " = %i\n", count);
```

which, after string concatenation is performed on the two adjacent strings, will become

```
printf ("count = %i\n", count);
```

So the # operator gives you a means to create a character string out of a macro argument. Incidentally, a space between the # and the parameter name is optional.

The ## Operator

This operator is used in macro definitions to join two *tokens* together. It is preceded (or followed) by the name of a parameter to the macro. The preprocessor takes the actual argument to the macro that is supplied when the macro is invoked and creates a single token out of that argument and whatever token follows (or precedes) the ##.

Suppose, for example, you have a list of variables `x1` through `x100`. You can write a macro called `printx` that simply takes as its argument an integer value 1 through 100 and that displays the corresponding x variable as shown:

```
#define   printx(n)    printf ("%i\n", x ## n)
```

The portion of the define that reads

```
x ## n
```

says to take the tokens that occur before and after the ## (the letter x and the argument n, respectively) and make a single token out of them. So the call

```
printx (20);
```

will be expanded into

```
printf ("%i\n", x20);
```

The `printx` macro can even use the previously defined `printint` macro to get the variable name as well as its value displayed:

```
#define   printx(n)    printint(x ## n)
```

The invocation

```
printx (10);
```

will first expand into

```
printint (x10);
```

and then into

```
printf ("x10" " = %i\n", x10);
```

and finally into

```
printf ("x10 = %i\n", x10);
```

The *#include* Statement

After you have programmed in C for a while, you will find yourself developing your own set of macros that you will want to use in each of your programs. But instead of having to type these macros into each new program you write, the preprocessor enables you to collect all your definitions into a separate file and then *include* them in your program, using the `#include` statement.

Suppose we were writing a series of programs for performing various metric conversions. We might want to set up some defines for all of the various constants that we would need for performing our conversions:

```
#define   INCHES_PER_CENTIMETER    0.394
#define   CENTIMETERS_PER_INCH     1 / INCHES_PER_CENTIMETER

#define   QUARTS_PER_LITER         1.057
#define   LITERS_PER_QUART         1 / QUARTS_PER_LITER
```

```
#define   OUNCES_PER_GRAM       0.035
#define   GRAMS_PER_OUNCE       1 / OUNCES_PER_GRAM
   ...
```

Suppose we entered the above definitions into a separate file on the system called `metric.h`. (The appendage `.h` is commonly used for files such as these, called *header* files.) Any program that subsequently needed to use any of the definitions contained in the `metric.h` file could then do so by simply issuing the preprocessor directive

```
#include "metric.h"
```

This statement must appear before any of the defines contained in `metric.h` are referenced and is typically placed at the beginning of the source file. The preprocessor will look for the specified file on the system and will effectively copy the contents of the file into the program at the precise point that the `#include` statement appears. So any statements inside the file will be treated just as if they had been directly typed into the program at that point.

The double quote signs around the include file name instruct the preprocessor to look for the specified file in one or more file directories (typically first in the same directory that contains the source file, but the actual places the preprocessor searches are system dependent). If the file isn't located, the preprocessor will automatically search other *system* directories as described below.

Enclosing the file name within the characters < and > instead, as in

```
#include <stdio.h>
```

causes the preprocessor to look for the include file in the special system include file directory or directories. Once again, these directories are system dependent. On UNIX systems, the system include file directory is `/usr/include`.

To see how include files are used in an actual program example, type the six defines given above into a file called `metric.h`. Then type in and run the following program in the normal manner.

Program 13.3

```
/* Illustrate the use of the #include statement
   Note: This program assumes that definitions are
   set up in a file called metric.h           */
#include <stdio.h>
#include "metric.h"

main ()
{
    float  liters, gallons;
```

continues

Program 13.3   Continued

```
    printf ("*** Liters to Gallons ***\n\n");
    printf ("Enter the number of liters: ");
    scanf ("%f", &liters);

    gallons = liters * QUARTS_PER_LITER / 4.0;
    printf ("%.2f liters = %.2f gallons\n",
                        liters, gallons);
}
```

Program 13.3 OUTPUT

```
*** Liters to Gallons ***

Enter the number of liters: 55.75
55.75 liters = 14.73 gallons.
```

The preceding example is a rather simple one because it only shows a single defined value (QUARTS_PER_LITER) being referenced from the included file metric.h. Nevertheless, the point is well made: Once the definitions have been entered into metric.h, they can be used in any program that uses an appropriate #include statement.

One of the nicest things about the include file capability is that it enables us to centralize our definitions, thus ensuring that all programs reference the same value. Furthermore, errors discovered in one of the values contained in the include file need only be corrected in that one spot, thus eliminating the need to correct each and every program that uses the value. Any program that referenced the incorrect value would simply have to be recompiled and would not have to be modified.

We can actually put anything we want in an include file—not just #define statements, as may have been implied.

QUICK TIP

Using include files to centralize commonly used preprocessor definitions, structure definitions, prototype declarations, and global variable declarations is good programming technique.

It is permitted to have more than one file included in a program. In such a case, separate #include statements must be used. Be careful, though, because if a statement contained in one include file references a value defined in another include file, then the latter file must be included in the program first.

One last point to be made about include files in this chapter: Include files may be nested. That is, an include file can itself include another file, and so on.

System Include Files

You have already encountered two system include files. stdio.h was included into your program to use the getchar function back in Chapter 10, "Character Strings." We noted the fact that the include file stddef.h contained a define for NULL and was often used for testing to see if a pointer has a null value or not.

The stdio.h header file contains information about the I/O routines contained in the standard library. This header file is described in more detail in Chapter 16, "Input and Output." You should include this file whenever you're using any I/O library routine other than printf and scanf (although it doesn't hurt to include it even if these are the only I/O routines you're using).

Two other useful system include files are limits.h and float.h. The first file, limits.h, contains system-dependent values that specify the sizes of various character and integer data types. For instance, the maximum size of an int is defined by the name INT_MAX inside this file. The maximum size of an unsigned long int is defined by ULONG_MAX, and so on.

The float.h header file gives information about floating-point data types. For example, FLT_MAX specifies the maximum floating-point number, and FLT_DIG specifies the number of decimal digits of precision for a float type.

Other system include files contain prototype declarations for various functions stored inside the system library. For example, the include file string.h contains prototype declarations for the library routines that perform character string operations like copying, comparing, and concatenating.

For more details on these header files, consult Appendix B.

Conditional Compilation

The C preprocessor offers a feature known as *conditional compilation*. If you have some experience with assembly language programming, then this concept may not be new to you. Conditional compilation is often used to have one program that can run on different computer systems. It is also often used to switch various statements on or off in the program, such as debugging statements that print out the values of various variables or trace the flow of program execution.

The #*ifdef*, #*endif*, #*else*, and #*ifndef* Statements

In our discussions of the C preprocessor, we described how we could make the `rotate` function from Chapter 12 more portable. We showed how the use of a define would help in this regard. So the definition

```
#define   INT_SIZE   16
```

was used to isolate the dependency on the specific number of bits contained in an `unsigned int`. We also noted in several places that this dependency does not have to be made at all, since the program can itself determine the number of bits stored inside an `unsigned int`.

Unfortunately, a program sometimes must rely on system-dependent parameters,—on a filename, for example—that may be specified differently on different systems or on a particular feature of the operating system.

If we had a large program that had many such dependencies on the particular hardware and/or software of the computer system (and this should be minimized as much as possible), we might end up with many defines whose values would have to be changed when the program was moved to another computer system.

We can help reduce the problem of having to change these defines when the program is moved and can incorporate the values of these defines for each different machine into the program by using the conditional compilation capabilities of the preprocessor. As a simple example, the statements

```
#ifdef   UNIX
#    define   DATADIR       "/uxn1/data"
#else
#    define   DATADIR       "\\usr\\data"
#endif
```

have the effect of defining `DATADIR` to `"/uxn1/data"` if the symbol `UNIX` has been previously defined and to `"\usr\data"` otherwise. As you can see here, you are allowed to put one or more spaces after the # that begins a preprocessor statement.

The `#ifdef`, `#else`, and `#endif` statements behave as you would expect. If the symbol specified on the `#ifdef` line has been already defined—through a `#define` statement or through the command line when the program is compiled—then lines that follow up to a `#else`, `#elif`, or `#endif` are processed by the compiler; otherwise, they are ignored.

In order to define the symbol `UNIX` to the preprocessor, the statement

```
#define   UNIX      1
```

or even just

```
#define  UNIX
```

will suffice. Most compilers also permit you to define a name to the preprocessor when the program is compiled by using a special option to the compiler command. The UNIX command line

```
cc -D UNIX program.c
```

will define the name UNIX to the preprocessor, causing all #ifdef UNIX statements inside program.c to evaluate as TRUE (note that the -D UNIX must be typed *before* the program name on the command line). This technique enables names to be defined *without* having to edit the source program.

A value can also be assigned to the defined name on the command line. For example,

```
tcc -D INT_SIZE=16 program.c
```

invokes the Turbo C compiler, defining the name INT_SIZE to be the text 16.

The #ifndef statement follows along the same lines as the #ifdef. This statement is used the same way the #ifdef statement is used, except that it causes the subsequent lines to be processed if the indicated symbol is *not* defined.

As already mentioned, conditional compilation is useful when debugging programs. We may have many printf calls embedded in our program that are used to display intermediate results and trace the flow of execution. These statements can be "turned on" by conditionally compiling them into the program if a particular name, say DEBUG, is defined. For example, suppose we had some program that set up some data into an array called data. We might want to display the values contained inside this array at the terminal as a way of verifying the proper operation of the program. A sequence of statements such as the following could be used to display the elements of data only if the program had been compiled with the name DEBUG defined.

```
#ifdef DEBUG
    printf ("data elements:\n");

    for ( i = 0; i < MAX_DATA_VALUES; ++i )
        printf ("%i  %f\n", i, data[i]);
#endif
```

We might have many such debugging statements throughout the program. Whenever the program is being debugged, it can be compiled with the -D DEBUG command-line option to have all of the debugging statements compiled. When the program is working correctly, it can be recompiled without the -D option. This will also have the added benefit of reducing the size of the program, since the debugging statements will not be compiled in.

The #*if* and #*elif* Preprocessor Statements

The #if preprocessor statement offers a more general way of controlling conditional compilation. The #if statement can be used to test whether a constant expression evaluates to nonzero or not. If the result of the expression is nonzero, then subsequent lines up to a #else, #elif, or #endif are processed; otherwise, they are skipped. As an example of how this may be used, assume we define the name OS, which is set to 1 if the operating system is Macintosh OS, to 2 if the operating system is MS-DOS, to 3 if the operating system is UNIX, and so on. We could write a sequence of statements to conditionally compile statements based upon the value of OS as follows:

```
#if    OS == 1  /* Mac OS */
  ...
#elif  OS == 2  /* MS-DOS */
  ...
#elif  OS == 3  /* UNIX  */
  ...
#else
  ...
#endif
```

With most compilers, we can assign a value to the name OS on the command line using the -D option discussed earlier. The UNIX command line cc -D OS=2 program.c compiles program.c with the name OS defined as 2. This will cause the program to be compiled to run under MS-DOS.

The special operator

```
defined (name)
```

can also be used in #if statements. The set of preprocessor statements

```
#if  defined (DEBUG)
  ...
#endif
```

and

```
#ifdef DEBUG
  ...
#endif
```

does the same thing. The statements

```
#if defined (MSDOS) ¦¦ defined (OS2)
#  define BOOT_DRIVE "C:/"
#else
#  define BOOT_DRIVE "D:/"
#endif
```

define BOOT_DRIVE as "C:/" if either MSDOS or OS2 is defined and as "D:/" otherwise.

The *#undef* Statement

On some occasions, you may need to cause a defined name to become undefined. This is done with the #undef statement. To remove the definition of a particular *name*, you write

```
#undef   name
```

So the statement

```
#undef   MSDOS
```

removes the definition of MSDOS. Subsequent #ifdef MSDOS or #if defined (MSDOS) statements will evaluate FALSE.

This concludes our discussion on the preprocessor. Some other preprocessor statements that weren't described here are described in Appendix A, "ANSI C Language Summary."

Exercises

1. If you have access to a computer facility that supports the C programming language, type in and run the three programs presented in this chapter, remembering to type in the include file associated with Program 13.3. Compare the output produced by each program with the output presented.

2. Locate the system header files stdio.h, limits.h, and float.h on your machine (on UNIX systems, look inside the /usr/include directory). Examine the files to see what's in them.

3. Define a macro MIN that gives the minimum of two values. Then write a program to test the macro definition.

4. Define a macro MAX3 that gives the maximum of three values. Write a program to test the definition.

5. Write a macro SHIFT to perform the identical purpose as the shift function of Program 12.3.

6. Write a macro IS_UPPER_CASE that gives a nonzero value if a character is an uppercase letter.

7. Write a macro IS_ALPHABETIC that gives a nonzero value if a character is an alphabetic character. Have the macro use the IS_LOWER_CASE macro defined in the chapter text and the IS_UPPER_CASE macro defined in Exercise 6.

8. Write a macro IS_DIGIT that gives a nonzero value if a character is a

digit `'0'` through `'9'`. Use this macro in the definition of another macro `IS_SPECIAL`, which gives a nonzero result if a character is a special character; that is, not alphabetic and not a digit. Be sure to use the `IS_ALPHABETIC` macro developed in Exercise 7.

9. Write a macro `ABSOLUTE_VALUE` that computes the absolute value of its argument. Make sure that an expression such as

    ```
    ABSOLUTE_VALUE (x + delta)
    ```

    is properly evaluated by the macro.

10. Test out the system library functions that are equivalent to the macros you developed in the preceding three exercises. The library functions are called `isupper`, `isalpha`, and `isdigit`. You'll need to include the *system* header file `ctype.h` in your program in order to use them.

14

CHAPTER

More on Data Types

This chapter discusses a data type that we have not yet described: the *enumerated* data type. Also described in this chapter is the typedef statement, which enables us to assign our own names to basic data types or to derived data types. Finally, this chapter discusses the precise rules that are used by the compiler in the conversion of data types in an expression.

Enumerated Data Types

One of the qualities of a variable used as a flag in a C program is that it will usually be assigned one of two values: either TRUE or FALSE. In the preceding chapter, we saw how we could define the names TRUE or FALSE to the preprocessor and then subsequently use these names when dealing with flags. This approach is a valid one; however, it does not prevent us from inadvertently assigning a value other than TRUE or FALSE to a variable that is used as a flag in a program. Furthermore, such variables are usually declared to be of type int or of type short int, thus somewhat obscuring their usage in the program. Wouldn't it be nice if we could define a variable to be of type flag, and then somehow specify that variables declared to be of this type could only be assigned the values TRUE and FALSE and nothing else? This is precisely the type of capability that is provided by the enumerated data type.

An enumerated data type definition is initiated by the keyword enum. Immediately following this keyword is the name of the enumerated data type, followed by a list of identifiers (enclosed in a set of curly braces) that define the permissible values that can be assigned to the type. For example, the statement

```
enum flag  { true, false };
```

defines a data type flag. This data type can be assigned the values TRUE and FALSE inside the program, *and no other values*. Any attempt to assign another value to such a variable will cause most compilers to issue an error message.

To declare a variable to be of type enum flag, we again use the keyword enum, followed by the enumerated type name, followed by the variable list. So the statement

```
enum flag  end_of_data, match_found;
```

defines the two variables end_of_data and match_found to be of type flag. The only permissible values that can be assigned to these variables are the names TRUE and FALSE. So statements such as

```
end_of_data = true;
```

and

```
if ( match_found == false )
   ...
```

are valid. As another example of an enumerated data type definition, the following defines the type enum month, with permissible values that can be assigned to a variable of this type being the months of the year:

```
enum  month  { january, february, march, april, may,
               june, july, august, september, october,
               november, december };
```

The C compiler actually treats enumeration identifiers as integer constants. Beginning with the first name in the list, the compiler assigns sequential integer values to these names, starting with 0. If your program contains these two lines:

```
enum month  this_month;
   ...
this_month = february;
```

the value 1 would be assigned to this_month (and not the name february), since it is the second identifier listed inside the enumeration list.

Program 14.1 shows a simple program using enumerated data types. The program reads a month number and then enters a switch statement to see what month was entered. Recall that enumeration values are treated as integer constants by the compiler, so they're valid case values. The variable days is assigned the number of days in the specified month, and its value is displayed after the switch is exited. A special test is included to see if the month is February.

Program 14.1

```c
/* print the number of days in a month */
#include <stdio.h>
main ()
{
    enum   month  { january, february, march, april, may,
                    june, july, august, september, october, november,
                    december };
    enum   month  amonth;
    int           days;

    printf ("Enter month number: ");
    scanf ("%i", &amonth);

    switch (amonth-1)
    {
        case january:
        case march:
        case may:
        case july:
        case august:
        case october:
        case december:
                    days = 31;
                    break;
        case april:
        case june:
        case september:
        case november:
                    days = 30;
                    break;
        case february:
                    days = 28;
                    break;
        default:
                    printf ("bad month number\n");
                    days = 0;
                    break;
    }

    if ( days != 0 )
        printf ("Number of days is %i\n", days);

    if (( amonth -1) == february )
    printf ("...or 29 if it's a leap year\n");
}
```

Program 14.1 OUTPUT

```
Enter month number: 5
Number of days is 31
```

Program 14.1 OUTPUT (Rerun)

```
Enter month number: 2
Number of days is 28
...or 29 if it's a leap year
```

If you want to have a specific integer value associated with an enumeration identifier, the integer can be assigned to the identifier when the data type is defined. Enumeration identifiers that subsequently appear in the list will be assigned sequential integer values beginning with the specified integer value plus 1. For example, in the definition

```
enum  direction  { up, down, left = 10, right };
```

an enumerated data type direction is defined with the values up, down, left, and right. The compiler assigns the value 0 to up, since it appears first in the list; 1 to down since it appears next; 10 to left since it is explicitly assigned this value; and 11 to right since it appears immediately after left in the list.

Enumeration identifiers can share the same value. For example, in

```
enum  boolean  { no=0, false=0, yes=1, true=1 };
```

assigning either the value no or false to an enum boolean variable assigns it the value 0; assigning either yes or true assigns it the value 1.

Explicitly assigning an integer value to an enumerated data type variable can be done with the type cast operator. So if month_value were an integer variable that had the value 6, for example, the expression

```
this_month = (enum month) (month_value - 1);
```

would be permissible.

QUICK TIP

When writing programs with enumerated data types, try not to rely on the fact that the enumerated values are treated as integers. Instead, try to treat them as distinct data types.

The variations permitted when defining an enumerated data type are similar to those permitted with structure definitions: The name of the data type can be omitted, and variables can be declared to be of the particular enumerated data type when the type is defined. As an example showing both of these options, the statement

```
enum { east, west, south, north }  location;
```

defines an (unnamed) enumerated data type with values east, west, south, or north, and declares a variable location to be of that type.

Enumerated type definitions behave like structure and variable definitions as far as their scope is concerned: Defining an enumerated data type within a function limits the scope of that definition to the function. On the other hand, defining an enumerated data type at the beginning of the program, outside of any function, makes the definition global to the file.

QUICK TIP

When defining an enumerated data type, you must make certain that the enumeration identifiers are unique with respect to other variable names and enumeration identifiers defined within the same scope.

The *typedef* Statement

C provides a capability that enables the programmer to assign an alternate name to a data type. This is done with a statement known as typedef. The statement

```
typedef  int  COUNTER;
```

defines the name COUNTER to be equivalent to the C data type int. Variables can subsequently be declared to be of type COUNTER, as in the statement

```
COUNTER  j, n;
```

The C compiler actually treats the declaration of the variables j and n, shown above, as normal integer variables. The main advantage of the use of the typedef in this case is in the added readability that it lends to the definition of the variables. It is clear from the definition of j and n what the intended purpose of these variables is in the program. Declaring them to be of type int in the traditional fashion would not have made the intended use of these variables at all clear.

In many instances, a typedef statement can be equivalently substituted by the appropriate #define statement. For example, we could have used the statement

```
#define  COUNTER  int
```

instead to achieve the same results as the previous statement. However, because the `typedef` is handled by the C compiler proper, and not by the preprocessor, the `typedef` statement provides more flexibility than does the `#define` when it comes to assigning names to derived data types. For example, the following `typedef` statement:

```
typedef  char  STRING[81];
```

defines a type called `STRING`, which is an array of 81 characters. Subsequently declaring variables to be of type `STRING`, as in

```
STRING  text, input_line;
```

has the effect of defining the variables `text` and `input_line` to be character arrays containing 81 characters. This is equivalent to the following declaration:

```
char  text[81], input_line[81];
```

You will note that, in this case, `STRING` could *not* have been equivalently defined with a `#define` preprocessor statement.

The following `typedef` defines a type name `STRING_POINTER` to be a `char` pointer:

```
typedef  char *STRING_POINTER;
```

Variables subsequently declared to be of type `STRING_POINTER`, as in

```
STRING_POINTER  buffer;
```

will be treated as character pointers by the C compiler.

QUICK TIP

In order to define a new type name with `typedef`, follow this procedure:

1. Write the statement as if a variable of the desired type were being declared.

2. Where the name of the declared variable would normally appear, substitute the new type name.

3. In front of everything, place the keyword `typedef`.

As an example of this procedure, to define a type called `DATE` to be a structure containing three integer members called `month`, `day`, and `year`, we write out the structure definition, substituting the name `DATE` where the variable name would normally appear (before the last semicolon). Before everything, we place the keyword `typedef`:

```
typedef  struct
        {
                int    month;
                int    day;
                int    year;
        } DATE;
```

With this `typedef` in place, we could subsequently declare variables to be of type `DATE`, as in

```
DATE   birthdays[100];
```

This defines `birthdays` as an array containing 100 `DATE` elements.

By convention, `typedef` names are usually written in uppercase letters to alert the reader of the program that they are user-defined type names. When working on programs in which the source code is contained in more than one file (as described in the next chapter), it's a good idea to place the common `typedef`s into a separate file that can be included into each source file with a `#include` statement.

As another example, let's say you're working on a graphics package that needs to deal with drawing lines, circles, and so on. You probably will be working very heavily with the coordinate system. Here's a `typedef` statement that defines a type named `POINT`, where a `POINT` is a structure containing two `float` members x and y:

```
typedef  struct
{
    float  x;
    float  y;
} POINT;
```

You can now proceed to develop your graphics library, taking advantage of this `POINT` type. For example, the declaration

```
POINT  origin = { 0.0, 0.0 }, currentpoint;
```

defines `origin` and `currentpoint` to be of type `POINT` and sets the x and y members of `origin` to 0.0.

Here's a function called `distance` that calculates the distance between two points.

```
#include <math.h>

double  distance (POINT p1, POINT p2)
{
   double  diffx, diffy;
```

```
    diffx = p1.x - p2.x;
    diffy = p1.y - p2.y;

    return ( sqrt (diffx * diffx + diffy * diffy) );
}
```

(sqrt is the square root function from the standard library. It is declared in the system header file math.h, thus the reason for the #include.)

QUICK TIP

Remember, the typedef statement does not actually define a new type—only a new type *name*.

So the COUNTER variables j and n, as defined in the beginning of this section, would in all respects be treated as normal int variables by the C compiler.

Data Type Conversions

In Chapter 4, "Variables, Data Types, and Arithmetic Expressions," we briefly addressed the fact that sometimes conversions are implicitly made by the system when expressions are evaluated. The case that we examined was with the data types float and int. We saw how an operation that involved a float and an int was carried out as a floating-point operation, the integer data item being automatically converted to floating point.

We have also seen how the type cast operator can be used to explicitly dictate a conversion. So in the statement

```
average = (float) total / n;
```

the value of the variable total is converted to type float before the operation is performed, thereby guaranteeing that the division will be carried out as a floating-point operation.

The C compiler adheres to strict rules when it comes to evaluating expressions that consist of different data types.

The following summarizes the order in which conversions take place in the evaluation of two operands in an expression.

Conversion of Operands in an Expression

Step 1: If either operand is of type `long double`, the other is converted to `long double`, and that is the type of the result.

Step 2: If either operand is of type `double`, the other is converted to `double`, and that is the type of the result.

Step 3: If either operand is of type `float`, the other is converted to `float`, and that is the type of the result.

Step 4: If either operand is of type `char`, `short int`, `int` bit field, or of an enumerated data type, it is converted to `int`.

Step 5: If either operand is of type `long int`, the other is converted to `long int`, and that is the type of the result.

Step 6: If this step is reached, both operands are of type `int`, and that is the type of the result.

This is actually a simplified version of the steps that are involved in converting operands in an expression. The rules get more complicated when `unsigned` operands are involved. For the complete set of rules, refer to Appendix A, "ANSI C Language Summary."

Keep in mind that whenever you reach a step that says "…that is the type of the result," you're done with the conversion process.

As an example of how to follow these steps, let us see how the following expression would be evaluated, where f is defined to be a `float`, i an `int`, l a `long int`, and s a `short int` variable:

```
f * i + l / s
```

Consider first the multiplication of f by i, which is the multiplication of a `float` by an `int`. From Step 3, we find that, since f is of type `float`, the other operand, i, will also be converted to type `float`, and that will be the type of the result of the multiplication.

Next we proceed to the division of l by s, which is the division of a `long int` by a `short int`. Step 4 tells us that the `short int` will be promoted to an `int`. Continuing, we find from Step 5 that since one of the operands (l) is a `long int`, the other operand will be converted to a `long int`, which will also be the type of the result. This division will therefore produce a value of type `long int`, with any fractional part resulting from the division truncated.

Finally, Step 3 indicates that if one of the operands in an expression is of type `float` (as is the result of multiplying `f * i`), the other operand will be converted to type `float`, which will be the type of the result. Therefore, *after* the division of `l` by `s` has been performed, the result of the operation will be converted to type `float` and then added into the product of `f` and `i`. The final result of the preceding expression will therefore be a value of type `float`.

QUICK TIP

Remember, the type cast operator can always be used to explicitly force conversions and thereby control the way that a particular expression is evaluated.

So, if we didn't want the result of dividing `l` by `s` to be truncated in the preceding expression evaluation, we could have type cast one of the operands to type `float`, thereby forcing the evaluation to be performed as a floating-point division:

```
f * i + (float) l / s
```

In this expression, `l` would be converted to `float` before the division operation was performed, since the type cast operator has higher precedence than the division operator. One of the operands of the division would then be of type `float`, the others would be automatically converted to type `float`, and that would be the type of the result.

Sign Extension

Whenever a signed `int` or signed `short int` is converted into an integer of a larger size, the sign is extended to the left when the conversion is performed. This ensures that a `short int` having a value of -5, for example, will also have the value -5 when converted to a `long int`. Whenever an `unsigned` integer is converted to an integer of a larger size, as you would expect, no sign extension occurs.

On some systems (such as on the PDP-11, the VAX-11, and the IBM PC), characters are treated as signed quantities. This means that when a character is converted to an integer, sign extension occurs. As long as characters are used from the standard character set, this fact will never pose a problem. However, if a character value is used that is not part of the standard character set, its sign may be extended when converted to an integer. For example, on the machines noted, the character constant `'\377'` will be converted to the value -1 because its value is negative when treated as a signed eight-bit quantity.

The C language permits character variables to be declared unsigned, thus avoiding this potential problem. That is, an unsigned char variable will never have its sign extended when converted to an integer; its value will always be greater than or equal to 0. For the typical eight-bit character, a signed character variable therefore has the range of values from -128 to +127, inclusive. An unsigned character variable can range in value from 0 to 255, inclusive.

If you want to force sign extension on your character variables (something you won't normally want to do if you're storing standard characters inside them), you can declare such variables to be of type signed char. This ensures that sign extension will occur when the character value is converted to an integer, even on machines that don't do so by default.

Argument Conversion

We have used prototype declarations for all the functions that we wrote in this book. In Chapter 8, "Functions," we said that this was wise because with a prototype declaration you can physically locate the function either before or after its call, or even in another source file. We also noted that the compiler will automatically convert your arguments to the appropriate types for you as long as it knows what types of arguments the function expects. The only way it can know this is by having previously encountered the actual function definition or a prototype declaration.

Recall that, if the compiler sees neither the function definition nor a prototype declaration before it encounters a call to a function, it will assume the function returns an int. The compiler will also make assumptions about its argument types. In the absence of information about the argument types to a function, the compiler automatically converts char or short arguments to ints and converts float arguments to double. This is done to be compatible with the pre-ANSI versions of C (for more details consult Appendixes A and C).

For example, assume that the compiler encounters in your program

```
float  x;
   ...
y = absolute_value (x);
```

Having not previously seen the definition of the absolute_value function, and with no prototype declaration for it either, the compiler will generate code to convert the value stored inside the float variable x to double and pass the result to the function. The compiler will also assume the function returns an int.

If the `absolute_value` function is defined inside another source file like this:

```
float   absolute_value (float   x)
{
    if ( x < 0.0 )
        x = -x;

    return x;
}
```

you're in trouble. First, the function returns a `float`, yet the compiler thinks it returns an `int`. Second, the function expects to see a `float` argument, and we know the compiler will be passing a `double`.

QUICK TIP

Remember, the bottom line here is that you should always include prototype declarations for the functions you use. This will prevent the compiler from making mistaken assumptions about return types and argument types.

Exercises

1. Define a type `FUNCTION_POINTER` (using `typedef`) that represents a pointer to a function that returns an `int` and that takes no arguments. Refer to Chapter 11, "Pointers," for the details on how to declare a variable of this type.

2. Write a function called `month_name` that takes as its argument a value of type `enum month` (as defined in this chapter) and returns a pointer to a character string containing the name of the month. In this way, we can display the value of an `enum month` variable with a statement such as:

    ```
    printf ("%s\n", month_name (amonth));  .xe
    ```

3. Given the following variable declarations:

    ```
    short int     s = 10;
    int           i = 25;
    long int      l = 50L;
    float         f = 0.5F;
    double        d = 1.5;
    ```

what would be the value and the type of the following expressions?

```
f + s * i - l
l + i / s
i / f + s * d
i / s * f
(double) i / s * f
l / i + (int) d / f
i * i + 0x100
```

15

Working with Larger Programs

The programs that we have illustrated throughout this book have all been very small and relatively simple. Unfortunately, the programs that you will have to develop to solve your particular problems will probably be neither as small nor as simple. Learning the proper techniques for dealing with such programs is the topic of this chapter. As you will see, C provides all the features necessary for the efficient development of large programs.

Separate Compilations

In every program that we have shown, we always assumed that the entire program was entered into a single file on the system—presumably via a text editor such as vi under UNIX—and then compiled and executed. In this single file was included all the functions that the program used—except, of course, for the system functions such as printf and scanf.

This approach works fine when dealing with small programs—that is, programs that contain up to 100 statements or so. However, when you start dealing with larger programs, this approach no longer suffices. As the number of statements in the program increases, so does the time it takes to edit the program and to subsequently recompile it. Not only that, large programming applications frequently require the efforts of more than one programmer. Having everyone work on the same source file, or even on their own copy of the same source file, would be unmanageable.

C very much supports the notion of modular programming in that it does not require that all the statements for a particular program be contained in a single file. This means that you can enter your code for a particular module into one file, for another module into a different file, and so on. Here, when we use the term *module*, we are referring either to a single function or to a number of related functions that we choose to group logically.

For example, suppose you have conceptually divided your program into two modules and have entered the statements for the first module into a file called mod1.c and the statements for the second module into a file called mod2.c. In order to tell the system that these two modules actually belong to the same program, you simply include the names of both files when you enter the command to compile the program. For example, under UNIX, the command

```
cc mod1.c mod2.c
```

would have the effect of compiling the code contained in mod1.c and the code contained in mod2.c. Errors discovered in either mod1.c or mod2.c would be separately identified by the compiler. For example, one compiler gives output that looks like this:

```
mod1.c:
mod2.c:
"mod2.c", line 3: i undefined
```

Here the compiler indicates that mod1.c has no errors, but mod2.c has an error at line 3.

Obviously, if there were errors discovered in both modules, you would have to edit both modules to correct the mistakes. But in this case, since an error was discovered only inside mod2.c, you have to edit only this file to fix the mistake. And, since you haven't made any changes to mod1.c since the last time it was compiled, you can tell the C compiler to recompile only mod2.c and *not* mod1.c. Under UNIX, this would be done as follows:

```
cc mod1.o mod2.c
```

Replacing the c from the filename mod1.c with an o instructs the C compiler to use the object file that was produced the last time mod1.c was compiled. The

UNIX C compiler places the resulting object code from compiling *mod*.c into the file *mod*.o by default. When a program consisting of only one module is compiled and linked—such as would be the case with all the program examples in this book—this object file is automatically deleted by the system. However, when the program is divided into multiple modules, these separate \&.o files are retained. Most MS-DOS compilers work similarly, only they place the resulting object code into .obj files instead of .o files.

So, not only do we not have to reedit mod1.c if no errors are discovered by the compiler, but we don't have to recompile it either. If no errors are discovered in compiling mod2.c, the UNIX C compiler will place the final executable object into the file a.out, which can then be executed by simply typing the command

```
a.out
```

at the terminal. Most MS-DOS C compilers will place the executable object into a file with the same name as the source, replacing the file name extension with exe. If more than one file is specified on the command line, the first file name is used. So in the example above, the executable object file would be called mod1.exe by default, since mod1.c is the first file listed on the command line. All popular C compilers provide command line options that enable you to specify an alternate name for the executable object. Check the documentation that comes with your particular compiler.

We should reiterate something we have mentioned on several occasions in this book: In either of the two files mod1.c or mod2.c (but not in both), there *must* exist a function called main to indicate to the system where program execution is to begin.

If we extend the preceding example to programs that consist of more than two modules, then you can see how this mechanism of separate compilations can enable us to develop large programs more efficiently. For example, the UNIX command

```
cc legal.c makemove.o exec.o enumerator.o evaluator.o
```

could be used to compile a program consisting of five modules, in which only the module legal.c is to be recompiled.

Communication Between Modules

There are several methods that can be used so that the modules contained in separate files can effectively communicate. If a function from one file needs to call a function contained inside another file, then the function call can be made in the normal fashion and arguments can be passed and returned in the usual way. Of course, in the file that calls the function you should *always make sure to include a prototype declaration so the compiler knows the function's argument types and the type of the return value.* As noted in the previous chapter, in the absence of any information about a function, the compiler will assume it returns an `int` and will convert `short` or `char` arguments to `int`s and `float` arguments to `double`s when the function is called.

It's important to remember that even though two or more modules may be specified to the compiler at the same time on the command line, *the compiler compiles each module independently*.

QUICK TIP

No knowledge about structure definitions, function return types, or function argument types is shared across module compilations by the compiler. It's totally up to you to ensure that the compiler has sufficient information about such things to correctly compile each module.

External Variables

Functions contained in separate files can also communicate through *external variables*, which are effectively an extension to the concept of the global variable that we discussed in Chapter 8, "Functions."

An external variable is one whose value can be accessed and changed by another module. Inside the module that wishes to access the external variable, the variable is declared in the normal fashion and the keyword `extern` is placed before the declaration. This signals to the system that a globally defined variable from another file is to be accessed.

Suppose we wished to define an `int` variable called `move_number`, whose value we wished to access and possibly modify from within a function contained in another file. In Chapter 8, we noted that if we wrote the statement

```
int   move_number = 0;
```

at the beginning of our program, outside of any function, then its value could be referenced by any function within that program. In such a case, `move_number` was defined as a global variable.

Actually, this same definition of the variable `move_number` also makes its value accessible by functions contained in other files. Specifically, the preceding statement defines the variable `move_number` not just as a global variable, but in fact as an *external* global variable. In order to reference the value of an external global from another module, we must declare the type of the variable to be accessed, preceding the declaration with the keyword `extern`, for example:

```
extern int  move_number;
```

The value of move_number can now be accessed and modified by the module in which the preceding declaration appeared. Other modules can also access the value of move_number by using a similar extern declaration in the file.

Here is an important rule that you must obey when working with external variables. The variable has to be *defined* in some place among your source files. This is done in one of two ways. The first way is to declare the variable outside of any function, *not* preceded by the keyword extern, as in

```
int  move_number;
```

Here, an initial value can be optionally assigned to the variable, as was shown previously.

The second way to define an external variable is to declare the variable outside of any function, placing the keyword extern in front of the declaration, and *explicitly assigning an initial value to it,* as in

```
extern int move_number = 0;
```

Note that these two ways are mutually exclusive.

QUICK TIP

When dealing with external variables, the keyword extern can only be omitted in one spot throughout your source files. If you don't omit the keyword in any one spot, in exactly one place, you must assign the variable an initial value.

Let's take a look at a small program example to illustrate the use of external variables. Suppose we type the following code into a file called main.c:

```
#include <stdio.h>
int  i = 5;

main ()
{
    printf ("%i  ", i);

    foo ();

    printf ("%i\n", i);
}
```

The definition of the global variable i in the above program makes its value accessible by any module that uses an appropriate extern declaration. Suppose we now type the following statements into a file called foo.c:

```
extern int i;

foo ()
{
    i = 100;
}
```

Compiling the two modules `main.c` and `foo.c` together under UNIX with the command

```
cc main.c foo.c
```

and subsequently executing the program with the command

```
a.out
```

would produce the following output at the terminal:

```
5   100
```

which would verify that the function `foo` was able to access and change the value of the external variable `i`.

Since the value of the external variable `i` is referenced *inside* the function `foo`, we could have placed the `extern` declaration of `i` inside the function itself, as in:

```
foo ()
{
    extern int  i;

    i = 100;
}
```

If many functions in the file `foo.c` needed to access the value of `i`, it would be easier to make the `extern` declaration just once at the front of the file. However, if only one function or a small number of functions needed to access this variable, there would be something to be said for making separate `extern` declarations in each such function; it would make the program more organized and would isolate the use of the particular variable to those functions that actually used it.

When declaring an external array, it is not necessary to give its size. Thus, the declaration

```
extern char  text[];
```

would enable us to reference a character array `text` that is defined elsewhere. As with formal parameter arrays, if the external array is multidimensional, all but the first dimension must be specified. Thus the declaration

```
extern int  matrix[][50];
```

would suffice to declare a two-dimensional external array `matrix` that contained 50 columns.

Some things are worth noting with respect to external variable names. On some systems, the number of characters that are significant for an external variable name may not be the same as the number that are significant for nonexternal variable names. For example, on the PDP-11, only the first seven characters of an external variable name are significant. External variables that have the same first seven characters (as in `pointera` and `pointerb`), will therefore not be distinguishable and will lead to an error on this machine. ANSI C only requires that a system be able to distinguish external variable names up to six characters in length. If you're interested in writing truly portable programs, you will have to abide by this limitation. That is, you'll have to make sure that all your external names are distinct within their first six characters.

A second point worth noting is that on some systems, lowercase and uppercase letters are indistinguishable in external variable names. On such systems, external variables called `stack` and `Stack`, for example, would be treated as the same variable. Check your system documentation to find out any limitations that may exist with respect to external variable names.

Static versus *Extern* Variables and Functions

We now know that any variable defined outside of a function is not only a global variable, but is an external variable as well. Many situations arise in which we would like to define a variable to be global but *not* external. In other words, we would like to define a global variable to be local to a particular module (file). It would make sense to want to define a variable this way if no functions other than those contained inside a particular file needed access to the particular variable. This can be accomplished in C by defining the variable to be `static`.

The statement

```
static int  move_number = 0;
```

if made outside of any function, makes the value of `move_number` accessible from any subsequent point in the file in which the definition appears, *but not from functions contained in other files*.

QUICK TIP

If you need to define a global variable whose value does not have to be accessed from another file, declare the variable to be `static`. This is a cleaner approach to programming: the `static` declaration more accurately reflects the variable's usage, there can be no conflicts created by two modules that unknowingly both use different external global variables of the same name, and the process of linking the program together will actually be more efficient.

We mentioned earlier in this chapter that we can directly call a function from another file. Unlike variables, no special mechanisms are required; that is, to call a function contained in another file, we don't need an `extern` declaration for that function.

When a function is *defined*, it can be declared to be either `extern` or `static`, the former case being the default. A static function can be called only from within the same file as the function appears. So if we had a function called `square_root`, placing the keyword `static` before the function header declaration for this function would make it callable only from within the file in which it is defined:

```
static double  square_root (double x)
{
    ...
}
```

The definition of the `square_root` function effectively becomes local to the file in which it is defined. It cannot be called from outside this file.

The same motivations previously cited for using static variables also apply in the case of static functions.

Figure 15.1 summarizes communication between different modules. Here we depict two modules, `mod1.c` and `mod2.c`.

In `mod1.c`, we define two functions: `dosquare` and `main`. The way things are set up here, `main` calls `dosquare`, which in turn calls `square`. This last function is defined in the module `mod2.c`.

Because `dosquare` is declared `static`, it can only be called from within `mod1.c`, and by no other module.

`mod1.c` defines two global variables: `x` and `result`, both of type `double`. `x` can be accessed by any module that is linked together with `mod1.c`. On the other hand, the keyword `static` in front of the definition of `result` means that it can only be accessed by functions defined inside `mod1.c` (namely `main` and `dosquare`).

When execution begins, the `main` routine calls `dosquare`. `dosquare` assigns the value 2.0 to the global variable `x` and then calls the function `square`. Since `square` is defined in another source file (inside `mod2.c`), and since it doesn't return an `int`, `dosquare` properly includes an appropriate declaration at the start of the function.

```
double x;
static double result;

static void dosquare (void)
{
  double square (void);

  x = 2.0;
  result = square ();
}

main ()
{
  dosquare ();
  printf ("%f\n", result);
}
```
mod1.c

```
extern double x;

double square (void)
{
  return (x * x);
}
```
mod2.c

Figure 15.1. *Communication between modules.*

The square function returns as its value the square of the value of the global variable x. Because square wishes to access the value of this variable, which is defined in another source file (in mod1.c), an appropriate extern declaration appears in mod2.c (and, in this case, it makes no difference whether the declaration occurs inside or outside the square function).

The value that is returned by square is assigned to the global variable result inside dosquare, which then returns back to main. Inside main, the value of the global variable result is displayed. This example, when run, will produce a result of 4.0 at the terminal (since that's obviously the square of 2.0).

QUICK TIP

Study the example until you feel comfortable with it. This small—albeit impractical—example illustrates very important concepts about communicating between modules, and it's necessary that you understand these concepts to work effectively with larger programs.

Include Files

In Chapter 13, "The Preprocessor," we introduce the concept of the include file. We state there that we could group all our commonly used definitions inside such a file and then simply include the file in any program that needed to use those definitions. Nowhere is the usefulness of the #include facility greater than in developing programs that have been divided into separate program modules.

If more than one programmer is working on developing a particular program, then include files provide a means of standardization: Each programmer will be using the same definitions, which have the same values. Furthermore, each programmer is thus spared the time-consuming and error-prone task of typing these definitions into each file that must use them. These last two points are made even stronger when we start placing common structure definitions, external variable declarations, typedef definitions, and function return type declarations into include files. Various modules of a large programming system will invariably deal with common data structures. By centralizing the definition of these data structures into one or more include files, we eliminate the error that would be caused by two modules that used different definitions for the same data structure. Furthermore, if a change had to be made to the definition of a particular data structure, it could be done in one place only—inside the include file.

16

Input and Output

All reading and writing of data up to this point has been done through the terminal. When we wished to input some information, we either used the scanf or getchar functions. All program results were displayed at the terminal with a call to the printf function.

The C language itself does not have any special statements for performing Input/Output (I/O) operations. Unlike FORTRAN, for example, which has the READ and WRITE statements defined as part of the language, all I/O operations in C must be carried out through function calls. These functions are contained in the standard C library.

You will recall the use of the include statement

```
#include <stdio.h>
```

from previous programs that used the getchar function. This include file contains declarations and macro definitions associated with the I/O routines from the standard library. Therefore, whenever using a function from this library, you should include this file at the front of your program.

In this chapter, we will describe many of the I/O functions that are provided in the standard library. Unfortunately, space does not permit us to go into too much detail about these functions or discuss each function that is offered. Refer to Appendix B for a list of most of the functions in the library.

Character I/O: *getchar* and *putchar*

The getchar function proved convenient when we wished to read data from the terminal a single character at a time. We saw how we could develop a function called read_line to read an entire line of text from the terminal. This function repeatedly called getchar until a newline character was read.

There is an analogous function for writing data to the terminal a single character at a time. The name of this function is putchar.[1]

A call to the putchar function is quite simple: The only argument it takes is the character to be displayed. So the call

```
putchar ;
```

where c is defined of type char, would have the effect of displaying the character contained in c at the terminal.

The call

```
putchar ('\n');
```

would have the effect of displaying the newline character at the terminal, which, as we know, would cause the cursor to move to the beginning of the next line.

Formatted I/O: *printf* and *scanf*

We have been using the printf and scanf functions throughout this book. In this section, we will summarize all the options that are available for formatting data with these functions.

The first argument to both printf and scanf is a character pointer. This points to the format string. The format string specifies how the remaining arguments to the function are to be displayed in the case of printf, and how the data that is read is to be interpreted in the case of scanf.

---

[1]*Even though* putchar *may actually be defined as a macro inside the header file* **stdio.h** *(as may be* getchar*), we will still refer to it as a function here.*

The *printf* Function

We have seen in various program examples how we could place certain characters between the % character and the specific so-called conversion character to more precisely control the formatting of the output. For example, we saw in Program 5.3A how an integer value before the conversion character could be used to specify a *field width*. The format characters %2i specified the display of an integer value right-justified in a field width of two columns. We also saw in Exercise 6 in Chapter 5 how a minus sign could be used to left justify a value in a field.

The general format of a printf conversion specification is

%[*flags*][*width*][.*prec*][hlL]*type*

Optional fields are enclosed in brackets and must appear in the order shown.

Table 16.1 summarizes all possible characters and values that can be placed directly after the % sign and before the *type* specification inside a format string.

Table 16.1. printf conversion modifiers.

Modifier		*Meaning*
flags	-	Left justify value
	+	Precede value with + or -
	(*space*)	Precede positive value with space character
	0	Zero fill numbers
	#	Precede octal value with 0, hexadecimal value with 0x (or 0X; display deciaml point for floats; leave trailing zeroes for g or G format
width		Minimum size of field; *means take next argument as field width
prec		Minimum number of digits to display for integers; number of decimal places for e or f formats; maximum number of significant digits to display for g; maximum number of characters for s format; *means take next argument as size
h		Display short integer
l		Display long integer
L		Display long double
type		Type conversion character

Table 16.2 lists all the conversion characters that may be specified in the format string.

Tables 16.1 and 16.2 may appear a bit overwhelming. As you can see, there are many different combinations that can be used to precisely control the format of your output. The best way to become familiar with the various possibilities is through experimentation. Just make sure that the number of arguments you give to the `printf` function matches the number of % signs in the format string (with %% the exception, of course). And, in the case of using an * in place of an integer for the field width or precision modifiers, remember that `printf` will be expecting an argument for each asterisk as well.

Table 16.2. `printf` conversion characters.

Char	Use for Printing
i or d	Integers
u	Unsigned integers
o	Octal integers
x	Hexadecimal integers, using a-f
X	Hexadecimal integers, using A-F
f	Floating-point numbers, to six decimal places by default
e	Floating-point numbers in exponential format, using E before exponent
g	Floating-point numbers in f or e format
G	Floating-point numbers in f or E format
c	Single characters
s	Null-terminated character strings
p	Pointers
n	Doesn't print anything; stores the number of characters written so far by this call inside the `int` pointed to by the corresponding argument
%	Percent signs

Program 16.1 shows some of the formatting possibilities using `printf`.

Program 16.1

```
/* Program to illustrate various printf formats */
#include <stdio.h>
main ()
{
    char            c = 'X';
    char            s[] = "abcdefghijklmnopqrstuvwxyz";
    int             i = 425;
    short int       j = 17;
    unsigned int    u = 0xf179U;
    long int        l = 75000L;
    float           f = 12.978F;
    double          d = -97.4583;
    char            *cp = &c;
    int             *ip = &i;
    int             c1, c2;

    printf ("Integers:\n");
    printf ("%i  %o  %x  %u\n", i, i, i, i);
    printf ("%x  %X  %#x %#X\n", i, i, i, i);
    printf ("%+i % i %07i %.7i\n", i, i, i, i);
    printf ("%i  %o  %x  %u\n", j, j, j, j);
    printf ("%i  %o  %x  %u\n", u, u, u, u);
    printf ("%ld  %lo  %lx  %lu\n", l, l, l, l);

    printf ("\nFloats and Doubles:\n");
    printf ("%f  %e  %g\n", f, f, f);
    printf ("%.2f  %.2e\n", f, f);
    printf ("%.0f  %.0e\n", f, f);
    printf ("%7.2f  %7.2e\n", f, f);
    printf ("%f  %e  %g\n", d, d, d);
    printf ("%.*f\n", 3, d);
    printf ("%*.*f\n", 8, 2, d);

    printf ("\nCharacters:\n");
    printf ("%c\n", c);
    printf ("%3c%3c\n", c, c);
    printf ("%x\n", c);

    printf ("\nStrings:\n");
    printf ("%s\n", s);
    printf ("%.5s\n", s);
    printf ("%30s\n", s);
    printf ("%20.5s\n", s);
    printf ("%-20.5s\n", s);

    printf ("\nPointers:\n");
    printf ("%p  %p\n\n", (void *) ip, (void *) cp);
```

continues

Program 16.1 Continued

```
    printf ("This%n is fun.%n\n", &c1, &c2);
    printf ("c1 = %i, c2 = %i\n", c1, c2);
}
```

Program 16.1 OUTPUT

```
Integers:
425   651   1a9   425
1a9   1A9   0x1a9 0X1A9
+425   425 0000425 0000425
17   21   11   17
-3719   170571   f179   61817
75000   222370   124f8   75000

Floats and Doubles:
12.978000  1.297800e+01  12.978
12.98  1.30e+01
13  1e+01
  12.98  1.30e+01
-97.458300  -9.745830e+01  -97.4583
-97.458
  -97.46

Characters:
X
  X  X
58

Strings:
abcdefghijklmnopqrstuvwxyz
abcde
    abcdefghijklmnopqrstuvwxyz
              abcde
abcde

Pointers:
81D0  84F4

This is fun.
c1 = 4, c2 = 12
```

It's worthwhile to take some time to explain the output in detail. The first set of output deals with the display of integers: short, long, unsigned, and "normal" ints. The first line displays i in decimal (%i), octal (%o), hexadecimal

(%x), and unsigned (%u) formats. You will notice that octal numbers are not preceded by a leading 0 when they are displayed.

The next line of output displays the value of i again. First, i is displayed in hexadecimal notation using %x. The use of a capital X (%#X) causes printf to use uppercase letters A-F instead of lowercase letters when displaying numbers in hexadecimal. The # modifier (%#x) causes a leading 0x to appear before the number and causes a leading 0X to appear when the capital X is used as the conversion character (%#X).

The fourth printf call first uses the + flag to force a sign to appear, even if the value is positive (normally, no sign is displayed). Then the space modifier is used to force a leading space in front of a positive value. (Sometimes this is useful for aligning data that may be positive or negative; the positive values will have a leading space, the negative ones a minus sign.) Next, %07 is used to display the value of i right-justified within a field width of seven characters. The 0 flag specifies zero fill. Therefore, four leading zeroes are placed in front of the value of i, which is 425. The last conversion in this call, %.7i is used to display the value of i using a minimum of seven digits. The net effect is the same as specifying %07i: Four leading zeroes are displayed, followed by the three-digit number 425.

The fifth printf call displays the value of the short int variable j in various formats. Any integer format can be specified to display the value of a short int.

The next printf call shows what happens when %i is used to display the value of an unsigned int. Since the value assigned to u was larger than the maximum positive value that could be stored in a signed int on the machine on which this program was run, it is displayed as a negative number when the %i format characters are used.

The last printf call in this set shows how the l modifier is used to display long integers.

The second set of output illustrates various formatting possibilities for displaying floats and doubles. The first output line of this set shows the result of displaying a float value using %f, %e, and %g formats. As we mentioned, unless specified otherwise, the %f and %e formats default to six decimal places. With the %g format, printf decides whether to display the value in either %e or %f format, depending upon the magnitude of the value and on the specified precision. If the exponent is less than -4 or greater than the optionally specified precision (remember, the default is 6), %e is used; otherwise, %f is used. In either case, trailing zeroes are automatically removed, and a decimal point is displayed only if nonzero digits follow it. In general, %g is the best format to use for displaying floating-point numbers.

In the next line of output, the precision modifier .2 was specified to limit the display of f to two decimal places. As you can see, printf was nice enough to automatically round the value of f for us. The line that immediately follows shows the use of the .0 precision modifier to suppress the display of any decimal places, including the decimal point, in the %f format. Once again, the value of f was automatically rounded for us.

The modifiers 7.2, as used for generating the next line of output, specify that the value is to be displayed in a minimum of seven columns, to two decimal places of accuracy. Since both values need fewer than seven columns to be displayed, printf right justifies the value (adding spaces on the left) within the specified field width.

In the next three lines of output, the value of the double variable d is displayed with various formats. The same format characters are used for the display of floats and double values, since, as you'll once again recall, floats are automatically converted to doubles when passed as arguments to functions. The printf call

```
printf ("%.*f\n", 3, d);
```

specifies that the value of d is to be displayed to three decimal places. The asterisk after the period in the format specification instructs printf to take the next argument to the function as the value of the precision. In this case, the next argument is 3. This value could also have been specified by a variable, as in

```
printf ("%.*f\n", accuracy, d);
```

which makes this feature useful for dynamically changing the format of a display.

The final line of the Floats and Doubles set shows the result of using the format characters %*.*f for displaying the value of d. In this case, both the field width and the precision are given as arguments to the function, as indicated by the two asterisks in the format string. Since the first argument after the format string is 8, this is taken as the field width. The next argument, 2, is taken as the precision. The value of d is, therefore, displayed to two decimal places in a field size of eight characters. You will notice that the minus sign as well as the decimal point are included in the field-width count. This is true for any field specifier.

In the next set of program output, the character c, which was initially set to the character X, is displayed in various formats. The first time it is displayed using the familiar %c format characters. On the next line, it is displayed twice with a field-width specification of 3. This results in the display of the character with two leading spaces.

A character can be displayed using any integer format specification. In the next line of output, the value of c is displayed in hexadecimal. The output indicates that on this machine the character X is internally represented by the number hexadecimal 58.

In the final set of program output, the character string s is displayed. The first time it's displayed with the normal %s format characters. Then, a precision specification of 5 is used to display just the first five characters from the string. This results in the display of the first five letters of the alphabet.

In the third output line from this set, the entire character string is once again displayed, this time using a field width specification of 30. As you can see, the string is displayed right-justified in the field.

The final two lines from this set show five characters from the string s being displayed in a field-width size of 20. The first time, these five characters are displayed right-adjusted in the field. The second time, the minus sign results in the display of the first five letters left-adjusted in the field. The vertical bar character was printed to verify that the format characters %-20.5s actually result in the display of 20 characters at the terminal (five letters followed by 15 spaces).

The %p characters are used to display the value of a pointer. The corresponding argument should be of type pointer to void (which is written as void *). This is the C language's *generic* pointer type and is described more in the next chapter. Here we are converting the integer pointer ip and the character pointer cp to be generic pointers to satisfy the argument type requirement.

The format of the output when using %p is implementation defined, but in this example, the pointers are displayed in hexadecimal format. According to the output, the pointer variable ip contained the address 81D0 hexadecimal, and the pointer cp contained the address 84FA.

The last set of output shows the use of the %n format characters. In this case, the corresponding argument to printf must be of type pointer to int. printf will actually store the number of characters it has written so far into the integer pointed to by this argument. So the first occurrence of %n causes printf to store the value 4 inside the integer variable c1, since that's how many characters have been written so far by this call. The second occurrence of %n causes the value 12 to be stored inside c2. This is because 12 characters had been displayed at that point by printf. Notice that inclusion of the %n inside the format string has no effect on the actual output produced by printf.

The *scanf* Function

Like the printf function, many more formatting options can be specified inside the format string of a scanf call than have been illustrated up to this point. As with printf, scanf takes optional modifiers between the % and the conversion character. These optional modifiers are summarized in Table 16.3. The possible conversion characters that may be specified are summarized in Table 16.4.

When the scanf function searches the input stream for a value to be read, it will always bypass any leading so-called *whitespace* characters, where *whitespace* refers to either a blank space, horizontal tab ('\t'), vertical tab ('\v'), carriage return ('\r'), newline ('\n'), or form-feed character ('\f'). The exceptions are in the case of the %c format characters—in which case, the next character from the input, no matter what it is, is read—and in the case of the bracketed character string read—in which case, the characters contained in the brackets (or *not* contained in the brackets) specify the permissible characters of the string.

Table 16.3. scanf conversion modifiers.

Modifier	Meaning
*	Field is to be skipped and not signed.
size	Maximum size of the input field.
h	Value is to be stored in a short int.
l	Value is to be stored in long int or double.
L	Value is to be stored in long double.
type	Conversion character.

Table 16.4. scanf conversion characters.

Character	Action
d	The value to be read is expressed in decimal notation; corresponding argument is a pointer to an int unless the l or h modifier is used, in which case the argument is a pointer to a long or short int, respectively.
i	Like %d, except numbers expressed in octal (leading 0) or hexadecimal (leading 0x or 0X) also can be read.
u	The value to be read is an integer, and the corresponding argument is a pointer to an unsigned int.
o	The value to be read is expressed in octal notation and may be optionally preceded by a 0. The corresponding argument is a pointer to an int, unless an l or an h precedes the letter o, in which case the argument is a pointer to a long or a short, respectively.

Character	Action
x	The value to be read is expressed in hexadecimal notation and may be optionally preceded by a leading 0x or 0X; the corresponding argument is a pointer to an int, unless a l or an h modifies the x.
e, f, or g	The value to be read is expressed in floating-point notation; the value may be optionally preceded by a sign and may optionally be expressed in exponential notation (as in 3.45 e-3); the corresponding argument is a pointer to float, unless an l or L modifier is used, in which case it is a pointer to a double or to a long double, respectively.
c	The value to be read is a single character; the next character that appears on the input is read, even if it is a space, tab, newline, or form-feed character. The corresponding argument is pointer to char; an optional count before the c specifies the number of characters to read.
s	The value to be read is a sequence of characters; the sequence begins with the first nonwhitespace character and is terminated by the first whitespace character. The corresponding argument is a pointer to a character array, which must contain enough characters to contain the characters that are read plus the null character that is automatically added to the end. If a number precedes the s, the specified number of characters is read, unless a whitespace character is encountered first.
[...]	Characters enclosed within brackets indicate that a character string is to be read, as in %s; the characters within the brackets indicate the permissible characters in in the string. If any character other than that specified in the brackets is encountered, then the string will be terminated; the sense of how these characters are treated may be "inverted" by placing a ^ as the first character inside the brackets. In such a case, the subsequent characters are taken to be the ones that will terminate the string; that is, if any of the subsequent characters are found on the input, then the string will be terminated.
n	Nothing gets read. The number of characters read so far by this call is written into the int pointed to by the corresponding argument.
p	The value to be read is a pointer expressed in the same format as is displayed by printf with the %p conversion characters. The corresponding argument is a pointer to void.
%	The next nonwhitespace character on input must be a %.

When scanf reads in a particular value, reading of the value will terminate as soon as the number of characters specified by the field width is reached (if supplied) or until a character that is not valid for the value being read is encountered. In the case of integers, valid characters are an optionally signed sequence of digits that are valid for the base of the integer that is being read (decimal: 0-9, octal: 0-7, hexadecimal: 0-9, a-f, or A-F). For floats, permissible characters are an optionally signed sequence of decimal digits, followed by an optional decimal point and another sequence of decimal digits, all of which may be followed by the letter e (or E) and an optionally signed exponent. For character strings read in with the %s format, any nonwhitespace character is valid. In the case of %c format, all characters are valid. Finally, in the case of the bracketed string read, valid characters are only those enclosed within the brackets (or not enclosd within the brackets if the ^ character is used after the open bracket).

When we wrote the programs in Chapter 9, "Structures," that prompted us to enter the time from the terminal, we mentioned there that any nonformat characters that were specified in the format string of the scanf call would be expected on the input. So, for example, the scanf call

```
scanf ("%i:%i:%i", &hour, &minutes, &seconds);
```

meant that three integer values were to be read in and stored into the variables hour, minutes, and seconds, respectively. Inside the format string, the : characters specified that colons were expected as separators between the three integer values. In order to specify that a percent sign is expected as input, double percent signs are included in the format string, as in

```
scanf ("%i%%", &percentage);
```

Whitespace characters inside a format string match an arbitrary number of whitespace characters on the input. So the call

```
scanf ("%i%c", &i, &c);
```

with the line of text

```
29    w
```

would assign the value 29 to i and a blank space character to c, since this is the character that appears immediately after the characters 29 on the input. If the following scanf call were made instead:

```
scanf ("%i %c", &i, &c);
```

and the same line of text entered, then the value 29 would be assigned to i and the character 'w' to c since the blank space in the format string would cause the scanf function to ignore any leading whitespace characters after the characters 29 had been read.

Table 16.3 indicates that an asterisk may be used to skip fields. If the scanf call

```
scanf ("%i %5c %*f %s", &i1, text, string);
```

were executed and the following line of text were typed in at the terminal:

```
144abcde    736.55       (wine and cheese)
```

then the value 144 would get stored into i1; the five characters abcde would get stored into the character array text; the floating value 736.55 would be matched but not assigned; and the character string "(wine" would be stored into string, terminated by a null. The next call to scanf would *pick up where the last one left off*. So a subsequent call such as

```
scanf ("%s %s %i", string2, string3, &i2);
```

would have the effect of storing the character string "and" into string2 and the string "cheese)" into string3 and would cause the function to wait for an integer value to be typed.

Remember that scanf expects pointers to the variables where the values that are read in are to be stored. We know from Chapter 11, "Pointers," why this is necessary: so that scanf can make changes to the variables; that is, store the values that it read into them. You will also remember that to specify a pointer to an array, only the name of the array need be specified. So if text is defined as an appropriately sized array of characters, then the scanf call

```
scanf ("%80c", text);
```

would read the next 80 characters from the input and store them into text.

The scanf call

```
scanf ("%[^/]", text);
```

indicates that the string to be read in can consist of any character except for a slash. Using the above call on the line of text

```
(wine and cheese)/
```

would have the effect of storing the string "(wine and cheese)" into text, since the string would not be terminated until the / was matched (which would also be the next character read by scanf on the next call).

To read an entire line from the terminal into the character array buf, you can specify that the newline character at the end of the line is your string terminator:

```
scanf ("%[^\n]\n", buf);
```

The newline character is repeated outside the brackets so that scanf will match it and not read it the next time it's called. (Remember, scanf always continues reading from the character that terminated its last call.)

When a value is read that does not match a value expected by scanf (for example, typing in the character x when an integer is expected), scanf does not read any further items from the input and immediately returns. Since the function returns the number of items that were successfully read and assigned to variables in your program, this value can be tested to determine if any errors occurred on the input. For example, the call

```
if ( scanf ("%i %f %i", &i, &f, &l) != 3 )
    printf ("Error on input\n");
```

will test to make sure that scanf successfully read and assigned three values. If not, an appropriate message is displayed.

Remember, the return value from scanf indicates the number of values read *and assigned*, so the call

```
scanf ("%i %*d %i", &i1, &i3)
```

returns 2 when successful and not 3, since we are reading and assigning *two* integers (skipping one in between). Note also that use of the %n (to obtain the number of characters read so far) does not get included in the value returned by scanf.

Experiment with the various formatting options provided by the scanf function. As with the printf function, a good understanding of these various formats will be obtained only by trying them in actual program examples. Consult *Topics in C Programming, Revised Edition* (Kochan & Wood, John Wiley & Sons, Inc.), for a more detailed discussion of scanf and its various peculiarities.

File I/O

Redirection of I/O to a File

Whenever a call was made to the scanf function by one of the programs in this book, the data that was requested by the call was always read in from the terminal. Similarly, all calls to the printf function resulted in the display of the desired information at the terminal.

The need frequently arises to either read in information from a file that is stored on the system, or to write data out to a file on the system. Both of these operations can be easily performed under many operating systems like UNIX and MS-DOS without anything special being done at all to the program. If we wished to write all our program results into a file called `data`, for example, then all that we would have to do under UNIX (or MS-DOS) would be to redirect the output from the program into the file `data` by executing the program with the following command:

```
a.out > data
```

This command instructs the system to execute the program `a.out` but to take all of the output that is normally written to the terminal by the program and redirect it into a file called `data` instead. So any values displayed by `printf` would not be appear at the terminal but instead would be written into the file called `data`.

To see how this works, type in the very first program we wrote, Program 3.1, and compile the program in the usual way. Now execute the program as you normally would by typing in the program name (assume it's called `prog1`)

```
prog1
```

If all goes well, you should get the output

```
Programming is fun.
```

at the terminal. Now issue the following command at the terminal:

```
prog1 > data
```

This time you will notice that you did not get any output at the terminal. This is because the output was redirected into the file called `data`. We can examine the contents of the file `data` under MS-DOS by issuing the command

```
type data
```

which will result in the display of the following at the terminal:

```
Programming is fun.
```

This verifies that the output from the program went into the file `data` as we described. You might want to try the preceding sequence of commands with a program that produces more lines of output to verify that the preceding process works properly in such cases.

We can do a similar type of redirection for the input to our program. Any call to a function that normally reads data from the terminal, such as `scanf` and `getchar`, can be easily made to read its information from a file. Program 5.8 was designed to reverse the digits of a number. The program uses `scanf` to read in the value of the number to be reversed from the terminal. We can have the program get its input from a file called `number`, for example, by redirecting the input to the program when the program is executed. If the program is called `reverse`, the following command line should do the trick:

```
reverse < number
```

If we typed the number 2001 into a file called number before issuing the above command, then the following output would appear at the terminal after this command was entered:

```
Enter your number.
1002
```

You will notice that the program requested that a number be entered but did not wait for you to type in a number. This is because the input to the program—but not its output—was redirected to the file called number. Therefore, the scanf call from the program had the effect of reading the value from the file number and not from the terminal. The information must be entered in the file the same way that it would be typed in from the terminal. The scanf function itself does not actually know (or care) whether its input is coming from the terminal or a file; all it cares about is that it is properly formatted.

Naturally, we can redirect the input and the output to a program at the same time. The command

```
a.out < number > data
```

causes execution of the program contained in a.out to read all program input from the file number and to write all program results into the file data. So if we executed the above command for Program 5.8, the input would once again be taken from the file number, and the output would be written into the file data.

The method of redirecting the program's input and/or its output is often practical. For example, suppose we were writing an article for a magazine and had typed the text into a file called article. Program 10.8 counted the number of words that appeared in lines of text entered at the terminal. We could use this very same program to count the number of words in our article simply by typing in the command

```
a.out < article
```

Of course, we would have to remember to include an extra carriage return at the end of the article file, since our program was designed to recognize an end-of-data condition by the presence of a single newline character on a line.

Note that I/O redirection, as described here, is not actually part of the ANSI definition of C. This means that you may find operating systems that don't support it. Luckily, most do.

End of File

The preceding point about end of data is worthy of more discussion. When dealing with files, this condition is called end of file. An end-of-file condition exists when the last piece of data has been read from a file. Attempting to read past the end of the file may cause the program to terminate with an error, or it may cause the program to go into an infinite loop if this condition is not checked by the program (the latter being the case for the UNIX system). Luckily, most of the functions from the Standard I/O Library return a special flag to indicate when a program has reached the end of a file. The value of this flag is equal to a special name called EOF, which is defined in the standard I/O include file <stdio.h>.

As an example of the use of the EOF test in combination with the getchar function, the following program will read in characters and echo them back at the terminal until an end of file is reached. Notice the expression contained inside the while loop. As you can see, an assignment does not have to be made in a separate statement.

Program 16.2

```
/* Program to echo characters until an end of file */

#include <stdio.h>

main ()
{
    int  c;

    while ( (c = getchar ()) != EOF )
        putchar (c);
}
```

If we were to compile and execute Program 16.2, redirecting the input to a file with a command such as

```
a.out < infile
```

the program would display the contents of the file infile at the terminal. Try it and see! Actually, the program serves the same basic function as the cat command under UNIX, or as the type command under MS-DOS, and we could use it to display the contents of any text file we chose.

In the while loop of Program 16.2, the character that is returned by the getchar function is assigned to the variable c and is then compared against the defined value of EOF. If the values are equal, this means that we have read the last character from the file. One important point must be mentioned with respect to the EOF value that is returned by the getchar function: The function actually returns an int and not a char. This is because the EOF value must be unique; that is, it cannot be equal to the value of any character that would normally be returned by `getchar`. Therefore, the value returned by `getchar` is assigned to an `int` and not a `char` variable in the preceding program. This works out okay, because C allows you to store characters inside `int`s, even though, in general, it may not be the best of programming practices.

If you store the result of the `getchar` function inside a `char` variable, the results will be unpredictable. On systems that do sign extension of characters, the code may still work okay. On systems that don't do sign extension, you may end up in an infinite loop.

QUICK TIP

Always remember to store the result of `getchar` inside an `int` so that you can properly detect an end-of-file condition.

The fact that we can make an assignment inside the conditional expression of the `while` loop illustrates the flexibility that C provides in the formation of expressions. The parentheses are required around the assignment because the assignment operator has lower precedence than the not equals operator.

Special Functions for Handling Files

It is very likely that many of the programs you will develop will be able to perform all their I/O operations using just the `getchar`, `putchar`, `scanf`, and `printf` functions and the notion of I/O redirection. However, situations do arise when you need more flexibility to work with files. For example, you may need to read data from two or more different files or to write output results into several different files. To handle these situations, special functions have been designed expressly for the purpose of working with files. Several of these functions will now be described.

The *fopen* Function

Before you can begin to do any I/O operations on a file, the file must first be *opened*. In order to open a file, we must specify to the system the name of the file. The system will then check to make sure that this file actually exists and, in certain instances, will create the file for you if it does not. When a file is opened, we must also specify to the system the type of I/O operations that we intend to perform with the file. If the file is to be used to read in data, then we would normally specify that the file be opened in *read mode*. If we wish to write data into the file, then the file must be opened in *write mode*. Finally, if we wish to append information to the end of a file that already contains some data, then the file must be opened in *append mode*. In the last two cases, write and append mode, if the specified file does not exist on the system, the system will create the file for you. In the case of read mode, if the file does not exist, the system will report an error.

Since a program can have many different files open at the same time, we need a way of identifying a particular file in the program whenever we wish to perform some I/O operation on the file. This is done by means of a *file pointer*.

The function called fopen in the standard library serves the function of opening a file on the system and of returning a unique file pointer with which to subsequently identify the file. The function takes two arguments: The first is a character string specifying the name of the file to be opened; the second is also a character string that indicates the mode in which the file is to be opened. The function returns a file pointer that is used by other library functions to identify a particular file.

If the file cannot be opened for some reason, the function returns the value NULL,[1] which is defined inside the header file <stdio.h>. Also defined in this file is the definition of a type called FILE. In order to store the result returned by the fopen function in our program, we must define a variable of type "pointer to FILE."

If we take the preceding comments into account, the statements

```
#include <stdio.h>

FILE  *input_file;

input_file = fopen ("data", "r");
```

will have the effect of opening a file called data in read mode. (Write mode is specified by the string "w", and append mode is specified by the string "a".) The fopen call will return an identifier for the opened file that will be assigned to the FILE pointer variable input_file. Subsequent testing of this variable against the defined value NULL

```
if ( input_file == NULL )
    printf ("*** data could not be opened.\n");
else
    /* read the data from the file */
```

will tell us if the open was successful or not.

---

[1] *Historically, NULL was defined only inside <stdio.h>. ANSI C places it in the file <stddef.h>. To make life easier, you'll most likely find it defined in both header files.*

> ### QUICK TIP
>
> You should always check the result of an `fopen` call to make sure it succeeded. Using a null pointer can produce unpredictable results.

Frequently, in the `fopen` call, the assignment of the returned `FILE` pointer variable and the test against the `NULL` pointer are combined into a single statement, as in

```
if ( (input_file = fopen ("data", "r")) == NULL )
    printf ("*** data could not be opened.\n");
```

The `fopen` function also supports three other types of modes, called *update* modes (`"r+"`, `"w+"`, and `"a+"`). All three update modes permit both reading and writing operations to be performed on a file. Read update (`"r+"`) opens an existing file for both reading and writing. Write update (`"w+"`) is like write mode (if the file already exists, the contents are destroyed; if one doesn't exist, it's created), but once again both reading and writing are permitted. Append update (`"a+"`) opens an existing file or creates a new one if one doesn't exist. Read operations can occur anywhere in the file, but write operations can only add data to the end.

On systems such as MS-DOS and Windows, which distinguish text files from binary files, a b must be added to the end of the mode string to read or write a binary file. If you forget to do this, you will get strange results, even though your program will still run. That's because on these systems, carriage return/ line feed character pairs are converted to return characters when they are read from or written to text files. Furthermore, on input, a file that contains a Control-Z character will cause an end-of-file condition if the file was not open as a binary file. So

```
input_file = fopen ("data", "rb");
```

would open the binary file `data` for reading.

The *getc* and *putc* Functions

The function `getc` enables you to read in a single character from a file. This function behaves identically to the `getchar` function that we have described. The only difference is that `getc` takes an argument: a `FILE` pointer that identifies the file from which the character is to be read. So if `fopen` were called as shown above, then subsequent execution of the statement

```
c = getc (input_file);
```

would have the effect of reading a single character from the file data. Subsequent characters could be read from the file simply by making additional calls to the getc function.

The getc function returns the value EOF when the end of file is reached, and as with the getchar function, the value returned by getc should be stored in a variable of type int.

As you might have guessed, the putc function is equivalent to the putchar function, only it takes two arguments instead of one. The first argument to putc is the character that is to be written into the file. The second argument is the FILE pointer. So the call

```
putc ('\n', output_file);
```

would write a newline character into the file identified by the FILE pointer output_file. Of course, the identified file must have been previously opened in either write or append mode (or in any of the update modes) in order for this call to succeed.

With the functions putc and getc, we can now proceed to write a program that will copy one file to another. The program will prompt the user for the name of the file to be copied and the name of the resultant copied file. This program is based upon Program 16.2. You may want to refer to that program for comparison purposes.

Let's assume that the following three lines of text have been previously typed into the file copyme:

```
This is a test of the file copy program
that we have just developed using the
fopen, getc and putc functions.
```

Program 16.3

```
/* Program to copy one file to another */

#include <stdio.h>

main ()
{
    char  in_name[25], out_name[25];
    FILE  *in, *out;
    int   c;

    printf ("Enter name of file to be copied: ");
    scanf ("%24s", in_name);
    printf ("Enter name of output file: ");
```

continues

Program 16.3 Continued

```
    scanf ("%24s", out_name);

    if ( (in = fopen (in_name, "r"))  ==  NULL )
        printf ("Can't open %s for reading.\n", in_name);
    else if  ( (out = fopen (out_name, "w"))  ==  NULL )
        printf ("Can't open %s for writing.\n", out_name);
    else
    {
        while ( (c = getc (in)) != EOF )
            putc (c, out);

        printf ("File has been copied.\n");
    }
}
```

Program 16.3 OUTPUT

```
Enter name of file to be copied: copyme
Enter name of output file: here
File has been copied.
```

Now examine the contents of the file here. The file should contain the same three lines of text as contained in the copyme file.

The scanf function call in the beginning of the program was given a field-width count of 24 just to ensure that we didn't overflow our in_name or out_name character arrays. The program then opens the specified input file for reading, and the specified output file for writing. If the output file already exists and is opened in write mode, then its previous contents will be destroyed under most systems.

If either of the two fopen calls is unsuccessful, then the program displays an appropriate message at the terminal and proceeds no further. Otherwise, the file is copied one character at a time, by means of successive getc and putc calls, until the end of the file is encountered.

The *fclose* Function

One operation that we can perform on a file, which must be mentioned, is that of closing the file. The fclose function, in a sense, does the opposite of what the fopen does: It tells the system that we no longer need to access the file. Whenever a file is closed, the system performs some necessary housekeeping chores (such as writing all the data that it may be keeping in a buffer in memory to the file) and then dissociates the particular file identifier from the file. Once a file has been closed, it can no longer be read from or written to unless it is re-opened.

Whenever you have completed your operations on a file, it is a good habit to close the file. We did not do so in Program 16.3 because when a program terminates normally, the system automatically closes any open files for us. It is generally better programming practice to close a file as soon as you are done with it. This can be beneficial if your program has to deal with a large number of files, as there are practical limits on the number of files that can be kept simultaneously open by a program. ANSI C guarantees that you can have at least eight different files open simultaneously. Many systems permit more. For example, UNIX allows 20 and MS-DOS defaults to 8 but can be increased by adding an appropriate `FILES=` command to your `config.sys` file.

By the way, the argument to the `fclose` function is the `FILE` pointer of the file to be closed. So the call

```
fclose (input);
```

would close the file associated with the `FILE` pointer `input`.

The *feof* Function

In order to test for an end-of-file condition on a file, the function `feof` is provided. The single argument to the function is a `FILE` pointer. The function returns an integer value that is nonzero, if an attempt has been made to read past the end of a file and is zero otherwise. So, the statements

```
if ( feof (in_file) )
    printf ("Ran out of data.\n");
```

will have the effect of displaying the message "Ran out of data" at the terminal if an end-of-file condition exists on the file identified by `in_file`.

Remember, `feof` tells you that an attempt has been made to read past the end of the file, which is not the same as telling you that you just read the last data item from a file. You have to read one past the last data item for `feof` to return nonzero.

The *fprintf* and *fscanf* Functions

The functions `fprintf` and `fscanf` are provided to perform the analogous operations of the `printf` and `scanf` functions on a file. These functions take an additional argument, which is the `FILE` pointer that identifies the file to which the data is to be written or from which the data is to be read. So to write the character string `"Programming in C is fun.\n"` into the file identified by `out_file`, we can write the statement

```
fprintf (out_file, "Programming in C is fun.\n");
```

Similarly, to read in the next floating-point value from the file identified by in_file into the variable fv, the statement

```
fscanf (in_file, "%f", &fv);
```

could be used. As with scanf, fscanf returns the number of arguments that are successfully read and assigned or the value EOF, if the end of the file is reached before any of the conversion specifications have been processed.

The *fgets* and *fputs* Functions

For reading and writing entire lines of data from and to a file, the fputs and fgets functions can be used. The fgets function is called as follows:

```
fgets (buffer, n, file_pointer);
```

buffer is a pointer to a character array where the line that is read in will be stored; *n* is an integer value that represents the maximum number of characters that are to be stored into *buffer*; and *file_pointer* identifies the file from which the line is to be read.

The fgets function reads characters from the specified file until a newline character has been read (which *will* get stored into the buffer) or until *n-1* characters have been read, whichever occurs first. The function automatically places a null character after the last character in *buffer*. It returns the value of *buffer* (the first argument) if the read is successful, and the value NULL if an error occurs on the read or if an attempt is made to read past the end of the file.

QUICK TIP

fgets can be combined with fscanf to perform line-oriented reading in a more orderly and controlled fashion than by using scanf alone.

The fputs function writes a line of characters to a specified file. The function is called as shown:

```
fputs (buffer, file_pointer);
```

Characters stored in the array pointed to by *buffer* are written to the file identified by *file_pointer* until the null character is reached. The terminating null character is *not* written to the file.

There are also analogous functions called gets and puts that can be used to read a line from the terminal and write a line to the terminal, respectively. These functions are described in Appendix B.

stdin, *stdout*, **and** *stderr*

Whenever a C program is executed, three files are automatically opened by the system for use by the program. These files are identified by the *constant* FILE pointers stdin, stdout, and stderr, which are defined in <stdio.h>. The FILE pointer stdin identifies the standard input of the program and is normally associated with your terminal. All standard I/O functions that perform input and do not take a FILE pointer as an argument get their input from stdin. For example, the scanf function reads its input from stdin, and a call to this function is equivalent to a call to the fscanf function with stdin as the first argument. So the call

```
fscanf (stdin, "%i", &i);
```

will read in the next integer value from the standard input, which will normally be your terminal. If the input to your program has been redirected to a file, this call will read the next integer value from the file to which the standard input has been redirected.

As you might have guessed, stdout refers to the standard output, which is normally also associated with your terminal. So a call such as

```
printf ("hello there.\n");
```

can be replaced by an equivalent call to the fprintf function with stdout as the first argument:

```
fprintf (stdout, "hello there.\n");
```

The putchar function on your system is probably implemented actually as a macro definition that simply calls the putc function with stdout as the argument for the FILE pointer:

```
#define  putchar     putc (c, stdout)
```

The same is most likely true for the getchar function with respect to the function getc:

```
#define  getchar()    getc (stdin)
```

On your system, putc and getc may be implemented as macro definitions as well.

The FILE pointer stderr identifies the standard error file. This is where most of the error messages produced by the system are written and is also normally associated with your terminal. The reason stderr exists is so that error messages can be logged to a device or file other than where the normal output is written. This is particularly desirable whenever the program's output is redirected to a file. In such a case, the normal output will be written into the file, but any system error messages will still appear at the terminal. You might want to write your own error messages to stderr for this same reason. As an example, the fprintf call in the following statement

```
if ( (in_file = fopen ("data", "r")) == NULL )
{
    fprintf (stderr, "Can't open data for reading.\n");
        ...
}
```

will write the indicated error message to stderr if the file data cannot be opened for reading. And if the the standard output had been redirected to a file, this message would still appear at the terminal.

The *exit* Function

At times, it may be desirable to force the termination of a program, such as when an error condition is detected by a program. We know that program execution is automatically terminated whenever the last statement in main is executed, but in order to explicitly terminate a function, the exit function can be called. The function call

```
exit (n);
```

has the effect of terminating (exiting from) the current program. Any open files will be automatically closed by the system. The integer value *n* is called the *exit status*. This exit status may be tested by other processes to determine whether the program successfully completed execution or not. For example, a UNIX shell program or MS-DOS .bat file can test the exit status of the program after it has run and alter the execution of the file based upon the result.

The standard header file <stdlib.h> defines EXIT_FAILURE as an integer value that you can use to indicate the program has failed and EXIT_SUCCESS to be one that you can use to indicate it has succeeded.

When a program terminates simply by executing the last statement in main, its exit status is undefined. If another program needs to use this exit status, you mustn't let this happen. In such a case, make sure that you exit from main with a defined exit status.

As an example of the use of the exit function, the following sequence of statements will cause the program to terminate with an exit status of EXIT_FAILURE if the file data cannot be opened for reading. If the program reaches the end, it will exit with a status value of EXIT_SUCCESS.

```
#include <stdlib.h>

main ()
{
   FILE  *in_file;
```

```
   ...
   if ( (in_file = fopen ("data", "r")) == NULL )
   {
   fprintf (stderr, "Can't open data for reading.\n");
       exit (EXIT_FAILURE);
   }

   ...

   exit (EXIT_SUCCESS);
}
```

The C language also supports the idea of *returning* from main. In this case, the exit status is taken from the returned value. So the above code could also be equivalently expressed using the idea of returning from main as shown:

```
#include <stdlib.h>

int main ()
{
   FILE  *in_file;

   ...

   if ( (in_file = fopen ("data", "r")) == NULL )
   {
       fprintf (stderr, "Can't open data for reading.\n");
       return EXIT_FAILURE;
   }

   ...

   return EXIT_SUCCESS;
}
```

There's no real difference here between the version that uses exit and the one that uses return. They both terminate the program, sending back an exit status. The main difference between exit and return is when they're executed from inside a function other than main. The exit call will terminate the program *immediately*; the return will simply transfer control back to the calling routine.

Renaming and Removing Files

The rename function from the library can be used to change the name of a file. It takes two arguments: the old filename and the new filename. If for some reason the renaming operation fails (for example, if the first file doesn't exist, or the system won't allow you to rename the particular file), rename returns a nonzero value. The code

```
if  ( rename ("tempfile", "database") )
{
    fprintf (stderr, "Can't rename tempfile\n");
    exit (EXIT_FAILURE);
}
```

will rename the file called `tempfile` to `database` and will check the result of the operation to ensure it succeeded.

The `remove` function deletes the file specified by its argument. It returns a non-zero value if the file removal fails. The code

```
if ( remove ("tempfile") )
{
    fprintf (stderr, "Can't remove tempfile\n");
    exit (EXIT_FAILURE);
}
```

will attempt to remove the file `tempfile` and will write an error message to standard error and exit if the removal fails.

Incidentally, you may be interested in using the `perror` function to report errors from standard library routines. For more details, consult Appendix B.

This concludes our discussion of I/O operations under C. As mentioned, we have not covered all the library functions here for reasons of space. You should check the documentation with your compiler to find out about other functions that are available—not just in the standard library, but in other function libraries as well. The standard library contains a wide selection of functions for performing operations with character strings, for *random* I/O, mathematical calculations, and dynamic memory management. Appendix B lists most of the functions inside this library.

Exercises

1. If you have access to a computer facility that supports the C programming language, type in and run the three programs presented in this chapter. Compare the output produced by each program with the output presented.

2. Go back to programs developed earlier in this book and experiment with redirecting their input and output to files.

3. Write a program to copy one file to another, replacing all lowercase characters with their uppercase equivalents.

4. Write a program that merges lines alternately from two files and writes the results to `stdout`. If one file has less lines than the other, the remaining lines from the larger file should be simply copied to `stdout`.

5. Write a program that writes columns m through n of each line of a file to stdout. Have the program accept the values of m and n from the terminal.

6. Write a program that displays the contents of a file at the terminal 20 lines at a time. At the end of each 20 lines, have the program wait for a character to be entered from the terminal. If the character is the letter q, then the program should stop the display of the file; any other character should cause the next 20 lines from the file to be displayed.

17

Miscellaneous and Advanced Features

This chapter discusses some miscellaneous features of the C language that we have not yet covered and also provides a discussion of some more advanced topics, such as command-line arguments and dynamic memory allocation.

Miscellaneous Language Statements

The *goto* Statement

Anyone who has learned about structured programming knows of the reputation afforded to the goto statement. Virtually every computer language has such a statement.

Execution of a goto statement causes a direct branch to be made to a specified point in the program. This branch is made immediately and unconditionally upon execution of the goto. In order to identify where in the program the branch is to be made, a *label* is needed. A label is a name that is formed with the same rules as variable names and must be immediately followed by a colon. The label is placed directly before the statement to which the branch is to be made and must appear in the same function as the goto.

So, for example, the statement

```
goto out_of_data;
```

will cause the program to branch immediately to the statement that is preceded by the label out_of_data:. This label can be located anywhere in the function, before or after the goto, and might be used as shown:

```
out_of_data:   printf ("Unexpected end of data.\n");
   ...
```

Programmers who are lazy will frequently abuse the goto statement to branch to other portions of their code. The goto statement interrupts the normal sequential flow of a program. As a result, programs are harder to follow. Using many gotos in a program can make it impossible to decipher. For this reason, goto statements are not considered part of a good programming style.

The *null* Statement

C permits a solitary semicolon to be placed wherever a normal program statement can appear. The effect of such a statement, known as the null statement, is that nothing is done. While this may seem useless, it is often used by C programmers in while, for, and do statements. For example, the purpose of the following statement is to store all the characters read in from the standard input into the character array pointed to by text until a newline character is encountered.

```
while ( (*text++ = getchar ()) != '\n' )
    ;
```

All of the operations are performed inside the looping-conditions part of the while statement. The null statement is needed because the compiler takes the statement that follows the looping expression as the body of the loop. Without the null statement, whatever statement that follows in the program would be treated as the body of the program loop by the compiler.

The following for statement copies characters from the standard input to the standard output until the end of file is encountered:

```
for (  ; (c = getchar ()) != EOF;   putchar  )
    ;
```

The next for statement counts the number of characters that appear in the standard input:

```
for ( count = 0;   getchar () != EOF;   ++count )
    ;
```

As a final example illustrating the `null` statement, the following loop copies the character string pointed to by `from` to the one pointed to by `to`.

```
while ( (*to++ = *from++) != '\0' )
    ;
```

The reader is advised that there is a tendency among certain programmers to try to squeeze as much as possible into the condition part of the `while` or into the condition or looping part of the `for`. Try not to become one of those programmers. In general, only those expressions involved with testing the condition of a loop should be included inside the condition part. Everything else should form the body of the loop. The only case to be made for forming such complex expressions might be one of execution efficiency. Unless execution speed is that critical, you should avoid using these types of expressions.

The preceding `while` statement is easier to read when written like this:

```
while ( *from != '\0' )
    *to++ = *from++;

*to = '\0';
```

Unions

One of the more unusual constructs in the C programming language is the *union*. This construct is used mainly in more advanced programming applications where it is necessary to store different types of data into the same storage area. For example, if we wanted to define a single variable called x, which could be used to store a single character, a floating-point number, or an integer, we would first define a union called, perhaps, `mixed`:

```
union  mixed
{
    char   c;
    float  f;
    int    i;
};
```

The declaration for a union is identical to that of a structure, except the keyword `union` is used where the keyword `struct` is otherwise specified. The real difference between structures and unions has to do with the way memory is allocated. Declaring a variable to be of type `union  mixed`, as in

```
union mixed  x;
```

does *not* define x to contain three distinct members called c, f, and i; rather it defines x to contain a *single* member that is called *either* c, f, or i. In this way, the variable x can be used to store either a `char` or a `float` or an `int`, but not all three (or not even two of the three). We can store a character into the variable x with the following statement:

```
x.c = 'K';
```

The character stored in x can subsequently be retrieved in the same manner. So to display its value at the terminal, for example, the following could be used:

```
printf ("Character = %c\n", x.c);
```

To store a floating-point value into x, the notation x.f is used:

```
x.f = 786.3869;
```

Finally, to store the result of dividing an integer count by 2 into x, the statement

```
x.i = count / 2;
```

could be used.

Since the float, char, and int members of x all exist in the same place in memory, only one value can be stored into x at a time. Furthermore, it is your responsibility to ensure that the value retrieved from a union is consistent with the way it was last stored in the union.

A union member follows the same rules of arithmetic as the type of the member that is used in the expression. So in

```
x.i / 2
```

the expression is evaluated according to the rules of integer arithmetic, since x.i and 2 are both integers.

A union can be defined to contain as many members as desired. The C compiler ensures that enough storage is allocated to accommodate the largest member of the union. Structures can be defined that contain unions, as can arrays. When defining a union, the name of the union is not required, and variables can be declared at the same time that the union is defined. Pointers to unions can also be declared, and their syntax and rules for performing operations are the same as for structures. Finally, a union variable can be initialized as follows: If it's a global, static, or automatic union variable, the *first* member of the union can be initialized to a constant expression. In such a case, the constant expression is listed inside a pair of braces, as in

```
union mixed  x = { '#' };
```

This sets the first member of x, which is c, to the character #.

An automatic union variable can also be initialized to another union variable of the same type:

```
void foo (union mixed x)
{
    union mixed  y = x;
    ...
}
```

Here the function `foo` assigns to the automatic union variable `y` the value of the argument `x`.

The use of a union enables you to define arrays that can be used to store elements of different data types. For example, the statement

```
struct
{
    char  *name;
    int   type;
    union
    {
        int   i;
        float f;
        char  c;
    } data;
}  table [TABLE_ENTRIES];
```

sets up an array called `table`, consisting of `TABLE_ENTRIES` elements. Each element of the array contains a structure consisting of a character pointer called `name`, an integer member called `type`, and a union member called `data`. Each `data` member of the array can contain either an `int`, a `float`, or a `char`. The integer member `type` might be used to keep track of the type of value stored in the member `data`. For example, we could assign it the value `INTEGER` (defined appropriately, we assume) if it contained an `int`, `FLOATING` if it contained a `float`, and `CHARACTER` if it contained a `char`. This information would enable us to know how to reference the particular `data` member of a particular array element.

To store the character `'#'` into `table[5]`, and subsequently set the `type` field to indicate that a character is stored in that location, the following two statements could be used:

```
table[5].data.c = '#';
table[5].type = CHARACTER;
```

When sequencing through the elements of `table`, we could determine the type of data value stored in each element by setting up an appropriate series of test statements. For example, the following loop would display each name and its associated value from `table` at the terminal:

```
#define   INTEGER   0
#define   FLOATING  1
#define   CHARACTER 2
    ...
```

```
for ( j = 0;   j < TABLE_ENTRIES;   ++j )
{
    printf ("%s  ", table[j].name);

    switch ( table[j].type )
    {
        case INTEGER:
            printf ("%i\n", table[j].data.i);
            break;
        case FLOATING:
            printf ("%f\n", table[j].data.f);
            break;
        case CHARACTER:
            printf ("%c\n", table[j].data.c);
            break;
        default:
            printf ("Unknown type (%i), element %i\n",
                        table[j].type, j );
            break;
    }
}
```

The preceding type of application illustrated might be practical for storage of a symbol table, for example, which might contain the name of each symbol, its type, and its value (and perhaps other information about the symbol as well).

The Comma Operator

At the bottom of the precedence totem pole, so to speak, is the comma operator. In Chapter 5, "Program Looping," we pointed out that inside a for statement we could include more than one expression in any of the fields by separating each expression with a comma. For example, the for statement that begins

```
for ( i = 0, j = 100;  i != 10;   ++i, j -= 10 )
    ...
```

initializes the value of i to 0 *and* j to 100 before the loop begins, and increments the value of i *and* subtracts 10 from the value of j each time after the body of the loop is executed.

The comma operator can be used to separate multiple expressions anywhere that a valid C expression can be used. The expressions will be evaluated from left to right. So in the statement

```
while ( i < 100 )
    sum += data[i], ++i;
```

the value of data[i] is added into sum and then i is incremented. Note that we don't need braces here since there is just one statement that follows the while statement. (It consists of two expressions separated by the comma operator.)

Since all operators in C produce a value, the value of the comma operator is that of the rightmost expression.

Note that a comma, used to separate arguments in a function call, or variable names in a list of declarations, for example, is a separate syntactic entity and is *not* an example of the use of the comma operator.

Variable Attributes

register

The C compiler provides a mechanism that enables the programmer to have some influence over the efficiency of the code that is generated by the compiler. If a function uses a particular variable heavily, then you can request that the value of that variable be stored in one of the machine's registers whenever the function is executed. This is done by prefixing the declaration of the variable by the keyword register, as in

```
register int    index;
register char   *text_pointer;
```

Both local variables and formal parameters can be declared as register variables. The types of variables that can be assigned to registers vary among machines. The basic data types can usually be assigned to registers, as well as pointers to any data type. As you would expect, arrays and structures cannot be declared as register variables.

Even if your compiler enables you to declare a variable as a register variable, it is still not guaranteed that it will in fact be assigned to a register. Each machine has different limitations on the number of register variables that are permitted. And some optimizing compilers simply ignore your requests anyway, preferring to make their own decisions as to what gets allocated to registers. In any case, variables that cannot be assigned to a register will not cause an error—the declaration will simply be ignored by the compiler.

It is worth noting that you cannot apply the address operator to a register variable. Other than that, register variables behave just as ordinary automatic variables.

const

The compiler allows you to associate the const attribute to variables whose values will not be changed by the program. That is, this tells the compiler that the specified variables have a *const*ant value throughout the program's execution. If you try to assign a value to a const variable after initializing it, or try to increment or decrement it, the compiler may issue an error message, although it is not required to do so. One of the motivations for the const attribute in the language is that it allows the compiler to place your const variables into read only memory. (Normally, the instructions of your program are also placed into read only memory.)

As an example of the const attribute, the lines

```
const   double   pi = 3.141592654;
const   char     *cp = &buffer;
```

declare two const variables, pi and cp. This tells the compiler that both of the variables will not be modified by the program.

volatile

This is sort of the inverse to const. It tells the compiler explicitly that the specified variable *will* change its value. It's included in the language to prevent the compiler from optimizing away seemingly redundant assignments to a variable, or repeated examination of a variable without its value seemingly changing. A good example is to consider an I/O port. Let's say you have an output port that's pointed to by a variable in your program called out_port. If you wanted to write two characters to the port, for example an O followed by an N, you might have the following code:

```
*out_port = 'O';
*out_port = 'N';
```

A smart compiler will notice two successive assigments to the same location and, since out_port isn't being modified in between, will simply remove the first assignment from the program. To prevent this from happening, you declare out_port to be a volatile pointer:

```
volatile char   *out_port;
```

Command-Line Arguments

Many times a program will be developed that requires the user to enter a small amount of information at the terminal. Based upon programs presented in this book, this information might consist of a number indicating the triangular number that we would like to have calculated or a word that we would like to have referenced in a dictionary.

Rather than having the program request this type of information from the user, we can supply the information to the program *at the time that the program is executed*. This capability is provided by what is known as *command-line arguments*.

We have pointed out that the only distinguishing quality of the function main is that its name is special; it specifies where program execution is to begin. In fact, the function main is actually *called* upon at the start of program execution by the C system (known more formally as the *runtime* system), just as you would call a function from within your own C program. When main completes execution, control is returned to the runtime system, which then knows that your program has completed execution.

When main is called by the runtime system, two arguments are actually passed to the function. The first argument, which is called argc by convention (for *arg*ument *c*ount), is an integer value that specifies the number of arguments typed on the command line. The second argument to main is an array of character pointers, which is called argv by convention (for *arg*ument *v*ector). There will be argc + 1 character pointers contained in this array, where argc always has a minimum value of 0. The first entry in this array is a pointer to the name of the program that is executing or is a pointer to a null string if the program name is not available on your system. Subsequent entries in the array point to the values that were specified in the same line as the command that initiated execution of the program. The last pointer in the argv array, argv[argc], is defined to be null.

In order to access the command-line arguments, the main function must be appropriately declared as taking two arguments. The conventional declaration that is used appears as follows:

```
int  main (int  argc, char  *argv[])
{
    ...
}
```

Remember, the declaration of argv defines an array that contains elements of type "pointer to char." As a practical use of command-line arguments, recall Program 10.10, which looked up a word inside a dictionary and printed its meaning. We can make use of command-line arguments so that the word whose meaning we wish to find can be specified at the same time that the program is executed, as in the UNIX command

```
a.out  aerie
```

This eliminates the need for the program to prompt the user to enter a word and also reduces the number of steps required on the part of the user to have a word looked up inside the dictionary.

If the command shown above were executed, the system would automatically pass to the main function a pointer to the character string "aerie" in argv[1]. As you will recall, argv[0] would contain a pointer to the name of the program, which in this case would be "a.out".

The `main` routine might appear as shown:

```
#include <stdlib.h>
#include <stdio.h>

int   main (int   argc, char   *argv[])
{
    struct entry  dictionary[100] =
      { { "aardvark",  "a burrowing African mammal"      },
        { "abyss",     "a bottomless pit"                },
        { "acumen",    "mentally sharp; keen"            },
        { "addle",     "to become confused"              },
        { "aerie",     "a high nest"                     },
        { "affix",     "to append; attach"               },
        { "agar",      "a jelly made from seaweed"       },
        { "ahoy",      "a nautical call of greeting"     },
        { "aigrette",  "an ornamental cluster of feathers" },
        { "ajar",      "partially opened"                } };

    int    entries = 10;
    int    entry_number;
    int    lookup (struct entry dictionary [], char   search[],
                   int   entries);

    if ( argc != 2 )
    {
        fprintf (stderr, "No word typed on the command line.\n");
        return (EXIT_FAILURE);
    }

    entry_number = lookup (dictionary, argv[1], entries);

    if ( entry_number != -1 )
        printf ("%s\n", dictionary[entry_number].definition);
    else
        printf ("Sorry, %s is not in my dictionary.\n", argv[1]);

    return (EXIT_SUCCESS);
}
```

The `main` routine tests to make sure that a word was typed after the program name when the program was executed. If it wasn't, or if more than one word was typed, then the value of `argc` will not be equal to 2. In that case, the program will write an error message to standard error and would terminate, returning an exit status of `EXIT_FAILURE`.

If `argc` is equal to 2, the `lookup` function will be called to find the word pointed to by `argv[1]` in the dictionary. If the word is found, its definition will be displayed.

By changing the name of the executable object to something more meaningful, such as `lookup`, the command to execute the program to find the word *addle* in the dictionary would be

```
lookup addle
```

The name of the executable file can be specified to be `lookup` when the program is compiled, or the executable file can easily be renamed with a simple command after the program has been compiled.

As another example of command-line arguments, Program 16.3 was a file-copying program. Program 17.1, which follows, takes the two file names from the command line, rather than prompting the user to type them in.

Program 17.1

```c
/* Program to copy one file to another — version 2 */

#include <stdlib.h>
#include <stdio.h>

int main (int  argc, char  *argv[])
{
    FILE  *in, *out;
    int   c;

    if ( argc != 3 )
    {
        fprintf (stderr, "Need two files names\n");
        return (EXIT_FAILURE);
    }

    if ( (in = fopen (argv[1], "r"))  ==  NULL )
    {
        fprintf (stderr, "Can't read %s.\n", argv[1]);
        return (EXIT_FAILURE);
    }
    if ( (out = fopen (argv[2], "w")) == NULL )
    {
        fprintf (stderr, "Can't write %s.\n", argv[2]);
        return (EXIT_FAILURE);
    }

    while ( (c = getc (in)) != EOF )
        putc (c, out);

    printf ("File has been copied.\n");

    return (EXIT_SUCCESS);
}
```

The program first checks to make sure that two arguments were typed after the program name. If so, the name of the input file will be pointed to by argv[1], and the name of the output file by argv[2]. After opening the first file for reading and the second file for writing, and after checking both opens to make sure they succeeded, the program copies the file character by character as before.

Note that there are four different ways for the program to terminate: incorrect number of command-line arguments, can't open the file to be copied for reading, can't open the file to place the copy into for writing, and successful termination. Remember, if you're going to use the exit status, you should *always* terminate the program with one. If your program terminates by falling through the bottom of main, it will return an *undefined* exit status.

If Program 16.3 were called copyf and the program was executed with the following command line:

```
copyf foo foo1
```

then the argv array would look like Figure 17.1 when main is entered.

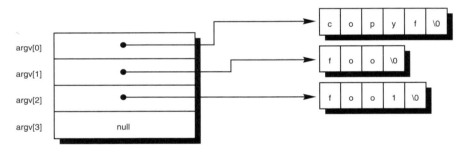

Figure 17.1. argv *array on startup of* copyf.

Remember that command-line arguments are *always* stored as character strings. Execution of the program power with the command-line arguments 2 and 16, as in

```
power 2 16
```

will store a pointer to the character string "2" inside argv[1], and a pointer to the string "16" inside argv[2]. If the arguments are to be interpreted as numbers by the program (as we suspect is the case in the power program), they must be converted by the program itself. There are several routines in the program library for doing such conversions, such as sscanf, atof, atoi, strtod, and strtol. These are described in Appendix B.

Dynamic Memory Allocation

Whenever we define a variable in C—whether it is a simple data type, an array, or a structure—we are effectively reserving one or more locations in the computer's memory to contain the values that will be stored in that variable. The C compiler automatically allocates the correct amount of storage for us.

It is frequently desirable, if not necessary, to be able to *dynamically* allocate storage while a program is running. Suppose we had a program that was designed to read in a set of data from a file into an array in memory. If we were unsure precisely how many data elements were contained in the file, or if the amount could vary from one run of the program to the next, then we would have to define our array to contain the maximum number of elements that would be read into the array, as in the following:

```
#define  MAX_ELEMENTS    1000

struct data_entry  data_array [MAX_ELEMENTS];
```

Now as long as the data file contains 1,000 elements or less, we're in business. But what happens when the number of elements exceeds this amount? In that case, we must go back to the program, change the value of MAX_ELEMENTS, and recompile it. Of course, no matter what value we select, we always have the chance of running into the same problem again in the future.

The preceding problem becomes much worse if we are dealing with many different arrays in our program, each of which can contain a variable number of elements. In order to handle the situation properly, we must reserve the maximum number of elements in each array. In many cases, this approach may be infeasible. We might know, for example, that the *total* number of elements that would be stored into three different arrays would be a maximum of 10,000, but that each individual array might contain up to 8,000 elements. Reserving 8,000 elements for each array might exceed the memory capacity of the computer system, whereas we know that 10,000 total elements could be easily handled. What could we do?

Dynamic memory allocation enables us to get storage as we need it. That is, this approach enables us to allocate memory as the program is executing, and thereby eliminates the need to completely define our storage requirements when the program is compiled. In order to use dynamic memory allocation, we must first learn about three functions and one new operator.

The *calloc* and *malloc* Functions

In order to allocate storage while a program is executing, a call must be made to a special function. In the standard C library, two functions, called calloc and malloc, can be used. The calloc function takes two arguments that specify the number of elements to be reserved and the size of each element in *bytes*. The function returns a pointer to the beginning of the allocated storage area in memory. The storage area is also automatically set to 0.

calloc returns a pointer to void, which is C's generic pointer type. Before storing this returned pointer inside a pointer variable in your program, it should be converted into a pointer of the appropriate type using the type cast operator.

The malloc function works similarly, except that it only takes a single argument—the total number of bytes of storage to allocate—and also doesn't automatically set the storage area to 0.

The dynamic memory allocation functions are declared in the standard header file <stdlib.h>, which should be included in your program whenever you want to use these routines.

The *sizeof* Operator

In order to determine the size of data elements to be reserved by calloc or malloc in a machine-independent way, the C sizeof operator should be used. The sizeof operator returns the size of the specified item in bytes. The argument to the sizeof operator can be a variable, an array name, the name of a basic data type, the name of a derived data type, or an expression. For example, writing

```
sizeof (int)
```

gives the number of bytes needed to store an integer. On the IBM PC, this will have the value 2, since an integer occupies a 16-bit compiler on that machine. If x were defined to be an array of 100 integers, the expression

```
sizeof (x)
```

would give the amount of storage required for the 100 integers of x (or the value 200 using a 16-bit compiler on the IBM PC). The expression

```
sizeof (struct data_entry)
```

will have as its value the amount of storage required to store one data_entry structure. Finally, if data is defined as an array of struct data_entry elements, the expression

```
sizeof (data) / sizeof (struct data_entry)
```

will give the number of elements contained in data (data must be a previously defined array, and not a formal parameter or externally referenced array). The expression

```
sizeof (data) / sizeof (data[0])
```

will also produce the same result. The macro

```
#define  ELEMENTS(x)   (sizeof(x) / sizeof(x[0]))
```

simply generalizes this technique. It enables you to write code like

```
if ( i >= ELEMENTS (data) )
   ...
```

and

```
for ( i = 0; i < ELEMENTS (data); ++i )
   ...
```

You should remember that sizeof is actually an operator, and not a function, even though it looks like one. This operator is evaluated at compile time and not at run time. This means that the compiler automatically calculates the value of the sizeof expression and replaces it with the result of the calculation; also, the value of this operator is a constant.

QUICK TIP

Use the sizeof operator wherever possible to avoid having to calculate and hard-code sizes into your program.

Getting back to dynamic memory allocation, if you wanted to allocate enough storage in your program to store 1,000 integers, you can call calloc as shown:

```
#include <stdlib.h>
   ...
int  *intptr;
   ...
intptr = (int *) calloc (sizeof (int), 1000);
```

Using malloc, the function call would look like this:

```
intptr = (int *) malloc (1000 * sizeof (int));
```

Remember that both malloc and calloc are defined to return a pointer to void and, as noted, this pointer should be type cast to the appropriate pointer type. In the preceding example, the pointer is type cast to an integer pointer and then assigned to int_pointer.

If you ask for more memory than the system has available, calloc (or malloc) will return a null pointer.

> ### QUICK TIP
>
> Whether you use `calloc` or `malloc`, be sure to test the pointer that is returned to ensure that the allocation succeeded.

The following code segment allocates space for 1,000 integer pointers and tests the pointer that is returned. If the allocation fails, the program writes an error message to standard error and then exits.

```c
#include <stdlib.h>
#include <stdio.h>
   ...
int  *intptr;
   ...
intptr = (int *) calloc (sizeof (int), 1000);

if ( intptr == NULL )
{
    fprintf (stderr, "calloc failed\n");
    exit (EXIT_FAILURE);
}
```

If the allocation succeeds, the integer pointer variable `intptr` can be used as if it were pointing to an array of 1,000 integers. So, to set all 1,000 elements to -1, you could write

```c
for ( p = intptr; p < intptr + 1000; ++p )
    *p = -1;
```

assuming p is declared to be an integer pointer.

To reserve storage for n elements of type `struct data_entry`, we would first need to define a pointer of the appropriate type

```c
struct data_entry  *data_pointer;
```

and could then proceed to call the `calloc` function to reserve the appropriate number of elements

```c
data_pointer = (struct data_entry *)
                 calloc (n, sizeof (struct data_entry));
```

Execution of the above statement proceeds as follows:

1. The calloc function is called with two arguments, the first specifying that storage for n elements is to be dynamically allocated and the second specifying the size of each element;

2. The calloc function returns a pointer in memory to the allocated storage area. If the storage cannot be allocated then the null pointer will be returned;

3. The pointer is type cast into a pointer of type "pointer to struct data_entry" and is then assigned to the pointer variable data_pointer.

Once again, the value of `data_pointer` should be subsequently tested to ensure that the allocation succeeded. If it did, then its value will be nonnull. This pointer could then be used in the normal fashion, as if it were pointing to an array of n `data_entry` elements. For example, if `data_entry` contained an integer member called `index`, we could assign 100 to this member as pointed to by `data_pointer` with the statement

```
data_pointer->index = 100;
```

The *free* Function

When you have finished working with the memory that has been dynamically allocated by `calloc` or `malloc`, you can give it back to the system by calling the `free` function. The single argument to the function is a pointer to the beginning of the allocated memory, as returned by a `calloc` or `malloc` call. So the call

```
free (data_pointer);
```

will return the memory allocated by the `calloc` call shown above, provided that the value of `data_pointer` still points to the *beginning* of the allocated memory.

The `free` function does not return a value.

The memory that is freed by `free` can be reused by a later call to `calloc` or `malloc`. For programs that need to allocate more storage space than would otherwise be available if it were all allocated at once, this is worth remembering.

QUICK TIP

Make sure you give the `free` function a valid pointer to the beginning of some previously allocated space.

Dynamic memory allocation proves very useful when dealing with linked structures, such as linked lists. Whenever we wish to add a new entry to the list, we can dynamically allocate storage for one entry in the list and link it into the list with the pointer returned by `calloc` or `malloc`. For example, assume that list_end points to the end of a singly linked list of type struct entry, defined as follows:

```
struct entry
{
    int         value;
    struct entry  *next;
};
```

Here is a function called add_entry that takes as its argument a pointer to the start of the linked list and that adds a new entry to the end of the list.

```
#include <stdlib.h>
#include <stddef.h>

/* add new entry to end of list */

struct entry *add_entry (struct entry *list_ptr)
{
    /* find the end of the list */

    while ( list_ptr->next != NULL )
        list_ptr = list_ptr->next;

    /* get storage for new entry */

    list_ptr->next = (struct entry *)
                        malloc (sizeof (struct entry));

    if ( list_ptr->next != NULL )
        /* add null to the new end of the list */
        (list_ptr->next)->next = (struct entry *) NULL;

    return (list_ptr->next);
}
```

If the allocation succeeds, a null pointer is placed in the next member of the newly allocated linked-list entry (pointed to by list_ptr->next).

The function returns a pointer to the new list entry, or the null pointer if the allocation fails (verify that this is in fact what happens). If you draw a picture of a linked list and trace through the execution of add_entry, it will help you to understand how the function works.

There is another function, called realloc, that is associated with dynamic memory allocation. It can be used to shrink or expand the size of some previously allocated storage. For more details, consult Appendix B.

A

ANSI C Language Summary

This section summarizes the C language in a format suitable for quick reference. It is not intended that this section be a complete definition of the language, but rather a more informal description of its features. You should thoroughly read the material in this section after you have completed the text. Doing so will not only reinforce the material you have learned, but will also provide you with a better global understanding of C.

For a complete description of the semantics of the language, consult Appendix A of the Second Edition of Kernighan and Ritchie's *The C Programming Language* (Prentice Hall, 1988).

1.0 Identifiers

An *identifier* in C consists of a sequence of letters (upper- or lowercase), digits, or underscore characters. The first character of an identifier must be a letter or an underscore character. The first 31 characters of an identifier are guaranteed to be significant, even though more characters may be used. On some systems, external names may be significant to as few as six characters. Furthermore, on some systems upper- and lowercase letters may not be distinguishable in an external name.

Table A.1 lists the identifiers that are reserved by the C compiler and cannot be otherwise used in a program.

2.0 Comments

A comment begins with the two characters /* and ends as soon as the characters */ are encountered. Any characters may be included inside the comment, which can extend over multiple lines of the program. A comment can be used anywhere in the program where a blank space is allowed. Comments cannot be nested.

Table A.1. Reserved Words.

auto	double	int	struct
break	else	long	switch
case	enum	register	typedef
char	extern	return	union
const	float	short	unsigned
continue	for	signed	void
default	goto	sizeof	volatile
do	if	static	

3.0 Constants

3.1 Integer Constants

An integer constant is a sequence of digits, optionally preceded by a plus or minus sign. If the first digit is 0, the integer is taken as an octal constant, in which case all digits that follow must be from 0 through 7. If the first digit is 0 and is immediately followed by the letter x (or X), the integer is taken as a hexadecimal constant, and the digits that follow may be in the range of 0-9 or a-f (or A-F).

The suffix letter l or L can be added to the end of an integer constant to make it a long int constant. If the value can't fit into a long int, it's treated as an unsigned long int.

The suffix u or U can be added to the end of an integer constant to make it un-signed. If the constant is too large to fit inside an unsigned int, it's taken as an unsigned long int.

Both an unsigned and long suffix can be added to an integer constant to make it an unsigned long int.

If an unsuffixed decimal integer constant is too large to fit into a signed int, it is treated as a long int. If it's too large to fit into a long int, it's treated as an unsigned long int.

If an unsuffixed octal or hexadecimal integer constant is too large to fit into a signed int, it is treated as an unsigned int, unless it's too large. If it's too large to fit into an unsigned int, it's treated as a long int. Finally, if it's too large to fit into a long int, it's treated as unsigned long int.

3.2 Floating-Point Constants

A floating-point constant consists of a sequence of decimal digits, a decimal point, and another sequence of decimal digits. A minus sign may precede the value to denote a negative value. Either the sequence of digits before the deci-mal point or after the decimal point may be omitted, but not both.

If the floating-point constant is immediately followed by the letter e (or E) and an optionally signed integer, then the constant is expressed in scientific notation. This integer (the *exponent*) represents the power of 10 that the value preceding the letter e (the *mantissa*) is multiplied by (for example, 1.5e-2 rep-resents 1.5×10^{-2} or .015).

Floating-point constants are treated as double precision values by the compiler. The suffix letter f or F can be added to specify a float constant instead of a double one. The suffix letter l or L can be added to specify a long double con-stant.

3.3 Character Constants

A character that is enclosed within single quotes is a character constant. How the inclusion of more than one character inside the single quotes is handled is implementation-defined.

3.3.1 Escape Sequences

Special escape sequences are recognized and are introduced by the backslash character. These escape sequences are listed below.

Character	Meaning
\a	audible alert
\b	backspace
\f	form feed
\n	newline
\r	carriage return
\t	horizontal tab
\v	vertical tab
\\	backslash
\"	double quote
\'	single quote
\?	question mark
\nnn	octal character value
\xnn	hexadecimal character value

In the next to last case, from one to three octal digits can be specified. In the last case, hexadecimal digits are used.

3.3.2 Wide Character Constants

Some compilers may support *wide character constants*. Such a constant is written as L'x'. The type of such a constant is wchar_t, as defined in the standard header file <stddef.h>. Wide character constants give a way to express a character from a character set that cannot be fully represented with the normal char type.

3.4 Character String Constants

A sequence of zero or more characters enclosed within double quotes represents a character string constant. Any valid character can be included in the string, including any of the escape characters listed above. The compiler automatically inserts a null character ('\0') at the end of the string.

Normally, the compiler produces a pointer to the first character in the string and the type is "pointer to char." However, when the string constant is used with the sizeof operator to initialize a character array, or with the & operator, the type of the string constant is "array of char."

Character string constants cannot be modified by the program.

3.4.1 Character String Concatenation

The preprocessor automatically concatenates adjacent character string constants together. The strings may be separated by zero or more whitespace characters. So the three strings

```
"a" " character "
    "string"
```

are equivalent to the single string

```
"a character string"
```

after concatenation.

3.4.2 Wide Character String Constants

Character string constants from an extended character set are expressed using the format L"...". The type of such a constant is "pointer to wchar_t", where wchar_t is defined in <stddef.h>.

3.5 Enumeration Constants

An identifier that has been declared as a value for an enumerated type is taken as a constant of that particular type and is otherwise treated as type int by the compiler.

4.0 Data Types and Declarations

This section summarizes the basic data types, derived data types, enumerated data types, and typedef. Also summarized in this section is the format for declaring variables.

4.1 Declarations

When defining a particular structure, union, enumerated data type, or typedef, the compiler does not automatically reserve any storage. The definition merely tells the compiler about the particular data type and (optionally) associates a name with it. Such a definition can be made either inside or outside a function. In the former case, only the function knows of its existence; in the latter case, it is known throughout the remainder of the file.

Once the definition has been made, variables can subsequently be declared to be of that particular data type. A variable that is declared to be of *any* data type *will* have storage reserved for it, unless it is an `extern` declaration, in which case it may or may not have storage allocated (see Section 6.0).

The language also allows storage to be allocated at the same time that a particular structure, union, or enumerated data type is defined. This is done by simply listing the variables before the terminating semicolon of the definition.

4.2 Basic Data Types

The basic C data types are summarized in Table A.2. A variable can be declared to be of a particular basic data type using the format

```
type  name = initial_value;
```

The assignment of an initial value to the variable is optional, and is subject to the rules summarized in Section 6.2. More than one variable can be declared at once using the general format

```
type  name = initial_value, name = initial_value, ... ;
```

Before the type declaration, an optional storage class may also be specified, as summarized in Section 6.2. If a storage class is specified, and the type of the variable is `int`, then `int` can be omitted. For example,

```
static  counter;
```

declares `counter` to be a `static int` variable.

Table A.2. Summary of basic data types.

Type	*Meaning*
`int`	Integer value; that is, value that contains no decimal point; guaranteed to contain at least 16 bits of accuracy.
`short int`	Integer value of reduced accuracy; takes half as much memory as an `int` on some machines; guaranteed to contain at least 16 bits of accuracy.
`long int`	Integer value of extended accuracy; takes twice as much memory as an `int` on some machines; guaranteed to contain at least 32 bits of accuracy.

Type	Meaning
unsigned int	Positive integer value; can store positive values up to twice as large as an int; guaranteed to contain at least 16 bits of accuracy.
float	Floating-point value; that is, a value that may contain decimal places; guaranteed to contain at least six digits of precision.
double	Extended accuracy floating-point value; guaranteed to contain at least 10 digits of precision.
long double	Extra-extended accuracy floating-point value; guaranteed to contain at least 10 digits of precision.
char	Single character value; on some systems, sign extension may occur when used in an expression.
unsigned char	Same as char, except ensures that sign extension will not occur as a result of integral promotion.
signed char	Same as char, except ensures that sign extension will occur as a result of integral promotion.
void	No type; used to ensure that a function that does not return a value is not used as if it does, or to explicitly "discard" the results of an expression.

Note that the signed modifier can also be placed in front of the short int, int, and long int types. Since these types are signed by default anyway, this has no effect.

4.3 Derived Data Types

A derived data type is one that is built up from one or more of the basic data types. Derived data types are arrays, structures, unions, and pointers. A function that returns a value of a specified type is also considered a derived data type. Each of these, with the exception of functions, is summarized in the following sections. Functions are separately covered in Section 7.0.

4.3.1 Arrays

Single-Dimensional Arrays
Arrays can be defined to contain any basic data type or any derived data type. Arrays of functions are not permitted, although arrays of function pointers are.

The declaration of an array has the following basic format:

> *type name*[*n*]   = { *initial_value, initial_value, ...* };

The constant expression *n* determines the number of elements in the array *name* and may be omitted, provided a list of initial values is specified. In such a case, the size of the array will be determined based on the number of initial values listed. Each initial value must be a constant expression. There can be fewer values in the initialization list than there are elements in the array, but there cannot be more.

If fewer values are specified, then only that many elements of the array will be initialized, beginning with the first element. The remaining elements will be set to 0.

A special case of array initialization occurs in the case of character arrays, which may be initialized by a constant character string. For example,

```
char today[] = "Monday";
```

declares `today` as an array of characters. This array will be initialized to the characters `'M'`, `'o'`, `\&'n'`, `'d'`, `'a'`, `'y'`, and `'\0'`, respectively.

If you explicitly dimension the character array and don't leave room for the terminating null, the compiler won't place a null at the end of the array:

```
char today[6] = "Monday";
```

This declares `today` as an array of six characters and sets its elements to the characters `'M'`, `'o'`, `'n'`, `'d'`, `'a'`, and `'y'`, respectively.

Multidimensional Arrays

The general format for declaring a multidimensional array follows:

```
type  name[d1][d2]...[dn] = initialization_list;
```

The array *name* is defined to contain *d1 x d2 x ... x dn* elements of the specified type, where *d1, d2, ..., dn* are constant expressions. For example,

```
int  three_d [5][2][20];
```

defines a three-dimensional array, `three_d`, containing 200 integers.

A particular element is referenced from a multidimensional array by enclosing the desired subscript for each dimension in its own set of brackets. For example, the statement

```
three_d [4][0][15] = 100;
```

stores 100 into the indicated element of the array `three_d`.

Multidimensional arrays can be initialized in the same manner as one-dimensional arrays. Nested pairs of braces can be used to control the assignment of values to the elements in the array.

The following declares `matrix` to be a two-dimensional array containing four rows and three columns:

```
int matrix[4][3] =
        {  { 1, 2, 3 },
           { 4, 5, 6 },
           { 7, 8, 9 } };
```

Elements in the first row of `matrix` are set to the values 1, 2, and 3, respectively; in the second row to 4, 5, and 6, respectively; and in the third row to 7, 8, and 9, respectively. The elements in the fourth row are set to 0, since no values are specified for that row. The declaration

```
static int matrix[4][3] =
        { 1, 2, 3, 4, 5, 6, 7, 8, 9 };
```

initializes `matrix` to the same values, since the elements of a multidimensional array are initialized in "dimension-order"; that is, from leftmost to rightmost dimension.

Finally, the declaration

```
int matrix[4][3] =
        {  { 1 },
           { 4 },
           { 7 } };
```

sets the first element of the first row of `matrix` to 1, the first element of the second row to 4, and the first element of the third row to 7. All remaining elements will be set to 0 by default.

4.3.2 Structures

General Format
```
struct name
{
    member_declaration
    member_declaration
          . . .
}  variable_list;
```

The structure *name* is defined to contain the members as specified by each *member_declaration*. Each such declaration consists of a type specification followed by a list of one or more member names.

Variables may be declared at the time that the structure is defined simply by listing them before the terminating semicolon, or they may subsequently be declared using the format

```
struct name   variable_list;
```

This format obviously cannot be used if *name* is omitted when the structure is defined. If that were the case, all variables of that structure type would have to be declared with the definition.

The format of initializing a structure variable is similar to that for arrays. Its members may be initialized by enclosing the list of initial values in a pair of curly braces. Each value in the list must be a constant expression. The declaration

```
struct   entry
{
   char   *word;
   char   *definition;
} dictionary[1000] =
      { { "a",          "first letter of the alphabet" },
        { "aardvark",   "a burrowing African mammal"   },
        { "aback",      "to startle"                   } };
```

declares `dictionary` to contain 1,000 `entry` structures, with the first three elements initialized to the specified character string pointers.

An automatic structure variable can also be initialized to another structure of the same type as follows:

```
struct date   tomorrow = today;
```

This declares the `date` structure variable `tomorrow` and assigns to it the contents of the (previously declared) `date` structure variable `today`.

A *member_declaration* that has the format

```
    type   field_name : n
```

defines a *field* that is *n* bits wide inside the structure, where *n* is an integer value. Fields may be packed from left to right on some machines and right to left on others. If *field_name* is omitted, the specified number of bits are reserved, but cannot be referenced. If *field_name* is omitted and *n* is 0, the field that follows is aligned on the next storage *unit* boundary, where a *unit* is implementation-defined. The type of a field may be `int`, `signed int`, or `unsigned int`. It is implementation-defined whether an `int` field is treated as signed or unsigned. The address operator (&) cannot be applied to a field, and arrays of fields cannot be defined.

4.3.3 Unions

General Format

```
union   name
{
    member_declaration
    member_declaration
        ...
} variable_list;
```

This defines a union called *name* with members as specified by each *member_declaration*. Each member of the union shares overlapping storage space, and the compiler ensures that enough space is reserved to contain the largest member of the union.

Variables can be declared at the time that the union is defined, or they may be subsequently declared using the notation

```
union   name   variable_list;
```

provided the union was given a name when it was defined.

It is the programmer's responsibility to ensure that the value retrieved from a union is consistent with the last value that was stored inside the union. The *first* member of a union can be initialized by enclosing the initial value, which must be a constant expression, inside a pair of curly braces:

```
union   shared
{
    long  int  l;
    int         w[2];
} swap = { 0xffffL };
```

This declares the union variable swap and sets the l member to hexadecimal ffff.

An automatic union variable can also be initialized to a union of the same type, as in

```
union shared swap2 = swap;
```

4.3.4 Pointers

The basic format for declaring a pointer variable is as follows:

```
type   *name;
```

The identifier *name* is declared to be of type "pointer to *type*," which can be a basic C data type, or a derived data type. For example,

```
int   *ip;
```

declares `ip` to be a pointer to an `int`, and the declaration

```
struct  entry  *ep;
```

declares `ep` to be a pointer to an `entry` structure.

Pointers that will point to elements in an array are declared to point to the type of element contained in the array. For example, the prededing declaration of `ip` would also be used to declare a pointer into an array of integers.

More advanced forms of pointer declarations are also permitted. For example, the declaration

```
char *tp[100];
```

declares `tp` to be an array of 100 character pointers, and the declaration

```
struct entry (*fn_pointer) (int);
```

declares `fn_pointer` to be a pointer to a function that returns an `entry` structure and that takes a single `int` argument.

A pointer can be tested to see if it's null by comparing it against a constant expression whose value is 0. The implementation may choose to internally represent a null pointer with a value other than 0. However, a comparison between such an internally represented null pointer and a constant value of 0 must prove equal.

Some programmers have the bad habit of interchangeably using pointers and `int`s. For example, they frequently omit the declaration for a function that returns a pointer. The manner in which pointers are converted to integers, and integers are converted to pointers, is machine dependent, as is the size of the integer required to hold a pointer.

The type "pointer to `void`" is the generic pointer type. The language guarantees that a pointer of any type can be assigned to a `void` pointer and back again without changing its value.

Other than this special case, assignment of different pointer types is not permitted.

4.4 Enumerated Data Types

General Format

```
enum  name { enum_1, enum_2, ... } variable_list;
```

The enumerated type *name* is defined with enumeration values *enum_1*, *enum_2*, ..., each of which is an identifier or an identifier followed by an equals sign and a constant expression. *variable_list* is an optional list of variables (with optional initial values) declared to be of type `enum` *name*.

The compiler assigns sequential integers to the enumeration identifiers starting at 0. If an identifier is followed by = and a constant expression, the value of that expression is assigned to the identifier. Subsequent identifiers are assigned values beginning with that constant expression plus one. Enumeration identifiers are treated as constant integer values by the compiler.

If it is desired to declare variables to be of a previously defined (and named) enumeration type, the construct

```
enum  name  variable_list;
```

can be used.

A variable declared to be of a particular enumerated type can only be assigned a value of the same data type, although the compiler might not flag this as an error.

4.5 *typedef*

The `typedef` statement is used to assign a new name to a basic or derived data type. The `typedef` does not define a new type but simply a new name for an existing type. Therefore, variables declared to be of the newly named type are treated by the compiler exactly as if they were declared to be of the type associated with the new name.

In forming a `typedef` definition, proceed as though a normal variable declaration were being made. Then, place the new type name where the variable name would normally appear. Finally, in front of everything, place the keyword `typedef`.

As an example,

```
typedef struct
       {
             float  x;
             float  y;
       }  POINT;
```

associates the name `POINT` with a structure containing two floating-point members called x and y. Variables can subsequently be declared to be of type `POINT`, as in

```
POINT  origin = { 0.0, 0.0 };
```

4.6 Type Modifiers *const* and *volatile*

The keyword `const` may be placed before a type declaration to tell the compiler that the value cannot be modified. So the declaration

```
const int x5 = 100;
```

declares x5 to be a constant integer (that is, it won't be set to anything else during the program's execution). The compiler can then specify that x5 be stored in read only memory, if desired.

The compiler is *not* required to flag attempts to change the value of a const variable.

The `volatile` modifier explicitly tells the compiler that the value changes (usually dynamically). When a `volatile` variable is used in an expression, its value will be accessed each place it appears. The `volatile` qualifier is used in the following declaration of `port17` to ensure that the compiler always evaluates any indirect access through the pointer.

```
#define   TTYPORT   0x17755U;

volatile char *port17 = (char *) TTYPORT;

*port17 = 'O';
*port17 = 'N';
```

Here the consecutive assignments to `*port17` might seem redundant to the compiler, and unless told otherwise, a good optimizing compiler might simply remove the first assignment. Since `port17` is of type "pointer to volatile `char`," the compiler will not remove the assignment.

To declare `port17` to be of type "volatile pointer to `char`"a different declaration, you would write `char *volatile port17`.

5.0 Expressions

Variable names, function names, array names, constants, function calls, array references, and structure references are all considered expressions. Applying a unary operator (where appropriate) to one of these expressions is also an expression, as is combining two or more of these expressions with a binary or ternary operator. Finally, an expression enclosed within parentheses is also an expression.

An expression of any type other than `void` that identifies an object is called an `lvalue`. If it can be assigned a value, it is known as a *modifiable lvalue.*

Modifiable lvalue expressions are required in certain places. The expression on the left side of an assignment operator must be a modifiable lvalue. Furthermore, the increment and decrement operators can only be applied to modifiable lvalues, as can the unary address operator `&` (unless it's a function).

5.1 Summary of C Operators

Table A.3 summarizes the various operators in the C language. These operators are listed in order of decreasing precedence. Operators grouped together have the same precedence.

As an example of how to use Table A.3, consider the expression

```
b ¦ c & d * e
```

Table A.3. Summary of C operators.

Operator	Description	Associativity
( )	Function call	
[ ]	Array element reference	
->	Pointer to structure member reference	Left to right
.	Structure member reference	
-	Unary minus	
+	Unary plus	
++	Increment	
- -	Decrement	
!	Logical negation	
~	Ones complement	Right to left
*	Pointer reference (indirection)	
&	Address	
sizeof	Size of an object	
(type)	Type cast (conversion	
*	Multiplication	
/	Division	Left to right
%	Modulus	
+	Addition	Left to right
-	Subtraction	
<<	Left shift	Left to right
>>	Right shift	

continues

Table A.3. Continued

Operator	Description	Associativity
<	Less than	
<=	Less than or equal to	Left to right
>	Greater than	
=>	Greater than or equal to	
==	Equality	Left to right
!=	Inequality	
&	Bitwise AND	Left to right
^	Bitwise XOR	Left to right
¦	Bitwise OR	Left to right
&&	Logical AND	Left to right
¦¦	Logical OR	Left to right
?:	Conditional	Right to left
= *= /= %= += -= &= ^= ¦= <<= >>=	Assignment operators	Right to left
,	Comma operator	Left to Right

The multiplication operator has higher precedence than both the bitwise OR and bitwise AND operators, since it appears before both of these in Table A.3. Similarly, the bitwise AND operator has higher precedence than the bitwise OR operator, since the former appears above the latter in the table. Therefore, this expression would be evaluated as

```
b ¦ ( c & ( d * e ) )
```

Now consider the following expression:

```
b % c * d
```

Since the modulus and multiplication operator appear in the same grouping in Table A.3, they have the same precedence. The associativity listed for these operators is left to right, indicating that the expression would be evaluated as

```
( b % c ) * d
```

As another example, the expression

```
++a ->b
```

would be evaluated as

```
++(a->b)
```

since the `->` operator has higher precedence than the `++` operator.

Finally, since the assignment operators group from right to left, the statement

```
a = b = 0;
```

would be evaluated as

```
a = (b = 0);
```

which would have the net result of setting the values of a and b to 0. In the case of the expression

```
x[i] + ++i
```

it is not defined whether the compiler will evaluate the left side of the plus operator or the right side first. Here, the way that it's done will affect the result, since the value of i may be incremented before `x[i]` is evaluated.

Another case in which the order of evaluation is not defined is in the expression

```
x[i] = ++i
```

In this situation, it is not defined whether the value of i will be incremented before or after its value is used to index into x.

The order of evaluation of function arguments is also undefined. Therefore, in the function call

```
f (i, ++i);
```

i may be incremented first, thereby causing the same value to be sent as the two arguments to the function.

The C language guarantees that the && and ¦¦ operators will be evaluated from left to right. Furthermore, in the case of &&, it is guaranteed that the second operand will not be evaluated if the first is 0; and in the case of ¦¦, it is guaranteed that the second operand will not be evaluated if the first is nonzero. This fact is worth bearing in mind when forming expressions such as

```
if ( data_flag  ¦¦  check_data () )
   . . .
```

since, in this case, `check_data` will only be called if the value of `data_flag` is 0. To take another example, if the array a is declared to contain n elements, then the statement that begins

```
if ( index >= 0  &&  index < n  &&  a[index] == 0 )
   ...
```

will reference the element contained in `a[index]` only if `index` is a valid subscript into the array.

5.2 Constant Expressions

A constant expression is an expression in which each of the terms is a constant value. Constant expressions are *required* in the following situations:

1. As the value after a case in a `switch` statement

2. For specifying the size of an array

3. For assigning a value to an enumeration identifier

4. For specifying the bit field size in a structure definition

5. For assigning initial values to external or `static` variables

6. For specifying initial values inside a pair of curly braces

7. As the expression following the `#if` in a `#if` preprocessor statement

In the first four cases, the constant expression must consist of integer constants, character constants, enumeration constants, and `sizeof` expressions. The only operators that can be used are the arithmetic operators, the bitwise operators, the relational operators, the conditional expression operator, and the type cast operator.

In the fifth and sixth cases, in addition to the rules cited earlier, the address operator can be implicitly or explicitly used. However, it can only be applied to external or static variables or functions. So, for example, the expression

```
&x + 10
```

would be a valid constant expression, provided that x is an external or static variable. Furthermore, the expression

```
&a[10] - 5
```

is a valid constant expression if a is an external or static array. Finally, since `&a[0]` is equivalent to the expression a,

```
a + sizeof (char) * 100
```

is also a valid constant expression.

For the last situation that requires a constant expression (after the `#if`), the rules are the same as for the first four cases, except the `sizeof` operator, enumeration constants, and the type case operator cannot be used. However, the special `defined` operator is permitted (see Section 9.2.1).

5.3 Arithmetic Operators

Given that

a, b are expressions of any basic data type except void;

i, j are expressions of any integer data type;

then the expression

-a   negates the value of a;

+a   gives the value of a;

a + b   adds a with b;

a - b   subtracts b from a;

a * b   multiplies a by b;

a / b   divides a by b;

i % j   gives the remainder of i divided by j.

In each expression, the usual arithmetic conversions are performed on the operands (see Section 5.16). If a is unsigned, -a is calculated by first applying integral promotion to it, subtracting it from the largest value of the promoted type, and adding 1 to the result.

If two integral values are divided, the result is truncated. If either operand is negative, the direction of the truncation is not defined (that is, -3 / 2 may produce -1 on some machines and -2 on others); otherwise, truncation is always toward 0 (3 / 2 will always produce 1). See Section 5.15 for a summary of arithmetic operations with pointers.

5.4 Logical Operators

Given that

a, b   are expressions of any basic data type except void, or are both pointers;

then the expression

a && b   has the value 1 if both a and b are nonzero, and 0 otherwise (and b is evaluated only if a is nonzero);

a ¦¦ b   has the value 1 if either a or b is nonzero, and 0 otherwise (and b is evaluated only if a is zero);

! a   has the value 1 if a is zero, and 0 otherwise.

The usual arithmetic conversions are applied to a and b (see Section 5.16). The type of the result in all cases is int.

5.5 Relational Operators

Given that

a, b   are expressions of any basic data type except void, or are both pointers;

then the expression

a < b   has the value 1 if a is less than b, and 0 otherwise;

a <= b   has the value 1 if a is less than or equal to b, and 0 otherwise;

a > b   has the value 1 if a is greater than b, and 0 otherwise;

a >= b   has the value 1 if a is greater than or equal to b, and 0 otherwise;

a == b   has the value 1 if a is equal to b, and 0 otherwise;

a != b   has the value 1 if a is not equal to b, and 0 otherwise.

The usual arithmetic conversions are performed on a and b (see Section 5.16). The first four relational tests are only meaningful for pointers if they both point into the same array or to members of the same structure or union. The type of the result in each case is int.

5.6 Bitwise Operators

Given that

i, j, n   are expressions of any integer data type;

then the expression

i & j   performs a bitwise AND of i and j;

i ¦ j   performs a bitwise OR of i and j;

i ^ j   performs a bitwise XOR of i and j;

~i   takes the ones complement of i;

i << n   shifts i to the left n bits;

i >> n   shifts i to the right n bits.

The usual arithmetic conversions are performed on the operands, except with << and >>, in which case just integral promotion is performed on each operand (see Section 5.16). If the shift count is negative or is greater than or equal to the number of bits contained in the object being shifted, the result of the shift is undefined. On some machines, a right shift is arithmetic (sign fill) and on others logical (zero fill). The type of the result of a shift operation is that of the promoted left operand.

5.7 Increment and Decrement Operators

Given that

l   is a modifiable lvalue expression, whose type in not qualified as `const`;

then the expression

++l   increments l and then uses its value as the value of the expression;

l++   uses l as the value of the expression and then increments l;

--l   decrements l and then uses its value as the value of the expression;

l--   uses l as the value of the expression and then decrements l.

Section 5.15 describes these operations on pointers.

5.8 Assignment Operators

Given that

l   is a modifiable lvalue expression, whose type is not qualified as `const`;

op   is any operator that can be used as an assignment operator (see Table A.3);

a   is an expression;

then the expression

l = a   stores the value of a into l;

l *op*= a   applies *op* to l and a, storing the result into l.

In the first expression, if a is one of the basic data types (except `void`), then it is converted to match the type of l. If l is a pointer, then a must be a pointer to the same type as l, a `void` pointer, or the *null* pointer.

If l is a `void` pointer, a can be of any pointer type. The second expression is treated as if it were written l = l *op* (a), except l is only evaluated once (consider x[i++] += 10).

5.9 Conditional Operator

Given that

    `a, b, c`   are expressions;

then the expression

    `a ? b : c`   has as its value b if a is nonzero, and c otherwise. Only expression b or c is evaluated.

Expressions b and c must be of the same data type. If they are not, but are both arithmetic data types, the usual arithmetic conversions are applied to make their types the same. If one is a pointer and the other is 0, the latter is taken as a null pointer of the same type as the former. If one is a pointer to void and the other is a pointer to another type, the latter will be converted to pointer to void, and that will be the resulting type.

5.10 Type Cast Operator

Given that

    `type`   is the name of a basic data type, an enumerated data type (preceded by the keyword enum), a typedef-defined type, or is a derived data type;

    `a`   is an expression;

then the expression

    `( type )`   converts a to the specified type.

5.11 *sizeof* Operator

Given that

    `type`   is as described above;

    `a`   is an expression;

then the expression

    `sizeof (type)`   has as its value the number of bytes needed to contain a value of the specified type;

    `sizeof a`   has as its value the number of bytes required to hold the result of the evaluation of a.

If *type* is char, the result is defined to be 1. If a is the name of an array that has been dimensioned (either explicitly or implicitly through initialization) and is not a formal parameter or undimensioned extern array, sizeof a gives the number of bytes required to store the elements in *a*.

The type of the integer produced by the `sizeof` operator is `size_t`, which is defined in the standard header file `<stddef.h>`.

Since the `sizeof` operator is evaluated at compile time, it can be used in constant expressions (see Section 5.2).

5.12 Comma Operator

Given that

    `a, b`   are expressions;

then the expression

    `a, b`   causes a to be evaluated, and then b to be evaluated. The type and value of the expression is that of b.

5.13 Basic Operations with Arrays

Given that

    `a`   is declared as an array of n elements;

    `i`   is an expression of any integer data type;

    `v`   is an expression;

then the expression

    `a[0]`   references the first element of a;

    `a[n - 1]`   references the last element of a;

    `a[i]`   references element number i of a;

    `a[i] = v`   stores the value of v into a[i].

In each case, the type of the result is the type of the elements contained in a. See Section 5.15 for a summary of operations with pointers and arrays.

5.14 Basic Operations with Structures[1]

Given that

    `x`   is a modifiable lvalue expression of type `struct s`;

    `y`   is an expression of type `struct s`;

---

[1] *Also applies to unions.*

m   is the name of one of the members of the structure s;

v   is an expression;

then the expression

x   references the entire structure and is of type
                   struct s;

y.m   references the member m of the structure y and
                   is of the type declared for the member m;

x.m = v   assigns v to the member m of x and is of the type declared
                   for the member m;

x = y   assigns y to x and is of type struct s;

f (y)   calls the function f, passing the structure y as the argu-
                   ment. Inside f, the formal parameter must be declared to
                   be of type struct s;

return (y)   returns the structure y. The return type declared for the
                   function must be struct s.

5.15 Basic Operations with Pointers

Given that

x   is an lvalue expression of type *t*;

pt   is a modifiable lvalue expression of type "pointer to *t*";

v   is an expression;

then the expression

&x   produces a pointer to x and has type "pointer to *t*";

pt = &   sets pt pointing to x and has type "pointer to *t*";

pt = 0   assigns the null pointer to pt;

pt == 0   tests to see if pt is null;

*pt   references the value pointed to by pt and has type *t*;

*pt = v   stores the value of v into the location pointed to by pt
                   and has type *t*.

Pointers to Arrays

Given that

a	is an array of elements of type *t*;
pa1	is a modifiable lvalue expression of type "pointer to *t*" that points to an element in a;
pa2	is an lvalue expression of type "pointer to *t*" that points to an element in a, or to one past the last element in a;
v	is an expression;
n	is an expression of an integer data type;

then the expression:

a, &a, &a[0]	each produce a pointer to the first element of a and have type "pointer to *t*";
&a[n]	produces a pointer to element number n of a and has type "pointer to *t*";
*pa1	references the element of a that pa1 points to and has type *t*;
*pa1 = v	stores the value of v into the element pointed to by pa1, and has type *t*;
++pa1	sets pa1 pointing to the next element of a, no matter what type of elements are contained in a and has type "pointer to *t*";
--pa1	sets pa1 pointing to the previous element of a, no matter what type of elements are contained in a, and has type "pointer to *t*";
*++pa1	increments pa1 and then references the value in a that pa1 points to, and has type *t*;
*pa1++	references the value in a that pa1 points to before incrementing pa1 and has type *t*;
pa1 + n	produces a pointer that points n elements further into a than pa1 and has type "pointer to *t*";
pa1 - n	produces a pointer to a that points n elements previous to that pointed to by pa1 and has type "pointer to *t*";

`*(pa1 + n) = v`	stores the value of v into the element pointed to by pa1 + n and has type *t*;
`pa1 < pa2`	tests if pa1 is pointing to an earlier element in a than is pa2 and has type int (any relational operators can be used to compare two pointers);
`pa2 - pa1`	produces the number of elements in a contained between the pointers pa2 and pa1 (assuming that pa2 points to an element further in a than pa1) and has integer type;
`a + n`	produces a pointer to element number n of a, has type "pointer to t," and is in all ways equivalent to the expression &a[n];
`*(a + n)`	references element number n of a, has type *t*, and is in all ways equivalent to the expression a[n].

The actual type of the integer produced by subtracting two pointers is specified by ptrdiff_t, which is defined in the standard header file <stddef.h>.

Pointers to Structures[2]

Given that

`x`	is an lvalue expression of type struct s;
`ps`	is a modifiable lvalue expression of type "pointer to struct s";
`m`	is the name of a member of the structure s and is of type *t*;
`v`	is an expression;

then the expression

`&x`	produces a pointer to x and is of type "pointer to struct s";
`ps = &x`	sets ps pointing to x and is of type "pointer to struct s";
`ps->m`	references member m of the structure pointed to by ps and is of type *t*;

---

[2]*Also applies to unions.*

`(*ps).m`	also references this member and is in all ways equivalent to the expression `ps->m`;
`ps->m = v`	stores the value of `v` into the member `m` of the structure pointed to by `ps` and is of type *t*.

5.16 Conversion of Basic Data Types

The C language converts operands in arithmetic expressions in a predefined order, known as the *usual arithmetic conversions*.

Step 1: If either operand is of type `long double`, the other is converted to `long double`, and that is the type of the result.

Step 2: If either operand is of type `double`, the other is converted to `double`, and that is the type of the result.

Step 3: If either operand is of type `float`, the other is converted to `float`, and that is the type of the result.

Step 4: If either operand is of type `char`, `short int`, `int` bit field, or of an enumerated data type, it is converted to `int`, if an `int` can fully represent its range of values; otherwise it is converted to `unsigned int`.

Step 5: If either operand is of type `unsigned long int`, the other is converted to `unsigned long int`, and that is the type of the result.

Step 6: If one operand is of type `long int` and the other is of type `unsigned int`, the `unsigned int` is converted to `long int` if a `long int` can represent all values of an `unsigned int`. In such a case, the type of the result will be `long int`. If a `long int` cannot represent all values of an `unsigned int`, both operands are converted to `unsigned long int`, and that is the type of the result.

Step 7: If either operand is of type `long int`, the other is converted to `long int`, and that is the type of the result.

Step 8: If either operand is of type `unsigned int`, the other operand is converted to type `unsigned int`, and that is the type of the result.

Step 9: If this step is reached, both operands are of type `int`, and that is the type of the result.

Step 4 is known more formally as *integral promotion*.

Conversion of operands is well-behaved in most situations, although the following points should be noted:

1. Conversion of a `char` to an `int` may involve sign extension on some machines, unless the `char` is declared as `unsigned`.

2. Conversion of a signed integer to a longer integer results in extension of the sign to the left; conversion of an unsigned integer to a longer integer results in zero fill to the left.

3. Conversion of a longer integer to a shorter one results in truncation of the integer on the left.

4. Conversion of a floating-point value to an integer results in truncation of the decimal portion of the value. If the integer is not large enough to contain the converted floating-point value, the result is not defined, as is the result of converting a negative floating-point value to an unsigned integer.

5. Conversion of a `double` to a `float` may or may not result in rounding the `double` before the truncation occurs.

6.0 Storage Classes and Scope

The term *storage class* refers to the manner in which memory is allocated by the compiler in the case of variables and to the scope of a particular function definition in the case of functions. Storage classes are `auto`, `static`, `extern`, and `register`. A storage class can be omitted in a function or variable declaration and a default storage class will be assigned, as discussed below.

The term *scope* refers to the extent of the meaning of a particular identifier within a program. An identifier defined outside a function can be referenced anywhere subsequent in the file. Identifiers defined within a function or block are local to the function or block and can locally redefine an identifier defined outside the function or block. Label names are known throughout the function, as are formal parameter names. Labels, structure and structure member names, union and union member names, and enumerated type names do not have to be distinct from each other or from variable or function names. However, enumeration identifiers *do* have to be distinct from variable names and from other enumeration identifers defined within the same scope.

Table A.4. Variables: summary of storage classes, scope, and initialization.

If Storage Class is	*And Variable is declared*	*Then it can be referenced*	*And can be initialized with*	*Comments*
static	Outside a function	Anywhere within the file	Constant expressions only	Variables are initialized only once at the start of program execution; values are retained through function calls; default initial value is 0
	Inside a function/block	Within the function/block		
extern	Outside a function	Anywhere within the file	Constant expressions only	Variable must be declared in at least one place without the extern keyword or in exactly one place with an initial value
	Inside a function/block	Within the function/block		
auto	Inside a function/block	Within the function/block	Any valid expression; arrays structs & unions to constant expressions only if {...} list is used	Varible is initialized each time the function/ block is entered; no default value
register	Inside a function/block	Within the function/block	Any valid expression	Assignment to register not guaranteed; varying restrictions on types of variables that can be declared; cannot take the address of a register variable; initialized each time function/block is entered; no default value
omitted	Outside a function	Anywhere within the file or by other files that contain appropriate declarations	Constant expressions only	This declaration can appear in only one place; variable is initialized at the start of program execution; default value is 0
	Inside a function/block	(See auto)	(See auto)	Defaults to auto

6.1 Functions

If a storage class is specified when a function is defined, then it must be either static or extern. Functions that are declared static can only be referenced from within the same file that contains the function. Functions that are specified as extern (or that have no class specified) may be called by functions from other files.

6.2 Variables

Table A.4 summarizes the various storage classes that may be used in declaring variables as well as their scope and methods of initialization.

7.0 Functions

7.1 Function Definition

General Format

```
return_type    name ( type1 param1, type2 param2, ... )
{
    local_variable_declarations

    program_statement
    program_statement
    ...
    return expression;
}
```

The function called `name` is defined, which returns a value of type `return_type` and has formal parameters `param1, param2, ....` `param1` is declared to be of type `type1`, `param2` of type `type2`, and so on.

If the function does not return a value, `return_type` is not specified or is `void`. If the function returns an `int` value, `return_type` may be omitted, although specifying an `int` as the return type is better programming practice.

If just `void` is specified inside the parentheses, the function takes no arguments. If ... is used as the last (or only) parameter in the list, the function takes a variable number of arguments, as in

```
int  printf (char *format, ...)
{
   ...
}
```

Declarations for single-dimensional array arguments do not have to specify the number of elements in the array. For multidimensional arrays, the size of each dimension except the first must be specified.

See Section 8.9 for a discussion of the `return` statement.

An older way of defining functions is still supported. The general format is

```
return_type    name (param1, param2, ... )
param_declarations
```

```
{
     local_variable_declarations

     program_statement
     program_statement
     ...
     return expression;
}
```

Here, just the parameter names are listed inside the pareneteses. If no arguments are expected, nothing appears between the left and right parentheses. The type of each parameter is declared outside the parentheses and *before* the opening curly brace of the function definition. For example,

```
unsigned int rotate (value, n)
unsigned int value;
int   n;
{
   ...
}
```

defines a function called `rotate` that takes two arguments called `value` and `n`. The first argument is an `unsigned int`, and the second is an `int`.

7.2 Function Call

General Format

```
name ( arg1, arg2, ... )
```

The function called *name* is called and the values *arg1*, *arg2*, ... are passed as arguments to the function. If the function takes no arguments, just the open and closed parentheses are specified (as in `initialize ()`).

If you are calling a function that is defined after the call, or in another file, you must include a *prototype declaration* for the function, which has the following general format:

```
return_type  name  (type1  param1, type2  param2, ... );
```

This tells the compiler the function's return type, the number of arguments it takes, and the type of each argument. As an example, the line

```
long double  power (double x, int n);
```

declares `power` to be a function that returns a `long double` and that takes two arguments, the first a `double` and the second an `int`. The argument names inside the parentheses are actually dummy names and can be omitted if desired, so

```
long double  power (double, int);
```

works just as well.

If the compiler has previously encountered the function definition or a proto-type declaration for the function, the type of each argument will be automatically converted to match the type expected by the function when the function is called.

If neither the function's definition nor a prototype declaration has been encountered, the compiler will assume the function returns a value of type int and will automatically convert all float arguments to type double, and arguments of type char or short int to type int before passing them to the function. Other function arguments will be passed without conversion.

Functions that take a variable number of arguments must be declared as such. Otherwise, the compiler is at liberty to assume the function takes a fixed number of arguments based upon the number actually used in the call.

If the function was defined with the old-style format (see Section 7.1), a declaration for the function takes the following format:

```
return_type  name ();
```

Arguments to such functions will be converted as described in the previous paragraph.

A function whose return type is declared as void will cause the compiler to flag any calls to that function that try to make use of a returned value.

All arguments to a function are passed by value; therefore, their values cannot be changed by the function. If a pointer is passed to a function, the function *can* change values referenced by the pointer, but it still cannot change the value of the pointer itself.

7.3 Function Pointers

A function name, without a following set of parentheses, produces a pointer to that function. The address operator can also be applied to a function name to produce a pointer to it.

If fp is a pointer to a function, the corresponding function can be called either by writing

```
fp ()
```

or

```
(*fp) ()
```

If the function takes arguments, they can be listed inside the parentheses.

8.0 Statements

A program statement is any valid expression (usually an assignment or function call) that is immediately followed by a semicolon, or it is one of the special statements described below. A *label* may optionally precede any statement, and consists of an identifier followed immediately by a colon (see the goto statement).

8.1 Compound Statements

Program statements that are contained within a pair of braces are known collectively as a *compound* statement or *block* and can appear anywhere in the program that a single statement is permitted. A block can have its own set of variable declarations, which override any similarly named variables defined outside the block. The scope of such local variables is the block in which they are defined.

8.2 The *break* Statement

General Format

```
break;
```

Execution of a break statement from within a for, while, do, or switch statement causes execution of that statement to be immediately terminated. Execution continues with the statement that immediately follows the loop or switch.

8.3 The *continue* Statement

General Format

```
continue;
```

Execution of the continue statement from within a loop causes any statements that follow the continue in the loop to be skipped. Execution of the loop otherwise continues as normal.

8.4 The *do* Statement

General Format

```
do
  program_statement
while ( expression );
```

program_statement is executed as long as *expression* evaluates nonzero. Note that, since *expression* is evaluated each time *after* the execution of *program_statement*, it is guaranteed that *program_statement* will be executed at least once.

8.5 The *for* Statement

General Format

```
for ( expression_1;  expression_2; expression_3 )
     program_statement
```

expression_1 is evaluated once when execution of the loop begins. Next, *expression_2* is evaluated. If its value is nonzero, *program_statement* is executed and then *expression_3* is evaluated. Execution of *program_statement* and the subsequent evaluation of *expression_3* continues as long as the value of *expression_2* is nonzero. Note that, since *expression_2* is evaluated each time before *program_statement* is executed, *program_statement* may never be executed if the value of *expression_2* is 0 when the loop is first entered.

8.6 The *goto* Statement

General Format

```
goto identifier;
```

Execution of the goto causes control to be sent directly to the statement labeled *identifier*. The labeled statement must be located in the same function as the goto.

8.7 The *if* Statement

Format 1

```
if ( expression )
     program_statement
```

If the result of evaluating *expression* is nonzero, *program_statement* is executed; otherwise, it is skipped.

Format 2

```
if ( expression )
     program_statement_1
else
     program_statement_2
```

If the value of *expression* is nonzero then *program_statement_1* is executed; otherwise *program_statement_2* is executed. If *program_statement_2* is another if statement, then an if-else if chain is effected:

```
if ( expression_1 )
    program_statement_1
else if ( expression_2 )
    program_statement_2
    ...
else
    program_statement_n
```

An `else` clause is always associated with the last `if` statement that does not contain an `else`. Braces can be used to change this association if necessary.

8.8 The *null* Statement

General Format

```
;
```

Execution of a `null` statement has no effect and is used primarily to satisfy the requirement of a program statement in a `for`, `do`, or `while` loop. For example, in the following statement, which copies a character string pointed to by `from` to one pointed to by `to`:

```
while ( *to++ = *from++ )
    ;
```

the `null` statement is used to satisfy the requirement that a program statement appear after the looping expression of the `while`.

8.9 The *return* Statement

Format 1

```
return;
```

Execution of the `return` statement causes program execution to be immediately returned to the calling function. This format can only be used to return from a function that does not return a value.

If execution proceeds to the end of a function and a `return` statement is not encountered, the function returns as if a `return` statement of this form had been executed. Therefore, in such a case, no value is returned.

Format 2

```
return  expression;
```

The value of `expression` is returned to the calling function. If the type of *expression* does not agree with the return type declared in the function declaration, its value will be automatically converted to the declared type before it is returned. By convention, *expression* is usually enclosed in parentheses.

8.10 The *switch* Statement

General Format

```
switch ( expression )
{
    case constant_1:
        program_statement
        program_statement
```

```
        . . .
    break;
case constant_2:
    program_statement
    program_statement
        . . .
    break;
    . . .
case constant_n:
    program_statement
    program_statement
        . . .
    break;
default:
    program_statement
    program_statement
        . . .
    break;
}
```

expression is evaluated and compared against the constant expression values *constant_1*, *constant_2*, ..., *constant_n*. If the value of *expression* matches one of these case values, the program statements that immediately follow are executed. If no case value matches the value of *expression*, the default case, if included, is executed. If the default case is not included, then no statements contained in the switch are executed.

The result of the evaluation of *expression* must be of integral type and no two cases can have the same value. Omitting the break statement from a particular case causes execution to continue into the next case.

8.11 The *while* Statement

General Format
```
while ( expression )
    program_statement
```

program_statement is executed as long as the value of *expression* is nonzero. Note that, since *expression* is evaluated each time *before* the execution of *program_statement*, *program_statement* may never be executed.

9.0 The Preprocessor

The preprocessor analyzes the source file before the compiler proper sees the code. Here is what the preprocessor does:

1. Replaces trigraph sequences (see Section 9.1) by their equivalents.

2. Joins any lines that end with a backslash character (\) together into a single line.

3. Divides the program into a stream of tokens.

4. Removes comments, replacing them by a single space.

5. Processes preprocessor directives (see Section 9.2) and expands macros.

6. Replaces escape characters in character constants and character string constants by their equivalent internal representation.

7. Concatenates adjacent constant character strings.

9.1 Trigraph Sequences

To handle non-ASCII character sets, the following three-character sequences (called *trigraphs*) are recognized and treated specially wherever they occur inside a program (even inside character strings):

Trigraph	Meaning
??=	#
??(	[
??)	]
??<	{
??>	}
??/	\
??'	^
??!	|
??-	~

9.2 Preprocessor Directives

All preprocessor directives begin with the character #, which must be the first nonwhitespace character on the line. The # can be followed optionally by one or more space or tab characters.

9.2.1 The #*define* Directive

Format 1

```
#define name   text
```

This defines the identifier name to the preprocessor and associates with it whatever text appears after the first blank space after name to the end of the line. Subsequent use of *name* in the program causes *text* to be substituted directly into the program at that point.

Format 2

```
#define name(param_1, param_2, ..., param_n)  text
```

The macro *name* is defined to take arguments as specified by *param_1*, *param_2*, ..., *param_n*, each of which is an identifier. Subsequent use of *name* in the program with an argument list causes *text* to be substituted directly into the program at that point, with the arguments of the macro call replacing all occurrences of the corresponding parameters inside *text*.

If a definition in either format requires more than one line, then each line to be continued must be ended with a backslash character. Once a name has been defined, it can be used subsequently anywhere in the file.

The # operator is permitted in `#define` directives that take arguments. It is followed by the name of an argument to the macro. The preprocessor puts double quotes around the actual value passed to the macro when it's invoked. That is, it turns it into a character string. For example, the definition

```
#define  printint(x)  printf (# x " = %d\n", x)
```

with the call

```
printint (count);
```

will be expanded by the preprocessor into

```
printf ("count" " = %d\n", count);
```

or, equivalently,

```
printf ("count = %d\n", count);
```

The preprocessor puts a \ character in front of any " or \ characters when performing this *stringizing* operation. So, with the definition

```
#define  str(x)  # x
```

the call

```
str (The string "\t" contains a tab)
```

expands to

```
"The string \"\\t\" contains a tab"
```

The ## operator is also allowed in `#define` directives that take arguments. It is preceded (or followed) by the name of an argument to the macro. The preprocessor takes the value that is passed when the macro is invoked and creates a single token from the argument to the macro and the token that follows (or precedes) it. For example, the macro definition

```
#define printx(n)  printf ("%d\n", x ## n );
```

with the call

```
printx (5)
```

produces

```
printf ("%d\n", x5);
```

The definition

```
#define printx(n) printf ("x" # n " = %d\n", x ## n );
```

with the call

```
printx(10)
```

produces

```
printf ("x10 = %d\n", x10);
```

after substitution and concatenation of the character strings.

Spaces are not required around the # and ## operators.

9.2.2 The *#error* Directive

General Format
```
#error text
    ...
```

The specified `text` is written as an error message by the preprocessor.

9.2.3 The *#if* Directive

Format 1
```
#if constant_expression
    ...
#endif
```

The value of `constant_expression` is evaluated. If the result is nonzero, then all program lines up until the `#endif` directive are processed; otherwise, they are automatically skipped and are not processed by the preprocessor or by the compiler.

Format 2
```
#if constant_expression_1
    ...
```

```
#elif constant_expression_2
  ...
#elif constant_expression_n
  ...
#else
  ...
#endif
```

If `constant_expression_2` is nonzero, all program lines up until the `#elif` are processed. Otherwise if `constant_expression_2` is nonzero, all program lines up until the next `#elif` are processed. If none of the constant expressions evaluates to nonzero, the lines after the `#else` (if included) are processed.

The special operator `defined` can be used as part of the constant expression, so

```
#if defined (DEBUG)
  ...
#endif
```

causes the code between the `#if` and `#endif` to be processed if the identifier `DEBUG` has been previously defined (see also `#ifdef` in Section 9.2.4). The parentheses are not necessary around the identifier, so

```
#if defined DEBUG
```

works just as well.

9.2.4 The *#ifdef* Directive

General Format
```
#ifdef identifier
  ...
#endif
```

If the value of `identifier` has been previously defined (either through a `#define` or with the `-D` command-line option when the program was compiled), then all program lines up until the `#endif` are processed; otherwise, they are skipped. As with the `#if` directive, `#elif` and `#else` directives can be used with a `#ifdef` directive.

9.2.5 The *#ifndef* Directive

General Format
```
#ifndef identifier
  ...
#endif
```

If the value of `identifier` has not been previously defined, then all program lines up until the `#endif` are processed; otherwise, they are skipped. As with the `#if` directive, `#elif` and `#else` directives can be used with a `#ifndef` directive.

9.2.6 The *#include* Directive

Format 1
```
#include "file_name"
```

The preprocessor searches an implementation-defined directory or directories first for the file `file_name`. Typically, the same directory that contains the source file is searched. If the file is not found there, a sequence of standard places is searched. Once found, the contents of the file is included in the program at the precise point that the `#include` directive appears. Preprocessor directives contained within the `#include` file will be analyzed, and therefore an included file can itself contain other `#include` directives.

Format 2
```
#include <file_name>
```

The preprocessor searches for the specified file only in the standard places. The action taken after the file is found is otherwise identical to that described above.

9.2.7 The *#line* Directive

General Format
```
#line  constant  "file_name"
```

This directive causes the compiler to treat subsequent lines in the program as if the name of the source file were `file_name`, and as if the line number of all subsequent lines began at `constant`. If `file_name` is not specified, the filename specified by the last `#line` directive, or the name of the source file (if no filename was previously specified), is used.

The `#line` directive is primarily used to control the filename and line number that are displayed whenever an error message is issued by the compiler.

9.2.8 The *#pragma* Directive

General Format
```
#pragma text
```

This causes the preprocessor to perform some implementation-defined action. For example, under Microsoft C, the pragma

```
#pragma loop_opt(on)
```

causes special loop optimization to be performed. If this pragma is encountered by a compiler that doesn't recognize the `loop_opt` pragma, it will be ignored.

9.2.9 The *#undef* Directive

General Format

```
#undef   identifier
```

The specified *identifier* becomes undefined to the preprocessor. Subsequent `#ifdef` or `#ifndef` directives will behave as if the identifier were never defined.

9.2.10 The # Directive

This is a null directive and is ignored by the preprocessor.

9.3 Predefined Identifiers

The following identifiers are defined by the preprocessor:

Identifier	Meaning
`__LINE__`	Current line number being compiled
`__FILE__`	Name of the current source file being compiled
`__DATE__`	Date the file is being compiled, in the format `"Mmm dd yyyy"`
`__TIME__`	Time the file is being compiled, in the format `"hh:mm:ss"`
`__STDC__`	Defined as 1 if the compiler conforms to the ANSI standard

For example, if the following code were contained in the file `getmem.c`

```
if ( charp == NULL )
{
    fprintf (stderr,
               "Software error at line %d, file %s\n.",
               __LINE__, __FILE__);
    exit (1);
}
```

the following output might be produced if `charp` was null when the code was executed:

```
Software error at line 369, file getmem.c.
```

Take a look at the system header file `<assert.h>` for a macro called `assert` that uses these predefined identifiers in a similar way.

B

A P P E N D I X

The Standard C Library

The standard C library contains a large selection of functions that may be called from a C program. This section does not list all these functions, but rather most of the more commonly used ones. For a complete listing of all the functions that are available, consult the documentation that was included with your compiler. Among the routines not described in this appendix are ones for manipulating the date and time (such as time, ctime, and localtime), performing non-local jumps (setjmp and longjmp), generating diagnostics (assert), handling a variable number of arguments (va_list, va_start, va_arg, and va_end), handling signals (signal and raise), and dealing with wide character strings.

Standard Header Files

This section describes the contents of three standard header files: <stddef.h>, <limits.h>, and <float.h>.

\<stddef.h\>

This header file contains some standard definitions:

Define	Meaning
NULL	A null pointer constant.
offsetof	*(structure, member)*
	Gives the offset in bytes of the member *member* from the start of the structure *structure*. The type of the result is size_t.
ptrdiff_t	The type of integer produced by subtracting two pointers.
size_t	The type of integer produced by the sizeof operator.
wchar_t	The type of the integer required to hold a wide character (see Appendix A).

\<limits.h\>

This header file contains various implementation-defined limits for character and integer data types. Certain minimum values are guaranteed. These are noted at the end of each description inside parentheses.

Define	Meaning
CHAR_BIT	Number of bits in a char (8).
CHAR_MAX	Maximum value for object of type char (127 if sign extension is done on chars, 255 otherwise).
CHAR_MIN	Minimum value for object of type char (-127 if sign extension is done on chars, 0 otherwise).
SCHAR_MAX	Maximum value for object of type signed char (127).
SCHAR_MIN	Minimum value for object of type signed char (-127).
UCHAR_MAX	Maximum value for object of type unsigned char (255U).
SHRT_MAX	Maximum value for object of type short int (32767).

Define	Meaning
SHRT_MIN	Minimum value for object of type short int (-32767).
USHRT_MAX	Maximum value for object of type unsigned short int (65535U).
INT_MAX	Maximum value for object of type int (32767).
INT_MIN	Minimum value for object of type int (-32767).
UINT_MAX	Maximum value for object of type unsigned int (65535U).
LONG_MAX	Maximum value for object of type long int (2147483647L).
LONG_MIN	Minimum value for object of type long int (-2147483647L).
ULONG_MAX	Maximum value for object of type unsigned long int (4294967295UL).

<float.h>

This header file defines various limits associated with floating-point arithmetic. Minimum magnitudes are noted at the end of each description inside parentheses. Note that all of the definitions are not listed here.

Define	Meaning
FLT_DIG	Number of digits of precision for a float (6).
FLT_EPSILON	Smallest value that, when added to 1.0, does not compare equal to 1.0 (1e-5).
FLT_MAX	Maximum size of a float (1e+37).
FLT_MAX_EXP	Maximum size of a float (1e+37).
FLT_MIN	Minimum size of a normalized float (1e-37).

Similar definitions exist for double and long double types. Just replace the leading FLT with DBL for doubles, and with LDBL for long doubles. For example, DBL_DIG gives the number of digits of precision for a double, and LDBL_DIG gives it for a long double.

String Functions

The following functions perform operations on character arrays. In the description of these routines, s, s1, and s2 represent pointers to null-terminated character arrays, c is an `int`, and n represents an integer of type `size_t` (defined in `stddef.h`). For the `strnxxx` routines, s1 and s2 can point to character arrays that aren't null-terminated.

To use any of these functions, you should include the header file `<string.h>` in your program:

```
#include <string.h>
```

`char *strcat (s1, s2)`

Concatenates the character string s2 to the end of s1, placing a null character at the end of the final string. The function returns s1.

`char *strchr (s, c)`

Searches the string s for the first occurrence of the character c. If it is found, then a pointer to the character is returned; otherwise a null pointer is returned.

`int strcmp (s1, s2)`

Compares strings s1 and s2 and returns a value less than 0 if s1 is less than s2, equal to 0 if s1 is equal to s2, and greater than 0 if s1 is greater than s2.

`char *strcpy (s1, s2)`

Copies the string s2 to s1, returning s1.

`size_t strlen (s)`

Returns the number of characters in s, excluding the null character.

`char *strncat (s1, s2, n)`

Copies s2 to the *end* of s1 until either the null character is reached or n characters have been copied, whichever occurs first. Returns s1.

`int strncmp (s1, s2, n)`

Performs the same function as `strcmp`, except that at most n characters from the strings are compared.

`char *strncpy (s1, s2)`

Copies s2 to s1 until either the null character is reached or n characters have been copied, whichever occurs first. Returns s1.

```
char *strrchr (s, c)
```

> Searches the string s for the last occurrence of the character c. If found, a pointer to the character in s is returned; otherwise the null pointer is returned.

```
int strstr (s1, s2)
```

> Searches the string s1 for the first occurrence of the string s2. If found, a pointer to the start of where s2 is located inside s1 is returned; otherwise if s2 is not located inside s1, the null pointer is returned.

Memory Functions

The following routines deal with arrays of characters. They are designed for efficient searching of memory and for copying data from one area of memory to another. They require the header file <string.h>:

```
#include <string.h>
```

In the description of these routines, m1 and m2 are of type void *, c is an int that gets converted by the routine to an unsigned char, and n is an integer of type size_t.

```
void  *memchr (m1, c, n)
```

> Searches m1 for the first occurrence of c, returning a pointer to it if found, or the null pointer, if not found.

```
void  *memcmp (m1, m2, n)
```

> Compares the corresponding first n characters from m1 and m2. Zero is returned if both arrays are identical in their first n characters. If they're not, the difference between the corresponding characters from m1 and m2 that caused the first mismatch is returned. So if the disagreeing character from m1 was less than the corresponding character from m2, a value less than 0 is returned; otherwise, a value greater than 0 is returned.

```
void  *memcpy (m1, m2, n)
```

> Copies n characters from m2 to m1, returning m1.

```
void  *memmove (m1, m2, n)
```

> Like memcpy, but is guaranteed to work even if m1 and m2 overlap in memory.

```
void  *memset (m1, c, n)
```

> Sets the first n characters of m1 to the value c. memset returns m1.

Note that these routines attach no special significance to null characters inside the arrays. They can be used with arrays other than character arrays provided you cast the pointers accordingly to `void *`. So if data1 and data2 are each an array of 100 `int`s, the call

```
memcpy ((void *) data2, (void *) data1, sizeof (data1));
```

would copy all 100 integers from data1 to data2.

Character Functions

The following functions deal with single characters. To use them, you must include the file `<ctype.h>` in your program:

```
#include <ctype.h>
```

Each of the functions that follow takes an `int(c)` as an argument and returns a TRUE value (nonzero), if the test is satisfied, and a FALSE (zero) value otherwise. The specific octal values, as listed, are for an ASCII character set.

Name	Test
isalnum	Is c an alphanumeric character?
isalpha	Is c an alphabetic character?
iscntrl	Is c a control character (octal 0-037 or 0177)?
isdigit	Is c a digit character?
isgraph	Is c a graphics character (octal 041-0176)?
islower	Is c a lowercase letter?
isprint	Is c a printable character (octal 040-0176)?
ispunct	Is c a punctuation character?
isspace	Is c a whitespace character (space, newline, carriage return, horizontal or vertical tab, or form-feed)?
isupper	Is c an uppercase letter?
isxdigit	Is c a hexadecimal digit character?

The following two functions are provided for performing character translation.

```
int tolower(c)
```

Returns the lowercase equivalent of *c*. If *c* is not an uppercase letter, *c* itself is returned.

```
int toupper(c)
```

>   Returns the uppercase equivalent of *c*. If *c* is not a lowercase letter, *c* itself is returned.

I/O Functions

The following describes some of the more commonly used I/O functions from the C library. You should include the header file `stdio.h` at the front of any program that uses one of these functions, using the statement

```
#include <stdio.h>
```

Included in this file are declarations for the I/O functions and definitions for the names `EOF`, `NULL`, `stdin`, `stdout`, `stderr` (all constant values), and `FILE`.

In the descriptions that follow, *file_name, file_name1, file_name2, access_mode,* and *format* are pointers to null-terminated strings, *buffer* is a pointer to a character array, *file_pointer* is of type "pointer to `FILE`", *n* and *size* are positive integer values of type `size_t`, and *i* and *c* are of type `int`.

```
void clearerr (file_pointer)
```

>   Clears the end of file and error indicators associated with the file identified by *file_pointer*.

```
int fclose (file_pointer)
```

>   Closes the file identified by *file_pointer* and returns zero if the close is successful, `EOF` if an error occurs.

```
int feof (file_pointer)
```

>   Returns nonzero if the identified file has reached the end of the file and zero otherwise.

```
int ferror (file_pointer)
```

>   Checks for an error condition on the indicated file and returns zero if an error exists, and nonzero otherwise.

```
int fflush (file_pointer)
```

>   Flushes (writes) any data from internal buffers to the indicated file, returning zero on success, and the value `EOF` if an error occurs.

```
int fgetc (file_pointer)
```

>   Returns the next character from the file identified by *file_pointer*, or the value `EOF` if an end of file condition occurs (remember that this function returns an `int`).

```
int fgetpos (file_pointer, fpos)
```

> fgetpos gets the current file position for the file associated with *file_pointer*, storing it into the fpos_t (defined in <stdio.h>) variable pointed to by *fpos*. fgetpos returns zero on success, and nonzero on failure. See also the fsetpos function.

```
char *fgets (buffer, i, file_pointer)
```

> Reads characters from the indicated file, until either *i* - 1 characters are read or a newline character is read, whichever occurs first. Characters that are read are stored into the character array pointed to by *buffer*. If a newline character is read, then it *will* be stored in the array. If an end of file is reached or an error occurs, then the value NULL is returned; otherwise *buffer* is returned.

```
FILE *fopen (file_name, access_mode)
```

> Opens the specified file with the indicated access mode. Valid modes are "r" for reading, "w" for writing, "a" for appending to the end of an existing file, "r+" for read/write access starting at the beginning of an existing file, "w+" for read/write access (and the previous contents of the file, if it exists, are lost), and "a+" for read/write access with all writes going to the end of the file. If the file to be opened does not exist, it will be created if the *access_mode* is write ("w", "w+") or append ("a", "a+"). If a file is opened in append mode ("a" or "a+"), then it is not possible to overwrite existing data in the file.

> On systems that distinguish binary from text files, the letter b must be appended to the access mode (as in "rb") to open a binary file.

> If the fopen call is successful, a FILE pointer will be returned to be used to identify the file in subsequent I/O operations; otherwise, a null pointer is returned.

```
int fprintf (file_pointer, format, arg1, arg2, ..., argn)
```

> Writes the specified arguments to the file identified by *file_pointer*, according to the format specified by the character string *format*. Format characters are the same as for the printf function (see Chapter 16 "Input and Output"). The number of characters written is returned. A negative return value indicates that an error occurred on output.

```
int fputc (c, file_pointer)
```

> Writes the value of *c* (converted to an unsigned char) to the file identified by *file_pointer*, returning *c* if the write is successful, and the value EOF otherwise.

```
int fputs (buffer, file_pointer)
```

Writes the characters in the array pointed to by `buffer` to the indicated file until the terminating null character in `buffer` is reached. A newline character is *not* automatically written to the file by this function. On failure, the value `EOF` is returned.

```
size_t fread (buffer, size, n, file_pointer)
```

Reads *n* items of data from the identified file into `buffer`. Each item of data is `size` bytes in length. For example, the call

```
numread = fread (text, sizeof (char), 80, in_file);
```

reads 80 characters from the file identified by `in_file` and stores them into the array pointed to by `text`. The function returns the number of data items successfully read.

```
FILE *freopen (file_name, access_mode, file_pointer)
```

Closes the file associated with `file_pointer` and opens the file `file_name` with the specified `access_mode` (see the `fopen` function). The file that is opened is subsequently associated with `file_pointer`. If the `freopen` call is successful, `file_pointer` will be returned; otherwise, a null pointer will be returned. The `freopen` function is frequently used to reassign `stdin`, `stdout`, or `stderr` in the program. For example, the call

```
if ( freopen ("input_data", "r", stdin) == NULL )
{
    ...
}
```

will have the effect of reassigning `stdin` to the file `input_data`, which will be opened in read access mode. Subsequent I/O operations performed with `stdin` will be performed with the file `input_data`, as if `stdin` had been redirected to this file when the program was executed.

```
int fscanf (file_pointer, format, arg1, arg2, ..., argn)
```

Data items are read from the file identified by `file_pointer`, according to the format specified by the character string `format`. The values that are read are stored into the arguments specified after `format`, each of which must be a pointer. The `format` characters that are allowed in `format` are the same as those for the `scanf` function (see Chapter 16 "Input and Output"). The `fscanf` function returns the number of items successfully read and assigned (excluding any `%n` assignments) or the value `EOF` if end of file is reached before the first item was converted.

```
int fseek (file_pointer, offset, mode)
```

Positions the indicated file to a point that is *offset* (a `long int`) bytes from the beginning of the file, from the current position in the file, or from the end of the file, depending upon the value of *mode* (an integer). If *mode* equals `SEEK_SET`, positioning is relative to the beginning of the file. If *mode* equals `SEEK_CUR`, positioning is relative to the current position in the file. If *mode* equals `SEEK_END`, positioning is relative to the end of the file. `SEEK_SET`, `SEEK_CUR`, and `SEEK_END` are defined in `<stdio.h>`.

On systems that distinguish between text and binary files, `SEEK_END` might not be supported for binary files. For text files, either *offset* must be 0 or must be a value returned from a prior call to `ftell`. In the latter case, *mode* must be `SEEK_SET`.

If the fseek call is unsuccessful, a nonzero value is returned.

```
int fsetpos (file_pointer, fpos)
```

`fsetpos` sets the current file position for the file associated with *file_pointer* to the value pointed to by *fpos*, which is of type `fpos_t` (defined in `<stdio.h>`). Returns zero on success, and nonzero on failure. See also `fgetpos`.

```
long ftell (file_pointer)
```

Returns the relative offset in bytes of the current position in the file identified by *file_pointer*, or -1L on error.

```
size_t fwrite (buffer, size, n, file_pointer)
```

Writes *n* items of data from *buffer* to the specified file. Each item of data is *size* bytes in length. Returns the number of items successfully written.

```
int getc (file_pointer)
```

Reads and returns the next character from the indicated file. The value `EOF` is returned if an error occurs or if the end of the file is reached.

```
int getchar ()
```

Reads and returns the next character from `stdin`. The value `EOF` is returned upon error or end of file.

```
char *gets (buffer)
```

Reads characters from `stdin` into *buffer* until a newline character is read. The newline character is *not* stored in *buffer*, and the character string is terminated with a null character. If an error occurs in performing the read, or if no characters are read, a null pointer is returned; otherwise, *buffer* is returned.

```
void perror (message)
```

Writes an explanation of the last error to stderr, preceded by the string pointed to by *message*. For example, the code

```
#include <stdlib.h>
#include <stdio.h>

if ( (in = fopen ("data", "r")) == NULL )
{
    perror ("data file read");
    exit (EXIT_FAILURE);
}
```

will produce an error message if the fopen call fails, possibly giving more details to the user about the reason for the failure.

```
int printf (format, arg1, arg2, ..., argn)
```

Writes the specified arguments to stdout, according to the format specified by the character string *format* (see Chapter 16). Returns the number of characters written.

```
int putc (c, file_pointer)
```

Writes the value of *c* as an unsigned char to the indicated file. On success, *c* is returned; otherwise EOF is returned.

```
int putchar(c)
```

Writes the value of *c* as an unsigned char to stdout, returning *c* on success and EOF on failure.

```
int puts (buffer)
```

Writes the characters contained in *buffer* to stdout until a null character is encountered. A newline character is automatically written as the last character (unlike the fputs function). On error, EOF is returned.

```
int remove (file_name)
```

The specified file is removed. A nonzero value is returned on failure.

```
int rename (file_name1, file_name2)
```

Renames the file *file_name1* to *file_name2*, returning a nonzero result on failure.

```
void rewind (file_pointer)
```

Resets the indicated file back to the beginning.

```
int scanf (format, arg1, arg2, ..., argn)
```

Reads items from stdin according to the format specified by the string *format* (see Chapter 16). The arguments that follow *format* must all be pointers. The number of items successfully read and assigned (excluding %n assignments) is returned by the function. The value EOF is returned if an end of file is encountered before any items have been converted.

```
FILE *tmpfile (void)
```

Creates and opens a temporary binary file in write update mode ("r+b"), NULL if an error occurs. The temporary file is automatically removed when the program terminates. (A function called tmpnam is also available for creating unique temporary filenames.)

```
int ungetc (c, file_pointer)
```

Effectively "puts back" a character to the indicated file. The character is not actually written to the file but is placed in a buffer associated with the file. The next call to getc will return this character. The ungetc function can only be called to "put back" one character to a file at a time; that is, a read operation must be performed on the file before another call to ungetc can be made. The function returns *c* if the character is successfully "put back," or the value EOF otherwise.

In-Memory Format Conversion Functions

The functions sprintf and sscanf are provided for performing data conversion in memory. These functions are analogous to the fprintf and fscanf functions, except a character string replaces the FILE pointer as the first argument. You should include the header file <stdio.h> in your program when using these routines.

```
int sprintf (buffer, format, arg1, arg2, ..., argn)
```

The specified arguments are converted according to the format specified by the character string *format* (see Chapter 16 "Input and Output") and are placed into the character array pointed to by *buffer*. A null character is automatically placed at the end of the string inside *buffer*. The number of characters placed into *buffer* is returned, excluding the terminating null. As an example, the code

```
int  version = 2;
char fname[125];
 ...
sprintf (fname, "/usr/data%i/1989", version);
```

will result in the character string "/usr/data2/1989" being stored into
fname.

int sscanf (*buffer, format, arg1, arg2, ..., argn*)

The values as specified by the character string *format* are read from
buffer and stored into the corresponding pointer arguments that
follow *format* (see Chapter 16). The number of items successfully
converted is returned by this function. As an example, the code

```
char  buffer[] = "July 16, 1990", month[10];
int   day, year;
 ...
sscanf (buffer, "%s %d, %d", month, &day, &year);
```

will store the string "July" inside month, the integer value 16 inside day,
and the integer value 1990 inside year. The code

```
#include <stdio.h>
#include <stdlib.h>

if ( sscanf (argv[1], "%f", &fval) != 1 )
{
    fprintf (stderr, "Bad number: %s\n", argv[1]);
    exit (EXIT_FAILURE);
}
```

will convert the first command line argument (pointed to by argv[1])
to a floating-point number, and will check the value returned by
sscanf to see if a number was successfully read from argv[1]. (See the
routines described in the next section for other ways to convert strings
to numbers.)

String-to-Number Conversion

The following routines convert character strings to numbers. To use any of the
routines described here, include the header file <stdlib.h> in your program:

```
#include <stdlib.h>
```

In the descriptions that follow, *s* is a pointer to a null-terminated string, *end* is
a pointer to a character pointer, and *base* is an int.

All routines skip leading whitespace characters in the string and stop their scan upon encountering a character that is invalid for the type of value being converted.

```
double atof (s)
```

> Converts the string pointed to by *s* into a floating-point number, returning the result.

```
int atoi (s)
```

> Converts the string pointed to by *s* into an integer, returning the result.

```
int atol (s)
```

> Converts the string pointed to by *s* into a long integer, returning the result.

```
double strtod (s, end)
```

> Converts *s* to `double`, returning the result. A pointer to the character that terminated the scan is stored inside the character pointer pointed to by *end*, provided *end* is not a null pointer.

As an example, the code

```
#include <stdlib.h>
   ...
char    buffer[] = "  123.456xyz",  *end;
double  value;
   ...
value = strtod (buffer, &end);
```

would have the effect of storing the value 123.456 inside `value`. The character pointer variable `end` would be set by `strtod` to point to the character in `buffer` that terminated the scan. In this case, it would be set pointing to the character `'x'`.

```
long int strtol (s, end, base)
```

> Converts *s* to `long int`, returning the result. *base* is an integer base number between 2 and 36, inclusive. The integer is interpreted according to the specified base. If *base* is 0, the integer can be expressed in either base 10, octal (leading 0), or hexadecimal (leading 0x or 0X). If *base* is 16, the value can optionally be preceded by a leading 0x or 0X.
>
> A pointer to the character that terminated the scan is stored inside the character pointer pointed to by `end`, provided `end` is not a null pointer.
>
> ```
> unsigned long int strtoul (s, end, base)
> ```
>
> Converts *s* to `unsigned long int`, returning the result. The remaining arguments are interpreted as for `strtol`.

Dynamic Memory Allocation Functions

The following functions are available for allocating and freeing memory dynamically. For each of these functions, n and *size* represent integers of type size_t, and *pointer* represents a void pointer. To use these functions, include the following line in your program:

```
#include <stdlib.h>
```

void *calloc (*n*, *size*)

Allocates contiguous space for *n* items of data, where each item is *size* bytes in length. The allocated space is initially set to all zeroes. On success, a pointer to the allocated space is returned; on failure, the null pointer is returned.

void free (*pointer*)

Returns a block of memory pointed to by *pointer* that was previously allocated by a calloc, malloc, or realloc call.

void *malloc (*size*)

Allocates contiguous space of *size* bytes, returning a pointer to the beginning of the allocated block if successful, and the null pointer otherwise.

void *realloc (*pointer*, *size*)

Changes the size of a previously allocated block to *size* bytes, returning a pointer to the new block (which may have moved), or a null pointer if an error occurs.

Math Functions

The following lists the math functions. To use these routines, include the statement

```
#include <math.h>
```

in your program. In the list of functions that follows, *x* and *y* are of type double, *r* is an angle expressed in radians and is of type double, and *n* is an int.

For more information about how errors are reported by these functions, consult your documentation.

double acos (*x*)

Returns the arccosine of *x*, as an angle expressed in radians in the range $[0, \pi]$. *x* is in the range $[-1, 1]$.

```
double asin (x)
```

Returns the arcsine of *x* as an angle expressed in radians in the range [-π/2, π/2]. *x* is in the range [-1, 1].

```
double atan (x)
```

Returns the arctangent of *x* as an angle expressed in radians in range [-π/2, π/2].

```
double atan2 (y, x)
```

Returns the arctangent of *y*/*x* as an angle expressed in radians in range [-π, π].

```
double ceil (x)
```

Returns the smallest integer value greater than or equal to *x*. Note that the value is returned as a `double`.

```
double cos (r)
```

Returns the cosine of *r*.

```
double cosh (x)
```

Returns the hyperbolic cosine of *x*.

```
double exp (x)
```

Returns e^x.

```
double fabs (x)
```

Returns the absolute value of *x*.

```
double floor (x)
```

Returns the largest integer value less than or equal to x. Note that the value is returned as a `double`.

```
double fmod (x, y)
```

Returns the floating-point remainder of dividing *x* by *y*. The sign of the result is that of *x*.

```
double frexp (x, exp)
```

Divides *x* into a normalized fraction and a power of two. Returns the fraction in the range [1/2, 1] and stores the exponent into the integer pointed to by *exp*. If *x* is 0, both the value returned and the exponent stored are 0.

```
double ldexp (x, n)
```

Returns $x \times 2^n$.

```
double log (x)
```

Returns the natural logarithm of x, $x \geq 0$.

```
double log10 (x)
```

Returns $\log_{10} x$, $x \geq 0$.

```
double modf (x, ipart)
```

Returns the fractional portion of x, storing the integral portion of x in the `double` pointed to by `ipart`.

```
double pow (x, y)
```

Returns x^y. If x is less than 0, y must be an integer. If x is equal to 0, y must be greater than 0.

```
double sin (r)
```

Returns the sine of r.

```
double sinh (x)
```

Returns the hyperbolic sine of x.

```
double sqrt (x)
```

Returns the square root of x, $x \geq 0$.

```
double tan (r)
```

Returns the tangent of r.

```
double tanh (x)
```

Returns the hyperbolic tangent of x.

General Utility Functions

Here are some routines from the library that didn't fit neatly into any of the previous categories. To use these routines, include the header file `<stdlib.h>`.

```
int abs (n)
```

Returns the absolute value of its `int` argument n.

```
void exit (n)
```

Terminates program execution, closing any open files and returning the exit status specified by its int argument *n*. EXIT_SUCCESS and EXIT_FAILURE, defined in <stdlib.h>, can be used to return a success or failure exit status, respectively.

Other related routines in the library that you may want to refer to are abort and atexit.

```
char *getenv (s)
```

Returns a pointer to the value of the environment variable pointed to by *s*, or a null pointer if the variable doesn't exist. This function operates in a system-dependent way.

As an example, under UNIX the code

```
char   *homedir;
     ...
homedir = getenv ("HOME");
```

could be used to get the value of the user's HOME variable, storing a pointer to it inside homedir.

```
long int labs (l)
```

Returns the absolute value of its long int argument *l*.

```
void qsort (arr, n, size, comp_fn)
```

Sorts the data array pointed to by the void pointer *arr*. There are *n* elements in the array, each *size* bytes in length. *n* and *size* are of type size_t. The fourth argument is of type "pointer to function that returns int and that takes two void pointers as arguments." qsort calls this function whenever it needs to compare two elements in the array, passing it pointers to the elements to compare. The function, which is user-supplied, is expected to compare the two elements and return a value less than zero, equal to zero, or greater than zero if the first element is less than, equal to, or greater than the second element, respectively.

Here is an example of how to use qsort to sort an array of 1,000 integers called data:

```
#include <stdlib.h>
     ...
main ()
{
   int data[1000], comp_ints (void *, void *);
     ...
```

```
        qsort (data, 1000, sizeof(int), comp_ints);
           ...
    }

    int comp_ints (void *p1, void *p2)
    {
        int  i1 = * (int *) p1;
        int  i2 = * (int *) p2;
        return  i1 - i2;
    }
```

Another routine called bsearch, which is not described here, takes similar arguments to qsort and performs a binary search of an ordered array of data.

int rand (void)

> Returns a random number in the range [0, RAND_MAX], where RAND_MAX is defined in <stdlib.h> and has a minimum value of 32767. See also srand.

void srand (*seed*)

> Seeds the random number generator to the unsigned int value *seed*.

int system (*s*)

> Gives the command contained in the character array pointed to by *s* to the system for execution, returning a system-defined value. If *s* is the null pointer, system returns a nonzero value if a command processor is available to execute your commands.

> As an example, under UNIX the call

```
system ("mkdir /usr/tmp/data");
```

will cause the system to create a directory called /usr/tmp/data.

C

Major Differences in ANSI C

This appendix summarizes the major differences between ANSI C and the "old" C. Unless noted otherwise, the UNIX System V Release 3 C compiler is used here as the reference for the old C. Just the differences in the language are summarized, and not the libraries or header files.

The section numbers that follow refer to corresponding sections from Appendix A.

1.0 Identifiers

ANSI C requires that identifiers be distinguishable in their first 31 characters (Section 1.0) and that external names be distinguishable to at least six characters. Older C compilers distinguish identifiers to various numbers of characters. The UNIX System V Release 3 C compiler distinguishes all identifiers (both internal and external), no matter how many characters they contain.

The keywords `asm` and `fortran` are no longer reserved. The keywords `const`, `signed`, and `volatile` now are (Section 1.0).

3.0 Constants
3.1 Integer Constants
The suffix letters u and U are new for integer constants. The rules for determining the type of an integer constant have been changed.

3.2 Floating-Point Constants
Old C treats all floating constants as double. The suffix letters f, F, l, and L are new for float and long double constants (Section 3.2).

3.3 Character Constants

3.3.1 Escape Sequences
The escape sequence \x followed by hexadecimal digits is new, as are the escape sequences \a and \?.

3.3.2 Wide Character Constants
These don't exist in old C.

3.4 Character String Constants
ANSI C explicitly forbids modification of character string constants.

3.4.1 Character String Concatenation
This isn't supported in old C.

3.4.2 Wide Character String Constants
These don't exist in old C.

4.0 Data Types and Declarations
4.2 Basic Data Types
The keyword signed is new, as is the type long double. A signed char forces sign extension, even on machines that don't do so with normal char variables.

4.3 Derived Data Types

4.3.1 Arrays

Old C doesn't allow automatic arrays to be initialized. Old C generates an error if you don't leave enough room for a terminating null in the array when initializing it. ANSI C simply doesn't store the terminating null.

4.3.2 Structures

Old C doesn't permit the members of automatic structure variables to be initialized.

4.3.3 Unions

Old C doesn't permit union variables to be initialized.

4.3.4 Pointers

The type "pointer to `void`" was added as a generic pointer type. Old C used the type "pointer to `char`" for this purpose.

Many old C compilers would generate a warning message when comparing a pointer against the constant 0. ANSI C explicitly permits it without the use of a cast. The capability of an implementation to internally represent a null pointer with a value other than 0 is new.

ANSI C also permits a pointer to an array to be obtained by applying the `&` operator to the array.

4.6 Type Modifiers *const* and *volatile*

These don't exist in old C.

5.0 Expressions

In old C, the compiler is allowed to evaluate

```
a + (b + c)
```

in any order (even adding `a` and `b` together first and adding the result to `c`). ANSI C forbids this rearrangement of operands that involve the same commutative associative operator.

5.3 Arithmetic Operators

The unary plus operator is new to ANSI C.

5.6 Bitwise Operators

Old C applies the usual arithmetic conversions to the left and right operand in a shift operation. In ANSI C, the type of the shift count has no bearing on the type of the result.

5.11 *sizeof* Operator

This operator is now defined to produce a value of type `size_t`. The expression `sizeof (char)` is defined to have the value 1, no matter how many bits are required to represent a character. Thus, the term "byte" (as defined to be the storage unit given by `sizeof`) is defined as the amount of storage needed to store a character.

5.16 Conversion of Basic Data Types

Old C doesn't follow as many steps when converting operands in an expression. ANSI C gives new rules for conversion with `unsigned` operands. Furthermore, many older C compilers automatically carried out all floating-point operations using double-precision arithmetic. ANSI C allows the implementation to use single precision.

7.0 Functions

7.1 Function Definition

Prototype declarations are not supported in old C. The argument's types are declared outside the list of formal parameter names, before the opening curly brace. Subsequent declarations for the function only indicate the function's return type. The compiler does not check or convert arguments when the function is called. However, it does automatically convert `short` or `char` arguments to `int`s and converts `float` arguments to `double`s.

7.3 Function Pointers

Old C does not allow the `&` operator to be applied to a function name to produce a pointer to it. Furthermore, a function can be called through a function pointer only by explicitly applying the indirection operator `*` to the pointer and following it by the function call operator `()`. ANSI C permits the function to be called without the need for the indirection operator.

In ANSI C, function pointers not only describe the return type but also the pointed-to function's arguments. So a pointer to a function that returns an `int` and that takes two `int` arguments is a different type than a pointer to a function that returns an `int` but only takes one `int` argument.

9.0 The Preprocessor

9.1 Trigraph Sequences

This is new to ANSI C.

9.2.1 The *#define* Directive

The # and ## operators are new to ANSI C.

9.2.2 The *#error* Directive

This is new to ANSI C.

9.2.8 The *#pragma* Directive

This is new to ANSI C.

9.2.10 The # Directive

This is new to ANSI C.

D

Common Programming Mistakes

The following list summarizes some of the more common programming mistakes made in C. They are not arranged in any particular order. Knowledge of these mistakes will hopefully help you avoid them in your own programs.

1. *Misplacing a semicolon.*

   Example

   ```
   if ( j == 100 );
       j = 0;
   ```

   In the previous statements, the value of j will always be set to 0 due to the misplaced semicolon after the closing parenthesis. Remember, this semicolon is syntactically valid (it represents the null statement), and therefore no error is produced by the compiler. This same type of mistake is frequently made in while and for loops.

2. *Confusing the operator = with the operator ==.*

   This mistake is usually made inside an `if`, `while`, or `do` statement.

   Example

   ```
   if ( a = 2 )
      printf ("Your turn.\n");
   ```

   The preceding statement is perfectly valid and has the effect of assigning 2 to a and then executing the `printf` call. The `printf` function will *always* be called since the value of the expression contained in the `if` statement will always be nonzero. (Its value will be 2.)

3. *Omitting prototype declarations.*

   Example

   ```
   result = square_root (2);
   ```

   If `square_root` is defined later in the program, or in another file, and is not explicitly declared otherwise, the compiler will assume that the function returns an `int`. Furthermore, the compiler will convert `float` arguments to `double`, and `char` and `short` arguments to `int`. No other conversion of arguments will be done. Remember, it's always safest to include a prototype declaration for *all* functions that you call, even if they're defined earlier.

4. *Confusing the precedences of the various operators.*

   Examples

   ```
   while ( c = getchar ()  !=  EOF )
      ...

   if ( x & 0xF   ==  y )
      ...
   ```

   In the first example, the value returned by `getchar` will be compared against the value `EOF` first. This is because the inequality test has higher precedence than the assignment operator. The value that will therefore be assigned to c will be the TRUE/FALSE result of the test: 1 if the value returned by `getchar` is not equal to `EOF`, and 0 otherwise. In the second example, the integer constant `0xF` will be compared against y first, since the equality test has higher precedence than any of the bitwise operators. The result of this test (0 or 1) will then be ANDed with the value of x.

5. *Confusing a character constant and a character string.*

   In the statement

   ```
   text = 'a';
   ```

   a single character is assigned to `text`. In the statement

   ```
   text = "a";
   ```

   a pointer to the character string `"a"` is assigned to `text`. Whereas, in the first case, `text` is normally declared to be a `char` variable, in the second case, it should be declared to be of type "pointer to `char`."

6. *Using the wrong bounds for an array.*

   Example

   ```
   int  a[100], i, sum = 0;
      ...
   for ( i = 1;  i <= 100;  ++i )
      sum += a[i];
   ```

   Valid subscripts of an array range from 0 through the number of elements minus one. Therefore, the above loop is incorrect since the last valid subscript of a is 99 and not 100. The writer of this statement also probably intended to start with the first element of the array; therefore, `i` should have been initially set to 0.

7. *Forgetting to reserve an extra location in an array for the terminating null character of a string.*

   Remember to declare character arrays so that they are large enough to contain the terminating null character. For example, the character string `"hello"` would require six locations in a character array if you wanted to store a null at the end.

8. *Confusing the operator* -> *with the operator* . *when referencing structure members.*

   Remember, the operator . is used for structure variables, while the operator -> is used for structure *pointer* variables. So, if x is a structure variable, the notation x.m is used to reference the member m of x. On the other hand, if x is a pointer to a structure, the notation x->m is used to reference the member m of the structure pointed to by x.

9. *Omitting the ampersand before nonpointer variables in a* scanf *call.*

   Example

   ```
   int   number;
        . . .
   scanf ("%i", number);
   ```

   Remember that all arguments appearing after the format string in a
   scanf call must be pointers.

10. *Using a pointer variable before it's initialized.*

    Example

    ```
    char   *char_pointer;
    *char_pointer = 'X';
    ```

    You can only apply the indirection operator to a pointer variable *after*
    you have set the variable pointing somewhere. In this example,
    char_pointer is never set pointing to anything, so the assignment is not
    meaningful.

11. *Omitting the* break *statement at the end of a case in a* switch *statement.*

    Remember that if a break is not included at the end of a case, then
    execution will continue into the next case.

12. *Inserting a semicolon at the end of a preprocessor definition.*

    This usually happens because it becomes a matter of habit to end all
    statements with semicolons. Remember that everything appearing to
    the right of the defined name in the #define statement gets directly
    substituted into the program. So the definition

    ```
    #define   END_OF_DATA   999;
    ```

    would lead to a syntax error if used in an expression such as

    ```
    if ( value == END_OF_DATA )
       . . .
    ```

13. *Omitting parentheses around arguments in macro definitions.*

    Example

    ```
    #define   reciprocal(x)   1 / x
          . . .
    w = reciprocal (a + b);
    ```

    The preceding assignment statement would be incorrectly evaluated as

    ```
    w = 1 / a + b;
    ```

14. *Leaving a blank space between the name of a macro and its argument list in the #define statement.*

    Example

    ```
    #define MIN (a,b)  ( ( (a) < (b) ) ? (a) : (b) )
    ```

    This definition is incorrect, as the preprocessor considers the first blank space after the defined name as the start of the definition for that name.

15. *Using an expression that has side effects in a macro call.*

    Example

    ```
    #define  SQUARE(x)  (x) * (x)
       ...
    w = SQUARE (++v);
    ```

    The invocation of the SQUARE macro will cause v to be incremented *twice*, since this statement will be expanded by the preprocessor to

    ```
    w = (++v) * (++v);
    ```

E

The ASCII
Character Set

The following table lists the characters in the ASCII character set and their octal and hexadecimal equivalents.

Char	Oct	Hex	Char	Oct	Hex	Char	Oct	Hex	Char	Oct	Hex
nul	0	0	sp	40	20	@	100	40	`	140	60
soh	1	1	!	41	21	A	101	41	a	141	61
stx	2	2	"	42	22	B	102	42	b	142	62
etx	3	3	#	43	23	C	103	43	c	143	63
eot	4	4	$	44	24	D	104	44	d	144	64
enq	5	5	%	45	25	E	105	45	e	145	65
ack	6	6	&	46	26	F	106	46	f	146	66
bel	7	7	'	47	27	G	107	47	g	147	67
bs	10	8	(	50	28	H	110	48	h	150	68
ht	11	9	)	51	29	I	111	49	i	151	69
nl	12	A	*	52	2A	J	112	4A	j	152	6A
vt	13	B	+	53	2B	K	113	4B	k	153	6B
np	14	C	,	54	2C	L	114	4C	l	154	6C
cr	15	D	-	55	2D	M	115	4D	m	155	6D
so	16	E	.	56	2E	N	116	4E	n	156	6E
si	17	F	/	57	2F	O	117	4F	o	157	6F
dle	20	10	0	60	30	P	120	50	p	160	70
dc1	21	11	1	61	31	Q	121	51	q	161	71
dc2	22	12	2	62	32	R	122	52	r	162	72
dc3	23	13	3	63	33	S	123	53	s	163	73
dc4	24	14	4	64	34	T	124	54	t	164	74
nak	25	15	5	65	35	U	125	55	u	165	75
syn	26	16	6	66	36	V	126	56	v	166	76
etb	27	17	7	67	37	W	127	57	w	167	77
can	30	18	8	70	38	X	130	58	x	170	78
em	31	19	9	71	39	Y	131	59	y	171	79
sub	32	1A	:	72	3A	Z	132	5A	z	172	7A
esc	33	1B	;	73	3B	[	133	5B	{	173	7B
fs	34	1C	<	74	3C	\	134	5C	|	174	7C
gs	35	1D	=	75	3D	]	135	5D	}	175	7D
rs	36	1E	>	76	3E	^	136	5E	~	176	7E
us	37	1F	?	77	3F	_	137	5F	del	177	7F

F

Answers To Odd-Numbered Exercises

Chapter 3

3. Testing   1   2   3

The output would all appear on the same line since a newline character is not printed until the last `printf` call.

5.

```
#include <stdio.h>

main ()
(                          Should be a {
    INT  sum;              INT should be lowercase

    /* COMPUTE RESULT      Missing closing */
    sum = 25 + 37 - 19     Missing semicolon
```

```
          /* DISPLAY RESULTS */
          printf ("The sum is %i\n" sum);        Missing comma
      }
```

Chapter 4

3. `0996`   *Digits 8 and 9 invalid in octal constant*
   `0x10.5`   *Decimal point not valid in integer constant*
   `98.7U`   *Unsigned qualifier only valid for integers*
   `1.2Fe-7`   *Can't use F and e together*
   `0X0G1`   *G is not a valid hexadecimal digit*
   `17777s`   *s is not a valid qualifier*
   `15,000`   *Commas not allowed in constants*

5. `d = d`

7.
```
#include <stdio.h>

main ()
{
   double  result;

   result = (3.31e-8 + 2.01e-7) / (7.16e+6 + 2.01e+8);
   printf ("result = %g\n", result);
}
```

Chapter 5

3.
```
#include <stdio.h>

main ()
{
   int     n, triangular_number;

   printf ("TABLE OF TRIANGULAR NUMBERS\n\n");
   printf (" n    Sum from 1 to n\n");
   printf ("---   --------------\n");

   for ( n = 5;  n <= 50;  n = n + 5)
   {
      triangular_number = n * (n + 1) / 2;
      printf ("%2i           %i\n", n, triangular_number);
   }
}
```

5.
```c
#include <stdio.h>

main ()
{
    int    n, two_to_the_n;

    printf ("TABLE OF POWERS OF TWO\n\n");
    printf (" n      2 to the n\n");
    printf ("---     ----------\n");

    two_to_the_n = 1;

    for ( n = 0;  n <= 10;   ++n )
    {
        printf ("%2i         %i\n", n, two_to_the_n);
        two_to_the_n = two_to_the_n * 2;
    }
}
```

7. The decimal point in the field width causes leading zeroes to be displayed before numbers. This is discussed in more detail in Chapter 16. In this case, it causes a leading zero to appear if the number of cents entered is less than 10 (for example, $29.05).

9. *Program 5.2a*

```c
/* Program to calculate the 200th triangular number */

/* (while statement version)   */
#include <stdio.h>
main ()
{
    int   n, triangular_number;

    triangular_number = 0;

    n = 1;

    while (  n <= 200 )
    {
        triangular_number = triangular_number + n;
        n = n + 1;
    }
```

```
    printf ("The 200th triangular number is %i\n",
                    triangular_number);
}
```

Program 5.3a

```
/* Program to generate a table of triangular numbers */
#include <stdio.h>
main ()
{
    int  n, triangular_number;

    printf ("TABLE OF TRIANGULAR NUMBERS\n\n");
    printf (" n    Sum from 1 to n\n");
    printf ("---    --------------\n");

    triangular_number = 0;

    n = 1;

    while ( n <= 10 )
    {
        triangular_number = triangular_number + n;
        printf (" %i          %i\n", n, triangular_number);
        ++n;
    }
}
```

Program 5.4a

```
#include <stdio.h>
main ()
{
    int  n, number, triangular_number;

    printf ("What triangular number do you want? ");
    scanf  ("%i", &number);

    triangular_number = 0;

    n = 1;

    while ( n <= number )
    {
```

```
            triangular_number = triangular_number + n;
            ++n;
        }

        printf ("Triangular number %i is %i\n", number,
                    triangular_number);
    }
```

Program 5.5a

```
#include <stdio.h>
main ()
{
    int  n, number, triangular_number, counter;

    counter = 1;

    while ( counter <= 5 )
    {
        printf ("What triangular number do you want? ");
        scanf  ("%i", &number);

        triangular_number = 0;

        for ( n = 1;  n <= number;  ++n )
            triangular_number = triangular_number + n;

        printf ("Triangular number %i is %i\n\n", number,
                    triangular_number);

        ++counter;
    }
}
```

11.
```
/* Program to sum the digits in a number */
#include <stdio.h>
main ()
{
    int  number, right_digit, sum = 0;

    printf ("Enter your number: ");
    scanf ("%i", &number);
```

```
    while ( number != 0 )
    {
        right_digit = number % 10;
        sum = sum + right_digit;
        number = number / 10;
    }

    printf ("The sum of the digits is %i\n", sum);
}
```

Chapter 6

3.
```
#include <stdio.h>
main ()
{
    int   n1, n2;

    printf ("Please enter two integers: ");
    scanf ("%i%i", &n1, &n2);

    if (n2 == 0)
        printf ("Division by zero.\n");
    else
        printf ("Result of %i / %i is %.3f\n",
                   n1, n2, (float) n1 / n2);
}
```

5. A negative number entered for Program 5.9 causes each digit to print out as a negative number. For example, if -123 is entered, the output would look like this:

```
-3-2-1
```

Here is a corrected version of that program.

```
/* Program to reverse the digits of a number (revised) */
#include <stdio.h>
main ()
{
    int   number, right_digit;
    int   was_negative = 0;

    printf ("Enter your number.\n");
    scanf ("%i", &number);
```

```
        /* if keyed-in number is negative, make it
           positive, but remember it was negative */

        if ( number < 0 )
        {
            number = -number;
            was_negative = 1;
        }

        do
        {
            right_digit = number % 10;
            printf ("%i", right_digit);
            number = number / 10;
        }
        while ( number != 0 );

        if (was_negative)
            printf ("-");

        printf ("\n");
    }
```

7.
```
    /* Program to generate a table of prime numbers (revised) */
    #include <stdio.h>
    main ()
    {

        int  p, is_prime, d;

        /* we start off knowing 2 is prime */

        printf ("2  ");

        /* now start testing odd numbers from 3 */

        for ( p = 3;  p <= 50;  p = p + 2 )
        {
            is_prime = 1;

            /* only test odd divisors */
```

```
            for ( d = 3;   d < p && is_prime;   d = d + 2 )
               if ( p % d   ==   0 )
                  is_prime = 0;

            if ( is_prime != 0 )
               printf ("%i  ", p);
         }

      printf ("\n");
   }
```

Chapter 7

3.
```c
/* Modified Program 7.2 -- uses break statement */
#include <stdio.h>
main ()
{
    int  rating_counters[11], i, response;

    for ( i = 1;   i <= 10;   ++i )
       rating_counters[i] = 0;

    printf ("Enter your responses\n");
    printf ("When you are done, enter 999\n");

    while (1)
    {
      scanf ("%i", &response);

      if (response == 999)
          break;

      if ( response < 1 || response > 10 )
          printf ("Bad response: %i\n", response);
      else
          ++rating_counters[response];
    }

    printf ("\n\nRating   Number of Responses\n");
    printf ("------   ------------------\n");

    for ( i = 1;   i <= 10;   ++i )
        printf ("%4i%14i\n", i, rating_counters[i]);
}
```

Some people prefer not to use the `break` statement since it disrupts the normal sequential flow of a program's execution. You can rewrite this program to not use the `break` statement by replacing the `while` in the above program with the following equivalent code:

```
...
do
{
    scanf ("%i", &response);
    if (response != 999)
      if ( response < 1 || response > 10 )
          printf ("Bad response: %i\n", response);
      else
          ++rating_counters[response];
}
while ( response != 999 );
...
```

5. Each array element is calculated as the sum of the preceding array elements. This produces the following output:

```
1 1 2 4 8 16 32 64 128 256
```

Chapter 8

3. Here is a modified `square_root` function, a sample `main` routine that takes the square root of 3 with different values of epsilon, and the output from these calls.

```
/* Function to compute the square root of a number */
#include <stdio.h>
float  square_root (float x, float epsilon)
{
    float  guess   = 1.0;

    while ( absolute_value (guess * guess - x) >= epsilon )
       guess = ( x / guess + guess ) / 2.0;
    return (guess);
}

main ()
{
    printf ("%f\n", square_root (3.0, .1));
    printf ("%f\n", square_root (3.0, .01));
```

```
        printf ("%f\n", square_root (3.0, .001));
        printf ("%f\n", square_root (3.0, .0001));
    }


    1.750000
    1.732143
    1.732143
    1.732051
```

5.
```
float   square_root (float x)
{
    float   guess   = 1.0;
    float   epsilon = .00001;

    while  ( absolute_value((guess * guess) / x  - 1.0) >=
                epsilon )
      guess = ( x / guess + guess ) / 2.0;

    return (guess);
}
```

7.
```
long int  x_to_the_n (int x, int n)
{
    long int  result = 1;

    while (n > 0)
    {
        result = result * x;
        --n;
    }
    return (result);
}
```

9.
```
int  lcm (int u, int v)
{
    int  gcd (int u, int v);

    if ( u < 0 || v < 0 )
        return (0);
    else
        return ( u * v / gcd (u, v) );
}
```

11.
```
long int  array_sum (int  values [], int  n)
{
    int       i;
    long int  sum = 0;

    for ( i = 0;  i < n;  ++i )
        sum = sum + values[i];

    return (sum);
}
```

13.
```
/* Sort an array of integers into  descending (order = -1) or
   ascending (order = 1)        */
#include <stdio.h>
void sort (int  a[], int  n, int  order)
{
    int  i, j, temp;

    for ( i = 0;  i < n - 1;  ++i )
        for ( j = i + 1;  j < n;  ++j )
            if ( (order == -1 && a[i] < a[j]) ¦¦
                 (order == 1  && a[i] > a[j]) )
            {
                temp = a[i];
                a[i] = a[j];
                a[j] = temp;
            }
}

main ()
{
    int  i;
    int  array[16] = { 34, -5, 6, 0, 12, 100, 56, 22,
                       44, -3, -9, 12, 17, 22, 6, 11 };
    void sort (int  a[], int  n, int  order);

    printf ("The array before the sort:\n");

    for ( i = 0;  i < 16;  ++i )
        printf ("%i ", array[i]);

    printf ("\n\nThe array in ascending order:\n");
```

```
        sort (array, 16, 1);

        for ( i = 0;  i < 16;  ++i )
            printf ("%i ", array[i]);

        printf ("\n\nThe array in descending order:\n");

        sort (array, 16, -1);

        for ( i = 0;  i < 16;  ++i )
            printf ("%i ", array[i]);

        printf ("\n");
    }
```

15. Here is a modified `get_number_and_base` routine. The rest of the program remains unchanged.

```
void  get_number_and_base (void)
{
    printf ("Number to be converted? ");
    scanf ("%li", &number_to_convert);

    do
    {
        printf ("Enter base value between 2 and 16: ");
        scanf ("%i", &base);
    }
    while ( base < 2  ||  base > 16 );
}
```

Chapter 9

3.
```
#include <stdio.h>
struct time
{
    int  hour;
    int  minutes;
    int  seconds;
};

/* calculate elapsed time (assume t2 is later than t1) */

struct time  elapsed_time (struct time  t1, struct time  t2)
{
```

```
        struct time  result = { 0, 0, 0 };

        /* first subtract the seconds */

        result.seconds = t2.seconds - t1.seconds;

        /* if seconds < 0, need to borrow one minute */

        if (result.seconds < 0)
        {
            result.seconds += 60;
            --t2.minutes;
        }

        /* now subtract the minutes */

            result.minutes = t2.minutes - t1.minutes;

        /* if minutes < 0, need to borrow one hour */

        if (result.minutes < 0)
        {
            result.minutes += 60;
            --t2.hour;

        }

        /* now subtract the hours */

        result.hour = t2.hour - t1.hour;

        /* if hour < 0, need to borrow one day (crossed midnight) */

        if (result.hour < 0)
            result.hour += 24;

        return  (result);
    }

main ()
{
    struct time  elapsed_time (struct time  t1, struct time  t2);
```

```
        struct time  t1 = { 3, 45, 15 }, t2 = { 9, 44, 03 },
                     t3 = {22, 50, 59 }, t4 = { 7, 30,  0 };
        struct time  result;

        result = elapsed_time (t1, t2);
        printf ("Time between %.2i:%.2i:%.2i and %.2i:%.2i:%.2i "
            "is %.2i:%.2i:%.2i\n",
            t1.hour, t1.minutes, t1.seconds, t2.hour, t2.minutes,
            t2.seconds,
            result.hour, result.minutes, result.seconds);

        result = elapsed_time (t2, t1);
        printf ("Time between %.2i:%.2i:%.2i and %.2i:%.2i:%.2i "
            "is %.2i:%.2i:%.2i\n",
            t2.hour, t2.minutes, t2.seconds, t1.hour, t1.minutes,
            t1.seconds,
            result.hour, result.minutes, result.seconds);

        result = elapsed_time (t3, t4);
        printf ("Time between %.2i:%.2i:%.2i and %.2i:%.2i:%.2i "
            "is %.2i:%.2i:%.2i\n",
            t3.hour, t3.minutes, t3.seconds, t4.hour, t4.minutes,
            t4.seconds,
            result.hour, result.minutes, result.seconds);
    }
```

Here is some sample output from the program:

```
Time between 03:45:15 and 09:44:03 is 05:58:48
Time between 09:44:03 and 03:45:15 is 18:01:12
Time between 22:50:59 and 07:30:00 is 08:39:01
```

7.
```
struct date_and_time  clock_keeper (struct date_and_time  dt)
{
    struct time          time_update (struct time  now);
    struct date          date_update (struct date  today);

    dt.stime = time_update (dt.stime);

    /* see if we have to go to the next day */

    if ( dt.stime.hour == 0  && dt.stime.minutes == 0  &&
        dt.stime.seconds == 0 )
      dt.sdate  = date_update (dt.sdate);
```

```
      return (dt);
}
```

Here is a sample main routine and output:

```
main ()
{
   struct date_and_time   dt1 = { { 12, 31, 1999 }, { 23, 59, 59
} };
   struct date_and_time   dt2 = { { 2,  28, 1996 }, { 23, 59, 58
} };

   printf ("Current date and time is %.2i/%.2i/%.2i "
           "%.2i:%.2i:%.2i\n",
            dt1.sdate.month, dt1.sdate.day, dt1.sdate.year,
            dt1.stime.hour,
            dt1.stime.minutes, dt1.stime.seconds);

   dt1 = clock_keeper (dt1);
   printf ("Updated date and time is %.2i/%.2i/%.2i "
           "%.2i:%.2i:%.2i\n\n",
            dt1.sdate.month, dt1.sdate.day, dt1.sdate.year,
            dt1.stime.hour, dt1.stime.minutes, dt1.stime.seconds);

   printf ("Current date and time is %.2i/%.2i/%.2i "
           "%.2i:%.2i:%.2i\n",
            dt2.sdate.month, dt2.sdate.day, dt2.sdate.year,
            dt2.stime.hour, dt2.stime.minutes, dt2.stime.seconds);

   dt2 = clock_keeper (dt2);

   printf ("Updated date and time is %.2i/%.2i/%.2i "
           "%.2i:%.2i:%.2i\n\n",
            dt2.sdate.month, dt2.sdate.day, dt2.sdate.year,
            dt2.stime.hour, dt2.stime.minutes, dt2.stime.seconds);

   printf ("Current date and time is %.2i/%.2i/%.2i "
           "%.2i:%.2i:%.2i\n",
            dt2.sdate.month, dt2.sdate.day, dt2.sdate.year,
            dt2.stime.hour, dt2.stime.minutes, dt2.stime.seconds);

   dt2 = clock_keeper (dt2);
```

```
printf ("Updated date and time is %.2i/%.2i/%.2i "
        "%.2i:%.2i:%.2i\n\n",
        dt2.sdate.month, dt2.sdate.day, dt2.sdate.year,
        dt2.stime.hour, dt2.stime.minutes, dt2.stime.seconds);
}


Current date and time is 12/31/1999 23:59:59
Updated date and time is 01/01/2000 00:00:00

Current date and time is 02/28/1996 23:59:58
Updated date and time is 02/28/1996 23:59:59

Current date and time is 02/28/1996 23:59:59
Updated date and time is 02/29/1996 00:00:00
```

Chapter 10

3. There are many different ways to solve this problem. Here, we replaced the alphabetic function with a function called wordchar that
   considers not only alphabetic characters but also apostrophes as part
   of a word. We also added a function called numchar that considers
   digits, decimal points, commas, and dashes as part of a number. These
   definitions aren't perfect, but they do work reasonably well without
   making the program overly complex.

```
/* Function to determine if a character is part of a word */

int  wordchar (char  c)
{
    if ( (c >= 'a'  &&  c <= 'z') || (c >= 'A'  &&  c <= 'Z') ||
        c == '\'' )
        return (1);
    else
        return (0);
}


/* Function to determine if a character is part of a number */

int    numchar (char  c)
{

    if ( (c >= '0' && c <= '9') || c == '.' || c == ',' ||
        c == '-' )
        return  (1);
```

```
        else
          return (0);
}


/* Function to count the number of words in a string */

int  count_words (char  string[])
{
    int  i, looking_for_word = 1, word_count = 0;
    int  wordchar (char  c);
    int  numchar (char  c);

    for ( i = 0;  string[i] != '\0';  ++i )
        if ( wordchar (string[i])  || numchar (string[i]) )
        {
            if ( looking_for_word )
            {
                ++word_count;
                looking_for_word = 0;
            }
        }
        else
            looking_for_word = 1;

    return (word_count);
}
```

Here's a sample main routine and associated output:

```
main ()
{
    char  text1[] = "The sum of $552,227 and $-1,204.50 is "
          "$551,002.50";
    char  text2[] = "It isn't that I don't understand you.";
    int  count_words (char  string[]);

    printf ("%s -- words = %i\n", text1, count_words (text1));
    printf ("%s -- words = %i\n", text2, count_words (text2));
}
```

```
The sum of $552,227 and $-1,204.50 is $551,002.50 -- words = 8
It isn't that I don't understand you. -- words = 7
```

5.
```
/* find s1 inside source, return index number
   if found, -1 if not found   */

int  find_string (char  source[], char  s[])
{
    int  i, j, foundit = 0;

    /* try each character in source */

    for ( i = 0;  source[i] != '\0'  &&  !foundit;  ++i )
    {
        foundit = 1;

        /* now see if corresponding chars from s match */

        for ( j = 0;  s[j] != '\0'  &&  foundit;  ++j )
            if ( source[j + i] != s[j] || source[j + i] == '\0' )
                foundit = 0;

        if (foundit)
            return  (i);
    }

    return  (-1);
}
```

7.
```
/* insert string s into string source starting at i
   This function uses the string_length function defined
   in the chapter.

   Note: this function assumes source is big enough
         to store the inserted string (dangerous!)   */

void  insert_string (char  source[], char  s[], int  i)
{
    int  j, len_s, len_source;

    /* first, find out how big the two strings are */

    len_source = string_length (source);
    len_s = string_length (s);
```

```
    /* sanity check here -- note that i == len_source
       effectively concatenates s onto the end of source */

    if (i > len_source)
        return;

    /* now we have to move the characters in source
       down from the insertion point to make room for s
       note that we copy the string starting from the end
       to avoid overwriting characters in source.
       We also copy the terminating null (j starts at len_s)
       as well since the final result must be null-terminated */

    for ( j = len_source;  j >= i;  --j )
        source [len_s + j] = source [j];

    /* we've made room, now copy s into source at
       the insertion point */

    for ( j = 0;  j < len_s; ++j )
        source [j + i] = s[j];
}
```

9.
```
int  replace_string (char  source [], char  s1[], char  s2[])
{
    int  index;

    /* first locate s1 inside the source */

    index = find_string (source, s1);

    if ( index == -1 )
        return (0);

    /* now delete s1 from the source */

    remove_string (source, index, string_length (s1));

    /* now insert the new string */

    insert_string (source, s2, index);
```

```
        insert_string (source, s2, index);

        return (1);
    }
```

11. ```
    /* Function to convert a string to an integer */

    int  string_to_integer (char  string[]) {

        int  i = 0, integer_value, result = 0;
        int  negative = 0;

        /* test for leading minus sign */

        if ( string[0] == '-' )
        {
            negative = 1;
            i = 1;
        }

        while ( string[i] >= '0' && string[i] <= '9' )
        {
            integer_value = string[i] - '0';
            result = result * 10 + integer_value;
            ++i;
        }

        if ( negative )
            result = -result;

        return (result);
    }
    ```

13. ```
    void  uppercase ( char str[] )
    {
        int  i;

        for ( i = 0;  str[i] != '\0';  ++i )
            if ( str[i] >= 'a'  &&  str[i] <= 'z' )
                str[i] = str[i] - 'a' + 'A';
    }
    ```

Chapter 11

3. We can solve this problem by setting up a "dummy" structure variable called list_head, for example

```
struct entry   list_head;
```

and we can then set it pointing to the head of the list by assigning the next member of list_head to point to the actual first entry of the list:

```
list_head.next = &entry1;
```

Now to insert a new entry called new_entry at the front of the list, we can write

```
insert_entry (&new_entry, &list_head);
```

5.
```
struct dentry
{
    int            value;
    struct dentry  *next;
    struct dentry  *prev;
};

main ()
{
    struct dentry  n1, n2, n3, *lptr;
    int            i;

    n1.value = 100;
    n2.value = 200;
    n3.value = 300;

    n1.next = &n2;
    n2.next = &n3;
    n3.next = (struct dentry *) 0;

    n1.prev = (struct dentry *) 0;
    n2.prev = &n1;
    n3.prev = &n2;

    /* forward search through list */

    lptr = &n1;
    while ( lptr != 0 )
    {
```

```
            printf ("%i ", lptr->value);
            lptr = lptr->next;
        }

        printf ("\n");

        /* backward search through list */

        lptr = &n3;
        while ( lptr != 0 )
        {
            printf ("%i ", lptr->value);
            lptr = lptr->prev;
        }

        printf ("\n");
}
```

Here's the output from the test program:

```
100 200 300
300 200 100
```

7.
```
/* Sort an array of integers into ascending order
   (pointer version )  */

void sort (int  *a, int  n)
{
    int  *aptr1, *aptr2, temp;


    for ( aptr1 = a;   aptr1 < a + n - 1;  ++aptr1 )
        for ( aptr2 = aptr1 + 1;   aptr2 < a + n;  ++aptr2 )
            if ( *aptr1 > *aptr2 )
            {
                temp = *aptr1;
                *aptr1 = *aptr2;
                *aptr2 = temp;
            }
}
```

9.
```
/* Function to read a line of text from the terminal
   (pointer version)    */
void  read_line (char  *buffer)
```

```
    {
        char  character;

        do
        {
            character = getchar ();
            *buffer++ = character;
        }
        while ( character != '\n' );

        *(buffer - 1) = '\0';
    }
```

11.
```
/* Function to calculate tomorrow's date
   (pointer version) */

void  date_update (struct date  *today)
{
    int  number_of_days (struct date  d);

    if ( today->day != number_of_days (*today) )
        ++today->day;
    else if ( today->month == 12 )  /* end of year */
    {
        today->day = 1;
        today->month = 1;
        ++today->year;
    }
    else
    {                                   /* end of month */
        today->day = 1;
        ++today->month;
    }
}
```

Chapter 12

3.
```
int  int_size (void)
{
    unsigned int  bits;
    int           size = 0;

    bits = ~0;
```

```
      while ( bits )
      {
         ++size;
         bits >>= 1;
      }

      return  (size);
   }
```

5. ```
   /* test bit n in word to see if it is on
      assumes words are 32 bits long          */

   int  bit_test (unsigned int  word, int  n)
   {
      if ( n < 0  || n > 31 )
         return  (0);

      if ( (word >> (31 - n)) & 0x1 )
         return (1);
      else
         return (0);
   }

   unsigned int  bit_set (unsigned int  word, int  n)
   {
      if ( n < 0  || n > 31 )
         return  (0);

      return  (word | (1 << (31 - n)));
   }
```

7. ```
   /* extract count bits from value beginning at bit n */

   unsigned int bitpat_get (unsigned int value, int n, int count)
   {
      int   word_size, i;

      word_size = int_size ();

      if ( n < 0  ||  n > word_size  ||
           count < 0  ||  count + n > word_size )
         return  (0);
```

```
        /* first shift value to the leftmost part of the word */

        value <<= n;

        /* now when we shift right, the bits to the left of value
           will be cleared */

        return  (value  >>  word_size - count);
    }
```

Chapter 13

3. #define MIN(x, y)   (((x) < (y)) ? (x) : (y))

5. #define SHIFT(value, n) (((n) > 0) ? ((value) << (n)) \
                                          : ((value) >> -(n)))

7. #define IS_ALPHABETIC (IS_LOWER_CASE (c) ¦¦ IS_UPPERCASE (C))

9. #define ABSOLUTE_VALUE(x) (((x) < 0) ? -(x) : (x))

Chapter 14

1. typedef int (*FUNCTION_POINTER) (void);

3.
Expression	Type	Value
f + s * i - L	float	200.5
l + i / s	long	52
i / f + s * d	double	65.0
i / s * f	float	1.0
(double) i / s * f	double	1.25
l / i + (int) d / f	float	4.0
i * i + 0x100	int	881

Chapter 16

1.
```
/* Program to copy one file to another */

#include <stdio.h>

/* convert lowercase to uppercase character */

#define  TO_UPPER ( (C>= 'a'  &&  C<= 'z') ?C- 'a' + 'A' :C )
```

```
main ()
{
    char  in_name[25], out_name[25];
    FILE  *in, *out;
    int   c;

    printf ("Enter name of file to be copied: ");
    scanf ("%24s", in_name);
    printf ("Enter name of output file: ");
    scanf ("%24s", out_name);

    if ( (in = fopen (in_name, "r"))  ==  NULL )
        printf ("Can't open %s for reading.\n", in_name);
    else if ( (out = fopen (out_name, "w"))  ==  NULL )
        printf ("Can't open %s for writing.\n", out_name);
    else
    {
        while ( (c = getc (in)) != EOF )
            putc (TO_UPPER (c), out);

        printf ("File has been copied.\n");
    }
}
```

5. ```
/* Program to extract columns from each line of a file
   (similar to the UNIX cut command) */

#include <stdio.h>

main ()
{

    char in_name[25];
    FILE *in;
    int   m, n, curcol, c;

    printf ("Enter name of file: ");
    scanf ("%24s", in_name);
    printf ("Enter starting and ending column numbers: ");
    scanf ("%i%i", &m, &n);
```
```

```
if ( (in = fopen (in_name, "r"))  ==  NULL )
    printf ("Can't open %s for reading.\n", in_name);
else
{
   curcol = 1;

   while ( (c = getc (in)) != EOF )
     {
        if ( c == '\n' )
        {
           putchar ('\n');
           curcol = 0;
        }
        else if ( curcol >= m  &&  curcol <= n )
           putchar (c);

        ++curcol;
     }
  }
}
```

I

Symbols